# WISDOM WON FROM ILLNESS

# Wisdom Won from Illness

## *Essays in Philosophy and Psychoanalysis*

JONATHAN LEAR

HARVARD UNIVERSITY PRESS
*Cambridge, Massachusetts & London, England*
2017

Printed in the United States of America

First printing

*Library of Congress Cataloging-in-Publication Data*

Names: Lear, Jonathan, author.
Title: Wisdom won from illness: essays in philosophy and psychoanalysis / Jonathan Lear.
Description: Cambridge, Massachusetts: Harvard University Press, 2017. | Includes bibliographical references and index.
Identifiers: LCCN 2016017882 | ISBN 9780674967847
Subjects: LCSH: Psychoanalysis and philosophy. | Reason. | Literature—Philosophy. | Philosophical anthropology. | Philosophy and social sciences.
Classification: LCC BF175.4.P45 L434 2017 | DDC 150.19/5—dc23
LC record available at https://lccn.loc.gov/2016017882

For GABRIEL, SOPHIA, and SAMUEL, with love

# Contents

Introduction / 1
ONE Wisdom Won from Illness / 11
TWO Integrating the Nonrational Soul / 30
THREE What Is a Crisis of Intelligibility? / 50
FOUR A Lost Conception of Irony / 63
FIVE Waiting for the Barbarians / 80
SIX The Ironic Creativity of Socratic Doubt / 103
SEVEN Rosalind's Pregnancy / 120
EIGHT Technique and Final Cause in Psychoanalysis / 138
NINE Jumping from the Couch / 159
TEN Eros and Development / 175
ELEVEN Mourning and Moral Psychology / 191
TWELVE Allegory and Myth in Plato's *Republic* / 206
THIRTEEN The Psychic Efficacy of Plato's Cave / 227
FOURTEEN The Ethical Thought of J. M. Coetzee / 244
FIFTEEN Not at Home in Gilead / 269

*Notes / 287*
*Acknowledgments / 317*
*Index / 321*

# WISDOM WON FROM ILLNESS

# Introduction

What is the appropriate relation of human reason to the human psyche taken as a whole? The essays in this volume range over literature and ethics, psychoanalysis, social theory, and ancient Greek philosophy. But, from different angles, they all address this question.

In the *Republic,* Socrates says it is appropriate for reason to rule over the whole psyche.[1] But much hangs on what we might mean by this. We humans have inflicted unimaginable suffering on each other, justified by arrogant conceptions of reason, and of ruling. The same is true of our treatment of other animals. False images of reason regularly blind us to the claims and reality of others. One way to react to all this pain and destruction is to denounce the very idea of reason—as nothing more than an ideological tool of power. I do not think that is the right way to go. We should not be too quick to dismiss our real human capacities just because they have so often been put to such poor uses. What we need is a philosophical anthropology and psychology that is adequate to who we are—and who we might legitimately hope to become.

The Greek term Plato uses for "reason" is *to logistikon*: our capacity to exercise and extend *logos.* This is a special form of thoughtfulness that works its way through language and speech. The Greek for "rule" is *archein,* which also means to *take the lead,* to *extend itself as a principle,* to *impose form* on the psyche as a whole.

Socrates's idea seems to be that it is appropriate for us to use our capacity for logos-filled, self-conscious thinking both to understand *and to organize* our overall psychic functioning. This suggests that reason ought to be a *practical* capacity of the psyche to shape the psyche according to its own thoughtful understanding of how the psyche should be shaped. Why should reason have this privileged role? Socrates says: because it is wise and has "foresight" over the whole psyche. The Greek for "foresight" is *promêtheian.* That is, our *logos*-filled thinking brings with it a *Promethean* ability with respect to the entire psyche. Self-conscious reason *brings the gift of fire*: it ought to *light up* the nonrational part of the soul.

So, what is it to let there be light? The wrong way to inherit Socrates's claim is to assume that we already know what reason is—and that our only problem is to figure out how to extend its domain over unruly areas of the soul. Rather, we should see Socrates as laying down a task that may take millennia fully to comprehend: we shall find out what reason is—indeed, we will find out what we mean by *rationality*—as we become better able to understand what is involved in appropriately extending thoughtful guidance to the whole soul.

A deep insight to be found in Aristotle is that the way reason takes the lead is *in conversation.* The other realms of the psyche are sufficiently organized so as to speak with their own voices; and, up to a point, they are capable of listening. The harmonious soul, the well-organized psyche, the flourishing human being is such because of excellent intrapsychic communication (see Chapters 1 and 2). But if reason is to take the lead *via conversation,* it must come to understand its interlocutors—what they are saying; how they are thinking; what, if anything, they want; and, truly important, how one might communicate successfully with them. As reason learns how to communicate well with the other parts of the soul, it is not just discovering what these other parts of the soul are like; it is discovering what its own proper activity consists in.[2] This means that human reason cannot understand itself a priori—independently of the experience of coming to understand what is involved in taking the lead in communicating.

It is this demand to communicate well that false images of reason tend to ignore. It is correct that reason should only be influenced by what is reasonable. It should not be unduly influenced "from the outside." But on this basis it is easy to imagine reason as a thoughtful but isolated monarch, tucked up in the castle thinking through what is best, with unruly desires pounding at the gates for satisfaction. What it is for reason "to rule," on this picture, is to decide which desires shall be admitted into the castle. This is a stultifying image of the human psyche and its possibilities. It restricts our conception of what is "reasonable" and what counts as "inside" or "outside" the domain of reason. For if the nonrational part of the soul is not just a container of desires thoughtlessly seeking satisfaction but, as Aristotle says, participates in reason *in a way*, then the question of what counts as inside or outside the domain of reason is more open-ended. It cannot be settled in advance of our best efforts to settle it.

Here is the place to locate the philosophical significance of psychoanalysis. Freud and the subsequent psychoanalytic tradition have developed an art—a practice—of communicating thoughtfully with the nonrational soul far beyond anything Socrates, Plato, or Aristotle could have imagined. It is reason's task to communicate *well* with the whole soul, but psychoanalysis teaches us what such communicating consists in. Indeed, it would seem that psychoanalytic practice *is* the activity of reason itself, in its communicating function.

I could not have written this book on the basis of scholarship alone. I began studying Aristotle in my twenties, and what captured my imagination was not only the brilliance of his thinking, but also his commitment to life. He was *for* it. This showed up in the meticulous detail with which he observed the natural world and the vibrant way his philosophy grew out of those observations. I wanted to imitate this way of living. The realm of the living world that most interests me is the human: who *are* we? It seems we are creatures who need to pose, but do not know how to answer, that question. This may seem odd, but I decided to train as a psychoanalyst. In part, I was attracted to the meticulousness of psychoanalytic listening; in part, I had an inchoate hunch that philosophy was overlooking something important. So, in addition to my philosophical research and teaching, in the early mornings I began working with patients in psychoanalysis. Three decades later, this clinical experience has given me a base from which to judge the writings of Freud. But, more important, it put me in a position to attend to aspects of human being that are, in some sense, nonobservational. My work is not scholarship plus empirical research. For when psychoanalysis is going well, there is a meeting of the minds, a sharing of observations, an attentiveness in working together for which the concepts *subject* and *object, observer* and *observed* are ill suited to capture what is going on. There is a thinking-together that, over time, helps the analysand develop an unusual practical capacity of mind: the capacity to change the way her own mind works via the immediate and direct understanding of how it works. It is a practical capacity of mind that one comes to understand by exercising it oneself. To use a deep but ultimately misleading metaphor, one learns about it "from the inside." Of course, one may be misled in all sorts of ways—it is constitutive of this kind of insight that there is risk of blindness. That said, on those occasions when we are exercising this capacity of mind—and we have developed the capacity to attend to our experience in this way—we can have immediate and direct awareness of what we are doing. We can have confidence about what we are doing in the "internal" world that is similar to our confidence of what we are doing in the "external" world when we, say, tie our shoes. (I discuss how this works in Chapters 1, 2, 4, 8, and 9.) The idea that psychoanalysis consists in testing empirical hypotheses about a hidden realm, the unconscious, based on shards of empirical evidence is misleading. Indeed, this picture can function as a resistance to psychoanalysis.

My life in philosophy has helped me as a psychoanalyst. Over time, I have come to see that the unconscious functions not unlike a philosopher. I would not have been able to see this if I had not spent my life in philosophy. The unconscious, like philosophy, begins in wonder. This is not just curiosity, but rather the Greek sense of wonder, *thaumazein*: *being struck* by a wondrous intrusion from the world. There is a disturbing, energizing, enigmatic sense that things do not make sense—for example, hearing an utterance from a parent that one does not yet understand. And, as it gets busy, the unconscious tries to address elemental issues of human finitude. How could it be that we are not omnipotent? If we are not gods, who are we, and how shall we be? Freud was right that the unconscious has something to do with hidden wishes, gratifications, and pleasures; but it is a mistake to think that that is all it consists in. Freud also teaches—and this, I think, is his deepest insight—that the unconscious is a different manner of thinking. In its peculiar way it seeks to understand (and shape) the world. It tries to grasp the being of human being, but it is a creative intelligence that regularly distorts that which it seeks to understand. Ironically, the unconscious is like a philosopher who—*bad luck!*—lacks the capacity of reason. This would be funny were it not for the fact that this is the source of so much human suffering.

That is why Socrates is right. It is fitting for reason to take the lead and extend its influence over the whole soul. But accept no substitutes! It is crucially important not to be seduced by some currently fashionable simulacrum of human reason.

This book goes against the grain of our times in that it acknowledges Freud's extraordinary insights and the generous spirit of his mind. But let me begin with my most basic disagreement. In taking stock of its significance, Freud compares psychoanalysis to the intellectual revolutions of Copernicus and Darwin.

> In the course of the centuries the *naïve* self-love of men has had to submit to two major blows at the hands of science. The first was when they learnt that our earth was not the center of the universe but only a tiny fragment of a cosmic system of scarcely imaginable vastness. This is associated in our minds with the name of Copernicus. . . . The second blow fell when biological research destroyed man's supposedly privileged place in creation and proved his descent from the animal kingdom and his ineradicable animal nature. This revaluation has been accomplished in our own days by Darwin, Wallace. . . . But human megalomania will have suffered its third and most wounding blow from the psychological research of the present time which seeks to prove to the ego that it is not even master in its own house, but must content itself with scanty information of what is going on unconsciously in its mind.[3]

To claim that psychoanalysis has the shape of a Copernican revolution is to claim that one's predecessors were deeply mistaken, disoriented. We are, in effect, given permission not to pay attention to them. The image of revolution thus serves to repress historical awareness. It is a form of splitting: in the name of historical progress we cut ourselves off from a past that, if only we knew about it, might influence us. I think this has happened.

Plato and Aristotle invented psychology to vindicate the intuition that ethical life is a happy life for human beings. The word "ethical" comes from Greek words that refer to a person's character and to social customs and practices. In psychoanalytic terms, the superego need not be involved in ethical life. And, for Plato as for Aristotle, in the best forms of human life, it won't be. The happy human life will be imbued with values and purposes, but such a life will be the expression of an integrated psyche, and not simply the outcome of a critical superego set against an obedient ego. For the Greek philosophers, psychological integration was a condition of human health. Indeed, Plato develops a serious psychodynamic account of the human psyche in order to prove this point. Genuine integration might be rare—health may be difficult to achieve—but the Greek philosophers were convinced it was a genuine human possibility. For them, *the* most persistent obstacle to such a healthy, fulfilling life was precisely that the ego is not "master in its own house." As they put it, reason is often overruled, and its vision distorted, by desire. In other words, at the founding of psychology in ancient Greece, the situation is the opposite of what Freud would have us believe about our predecessors.[4] My point is not that there is nothing new under the sun. Freudian psychoanalysis does illuminate the human condition in the most remarkable ways. But we cannot understand what is genuinely new if we stick with fantasies of revolution. Nor can we understand how psychoanalysis might make a contribution to a long-standing vision of what is possible for human beings if we remain ignorant of what that vision is. (I discuss this in Chapter 2). In short, it is time to bid adieu to the fantasy of psychoanalysis as a Copernican revolution of the mind.

If psychoanalysis were merely a theory putting forward some strange claims about human beings, then philosophers might occupy themselves with its "foundations," or they might question the empirical warrant for its claims. This form of engagement does not bear much fruit. In this book, I want to take a different approach: psychoanalysis makes manifest aspects of the being of human beings we could not otherwise comprehend.

Properly understood, psychoanalysis is constituted by its "fundamental rule": try to say whatever comes to mind without censorship or inhibition. It is this injunction that binds psychoanalysis to the Socratic tradition of philosophical longing. It seems to me almost miraculous that Freud hit upon this rule. It is so simple, yet it is such an unlikely response to the pleas for help that confronted him. People came to him with every sort of physical ailment, with compulsive rituals and intrusive thoughts of torture, murder, and suicide. How could one ever think that this plethora of complaint deserved a uniform response? And, what an odd response to those sorts of complaints!

There are, I think, three reasons for treating the fundamental rule as fundamental. First, it gives one determination of what we might mean by the *free flow of self-consciousness.* Before we know any empirical results, before we have any outcome studies, we can tell simply by looking at the structure of the fundamental rule that psychoanalysis is a "cure" for constrictions of self-consciousness. This matters, for self-consciousness is not simply one capacity we have among others. Part of what it is to lead a distinctively human life is to have a self-conscious role in shaping the life that one understands to be the life that it is. Thus it is a discovery of some consequence that no one can follow the fundamental rule.[5] As Freud said, "there comes a time in every analysis when the patient disregards it."[6] In my experience, that time comes pretty much immediately and recurs constantly throughout the analysis. This suggests that there is something internal to the spontaneous unfolding of self-consciousness that opposes it.[7]

This brings us to the second reason for treating the fundamental rule as fundamental. It is as though simply laying down the fundamental rule instantiates its own blocks and disruptions. This is because the fundamental rule in effect sets up a membrane across which unconscious meanings can flow. As the analysand tries to speak his or her mind, that speech will inevitably be disrupted by intrusive thoughts, slips of the tongue, and so on. The unconscious will thus be breaking through into consciousness. This gives an extraordinary opportunity to listen to the unconscious speaking in its own voice. One way to view the development of psychoanalysis is that it has been learning to understand a foreign language that we have been speaking all along.

Freud emphasized the discovery of the unconscious as well as certain substantive claims—for example, the ubiquity of the Oedipus complex. But if we focus on the fundamental rule, the emphasis shifts away from any particular discovery and toward process or method. If there are any substantive discoveries to be had, they ought to be discoverable over and over again by using the appropriate method. And what is the psychoanalytic process if not the development and enhancement of our capacity for self-conscious awareness? Self-conscious awareness is extended to realms of mental activity that hitherto were seen through a glass darkly. Psychoanalysis is an attempt to listen to and address the whole psyche. Seen this way, psychoanalysis begins to look as though it is the development of an ancient ideal.

The third reason for thinking the fundamental rule is fundamental is that it promotes the fundamental value of psychoanalysis: truthfulness. I need to say a word about what I mean by this. It has long been a question why truth should cure. And Freud noticed early that simply stating truths about a person to that person might provoke all sorts of reactions: protest, intensification of symptoms, breaking off treatment—anything *but* a cure.[8] Obviously, we need a conception of truth that is not merely correspondence to facts. In fact, we need a conception of truth in which truth cures because truth *is* the cure.

The opening entry for "truthfulness" in the *Oxford English Dictionary* defines the word in terms of fidelity. One is true "to a person or a principle cause," and it explicates this in terms of "faithfulness, fidelity, loyalty, constancy, steadfast allegiance."[9] The question becomes: what would it mean to maintain fidelity or steadfastness toward oneself? At least one answer is: maintain an analytic life in which one holds oneself to the fundamental rule and to analyzing the inevitable breakdowns. For what we have learned over generations of psychoanalytic work is that attempting to speak one's mind according to the fundamental rule is *itself* an integrating psychic activity. This is a form of truthfulness: a fidelity to oneself expressed in the activity of becoming oneself via increasing psychic integration. This is what psychoanalytic activity consists in. And so understood, truthfulness must itself be the cure, for the relevant form of fidelity to oneself is psychic integration.

This brings us back to the project of the ancient Greek philosophers. It has long been thought that psychoanalysis could have nothing to do with ethics—indeed, that it should not. Plato and Aristotle promoted particular virtues such as justice and temperance; and psychoanalysis, it is plausibly thought, should not be in the business of promulgating any table of virtues. To give one example, Aristotle insists there is no right way to commit adultery.[10] But should analysands start discussing their adulterous affairs, the analyst's job is not to dissuade or criticize them, but rather to help them understand the deeper meanings of the adultery for them. Because of that, psychoanalysis has often struck outsiders as, at best, amoral and perhaps immoral. This is the wrong lesson to take away. Psychoanalysis is constituted by its commitment to truthfulness; and truthfulness is not simply one value among others. Truthfulness is the condition for the possibility of other ethical virtues. Consider this Aristotelian-spirited intuition: for anything to count as a genuine virtue, it must be possible for it to be an expression *of me*—that is, it must be the expression of an integrated psyche. And so, psychoanalysis, with its concern for truthfulness, far from being amoral or immoral, is a necessary condition for any robust approach to ethics based on virtues. To borrow a phrase from Kierkegaard, psychoanalysis turns out to be a teleological suspension of the ethical *for the sake of the ethical.*[11]

It seems to me that we are still in early days in terms of understanding what we mean by truthfulness, psychic integration, or unity. Psychoanalysis has taught us an enormous amount about this, but it has also laid down a challenge. We need to understand what psychic unity consists in when the nonrational part of the psyche—what Freud called the unconscious—has its own, peculiar principles of activity and change. Unity would have to consist not only in toleration but also in facilitation of certain forms of unconscious mental activity. Without a rich understanding of what this amounts to, we can only gesture in the direction of human flourishing.

Socrates famously expelled the best-loved poets from the polis, but he said they would be allowed back if they gave a good reason for poetry's existence. Many of the essays in this book—Chapters 3, 4, 5, 7, 12, 13, 14, and 15—try to do just that. Basically, we need poets and novelists and playwrights and artists to help us develop and exercise our practical and poetical capacities of mind. This can make an ethical and a political difference. To give one example: survivors of cultural catastrophe suffer all sorts of degradation—among which are attacks on the very concepts with which they understand themselves. There are attacks on the concepts with which they understand life to be worth living. Trauma does not befall individuals alone; the conceptual life of a culture may suffer a traumatic blow. Poets are needed to restore concepts to health and thereby reanimate a devastated culture. Irony, too, can play a crucial role in this restorative process; and if that sounds strange, it is because we have inherited a flattened conception of what irony is and why it should matter (see Chapters 4, 6, and 7). To give another example: if we live in an unjust society, we have reason to think that our own thought-processes have been distorted. I am not talking merely about psychological damage—as, for example, Plato examines the distorted psychological functioning of those raised in oligarchical societies—but about disfiguration of the very concepts with which we think.[12] Could it be that our concept of justice is unjust? If so, how would we be able to think this if the very concepts with which we think are distorted? We need somehow to be able to recognize the injustice *from inside* the unjust thinking—and do so in a way that at least holds out the prospect of rectifying our thought. Literature has a special way of addressing this problem (see Chapters 5, 14, and 15).

I shall close with a thought about the place of suffering in human life. Great literature—poetry, drama, the novel—shares with psychoanalysis the intuition that certain forms of suffering can be transformed via self-conscious appropriation. One literally gives suffering a different form by coming to grasp what it means. One thereby creates a possibility for living with the suffering in a better way—and sometimes for leaving it behind. This process at once makes life human and makes human life worthwhile. It is, I suspect, what Freud was gesturing at when he spoke of making the unconscious conscious. The essays in this book aim to shed light on what this means.

CHAPTER ONE

# Wisdom Won from Illness

**1.** From its inception, psychoanalysis claimed not merely to be an effective therapy for psychological suffering, but to shed light on the human condition. But what kind of insight is this? To be sure, psychoanalysis opened up vistas of psychopathology. But is the sum total of our insight *into* illness, or is there wisdom to be won *from* illness? The ancient Greeks bequeathed us a concept of wisdom (*sophia*) that makes it problematic that any such wisdom is possible. For Aristotle, theoretical wisdom is a deep understanding of how things are. It includes a grasp of the truth, as well as of the correct scientific theory in which the truth is embedded—a grasp of the causal connections and basic structure in terms of which it all fits together.[1] For living organisms, Aristotle thought that what they are shows up in conditions of health. From this perspective, wisdom is essentially about health and well-being. Pathology is a falling away from health, and there are indefinitely many ways in which that might happen. Such multiplicity and falling short is not the stuff of wisdom—at least, so Aristotle thought.

Aristotle also marked off a special form of wisdom, "practical wisdom" (*phronêsis*), appropriate for humans, which is the capacity to think effectively and well about how to live. A practically wise person can grasp what goods are worth pursuing in a fulfilling life: she can think through how to attain them, and she can make her thinking effective in living a good life. For Aristotle, the conclusion of practical reasoning is not a theoretical proposition about what to do, but rather *the very doing* of that act.[2] This is a different kind of wisdom than theoretical wisdom, and Aristotle mentions Thales as an example of a person who understood the principles of the universe but accidentally fell into a well while thinking.[3] At first glance, it would seem that psychoanalysis could have nothing to do with practical wisdom either. For, practical wisdom aims at and exemplifies human flourishing. A practically wise person, Aristotle thought, is capable of happiness (*eudaimonia*)—a full, rich, meaningful life lacking in nothing that is needed for the happy life that it is. By contrast, psychoanalysis is concerned with the myriad ways people fall ill psychologically. It addresses people who are suffering, failing to thrive. There are, Aristotle thought, indefinitely many ways that can happen, and grasping some of these failures does not count as wisdom.

There are two familiar modes of response—one deriving from Plato, the other from Nietzsche. In the *Republic,* Plato offered a rich account of psychopathology as a way of delineating by contrast what psychic health consists in. The accounts of disease bring into relief an image of psychological flourishing. The Nietzschean route is to insist that humans are uncanny animals, sick in their own nature. Wisdom thus must be won *through* the sickness; indeed, wisdom *is* the sickness that constitutes us as human. There are intimations of both lines of thought in Freud's work.

In this essay, I want to take a different tack. I want to argue that wisdom is about health *and* that psychoanalysis can be both an understanding *and a manifestation* of human health. Wisdom can be won from illness—and not simply in the sense that pathology lends insight into health, but in that it gives us direct and immediate insight into who and what we are.

**2.** From early on, Freud encouraged his patients to try to say whatever came into their minds, but by 1912 he had formalized this into a principle of technique he called *the fundamental rule* of psychoanalysis.[4] The analysand was enjoined to speak his or her mind without inhibition or censorship. By calling this rule fundamental and attaching the definite article—it was *the* fundamental rule—Freud placed it at the center of psychoanalytic practice. And in "Remembering, Repeating and Working-Through," written in 1914, he advanced a history of the development of psychoanalytic technique that emphasized abandoning deep interpretation in favor of facilitating the analysand's own associations:

> Finally, there was evolved the consistent technique used today, in which the analyst gives up the attempt to bring a particular moment or problem

> into focus. He contents himself with studying whatever is present for the time being on the surface of the patient's mind, and he employs the art of interpretation mainly for the purpose of recognizing the resistances which appear there, and making them conscious to the patient. From this there results a new sort of division of labor: the doctor uncovers the resistances which are unknown to the patient; when these have been got the better of, the patient often relates the forgotten situations and connections without any difficulty.[5]

We can see here a shift in Freud's image of psychoanalytic expertise: away from a claim to knowledge of hidden contents of the mind and toward a claim to practical knowledge—namely, the ability to facilitate a process that would otherwise be stuck, impeded, or conflicted. This is the process of the analysand coming to speak his or her mind. The analyst does not abandon a claim to expert knowledge, but, for Freud, the expertise is now focused on method: how to facilitate the free flow of consciousness in another.

In that same year, Freud added a footnote to a new edition of *The Interpretation of Dreams:*

> The technique [of dream-interpretation] which I describe in the pages that follow differs in one essential respect from the ancient method: it imposes the task of interpretation upon the dreamer himself. It is not concerned with what occurs to the interpreter in connection with a particular element of the dream but with what occurs to the dreamer.[6]

By this stage in his theorizing, Freud thinks the therapeutic method of psychoanalysis works through the self-conscious awareness and understanding of the analysand.

With the benefit of hindsight, Freud's picture of technique seems a bit wishful. One way to view the development of psychoanalytic technique since Freud is as a response to analysands who could not be helped simply by such straightforward treatment.[7] Still, as with any great thinker, one can read Freud as reaching beyond himself. Whatever the revisions of technique (and these may be considerable) and however limited the achievement in any particular case, the broadscale aim that Freud laid down for psychoanalysis is the unfettered movement of the self-conscious mind in its own activity. When, in his maturity, Freud famously wrote, "Where id was, there ego shall be,"[8] his injunction was not that the repressed unconscious should be replaced by unconscious defensive ego strategies[9] but that self-conscious awareness and understanding should attend and inform the workings of the mind. Let us call this aim "Freud's legacy."

What shall we do with it? We, of course, have a choice of inheritance. There is room for interpretation of what we might mean by the claim that psychoanalysis facilitates the development of self-consciousness; and there is room to decide whether we want to accept the claim under any interpretation. There is no reason to stick to Freud's legacy simply because it comes from Freud. Our relationship to this legacy ought to be shaped by what, on reflection, seem to be good reasons. And yet, psychoanalysis teaches that legacies tend to be fraught—often in ways we do not fully understand. We ought thus to be wary of quick dismissals. So, for example, the term *self-consciousness* can be used to pick out any of a family of phenomena—a bare awareness of oneself, a sense of embarrassment in the presence of others, apperception, an awareness of an act as one's own, or a sense of oneself as a certain type of person—and one can choose any of these meanings and insist that psychoanalysis is not particularly about *that.* Or, one can decide that self-consciousness is a purely cognitive state, decide that such cognitive states are distinct from emotional states or from states of desire and again conclude that psychoanalysis could not possibly be so confined or confining. But there is no need to legislate such a division of psychic life. In human beings, emotional and desiring life can be shot through with self-consciousness (though it need not be). There is, of course, a picture of the mind in which self-consciousness stands over our emotional and desiring life, as though from a distance, observing it. And some experiences make it seem as though this picture is accurate. But there are powerful reasons for thinking this is a misleading image of our conscious mental life.[10] Properly understood, self-consciousness can be, in itself, emotional and desiring.

**3.** A more powerful objection to Freud's legacy takes the form of a dilemma. *Either* we take the claim that psychoanalysis facilitates the development of self-consciousness and tie it tightly to Freud's own understanding of facilitating free association according to the fundamental rule—in which case it is too narrow to cover the important psychoanalytic work that has burgeoned out from there. *Or* we interpret this claim broadly to include a wide range of techniques—for example, the naming of states that have remained unnamable for the analysand, or repairing the damaged capacity to represent one's mental states, or drawing attention to projective identifications or the total transference situation. These are situations in which the analyst says things that would never simply flow from the associations of the analysand, by identifying resistances à la Freud, in which case the claim that psychoanalysis facilitates self-consciousness becomes vague. Precisely by covering such a wide range of phenomena, it is not clear what work the claim does.

I want to place psychoanalysis on *both sides* of this dilemma—and argue that, ironically, that is the solution to the problem. The fundamental rule is an important paradigm, both because it gives us a way to look carefully into the microcosm—to see how a person's mind unfolds as he tries to speak it out loud—and because thereby it gives us a basis for branching out by expanding and enriching technique.

If we think about what makes human life valuable, we come upon a handful of terms: *freedom, happiness, reason, love, truthfulness, being in touch with reality, and self-consciousness.* What they have in common is that while they can be found in the details of life, they are also overarching terms—life-values, really—that have an essential vagueness about them. That is why we need poets and playwrights and novelists and philosophers: to help us reimagine and rethink what these values might consist in, how they might be lived. We need to be able to link the details of our lives with our most significant overarching concerns. That need is not going to go away—at least so long as there is something recognizable as the human condition. Our humanity—not merely the biological species *human* but what makes human life distinctive and valuable—partially consists in wrestling, both individually and communally, with what these values mean and how they actually fit into a life well lived. One way to live a meaningful human life is to give *determination* in one's life to these *determinable* (and thus somewhat vague) categories.[11]

In effect, Freud's legacy is to bind psychoanalysis to the Western humanistic tradition by offering a remarkable determination of what we might mean by *self-consciousness.* In this way, psychoanalysts ought to join the ranks of poets, playwrights, novelists, and philosophers who help us understand the most basic values of human life. In this essay, I want to sketch out how that might be.

The fundamental rule is one determination of what we might mean by *self-consciousness:* one that brings self-consciousness into the microcosm by enjoining the analysand to speak *everything* that comes to mind, no matter how small or trivial. There is elegance in the simplicity of this rule. Prima facie, the task looks easy: all one has to do is speak one's mind. And if, following Freud, one thinks of the fundamental rule as partially constituting psychoanalysis, then one can see simply by looking at the activity that it is structured so as to promote self-consciousness in the analysand.

As I said in the introduction, no one can follow the fundamental rule.[12] This is an empirical discovery of some magnitude. Freud insists that this inability to follow the rule flows from a difficult-to-understand *refusal* to follow it. That is, we are motivated not to allow self-consciousness to unfold in this way. Sometimes these resistances are themselves unconscious—and thus Freud came to recognize that the psychoanalytically significant unconscious cannot simply be identified with the repressed. He introduces the concept *ego* in part because he recognizes that the unconscious lies on both sides of the repressing-repressed divide.[13] But, he also notes, on occasion we can *experience* the resistance as itself an aspect of the unfolding self-conscious experience. So, for example, he instructs analysts to tell their analysands:

> You will notice that as you relate things various thoughts will occur to you which you would like to put aside on the ground of certain criticisms and objections. You will be tempted to say to yourself that this or that is irrelevant here, or is quite unimportant, or nonsensical, so that there is no need to say it. You must never give into these criticisms, but must say it in spite of them—indeed, you must say it precisely *because* you feel an aversion to doing so.[14]

And in a footnote he recalls his own experience:

> We must remember from our own self-analysis how irresistible the temptation is to yield to these pretexts put forward by critical judgment for rejecting certain ideas.[15]

This means that not only is the spontaneous unfolding of self-consciousness fraught, but that on occasion we can become immediately and directly aware of the conflict. It need not be merely an empirical hypothesis, an inference based on evidence such as a pause or a sudden change of subject.

It is here that the psychoanalyst begins to have something significant to say to the philosopher. When Aristotle said that humans are by nature rational animals, he did not mean that humans were just like other animals, except that they had a special added-on capacity—rationality.[16] Rather, he meant that rationality is the *form* of human life. That is, it is a transformative capacity. We are creatures for whom, when we are flourishing, thoughtful self-consciousness can shape our lives. Now, Aristotle was certainly aware of the possibility of intrapsychic conflict, and he knew that conflict can show up in self-conscious awareness. He thought there was what he called a nonrational part of the soul—through which we express emotion and desire—that *in a way* participates in reason.[17] One of the central tasks in human life, he thought, is to train the nonrational soul to "speak with the same voice" (*homophôneô*) as the rational part.[18] This is a remarkable achievement of intrapsychic harmony, but often we fall short, in which case the rational and nonrational parts of the soul speak with different voices. In this situation, a person can *feel* the conflict between judgment and desire—or between judgment and emotion. Philosophers tend to look on psychoanalysis as offering an extension of this picture: that the conflict often escapes conscious awareness because the desire is unconscious, and the desire is unconscious because it is in some way unacceptable and therefore repressed. If that were an accurate picture, psychoanalysis' ability to make a contribution to the philosophical tradition would be limited. Even Plato recognized that we have desires of which we are unconscious in waking life, that only come to the surface in dreams:

> Those [desires] that are awakened in sleep, when the rest of the soul—the rational, gentle and ruling part—slumbers. Then the beastly and savage part, full of food and drink, casts off sleep and seeks to find a way to gratify itself. You know that there is nothing it won't dare to do at such a time, free of all control by shame or reason. *It doesn't shrink from trying to have sex with a mother as it supposes, or with anyone else at all,* whether man, god or beast. It will commit any foul murder, and there is no food it refuses to eat. In a word, it omits no act of folly or shamelessness.[19]

But Freud's recognition that we are constitutionally unable to follow the fundamental rule makes an importantly different point: not simply that there is forbidden desire beyond the horizon of self-conscious awareness, but that the domain of self-consciousness is itself disrupted and distorted in ways it usually does not recognize and certainly does not understand.

But the real challenge to philosophy comes with Freud's second major discovery: that the unconscious is active according to its own form of mental activity. Freud puts it concisely:

> To sum up: *exemption from mutual contradiction, primary process* (mobility of cathexes), *timelessness,* and *replacement of external by psychical reality*—these are the characteristics which we may expect to find in processes belonging to the system *Ucs.*[20]

To understand the challenge, we need better to understand these conditions, but right away we can see the broad outline of the problem. Philosophers have found deep conceptual links between *freedom, rationality,* and *self-consciousness.* In a nutshell: our freedom consists in our ability to act on the basis of reasons (not merely to be tossed about by mindless causes); and these reasons manifest our freedom by working through our self-conscious understanding. But if, following Aristotle, one takes it to be reason's task to *inform* human life, how is reason to appropriate not merely a hidden and recalcitrant realm of desire, but also an alternative, nonrational form of mindedness? Without a good answer to this question, the philosophical conception of human being is cut from its moorings and floats free of human life.

The ancient Greek philosophers bequeathed us a tradition now known as moral psychology. They thought we could ground a conception of what it is for us to live *well* by giving us a nuanced psychological account of who we are. And they thought we could then better understand what it is for us to live well with each other. But if we are partially constituted by another form of mindedness, this raises altogether new questions of what it would be for us to live well. Psychoanalysis not only brings the problem into view, but it also begins to offer a solution. And if practical wisdom is the efficacious understanding of how to live well, then psychoanalysis might have a claim to be a wisdom won from illness.

**4.** Let us look more closely at this form of other-mindedness. Ms. A came into analysis seeking help with intimacy. Over time I came to see her as inhabiting a disappointing world. No matter what happened to her, she would interpret it under an aura of disappointment. Obviously, real-life disappointments and frustrations would focus her attention. But even if something she wanted occurred—getting promoted at work, asked out on a date by someone who interested her—she would diminish it: "The boss only promoted me because he wanted to promote my colleague, and he was too embarrassed not to include me" or "He invited me out because he got turned down by the person he really wanted to date." In short, no matter what happened in life—invited out / not invited out—Ms. A would tend to experience it as disappointing. I came to think of her as inhabiting a geodesic dome of disappointment, because each particular disappointment would be constructed out of a petite triangle. There would be two others—whether two parents, or two siblings, or a parent and a sibling, or two colleagues, or friends, etc.—in relation to whom she felt excluded and let down. She was unaware of how active she was in constructing the triangle and inflicting the painful disappointment on herself.

We are, of course, familiar with the idea of unconscious repetition, but in calling the unconscious *timeless,* Freud asks us to envision what the repetitions are all about. Each of the individual disappointments—over and over again—supports a structure of repetition. But the structure of repetition itself expresses a timeless thought: *that life shall be disappointing.* The thought functions as though it is an injunction, and its temporality is different from the familiar narratives of conscious life. Instead of a historical narrative of past, present, and future using familiar tensed verbs—"When I was a baby my mother wasn't there for me, now the boss at work lets me down"—the injunction hangs over all narratives, informing them with a timeless quality of disappointment. In this way, whatever the particular conscious narrative, a primordial structure of disappointment is timelessly held in place.

The timelessness of the unconscious can thus lend shape and durability to a life. From this perspective, the repetitions are manifestations of an underlying timeless persistence. This can contribute an uncanny sense that life is fated—for example, to be isolated and disappointing.[21] And the durability of this life-structure is reinforced by the unconscious also being, as Freud put it, "exempt from contradiction." Philosophers have interpreted this to mean that a person can at the same time believe both P and *not-P,* just so long as one of the beliefs is unconscious.[22] But that is not what Freud is getting at. Rather, in the grips of feeling disappointed, the countervailing evidence loses salience. It is not so much that the person has contradictory beliefs; it is that she loses the ability to experience herself as confronted with a contradiction. Freud's point is that unconscious productions tend to present themselves as *unopposed.*[23]

This gives us a plausible way to understand the "psychic determinism" of unconscious mental life. The point ought not to be that there will always be a hidden, antecedent mental cause determining the will—how could we ever know that?—but that disappointment functions as a formal cause, casting an aura over the events that do occur and providing them with a misleading and unhappy-making interpretation. We cannot know with confidence what the chain of efficient causes has been, from past to present to future. But we can have confidence for thinking that *whatever* happens, and *however* it comes about, there will be a tendency to incorporate it into an interpretive frame in which a sense of disappointment rules.

These features of the unconscious—timelessness and exemption from contradiction—have a peculiar upshot: namely, that by the time people try to take self-conscious account of themselves, figure out who they are and what matters to them, they are *already* working with a largely unconscious sense of a world and their place in it. If, in trying to take stock of their lives, they overlook this aspect of life, they are in danger of constructing an illusion of self-understanding. This is of obvious clinical significance, for it means that the risk of going through a pseudotherapy is significant. But this insight also has philosophical import. We cannot legitimately think of the self as constructed by self-conscious judgments—about how to act, which desires to satisfy, what to believe, and so on.[24] For these judgments are themselves haunted by a core unconscious fantasy—for example, *that life shall be disappointing*—that provides its own source of unity for the self. In the case of Ms. A, disappointment was the most active principle constituting her life. The temptation to think otherwise derives, I suspect, from an inadequate anthropology: one that assumes that, but for the organizing principle of self-conscious judgment, we are threatened by an unstructured chaos of unruly desires. This is a philosopher's picture that goes back to Plato, but it does not capture who we are, and it ought to be abandoned. If a person is genuinely to take herself self-consciously into account, there must be a way of taking such a core fantasy into account. Psychoanalysis is aimed at doing this in an effective way.

These core fantasies tend to have a philosophical air about them. They began to form in childhood as an imaginative yet ultimately nonrational attempt to address a basic problem of human vulnerability. And then, precisely because the unconscious is timeless and exempt from contradiction, the fantasies persist into adult life. The fact that they develop through the loose associations and condensations of primary process, that they embed hidden sources of satisfaction, and that they are regularly experienced as real adds to their durability. Ironically, our imaginations thus act like a resourceful philosopher who happens to lack the capacity for rational thought. As finite, nonomnipotent creatures, we are constitutively vulnerable in a world over which we have, at best, limited control. How disappointing that we cannot render ourselves invulnerable to disappointment! An imaginary strategy that the young Ms. A chanced upon was to render herself invulnerable to the world's disappointments by getting there first and, in fantasy, inflicting the disappointment upon herself. This is an omnipotent "victory"—being in control of the disappointment—that consists in a lifetime of suffering disappointment. It has this illusory benefit: it protects a childish sense of omnipotence from the slings and arrows of outrageous fortune. There is, as it were, a hiding place for her omnipotence, and the disappointments paradoxically reinforce her sense of power and control. Obviously, from the point of view of living *well,* this is a disastrous outcome. But to address this problem adequately, we need to find a way to acknowledge that the Freudian unconscious has a tendency to turn us, unbeknownst to ourselves, into misguided but stubbornly insistent interpreters of the world. How could one ever undo *that?*

**5.** At the beginning of a session several years into the analysis, I could hear Ms. A fall repeatedly into silence. She would break the silence with mundane stories about work, or superficial accounts of how she was feeling—and then she would fall into silence again. I let this go on for a while: I had a hunch that Ms. A was experiencing some internal pressure, and I wanted her to live with it for a while so that she might notice it. But at some point—as she was living inside a pause—I asked her if she was aware she was pausing, and whether there might be something on her mind. She said that actually she had been thinking about asking me if I could reschedule an hour. But she was reluctant to ask because she thought I would just say no. A little bit later, she admitted that she had had a daydream that I would be with another analysand, whom I preferred. So, here in the living present of the analytic situation was one of those petite triangles of disappointment that made up her geodesic dome, only this time I was included. Obviously, this is an instance of what Freud called *transference*—an attempt to draw the analyst inside an unconscious drama. And, as we have seen, this means that the analyst and the analysand are together drawn into direct contact with that other form of mindedness that helps constitute who we are. Freud said, "Transference presents the psychoanalyst with the greatest difficulties."[25] He meant both the technical difficulties of handling it and the emotional difficulties of tolerating it. Freud came to see that this was the key to the efficacy of psychoanalytic treatment:

> But it should not be forgotten that it is precisely [transferences] that do us the inestimable service of *making the patient's hidden and forgotten impulses immediate and manifest.* For when all is said and done, *it is impossible to destroy anyone in absentia or in effigy.*[26]

Ms. A associated to a litany of times throughout her life when she had wanted to speak but stopped herself for fear of disappointment, thereby disappointing herself. She could see for herself that this was a fractal moment: immediately graspable in the present, but containing in itself the large-scale structure of her life. She associated to any number of occasions in her life when she inhibited herself in this way. She could see—not just as a theoretical insight, but as an emotionally laden moment in the living present—that she was protecting herself from being disappointed *by me* by anticipating it and inflicting the disappointment *on herself.* She also grasped immediately and from the inside that her sense of rationality had been skewed. She knew with clarity and immediate availability to consciousness: *this triangle was her creation.* She then made a comment of unusual emotional intensity: "The rage I anticipate, the rage if you say no . . . no one has even said no. *It feels like an eternal obstacle, a weight on my throat,* keeping me from speaking." The power of these words cannot be gleaned from their content alone. To be sure, the statement was a sincere, accurate, and insightful account of her feelings; they also expressed her feelings and were uttered by her in the process of coming to self-understanding. As such, the statement might have therapeutic value. But, on this occasion, the power of the words went beyond that. It was as though a weight was literally lifted off her throat. One could hear her larynx open, her throat clear. Freud taught that the unconscious often speaks in corporeal terms, with bodily symptoms and corporeal representations of mental activity.[27] In this moment, Ms. A is self-consciously describing her experience, and she is using a metaphor to do so: it feels as though a weight has been lifted from her throat. This is the voice of self-conscious experience. But in the same moment, her unconscious also speaks in its own form of mindedness. In a funny way, however, conscious and unconscious are, to use Aristotle's term, speaking with the same voice (*homophôneô*). It is as though the word has become flesh. Ms. A could feel the various voices in her psyche come together. She had a sense of vibrancy and efficacy: she could *feel* that she was actively taking this particular triangle apart. Her awareness of her efficacy was constitutive of this efficacy. That is, her ability to break this triangle down was flowing immediately through her self-conscious grasp of the artificiality of the triangle.

Do that again and again and again with the petite triangles as they keep coming up over time and you have the process that Freud called *working-through*. It is too simple to call this a step-by-step process, but it is sufficiently discrete that it takes the mystery out of the thought that over time the analysand herself can take apart a world that had hitherto held her captive. This is ethically significant in that it enables a person to live more realistically and truthfully.

**6.** When Aristotle isolates a special kind of wisdom (practical wisdom, *phronêsis*) and distinguishes it from theoretical wisdom, he is not trying to specify a certain subject matter (the practical) but rather a peculiar *form of causality*—one in which self-conscious understanding is itself efficacious in bringing about what it understands. This requires explication, of course. But grasping this point is important for understanding the peculiar efficacy of psychoanalysis, and thus the broadscale place of psychoanalysis in the Western humanistic tradition.

Even my simplest intentional action requires some degree of self-conscious awareness. Of course, it is this very awareness that often breaks down or goes missing in the myriad acts with which psychoanalysis deals. But we can understand such breakdowns better if we grasp the straightforward case. So, for example, in going to the store to buy food for dinner, I must be to some degree aware that that is what I am doing. That awareness helps constitute the intentional act as the very act that it is.[28] With a different understanding, I might perform the same physical acts but be doing something different: for example, exercising; retracing my steps from a previous trip; taking a walk; hoping to meet a stranger; sending a message to a spy. I am also aware that my understanding of what I am doing is itself efficacious in bringing about the very thing I am doing.[29] Throughout the time I am shopping, my awareness of what I am doing is causally efficacious in the doing and is at the very same time an awareness of that causal efficacy as my own. The doing and the awareness of the doing are thus internally related to each other: they are, as Sebastian Rödl put it, "the same reality."[30] In normal psychic conditions, it is impossible that there should be one thing (my shopping for dinner) and another thing (my conscious awareness of shopping for dinner), as though I stood in relation to my acts as an observer. Of course, I can relate to myself as an observer, but it is precisely then that the normal psychic conditions of intentional action break down. Part of what it is for me to be shopping for dinner is that I must be immediately and nonobservationally aware that that is what I am doing. This awareness contains within itself an immediate and nonobservational awareness of my efficacy. I am aware that this is *my doing.*

There are three points to take away from this simplified example: (1) In ordinary intentional action, one is (to some degree, in some manner) self-consciously aware that one is performing the action. (2) This self-consciousness is internal to the action. (3) The self-conscious understanding of the action is causally efficacious in bringing about the very action it helps constitute.

Practical wisdom, for Aristotle, is excellence with respect to this peculiar form of causality: the ability to live well based on, and flowing from, one's correct understanding of how to live well. Practical wisdom is itself efficacious in bringing about the life it understands to be a good life. But then Aristotle thought that the good life must be one of psychic harmony, and this requires that the nonrational part of the psyche "listen well to" and "speak with the same voice as" the thoughtful, self-conscious judgments of practical wisdom.[31] But how does one bring this integration about? Aristotle approached this at the level of education and public policy: we need to train children from early youth into the right sort of habits (thus educating the nonrational soul to obey), so that by the time a person can make judgments about how to live, he will be wholehearted in his decision. But on how precisely this psychic unity is achieved, Aristotle is silent. That is, he tells us how to educate the youth, and he tells us that success consists in the nonrational soul "speaking with the same voice as" or "listening better to" or "obeying" the reason's judgment. But he gives us no textured psychological account of what any of these conditions consist in. This, I think, is the place where Aristotle's moral psychology runs out of steam, though it is not clear that Aristotle sees that anything is missing. But an adequate moral psychology ought to be able to tell us more about what psychic integration consists in.

Our challenge is of course significantly different from Aristotle's. In particular, we are concerned with incorporating an unconscious, nonrational part of the soul that, as Freud teaches us, proceeds according to its own unusual form of mental activity. And we are often concerned with moments in the microcosm of an individual's life, when life is not going particularly well. But Aristotle's account of the practical shows us how self-consciousness can have its own immediate efficacy. Practical understanding is the cause of what it understands. This is a good place to start. And if we now go back to Freud's fundamental rule, we can see that it is designed to bring enhanced self-awareness to the mind's emerging productions. Some of those productions express the voice of the unconscious, and on favorable occasions self-consciousness can, via its own activity, effect an immediate transformation. One can see this transformation in Ms. A's utterance. Until that moment, Ms. A had gone through life—repetitively, timelessly—inhibiting herself by unconsciously anticipating her own rage. Ironically, it is precisely by speaking the truth of her condition that she was able to undo it. And she undid it via a direct and immediate understanding of what she had previously done unconsciously. This provides an example of self-conscious awareness *informing* the hitherto unconscious, nonrational part of the soul.

By now it should be clear that psychoanalysis aims at more than theoretical insight into oneself (however far-reaching and accurate). And it aims at more than the practical ability to take ameliorative steps when one notices a problem arising. All this may be of genuine help, but from a psychoanalytic point of view, more far-reaching psychological change is possible. The analysand can come over time to apprehend her activity *directly and immediately*—an activity that had hitherto been unconscious. This is why transference, and the handling of the transference, is invaluable. If the analysand is creating a disappointing world, she will bring that activity into the transference. And this puts her in a position to bring about her own psychic change—*actively, directly, immediately via the efficacy of her own self-conscious understanding.* This is a different mode of self-consciousness than the theoretical understanding that, say, I have a tendency to experience events in disappointing ways. It is, rather, an immediate apprehension of self-consciousness informing her life. And it makes possible a change of psychic structure *via* a self-conscious grasp of what that structure has been and what it might become. I think of it as a practical efficacy of the self-conscious mind.

**7.** This raises some questions about our most basic values: Are we to be creatures whose humanity partially consists in taking responsibility for our humanity? In particular, are we to continue to be creatures who take responsibility for shaping who we are via a self-conscious grasp of who we might become? Or is the category *human* to be emptied out—evacuated of the struggles with meaning and value that, over the past several thousand years, we have come to see as constituting the distinctively human mind? At the limit, *human* becomes a merely biological category, the name for a species that can continue reproducing itself regardless of the quality of mind it instantiates. It is a contingent question whether the human mind, as we have come to know it, will continue to exist. It is a question that lies at the heart of the Western humanistic tradition; and it is here that psychoanalysis is poised to make an invaluable contribution.

It is these days fashionable to be concerned with outcome studies—for example, trying to measure how well psychoanalysis stacks up against other treatment modalities. I want to make a claim that is as earnest as it is ironic: the aim of psychoanalysis is psychoanalysis. And when it comes to this aim, no other treatment modality can match it!

Think of Aristotle's famous distinction between a process (*kinêsis*), like building a house, and an activity (*energeia*), like living in a home.[32] Building a house is a process that has a beginning, a middle, and an end; in this case, the process comes to an end when the house is built. Living in a home, by contrast, is an open-ended activity that can manifest a fulfilling way of life. Psychoanalysis, I want to claim, is both process and activity. As a process, it aims, in the first instance, to address specific problems the analysand is facing, or problems that become clearer as the analysis progresses. But ultimately, psychoanalysis (as process) aims at its own activity. Psychoanalysis as activity is precisely self-consciousness appropriating and finding creative ways of living with the creations of one's own unconscious mental activity. Psychoanalysis has been shaped, and continues to be shaped, so that we might address the unconscious, nonrational aspects of the psyche in humane and understanding ways. This is an ongoing aspect of a full, rich, meaningful life.

Aristotle tells us that when it comes to living organisms, the psyche is the form or principle of unity of such creatures.[33] When it comes specifically to humans, that principle is to be understood in terms of the psyche's rational activity in an active and full life.[34] This, he concludes, is the characteristic activity of human life; it gives us the conditions of our flourishing.[35] His point is *not* that human life should be consumed with rational thinking. Rather, he thinks it is given to us to be thoughtful, self-conscious creatures. This includes a thoughtful, self-conscious appropriation of the nonrational parts of our psyches.[36] That is, our emotional lives and our desires should not be strangers to us, dominating us through our ignorance, but should be aspects of our lives that we, in one way or another, appreciate and comprehend. For Aristotle, this is what it is to be human. And to live well in this way is what it is for us to flourish. But psychoanalysis *considered as activity* is just this characteristic human activity: the thoughtful, self-conscious appropriation of the unconscious, nonrational parts of the psyche. Of course, we know much more than Aristotle did about what is involved in taking on such a task. Nevertheless, psychoanalysis is carried out in the service of living a flourishing human life. And it is itself a manifestation of such a life. Psychoanalysis is a way humans flourish as the active, thoughtful, self-conscious creatures that we are.

By now it should be clear that psychoanalysis gives us a new sense in which wisdom can be won from illness. Psychoanalysis provides significant insight into hitherto poorly understood forms of human suffering; but it is also an exemplification of human health. For the task of living well with one's own unconscious does not go away when, say, the acute suffering of neurosis has been eased. Living well with one's unconscious is a life task, one that is appropriate to thoughtful, self-conscious activity. And we come to understand better what this task consists in as we watch psychoanalysis itself deepen and enrich its own techniques, in response to the myriad challenges that arise in the treatment situation. This is the activity of determination that helps us better comprehend this determinable: *psychoanalysis is the activity of thoughtful self-consciousness informing human life.* That is, as psychoanalysis develops, we should come to better understand what it means for self-consciousness to inform human life. Certainly what psychoanalysis has already taught us is that we should expect psychic integration to be improvisational, ironic, syncopated, jazzy, and creative.[37] Philosophers need to understand that any plausible sense of "psychic unity" will be to some extent uncanny. We should not expect or want the "unity" of a marching band.

It would seem, then, that in the first and primary instance, the wisdom that psychoanalysis offers is practical and, one might even say, poetical. For the person who inhabited a disappointing world, psychoanalytic transformation did not consist primarily in the theoretical insight that she had been inhabiting a disappointing world (though that was a moment in the treatment), but in the creative opening up of new possibilities for living. These are possibilities that came into being for her via her developing practical and poetical awareness that those possibilities exist. It is, as we have seen, an immediate and direct grasp of one's own efficacy in the self-conscious creation of new possibilities. Unlike theoretical wisdom, whose knowledge is caused by what it knows, practical and poetical wisdom *is* the cause of what it knows. Self-conscious thought comes to understand that it has new possibilities for living by creating those possibilities, and it creates those possibilities precisely by self-consciously coming to grasp what they are. This creative opening-up is constituted by self-consciously *appropriating* the creative powers of (hitherto unconscious) imagination. Creativity here is not simply the recognition of a new possibility; it is a creative manner of thinking that itself opens new possibilities for living. This is why the emerging wisdom is practical and poetical: it is the cause of what it understands.

The philosopher Søren Kierkegaard famously said that to become human or to learn what it means to become human does not come that easily. By now we can begin to grasp what this might mean. Think of becoming human not in terms of biological birth, but in terms of what Aristotle considered our characteristic activity: thoughtful, self-conscious activity of the psyche that takes responsibility for living a human life. Psychoanalysis is a manifestation of just such activity. The same is true of learning what it means to be human. Kierkegaard is not concerned with the theoretical mastery of a difficult subject matter, the "human condition"; rather, he is concerned with what we learn practically and poetically when we go through the process of becoming human. Kierkegaard's use of "or" is exegetical: "to become human" and "to learn what it means to become human" are two ways of naming the same activity of psyche. What Freud and subsequent generations of psychoanalysts have discovered is that that very activity of psyche is, to a significant extent, the activity of psychoanalysis itself. No wonder it has not come that easily.

CHAPTER TWO

# Integrating the Nonrational Soul

**1.** Aristotle says that "there seems to be some other nature of the soul (*allê tis physis tês psychês*) that is nonrational, but which in a way participates in reason."[1] The Oxford and Loeb translations give us a nonrational "element" of the soul, and the Rowe translation gives us another "kind" of soul, so these translations flatten out the thought that with *"physis"* Aristotle is here talking about a different nature.[2] Since nature, for Aristotle, is an inner principle of change and rest, this would suggest that the nonrational soul on which Aristotle is focusing has its own principle of functioning. This is a thought that is in danger of getting lost in translation. For Aristotle, we are in the best position to understand what a principle is when we grasp the excellent functioning of that of which it is a principle. For the virtuous person—in this case, Aristotle mentions the temperate and courageous person—Aristotle gives us two criteria: first, the nonrational soul is better able and more willing to listen (*euêkoôteron*) to reason; second, with respect to all things, the nonrational soul speaks with the same voice (*homophônei*) as reason.[3] That is, the excellence of this nonrational part of the soul consists in communicating—listening *to* and speaking *with* reason. So, the nonrational soul has a distinctive form of activity, but that activity is nevertheless communicative: it listens and it speaks. And performing that communicative activity well is nothing other than ethical virtue, according to Aristotle. For ethical virtue is the excellence of the nonrational soul.[4]

This communicating function—the nature of this nonrational soul—also tends to get flattened out in translation. So, instead of drawing attention to listening, the Oxford translation says that the nonrational soul of the virtuous person is "still more obedient" to reason than the soul of the merely continent person. Of course, in a sense that is true; but it gives the misleading impression that the breakthrough from continence to virtue consists in the degree of obedience. For the virtuous person, however, the issue is not the *degree* of obedience per se—think of fanatical compliance—rather it is the *manner* in which the obedience takes shape. It is obedience that flows from listening well and willingly to what reason says. As another example, the Rowe translation says that this nonrational soul of the virtuous person "always chimes with reason." Again, true in a sense, but one bell can chime with another without being in communication. Etymologically, the verb *phôneô* paradigmatically means not the sounds of chimes or bells, but rather the sound made by voice, by speaking or crying out. This voice need not be endowed with *logos.* Aristotle uses the term to cover the cries and calls of other animals. Among other applications, Aristotle uses *phônê* for the voice of the nonrational soul.[5] So, when the nonrational soul *homophônei* with reason, it is not just chiming in; it is speaking with the same voice. This shows up in the wholeheartedness of the virtuous person acting virtuously, but Aristotle suggests that this is both the outcome and the manifestation of excellent intrapsychic communication.

There are, I suspect, two reasons for this flattening. First, in this passage, Aristotle is not concerned exclusively with the excellent use of this nonrational soul, but also with a range of less-than-excellent manifestations. That is because he is concerned to make a large-scale distinction between the nutritive soul—a nonrational part of the soul that, he thinks, in no way participates in reason—and the nonrational part that participates in reason to some degree or other. Of course, this includes nonvirtuous people, notably the merely continent person. The nonrational soul of the continent person never rises above obedience, though he is susceptible to admonishment, reprimand, and encouragement. For him, excellent communication between the rational and nonrational parts of the soul is the very thing he is missing. Second, to a contemporary English speaker, the phrase "speak with the same voice as" or "listening better and more willingly to" may, on a superficial first hearing, sound as though it leaves out the active living that is the life of the virtuous person. But, for Aristotle, the courageous person acting courageously is precisely an instance of the nonrational soul listening better and more willingly to, and speaking with the same voice as, reason. The courageous person's courageous act is a manifestation of this excellence of intrapsychic communication.

More is at stake here than the interpretation of a short passage from Aristotle. The question is what Aristotelian virtue consists in. Aristotle delineates an intermediate part of the soul that, depending on the way one looks at it, can be considered either rational or nonrational.[6] It is nonrational in that it lacks the proper capacities of reason; but it is rational in that it can participate in reason's activities, and at its best can listen well to and speak with the same voice as reason. It is on this distinction that Aristotle grounds his further distinction between intellectual and ethical virtues.[7] Ethical virtue is of the nonrational soul. And, as we have seen, the nonrational soul has a nature—its own inner principle of change—that consists in excellent communication (of the appropriate sort) with reason. This communication is what the integration of the nonrational soul consists in. We may not yet know much about it, but we are in a position to see that anything less must be something less than Aristotelian ethical virtue.

**2.** It is this possibility of the rational and nonrational parts of the soul speaking with the same voice that lends insight into why, for both Plato and Aristotle, psychic harmony should have ethical value.[8] If we were creatures such that psychic harmony was a real option only when our capacity for reason was enfeebled, it would lose its appeal. What makes harmony attractive for these thinkers is that they see the possibility of reason being instantiated in an individual human being, and the nonrational soul trained in such a way that reason can successfully communicate with the nonrational soul—thus manifesting itself in a life lived according to reason, untroubled by countervailing factors.

It is another question what this possible harmony consists in. Plato and Aristotle are explicit—at least, at the level of public policy, general education, and politics—about how this condition might be achieved. But they are skimpy about what it is composed of beyond saying it is a speaking-with-the-same-voice. In particular, as we have seen, Aristotle says the nonrational soul has its own nature, and that means it has its own internal principle of change, even though he also says that in a way it participates in reason. If it participates in reason, it must be a form of mindedness; but if it has a different nature—a different principle of change—this implies that it is a different form of mindedness from that of the rational soul. But how can two distinct forms of mindedness communicate with each other? How could there be a harmony of different natures? It is not enough to say that each participates in reason; we need to know how they participate, and how that makes effective communication possible.

This is the point, I think, where Aristotle's moral psychology peters out. For a moral psychology to be robust, Bernard Williams taught us, it must stake out a space that, on the one hand, allows in normatively laden concepts such as freedom, integrity, or truthfulness as values but, on the other, avoids collapsing into a *moralizing* psychology, one that simply assumes the very categories it seeks to vindicate.[9] This space is under pressure when Aristotle tells us that the nonrational soul of the virtuous person is *obedient* to reason.[10] Aristotle is here using the concept he wishes to valorize without giving us a sufficiently rich account of what the right kind of obedience consists in. Aristotle does say that the obedient nonrational soul *listens well to* and *speaks with the same voice as* the rational soul, but within his philosophy these terms serve as suggestive placeholders. If one could fill them in with real content, one would have a robust moral psychology. But without that filling-in, it is difficult to avoid the charge that one is merely moralizing.

Aristotle does offer an intriguing model. The nonrational soul, he says, participates in reason as though it were listening and obedient to a father.[11] To be sure, this is a patriarchal image, but the important point for now is that the nature of the nonrational soul is portrayed as essentially childish. It is as though it is permanently en route to maturity, but its excellence does not consist in actually reaching adulthood. Rather, the excellent nonrational soul is a fine instance of a childish soul. Its excellence consists not in "what it will be when it grows up," but in a distinctively *non*rational ability to listen to and communicate with reason. The external, social model of intrapsychic speaking-with-the-same-voice would thus be good parent–child communication. The child who is developing well is good at attending to his parent's communication; a good parent knows not only what to say, but also how to communicate it well to the child. Still, Aristotle's psychology leaves us without the resources to understand what such a communicative relationship consists in.

A distinctively *moral* psychology, Williams says, "uses the categories of meaning, reason and value, *but leaves it open, or even problematical,* in what way moral reasons and ethical values fit with other motives and desires, how far they express those other motives and how far they are in conflict with them." Williams thought that neither Aristotle's psychology nor

Plato's could live up to this task, and he looked elsewhere for inspiration: "Thucydides and (I believe) the tragedians, among the ancient writers, had such a psychology, *and so in the modern world did Freud.*"[12] This is a suggestion I would like to take up, but take it in a different direction than Williams envisaged.

**3.** Unlike Williams, I do not see Aristotle's psychology as inevitably moralizing, but rather as unfinished. So, instead of using Freud as a way of leaving Aristotle's moral psychology behind, I want to argue that psychoanalysis can provide valuable insight into the communicative relations between the rational and nonrational parts of the soul. It should thus be taken seriously by anyone who wishes not simply to study Aristotle but to extend a broadly Aristotelian approach to contemporary ethical life. It might at first seem strange that I am linking Aristotle's nonrational soul to the Freudian unconscious, since the major activity of Aristotle's nonrational soul is manifest in emotional life, and our emotions tend to be conscious experiences. However, Freud's discovery is that the nonrational soul has a significant unconscious dimension *and* that it proceeds according to its own form.

Indeed, I believe Freud's most significant discovery is not of the unconscious per se but that unconscious mental activity has a distinctive nature. The unconscious, Freud teaches, proceeds according to the loose associations and condensations of primary process mental activity. It works in a mode that is exempt from contradiction and in a temporality of timelessness; it substitutes psychical reality for external reality.[13] By coming to understand this alternative form of mental activity, we can work out in significant detail the voice of the nonrational soul. It also emerges from Freud's case studies that the nonrational soul—the part he called the "unconscious"—is typically engaged in a basic project: trying to address a problem of human existence, albeit in a nonrational and childish way. Thus it makes sense to think of the Freudian unconscious as "another nature of the soul" in Aristotle's sense. It has its own principles of change as well as a *telos*—namely, negotiating a fundamental problem of human existence (albeit in a fantasized, imaginative, nonrational way). In this sense, Freud's discovery is an enrichment of that original Aristotelian intuition. And psychoanalysis, the *praxis,* is the attempt to facilitate communication between the nonrational and the rational soul.

This has not been appreciated due to a widespread misconception of what psychoanalysis is. The misconception has various manifestations, but at its core is the idea of the psychoanalyst as an expert on what is hidden in another person's unconscious mind. In contemporary philosophy, psychoanalysis is often invoked as a contrast-case to the nonobservational, first-person authority we ordinarily have with respect to our beliefs. So, David Finkelstein invites us to:

> Imagine someone—call him Harry—who says: "My therapist tells me that I unconsciously believe no one could ever fall in love with me, and she's generally right about such things, so I suppose I must have that belief." Let's imagine Harry's therapist *is* right about him and that Harry is justified in believing that she's right about him. Harry is, then, aware of his belief that no one could ever fall in love with him; he knows about it. . . . But we can imagine that Harry holds no such conscious belief.[14]

He continues:

> We speak with first-person authority not about all our mental states, but only our conscious ones. I might learn in therapy that I harbor unconscious anger toward my sister, and having learned this, I might say to a friend, "I've discovered that I'm unconsciously angry with my sister." In such a circumstance I would not speak with first-person authority. If a friend were to ask me why I take myself to harbor unconscious anger toward my sister, it wouldn't make sense for me to reply, "What do you mean? I'm just really angry with her." . . . *[T]he claims I make about my unconscious states of mind are only as good as the evidence that backs them up.*[15]

And Richard Moran invokes analysis as an arena in which one can acquire nontransparent beliefs about oneself.

> In various familiar therapeutic contexts, for instance, the manner in which the analysand becomes aware of various of her beliefs and other attitudes does not necessarily conform to the Transparency Condition. The person who feels anger at the dead parent for having abandoned her, or who feels betrayed or deprived of something by another child, *may*

> *only know of this attitude through the eliciting and interpreting of evidence of various kinds.* She might become thoroughly convinced, both from the constructions of the analyst, as well as from her own appreciation of the evidence, that the attitude must indeed be attributed to her. And yet, at the same time, when she reflects on the world-directed question itself, whether she has indeed been betrayed by this person, she may find that the answer is no or can't be settled one way or the other. So transparency fails because she cannot learn of this attitude of hers by reflection on the object of that attitude. *She can only learn of it in a fully theoretical manner, taking an empirical stance toward herself as a particular psychological subject.*[16]

On this model, the psychoanalyst is an expert at taking an empirical stance with respect to the analysand, perhaps picking up unusual bits of available evidence and then making an inference to what must be going on in the analysand's unconscious mind. The analyst might also be good at encouraging the analysand to take just such an empirical stance with respect to herself.

Of course, in popular culture there are the familiar images of the analyst as someone relentlessly searching for repressed memories, or the analyst who somehow has the keys to unlock the psychic basement and a special light to shine under the cobwebbed stairs.

All of these images are based on something, but they misrepresent the psychoanalytic situation. Aristotle tells us that if we are to grasp an area of knowledge adequately, it is important to find the right starting point.[17] And we must also distinguish the order in which we discover a field of knowledge from the order in which we set it out when we understand its mature form.[18] At the beginning of his career, Freud was on the hunt for repressed memories, and he was willing to make so-called deep interpretations of what was purportedly going on in the analysand's mind. An interpretation is considered "deep" if it is not easily available to the analysand's own self-conscious experience. But Freud fairly quickly realized that simply telling a person the contents of her unconscious not only had no positive therapeutic effect, but it also regularly provoked irritation and resistance; on occasion it led to the analysand breaking off treatment. In effect, he recognized that simply telling another person the truth about himself was not a therapeutic method. And, as we saw in the last chapter, the more Freud thought about therapeutic efficacy the more he was led to abandon deep interpretations or the search for the historic truth about a moment in the past, and concentrate instead on facilitating the analysand's own associations.[19] On this conception, the psychoanalyst is not an expert about the hidden contents of another's mind. Rather, the analyst is a facilitator of the free thought and free speech of another. The emphasis now is on the analyst facilitating a process through which the analysand himself or herself will come to be able to speak its meaning. In this sense, psychoanalysis stands in a tradition of Socratic midwifery.

From the beginning, Freud encouraged his patients to say what was on their minds, but by 1912 he had explicitly formulated what he called "the fundamental rule" of psychoanalysis: namely, that the analysand should try to say whatever comes into conscious awareness without censorship or inhibition.[20] In calling this rule *fundamental,* Freud signals that this is the basic norm of psychoanalysis: the analysand is to try to speak his mind; the analyst is to facilitate the process. I take this to be a constitutive norm: we come over time to understand what psychoanalysis is as we come to understand what is genuinely involved in facilitating a process by which the analysand develops the capacity to speak his or her mind in an unfettered way. Whatever the complexities of technique, it is worth noticing a great simplicity here: a single norm to speak one's mind freely. And there is this humanistic elegance: whatever therapeutic value psychoanalysis has, it flows through the self-conscious understanding of the analysand. Obviously, there are myriad phenomena one might use the term *self-consciousness* to describe. But the fundamental rule gives us a basis for an unusual, and perhaps surprising, claim: *psychoanalysis is the activity of facilitating the free flow of self-consciousness.* This claim is more illuminating than the (ultimately misleading) claim that psychoanalysis concerns the discovery of hidden contents of the mind.[21]

It is also misleading to characterize this relationship in terms of one person being an especially good observer of empirical evidence inadvertently disclosed by the other. The psychoanalytic relationship is one of emotional intimacy and mutual, concerned engagement—more like a second-personal, I-thou relation. As a formal matter, psychoanalysis begins with one person asking another person for help and the other person responding that he thinks he can be of help precisely through offering psychoanalysis. Whatever the demands of psychoanalytic neutrality, it is not a stance of detached, empirical observation. So, an analyst may be on the lookout for empirically available evidence, notably a pause in the flow of speech—but it is in the context of a committed engagement to help. This help does not consist in using such an occasion to formulate an empirically grounded hypothesis to present to the analysand. Rather, it is an occasion to ask the analysand if she is aware that she has paused, and to wait to hear the analysand's own reports of what she was thinking during the pause, where her mind wandered, and whether she had an internal sense of whether the pause was somehow related to what she was thinking. It is astonishing how much will come to the analysand's mind in this way.[22] In such cases, the analyst is not proposing an empirically grounded hypothesis about the hidden contents of another's mind; he is facilitating a process by which the analysand expands and deepens her own capacity for first-person authority on the contents of her mind.

**4.** But, as we have seen, there is a characteristic problem.[23] Very early on in an analysis, there will be some kind of disruption to the free flow of speaking one's mind: a pause or silence; a sudden change of subject; intense fatigue; the eruption of a somatic issue like coughing, stomachache, headache, bowel troubles; and so on. These disruptions are not merely accidental but are motivated in various ways. They tend to function as inhibitions—sometimes under the guidance of self-conscious will, often bypassing the will, often just outside of conscious awareness, though it is relatively easy to draw a person's attention to them. These moments are of philosophical significance. They show, first, that there is something internally conflicted about the spontaneous unfolding of self-consciousness. Psychoanalysis promotes self-conscious awareness of these specific moments of internal conflict within self-consciousness. Second, these are moments in which the rational and nonrational parts of the soul are speaking in manifestly different voices. It is as though the unconscious is interrupting the flow of self-conscious speech. Psychoanalysis takes up these moments when the nonrational and rational parts of the soul speak discordantly. It thus works on the obverse side of virtue.

It is a mistake to think that these moments of conflicting voices always take the form of threatened *akrasia*—whether the person will stand by her judgment or give in to temptation. They can be moments that call into question the faculty of judgment. Freud formulated the concept of *ego* precisely because he came to see that the repressed unconscious is only part of the story. There are, in addition, motivated strategies for living, for dealing with uncomfortable material, for keeping the repressed at bay that are themselves unconscious. And these modes of ego-functioning themselves resist self-conscious understanding. Thus "the unconscious" lies on both sides of the repressing / repressed divide.

> We find ourselves in an unforeseen situation. We have come upon something in the ego itself which is also unconscious, which behaves exactly like the repressed—that is, which produces powerful effects without itself being conscious and which requires special work before it can be made conscious.[24]

And he concludes, "We must admit that the characteristic of being unconscious begins to lose significance for us. It becomes a quality which can have many meanings."[25]

From an Aristotelian perspective, this is important because it means that "the unconscious" can show up as something that looks like character. We are not just dealing with hidden forbidden wishes. It would require an essay of its own to delineate how the Aristotelian and Freudian divisions of the psyche map onto each other. For now, the important point is this: the ego is and takes itself to be the voice of reason in that it is the capacity for self-conscious deliberation and intentional action, for forming conscious beliefs on the basis of perception and argument, and for giving reasons to others. It takes itself to be rational and reality-governed; and when all is going well, that is correct. However, Freud's point is that a person's capacity for reason can be pervaded by unconscious, nonrational, mental forces; and when that happens, reason can be pervasively distorted by a nonrational form of thinking. The issue is not just about repressed desires. And this complicates the question of what it would be for the rational and nonrational parts of the soul to speak with the same voice.

Here is a brief, clinical vignette. It illustrates, I think, the power of mind that develops when the psyche comes to speak with a unified voice. Mr. B had been in analysis with me for five years. He is a successful academic and had arranged to do further training in his field. He associates to me: I seem to him to be someone trying to learn new things. He comes to a session and begins to report a dream he had the night before:

> I'm watching cars that drive through red lights. They keep on going through. I have a series of reactions. They're getting away with something. They shouldn't be doing that. I feel angry; why didn't I do that? Could I get away with it? What stands out is: they got away with it. There's no accident, no police siren.

At first he does not associate to the dream; he talks instead about problems at work. He then moves on to discuss the program for his further education. He is excited to be able to start something new. But he called a friend who lives in a different part of the country, who had earlier gone through the program. His friend said that it was a shame Mr. B had not done this program a long time ago, when other faculty were teaching. And then Mr. B said:

> Maybe that's why I'm having dreams, seeing other cars racing through red lights. I'm not doing that. It makes me mad. I'm the one who stops for the green light. I even stop for the yellow light. Other people don't and they even get away with it.

I was struck by his slip of the tongue; and I had a sense that Mr. B had not noticed it. This is a moment in which the unconscious breaks through the membrane established by the fundamental rule and speaks with its own voice. I said:

> You said you're the one who stops for the *green* light.

Mr. B responded:

> No! I didn't know I said that. As I was waiting outside for you to come down, I was thinking, there's a lot of exciting things happening. So why do I feel so down. Green is the go light, and unbeknownst to myself I'm staying. That's where I stop.

This was a brief moment, but the more Mr. B associated to it, the more he came to see it reflected a world. It began with him recognizing he had telephoned someone *who could be expected to* run down the program. He also felt a pang of envy, for this other person was enjoying her academic training. Mr. B fantasized about moving to the part of the country where his friend lives and entering the very same program she is in. He began to associate to all sorts of examples, throughout his life, in which he had stopped himself at green lights—countless opportunities that he blocked, though he was hitherto unaware of doing this. Consciously, he spent his time envious and angry with other people who could go through red lights—get away with things—and not get caught. He was unaware that he had spent his life—over and over again—wary and hesitating in front of green lights. This is an example of what Freud called the "timelessness of the unconscious." It is a timelessness *of form.* Consciously, history and human development proceed apace; but unconsciously, Mr. B was on the lookout for events and opportunities that could be interpreted as "green lights," and he enveloped them in an aura of suspicion. It was the manner in which he inhibited himself from potential successes. From one perspective, this looks like repetition; the same thing happens over and over again. But if we think of the unconscious as actively imposing a form on life's passing events—creating a structure of hesitation before "green lights" and envy at others who get to go through "red lights"—we can see that this structure is being timelessly maintained.[26]

Aristotle, remember, told us that the nonrational part of the soul had its own nature: its own principle of movement. Here, in the microcosm, we can see the workings of a principle of unconscious mental activity more detailed than anything Aristotle could have envisaged. This presents an unusual opportunity for intervention, but it also poses a challenge. For it is clear that the problem Mr. B faced was not this or that unconscious wish or fear, but a principle of mental functioning that had shaped his life. How is one to intervene effectively in such well-organized mental activity—activity that seems to flow of its own accord, outside the reach of self-conscious reason? How could psychoanalysis undo such a formally organizing principle of mental life?

In the case of Mr. B, the "red-light/green-light" structure came into the transference in this way: the current green light was about furthering his academic training. I was an academic who, he thought, seemed to have no trouble going through my green lights and probably went through red lights too—and never got caught. He also wondered what I thought of his decision; perhaps I disapproved because it might take time away from his analytic work, and that too made him wary.

I pointed out that either way, he would feel stuck. Either he has a red light and he is full of frustrated and tantalizing thoughts that he will not let himself act on—all the while feeling envious of others who seem to get away with going through red lights—or he has a green light, in which case he feels wary and hesitant to go through it, fearing some danger of disappointment. And he looks to me—with envy, resentment, and admiration—as if I am able to go through both red and green lights.

At that point, Mr. B said, *"Ah, what would it be for me to just let myself go through a green light!?"* He sighed, and the muscles in his hands—which he had been rubbing together vigorously—relaxed. I sensed an overall relaxation in his body. It was as though, in body-and-mind, Mr. B was coming to some sort of summing up.[27]

There are, of course, different *manners* in which Mr. B might have made that utterance, and one cannot tell from the content of the utterance alone the manner in which Mr. B deployed it. I cannot tell you with absolute confidence what manner that was. But I would like to make a suggestion. Although I think I am right, what matters to me most is *the possibility* that Mr. B might have uttered it in this way. On the surface, it looks as though Mr. B had expressed a wish—a wish to be able to go through green lights without hesitation. But due to his years-long work in analysis, it was more than the expression of a wish. It was also more than an imaginary disappointment. Over the course of the analysis, Mr. B developed a capacity of mind such that, in expressing the wish consciously, he was in the same act of mind able to give himself permission to go through such lights. That is, the analysis gave him the ability not merely to formulate such a wish, but, in the same act, to convert the wish into a desire he could act upon. His activity was in the realm of the self-conscious mental. Through the immediate and direct efficacy of his self-conscious understanding, Mr. B was able to begin to open the traffic lanes of his life.

Of course, this is not something one can accomplish in a moment. The process of working-through is precisely the process of developing a capacity to recognize, again and again, that one has come, perhaps unbeknownst to oneself, to another traffic light. It is the capacity to grasp the underlying significance of the particularities of life—and, once grasped, to respond to them effectively. Working-through is typically a years-long activity. But it is one in which the analysand develops a power of the mind.

We need to know more about how this power works. But three of its features are already clear. First, this efficacy of mind is essentially self-conscious. The self-conscious mind becomes genuinely effective in giving permission through its self-conscious understanding that giving permission is precisely what it is doing. In this case, self-conscious understanding is causally efficacious in bringing about what it understands. Thus I think it is an unfamiliar form of what Kant called "practical reason." Practical reason, as we normally understand it, is concerned with making changes in the external world. This power of mind brings about changes in the internal world.[28] Second, self-conscious efficacy is possible in this instance because conscious and unconscious are in effective communication with each other. In the analytic situation, the conscious minds of analyst and analysand working together can hear the "voice" of the unconscious as it breaks through the membrane set up by the fundamental rule—in this case, a slip of the tongue using the vocabulary of red and green lights. The efficacy of self-conscious mind is possible on this occasion because *that very occasion* is at one and the same time an integrating activity of self-conscious and unconscious. Self-consciousness is efficacious because, on this occasion, it is, to use Aristotle's phrase, "speaking with the same voice" as the unconscious. Third, the development of this power of mind takes practice. It is the development of a mental skill, a *self-conscious* power of mind to change the shape of unconscious structures that have hitherto been dominating a life.

**5.** Obviously, more needs to be said to elaborate and defend these ideas, but I hope I have said enough to vindicate Bernard Williams's suggestion that Freudian psychoanalysis has the resources to help us in the formulation of a robust, nonmoralizing moral psychology. In the case we have been examining, psychoanalysis gives us the resources to give content to Aristotle's conception of the nonrational and rational parts of the soul speaking with the same voice—without simply assuming an unexplained obedience of the former to the latter. This is crucial for the possibility of a nonmoralizing Aristotelian moral psychology.

Aristotle is clear that the ethical virtues are excellences of the nonrational part of the soul, while practical wisdom (*phronêsis*) is an intellectual virtue.[29] Yet the possibility of happiness depends on getting these excellences to work together. Without ethical virtue, Aristotle suggests, practical wisdom degenerates into mere cleverness—the skill of obtaining poorly chosen goals.[30] Conversely, the development of true ethical virtues requires the aid of practical wisdom.[31] Aristotle begins by saying that the ethical virtues must *accord* with right reason, but then he makes an important qualification: "But it is necessary to take another small step forward: virtue is not merely a state *in accord (kata)* with right reason but is *with (meta)* right reason."[32] Aristotle takes this relation of *being with* right reason to be distinctive of his moral psychology: it is that which Socrates did not grasp as he mistakenly identified the ethical virtues as forms of reason.[33] The Freudian contribution is to offer a rich account of what this *being-with* relation might consist in.

Aristotle is clear that *eudaimonia*—regularly translated as "happiness"—is possible for humans, but not for other animals.[34] For Aristotle, the nonrational souls of other animals lack the capacity to *be with* reason in the right sort of way. This is the capacity for the rational and nonrational parts of the soul to speak with the same voice. Without a substantial understanding of what this consists in, Aristotle's conception of *eudaimonia,* the highest human good, remains a placeholder. Freud thus gives us resources to flesh out the distinctive nature of Aristotle's moral psychology. And this can open up possibilities for philosophy.

To give one example, it is a familiar thought in contemporary philosophy that our rationality, and thus our freedom, consists in our ability to step back in reflection and consider whether the evidence before us gives us a reason to believe, or whether in the face of a certain desire we have a reason to act.[35] This conception fits a moral psychology in which the threat to rationality comes from a sea of unruly desires—some conscious, some unconscious—pushing for satisfaction. These are treated as *outside,* though reason can either rule them in or rule them out. This psychology also makes plausible the thought that by this very activity we constitute ourselves.[36] On this model, in the absence of our self-conscious commitments, all that remains are unorganized desires.

But Mr. B's desires were not disorganized—indeed, that was a significant part of his problem. His nonrational desires were all too organized, refusing opportunities and imagining himself as inhibited by an outside force, frustrated and left behind. And his capacity for reason had itself been infiltrated and shaped by his nonrational soul. Mr. B was adept at stepping back in reflection and judging that he really was stuck in life's unfairness. It was in this very act of stepping back in purportedly rational deliberation that he unwittingly manifested his unfreedom. What Mr. B needed in order to move in the direction of psychic freedom and rationality was a *break* in the structure he experienced as reason, a break in his familiar activity of stepping back and reflecting, a break in the ordinary exercise of his capacity to judge.

It does not do justice to the phenomena to think of Mr. B as constituting himself through those self-conscious judgments in which he "accepted" or "adjusted to" the frustrations in life. Those judgments themselves were surface manifestations of a powerful nonrational, unconscious structure—and they added a misleading patina of rational reflection. It defies plausibility to insist that this nonrational structure of desire has nothing to do with him—on the grounds that it is not the expression of his rational judgment.[37] The unconscious structure is itself the manifestation of nonrational, but imaginative attempts to address a basic problem of how to live. We should not rule out the thought that the expressions of this structure are coming *from him* simply because it does not fit a psychology that is inadequate to capture who we are.

Aristotle's conception of the rational and nonrational parts of the soul speaking with the same voice provides a more illuminating model of what our rationality—and thus our *eudaimonia*—consists in. Here the central image is not of reflective distance, but a coming-together of voices into one. Rationality, on this model, is manifested in a *lack of distance* between the voices. Obviously, as rational animals, there will be important moments of stepping back and reflecting. But in those moments, there will always be a further question of *the manner* in which that stepping back takes place. Is this moment of stepping back one in which the rational and nonrational parts of the soul are in the process of coming to speak with the same voice? Or is a cruel superego punitively holding desire in place? Or is the reflection just one more move in a pseudorational life, dominated by exaggerated acts of "rationality"? Certainly, the bare fact that self-conscious judgment has ruled a desire in or out is not sufficient to determine whether the voices of the soul are thereby coming to speak together. And this opens room for us to consider *genuine* acts of reflection to nevertheless be mere *appearances* of rationality or freedom.

They can also be mere appearances of our happiness. Aristotle's insistence that reason speak with the same voice as the nonrational soul manifests a deep intuition of what *eudaimonia* consists in. For Aristotle, our happiness consists in part in the knowledge that we are happy. For the virtuous person grasps the appropriate good and the appropriate means, and he understands that he is doing such. And in a happy life, he grasps that the happy life consists in just such excellent activity in accordance with reason. Of course, even within a happy life, one ought to be aware of the possibility of overwhelming tragedy, like Priam's, that could ruin one's happiness. But that awareness does not impugn the thought that our happiness partially consists in the correct, appropriately grounded, self-conscious comprehension of our happiness. Part of what it is for a happy life to be "lacking in nothing"—to be a "complete life," a life of excellence according to reason—is that it possesses within itself the knowledge that it is the happy life that it is. Now this knowing that constitutes our happiness is not just the propositional knowledge *that* we are living a happy life; it is also the rational, self-conscious awareness of the various voices in our soul speaking with the same voice. This is an immediate, nonreflective knowing—a self-conscious experience of our rational and nonrational voices speaking with the same voice, that is in turn open to reflective, self-conscious understanding. This is a kind of knowing that is foreclosed to other animals, and it is one of the reasons Aristotle excludes them from *eudaimonia.*

Psychoanalysis is a form of self-conscious speech that aims to enhance the efficacy of thoughtful, self-conscious speech—an efficacy that runs through a self-conscious grasp of this efficacy, and one that can change the structure of the psyche. It is a form of psyche-formation that proceeds essentially through the psyche's own understanding of itself. This understanding has a theoretical as well as a practical aspect to it, but it is also poetic in the sense of self-creating through its own self-conscious grasp of its own meaning-making. In this way, psychoanalytic practice seems to me the best model we have of what is involved in reason coming to communicate with and thus *inform* the human soul. When Aristotle said that humans are by nature rational animals, he was isolating a distinctive capacity of the human soul.[38] Psychoanalysis shows us what is involved in bringing that capacity to fruition.

This is a humanistic value. Do we wish to be creatures who take this peculiar responsibility for shaping our own psyches? To put it in Aristotelian terms, psychoanalysis is both *kinêsis* and *energeia,* process and activity. It aims to help a person shape his mind in such a way that he can continue the life-activity of taking the nonrational part of his soul into harmonious and creative relations with his thoughtful self-conscious understanding. To put it in Freudian terms, psychoanalysis is both terminable (as *kinesis*) and interminable (as *energeia*). Psychoanalysis is the flourishing human activity of the rational soul taking immediate, poetic, and practical responsibility for the nonrational soul. Other names for this activity are, I think, truthfulness, rationality, freedom, and *eudaimonia.*

**6.** I conclude by considering a pair of objections: that psychoanalysis comes both too soon and too late to be part of a broadly Aristotelian approach to ethical life. It comes too soon in the sense that it is not concerned with promoting the list of Aristotelian ethical virtues.[39] And it can also seem that psychoanalysis comes too late in the sense that Freud stands on the other side of a divide—between modernity and the ancient world, or between postmodernity and premodernity—such that on this side we can no longer assume any set of purportedly inscribed values.[40] The "virtues" of any civilization, so the objection goes, are just manifestations of power relations by which one social class dominates others. And what philosophers of any given period call "reason" is a hodgepodge of valorizing self-justifications for the dominating ideology of the time. The divide between Aristotle and Freud can seem unbridgeable when one considers their differing views of political society. For Aristotle, the good polis should function to promote the happiness of its citizens, and vice versa. For Freud, it is an illusion to think that civilization is in place to make humans happy; rather, it secures a basic order, indifferent to the human costs, and is the source of neurotic discontent.[41] Moreover, there is Freud's postulation of the so-called death drive—purportedly, a principle within us that works against our flourishing.[42] This is a paradigm of a non-Aristotelian principle.

These challenges are important, but not definitive. As a "talking cure," psychoanalysis does differ from its famous philosophical predecessor, Socratic elenchus, in that it is not trying to promote any particular ethical value beyond the value of truthfulness—truthfulness in speech in which nonrational and rational parts are integrated. By contrast, although Socrates repeatedly says he does not know what the virtues consist in, he does not doubt that courage, temperance, justice, and piety are virtues, and he is convinced that his method promotes their development. Nevertheless, Aristotelian ethics holds out the prospect of virtue—in contrast to mere continence—and virtue requires that the nonrational soul speak with the same voice as the rational soul. Psychoanalysis is manifestly not a training in Aristotle's virtues, but it does help a person avoid an outcome Aristotle would find unfortunate: a person who lives a life of continence but who takes himself to be virtuous as he promotes the established norms of the day. In that sense, psychoanalysis may be prior, but it does not come "too soon"; it can help open the possibility of a distinctively human flourishing life.

Politically speaking, Aristotle insists that ethical life must be understood in the context of adequate politics that reflects and supports that life.[43] One can insist on this principle, while rejecting the specific aristocratic values Aristotle defended. In a similar vein, there are two ways to read Freud's critique of civilization: either that it is inevitable that civilization frustrate human happiness or that, in the conditions of bourgeois modernity in which he lived, the discrepancy between the conditions needed for humans to flourish and the demands imposed by political society had become too great. On this latter view, the aim would not be Stoic *ataraxia* in the face of an inevitable, tragic human condition, but rather political commitment to change the social conditions so as to support ethical human flourishing. Here, it is too quick to move from the recognition that the concept of reason has regularly been used for ideological purposes to the conclusion that that is its inevitable fate. When Socrates tells us it is appropriate for reason to rule the whole soul, and Aristotle follows suit, the politically appropriate way to understand these claims is not as stating an already-well-understood condition, but as setting out a task: we will come better to understand what reason is as we come better to understand what is involved in rejecting false images of reason. It remains a psychopolitical challenge to work out what it is for thoughtful self-consciousness to inform the human soul well. And even if Freud is correct that there is something inherently destructive in our natures—and we are still at an early stage of reflection about this—the task remains basically the same: how to take this into account in the living of a worthwhile life that is self-consciously grasped as such.

Psychoanalysis can be seen as a constituent moment in this process of figuring out—in theoretical, practical, and poetic ways—what would be involved in a life of *eudaimonia.* It is an attempt to listen to and communicate with the nonrational part of a soul in a manner that is up to the challenge. Freud added depth to the Aristotelian insight that the nonrational soul has its own nature that will inevitably complicate as it enriches what we might mean by the rational and nonrational parts of the soul speaking with the same voice. We risk yet another moralizing psychology if we assume we already know what speaking with the same voice must be. In particular, do not assume we need a marching band of the soul. Think instead of marvelous improvisational jazz: there are syncopated voices; some in the moment might appear at the edge of breaking the composition apart, but then they come spectacularly together—and the experience as a whole teaches us something about what it might be to come together into a single voice. If the voices of the nonrational soul are an occasion for a creative, in-tune, and thoughtful response from reason—and if, in turn, reason is able to enliven and free up the voices of the nonrational soul as it channels them into a life worth living—we can give content to the thought that this is a rich form of speaking with the same voice. This, I think, is a route for an Aristotelian ethics.

CHAPTER THREE

# What Is a Crisis of Intelligibility?

---

**1.** We are creatures who—at least up to a point—seek to understand ourselves and the world we inhabit. This is not just a deep psychological or social need; it is who we are. And, essentially and a priori, we make sense of who we are in part by making sense of who we were. Obviously, we are creatures who construct historical narratives, individual and social. But even when we are not explicitly thinking about our pasts, even when we are absorbed in the present or looking toward the future, a shadow of the past, as it were, illuminates self-conscious life. Thinking is paradigmatically with concepts; and the capacity to acquire and deploy a concept is in part a capacity to acquire a sense of how the concept has been used. Even when the concept undergoes change, even when the past has been significantly misunderstood, our current use of concepts carries with it a sense of the past. So, for example, even to understand myself as, say, currently reading a book is to understand myself as engaged with an artifact the likes of which others have engaged with before me—and, indeed, to be engaging with it in similar ways. To lose that sense of the past (however inchoate or implicit it might be) would be for self-consciousness to fall apart. This is not just an empirical, psychological point; it is a logical point about the structure of self-consciousness.

Ever since the work of Hegel, Wittgenstein, and Heidegger, we have become familiar with the thought that the meaningfulness of concepts depends on their being embedded in a living form of life. Even so, there is a tendency to overlook a peculiar loss that I am going to call a loss of intelligibility. Basically, the concepts and categories by which the inhabitants of a form of life have understood themselves—their acts, projects, and ideals—cease to make sense as ways to live. This is not a psychological claim—that when people try to make sense of their lives they fail. The claim is rather that insofar as they fail to make sense of their lives (psychologically speaking), the reason is that their lives no longer make sense. Nor is this simply a social claim—that, as a matter of social fact, it is no longer possible to live in these ways. No doubt the fact that there has been a breakdown in a form of life plays a crucial role in explaining the loss of intelligibility. But the phenomena are not identical: a traditional life might become impossible yet its core concepts remain intelligible. And the causality does not run in only one direction: it is not only because a form of life becomes impossible that its core concepts become unintelligible; the breakdown in intelligibility can contribute to the impossibility of a way of life. Thus we need to get a clear view of what this breakdown of intelligibility consists in. In this essay, I shall give an account of this loss, and I shall also offer a diagnosis of why it is often misidentified. When we speak of "appropriating the past," it is easy to conflate the theoretical and the practical demands of this task. At first, this claim might look absurd: what could be more different than thinking about a catastrophe (from a theoretical point of view) and having to live through it? But those who live through a catastrophe have to think about what they are living through; and those who think about a catastrophe (from a theoretical distance) have to think about the thinking of those who live through it. But the thinking of those who live through it is quintessentially practical thinking. And, as the philosopher Elizabeth Anscombe warned us, there is an overwhelming tendency in the modern age to treat practical thinking as though it were simply a species of theoretical thinking about a special subject matter, the practical.[1] It is only when we recognize that practical thinking is a different form of thinking that we can grasp what a loss of intelligibility is.

**2.** My imagination was captured by a series of haunting claims made by leaders of the Crow Nation after they moved onto the reservation.[2] Plenty Coups, the last great chief of the Crow, refused to speak to his biographer about his life after this move. And when repeatedly pushed, he finally said, "When the buffalo went away the hearts of my people fell to the ground, and they could not lift them up again. After this nothing happened."[3] Two

Leggings, a chief of one of the clans, told his biographer, "Nothing happened after that. We just lived. There were no more war parties, no capturing of horses from the Piegans and the Sioux, no buffalo to hunt. There is nothing more to tell."[4] And Pretty Shield, a respected medicine woman, would repeatedly tell her granddaughter, "I'm living a life I don't understand." "Why has this thing come upon us. . . . I feel like I am losing my children to this new world of life that I don't know."[5]

Of course, there are many ways one might interpret these statements. And I make no claim that the one I offer is the correct one in terms of historical accuracy or psychological insight into these particular individuals. I approach this moment not as an historian, anthropologist, or psychologist, but as a philosopher. Although I have respect for the historian's task of understanding what happened, and think my work should be constrained by what we do know, my primary concern is with investigating a possibility. What might they have meant? But this is not just a thought experiment. This possibility is an important one for human life—it discloses a vulnerability to which we are all subject—and learning to live with it well is an ethical task.

So, the possibility I want to explore is that Plenty Coups, Two Leggings, and Pretty Shield were each standing as witness—first-personal witness—within a form of life to the breakdown of intelligibility within it. After this, nothing happened—in the sense that nothing that had hitherto been happening any longer made sense as something that might happen or something that one might do. And Pretty Shield's claim is not just a subjective report of her psychological state: she is reporting that the concepts and categories with which she had hitherto understood her life are no longer intelligible ways to live, and thus that she is forced to live on deprived of the concepts with which she would have hitherto understood her life. How might we understand this as authentic witness to a collapse in intelligibility?

The Crow are a people on the northwest plains of (what is now) the United States who flourished as a nomadic tribe for about five hundred years. In the spring of 1884, they moved onto a reservation—and their traditional way of life came to an abrupt end. The Crow had a conception of the good life: unfettered hunting in a nomadic life on sacred land that God had given them as a chosen people; participating in sacred rituals of thanks, pleas, and preparation; opportunities for behaving bravely and supporting the tribe. Traditionally, war was not itself a good, but it was inevitable; and thus behaving bravely in that context was a culturally established way of flourishing. All this became impossible when the Crow moved onto the reservation. Intertribal warfare was forbidden and, more important, it was effectively shut down by the U.S. Government, as was the nomadic way of life. Obviously, an individual or a few individuals might stray off the reservation and hunt animals, but hunting as it had traditionally been understood became impossible. Indeed, as is well known, the traditional object of the hunt, the buffalo, had—through a combination of human greed and deliberate policy—been all but destroyed. There was thus no longer a way to live according to the traditional understanding of the good life. Basically, there was a breakdown in the *telos* of a form of life, and as a result the concepts and categories that had been organized in relation to that *telos* ceased to make sense as ways to live.

To take an example from my book *Radical Hope,* by 1885 nothing any longer made sense as planting a coup-stick. One might still have the physical object that used to be a coup-stick, and one might stick it in the ground—but neither that nor anything else could be understood or interpreted as the planting of a coup-stick. And nothing any longer made sense as trying to plant a coup-stick, preparing to plant a coup-stick, or intending to plant a coup-stick. Although the token movements that—in another context—used to be the planting of a coup-stick are still possible, neither they nor any other act is any longer intelligible as the planting of a coup-stick. One's acts are haunted by mimesis: a nostalgic reenactment of what the act used to be like when it was part of a viable way of life. As a matter of historical fact, the activity of planting coup-sticks fell out of existence.[6] So also did the Sun Dance, a traditional dance seeking spiritual inspiration and support before battle. The issue is not just a matter of impossibility; it is a matter of unintelligibility: although people could still certainly get up and dance, and people in 1885 certainly could go through all the physical motions that used to be the Sun Dance, neither that nor anything else could make sense—be understood or interpreted—as doing the Sun Dance. Again, the reason is that the form of life in which the Sun Dance was located, and in terms of which it had meaning, was no longer viable. As an historical indication that this is the right way to understand the situation, the Crow themselves stopped doing the Sun Dance. Though the Sun Dance—or rather *a* Sun Dance—is now a part of Crow life, there was a seventy-five-year gap in which the Sun Dance fell out of existence. It is this seventy-five-year gap whose cultural and conceptual ontology I wish to understand. At the end of World War II, it was thought that it would again be appropriate to dance the Sun Dance—as a way of praying for important outcomes. But by then no one could remember the steps; it had gone out of practical memory. The tribe invited a Shoshone Sun Dance leader to teach the people the steps of what had been the Shoshone Sun Dance.[7] I have Crow friends who refuse to dance the Sun Dance on the grounds that it is not sufficiently Crow.

Basically, if going on a hunt and going into war and going on a nomadic migration all become impossible, then there are no longer any acts that can intelligibly count as preparing to go to war, on a hunt, on a migration. Nor can anything intelligibly count as intending to perform such acts. Again, one might saddle up a horse, arm oneself, and ride off the reservation; but neither that nor any other act can be understood in these terms. But everything in traditional Crow life had been understood in terms of being oriented to hunts, migration, and battle. And thus if we think of events or happenings in traditional Crow terms—which, of course, one would do if one were a Crow—then Plenty Coups's claim "After this, nothing happened" starts to make poignant sense. If we follow Heidegger and Aristotle in thinking that time is dateable—that every now is a now-when—then we can also see that there is a sense in which the Crow ran out of time. For they could no longer say, "Now-when we are about to go into battle," "Now-when we are planning our nomadic migration," "Now-when I am counting coups," and so on. And if one wanted to stand witness to these being the "nows" that really matter—these are what count as happenings—one way to do this would be to say, "After this, nothing happened." This is what it would be to witness the breakdown of intelligibility from within the form of life.

**3.** To understand why this crisis represents a breakdown in intelligibility, it is helpful to think through certain objections. So, one might object:

> Just because a form of life is no longer possible that does not mean that the concepts that were used within it have become unintelligible. It may no longer be possible to be a chief or a warrior as those concepts were traditionally understood; but that does not imply that the concepts have become unintelligible. After all, the Crow can look back on their past;

> and they can certainly understand what it was to be a chief or a warrior. This is only possible, of course, if the concepts remain intelligible. If the concepts really became unintelligible, then even when the Crow looked back on their past, they would have to do so with puzzlement and bewilderment. They would have to be unable even to make sense of their past in those terms because the terms had ceased to make any sense to them.

The plausibility of this objection stems from a conflation of theoretical and practical reason. The point about unintelligibility as a practical concern is not that I can make no sense of my past, or my people's past, or of my culture's past theoretically understood; it is that I can make no sense of my past, or my people's past, or my culture's past practically understood: that is, as a way of going forward in my deliberations, choices, actions, aspirations, and identifications. Again, the issue is not primarily a psychological one; it is ontological. Because the culture has been devastated, I can no longer render myself intelligible (to myself or to others) in its terms. This form of unintelligibility does not imply that the past is incomprehensible to me as a matter of contemplation: it means that the concepts with which one had hitherto rendered oneself and others intelligible are no longer available to do that work.

The strands of impossibility and unintelligibility are intertwined in complex ways. I want to claim both:

- that it is because the traditional nomadic way of life became impossible that the central concepts, rituals, and activities within that form of life became unintelligible as ways to live, to understand oneself, and to be understood by others; and
- that this opened up a new way in which, say, the planting of a coup-stick became impossible; it became impossible because it had become unintelligible.

In the first case, the flow is from impossibility to unintelligibility; in the second, it is from unintelligibility to impossibility. In the catastrophe that confronted the Crow, the flow is moving in both directions at once. In trying to bring the polyvalence of impossibility to light, I used an example in *Radical Hope* of two different senses in which one might say, "It is no longer possible to order buffalo." The first is one in which the restaurant runs out of its supply of buffalo, perhaps because the world supply of buffalo is exhausted; the other, one in which the historical institution of restaurants goes out of existence, as do all other institutions of having one group of people serve upon the needs of another. In the former case, it is no longer possible to order buffalo; in the latter case, it is no longer possible to order. But in this latter case, the problem is not simply one of impossibility—it is one of intelligibility. In no act could I legitimately understand myself as ordering, in no act could I legitimately be understood as ordering, in no act could I make myself intelligible to others as ordering. This is a very robust sense of unintelligibility; and note that, in the first instance, it has nothing to do with my psychological state. And nothing about this kind of example need prevent me from remembering an earlier world in which ordering was not only intelligible, but it was a matter of course.

Note that the question of psychology—of the individual or the group—is a different question. One might recognize that there has been trauma to meaning and still not know what the psychological reaction to this trauma has been. It is true that there has been a trauma to the group—in the sense of a traumatic disruption of practical reason, a breakdown of intelligibility—but it is a further question what the psychological reaction(s) to this trauma are. It might be trauma in the psychological sense—and, given that these breakdowns often occur in the midst of human tragedy, one should not be surprised to find psychological trauma as well—but it might not. And the reactions might be various. The relation between trauma *to meaning* and trauma *to psyche* is not one to one.

Pretty Shield says, "I am living a life I no longer understand," and her granddaughter reports that she would often repeat this phrase, accompanied by a sigh.[8] An interpreter might hypothesize that she is sad, wistful, melancholy. Plenty Coups says, "After this, nothing happened," and an interpreter might interpret him as speaking metaphorically, perhaps about a depression or a lack of orientation that has overcome the group. And there might or might not be other evidence for such claims. I have no objection to psychological interpretation per se, just so long as it does not obscure from view a different kind of possibility: that they might be standing witness to a crisis of intelligibility.

As I said at the beginning, I do not claim to know what Pretty Shield, Two Leggings, and Plenty Coups meant by their utterances. I have merely been exploring the possibility that they were standing witness. Nevertheless, there is reason for thinking that this possibility is robust. For Pretty Shield, Plenty Coups, and Two Leggings had a peculiar form of authority to speak for the form of life—one that transcends their social, leadership roles. It is a priori that, in general and for the most part, agents can say what they are doing. That is, it is a priori that they can, for the most part, give a self-conscious account of what they are doing, using concepts that are being realized in their actions.[9] Thus it can be inferred that Crow leaders ought to be able to give an account of what they are doing in Crow terms. So when Pretty Shield says, "I am living a life I don't understand," she might be reporting that the concepts with which life would make sense—namely, Crow concepts—no longer make sense in terms of possible ways she might live. Her authority is, I think, first person and a priori; only in this case she is not only speaking on behalf of herself—that is, what she expresses by saying "I"—but also is expressing what would be expressed by her saying "We." Similarly, when Plenty Coups says, "After this, nothing happened," I take him to be speaking on behalf of the tribe, and with the authority of the first-person plural. If the Crow themselves say that Crow concepts no longer describe what we outsiders would see as unfolding events, then we ought to respect that claim, not merely as a matter of moral courtesy, but as having genuine authority. For Crow concepts to hang onto their intelligibility, there have to be Crow who can find ways to live by understanding themselves in those terms. This is just what the Crow leaders themselves seem to have called into question. One sign, then, that there has been a genuine loss of intelligibility is that the agents themselves cannot see how to take up the concepts of their past and project them into their futures. This is what it is to take seriously the Crow's own sense of loss of intelligibility.

**4.** When we speak about the "collapse of a world" there are various things we might mean; but one of them is a breakdown in intelligibility in the sense that I have been trying to isolate. By way of contrast: if the Crow tribe had been devastated when the Sioux launched a massive attack in the early 1820s, with a few survivors taken into captivity, there is a sense in which, though the tribe had been destroyed, the Crow way of life would have remained intelligible. The Crow who survived would have understood quite well what their position was: they were now slaves, captives; maybe some of them would be adopted into the Sioux tribe. A person in that situation would not say, as Pretty Shield did, "I am living a life I do not understand." Her pain would arise from the fact that she was living a life she understood all too well. These were understandings that were part of Crow life. So too was the larger world of nomadic life on the plains, where hunting, counting coups, and doing the Sun Dance continued to be ways people could live and understand themselves. We can imagine the survivors dreaming that one day they would escape from captivity and reestablish the Crow tribe. And however wishful and unlikely those dreams might have been, they would have had an entirely different status than a dream with the same content dreamt on the reservation today. In such a situation, continued Crow life might have become impossible, but it would have remained intelligible. For in the 1820s the larger world of nomadic tribes hunting and fighting each other on the northwest plains was still vibrant. And even if it were practically impossible for the dreamer's dream to come true, the kinds of things the dreamer would be dreaming—escaping from captivity, raising children in Crow ways—would be intelligible within the larger context of nomadic life on the plains. Even if the dreamer could not possibly pull it off, he would know what his next step would have to be. By contrast, when one suffers a crisis of intelligibility, the problem is not simply that one does not know what one's next step would have to be—as though this were a particularly difficult problem for practical reason—it is that nothing any longer counts as a next step.

Within classical logic it is a familiar idea that the law of excluded middle gives expression to our confidence that the world exists independently of us.[10] Obviously, classical logic was formalized primarily with the aim of capturing the timeless truths of arithmetic. But if we try to capture an existential version of the law of excluded middle—that is, one that captures a shared confidence in the determinacy of a range of possibilities manifested in a living way of life—then we need a version that is directed toward the future from now. So, on an evening in the early 1820s, a young Crow warrior could think:

> In tomorrow's battle, either I will be brave or I will not.[11]

The warrior's aim would be to acquit himself bravely, but his commitment would be viewed against background knowledge of what the possibilities were. It is over this range of future possibilities that the Crow concept for "brave" and "not brave" served as an exhaustive partition: on the eve before battle, a warrior would know that any failure to be brave would be a way of not being brave. This is the background knowledge that gives content to the idea of inhabiting a world—a world that is open-ended in the sense that various things might happen to one, and one might behave in various ways in response, but all of this remains within the range of what is intelligible. But by the 1920s, the intelligibility of the predicates that had hitherto been used to describe events—and thus the intelligibility of there being events—had broken down. So, for instance, the paradigm of Crow bravery was to plant a coup-stick in battle, from which point a warrior signaled that he would never willingly retreat. Within the traditional Crow form of life, that or anything like it counted as brave. However, with the move onto the reservation and the suppression of intertribal warfare, the act of planting a coup-stick ceased to make sense. One might take the very physical object that used to be a coup-stick and stick it in the ground, but neither that nor anything else could count as planting a coup-stick. Again, at most it could serve as a dramatic mimesis: an enactment of what warriors used to do when there used to be warriors. So when one now says, "that or anything like it": one fails with "that" to pick out any possible act; and one fails with "anything like it" to pick out any intelligible relation of similarity.

Now someone who has been exposed to classical logic might be tempted to say that classical negation is such that any failure to be brave is a way of not being brave—so the law of excluded middle holds even in the situation I have described. Again, I think the plausibility of this objection flows from imposing a demand of theoretical reason on a domain that is practical and existential. In classical logic one simply assumes a determinate range of objects over which the quantifiers range and a determinate set of predicates that either hold or fail to hold of those objects. But in the situation we are envisaging, both of these assumptions come into question. What we are trying to capture is an existential version of the law of excluded middle as it manifested itself in the Crow way of life. Thus we need to understand the quantifier as ranging over all future possibilities—as understood by and manifested in the Crow way of life. These are possibilities for living and for understanding life and the world in certain sorts of ways. This is what gives content to the idea of the "world of the Crow." Thus the possibility that we are now investigating—namely, that the entire range of possibilities ceases to make sense as ways to live—was not itself within that range. The Crow had a vivid idea of what it would be to be defeated in battle, decimated, destroyed, taken into slavery, and so on; but they had no idea what it would be for their way of life to cease making sense. That possibility was not in any way manifested in their living sense of all possibilities. Moreover, the Crow predicate we translate with the English word "brave" was one that was taught and understood in terms of the range of possibilities as understood by the Crow. We should not assume that the predicate will retain its determinacy—applying or not applying to an independently specifiable range of events—even after the form of life in which it gained its meaning becomes moribund. It is one thing for the predicate (which we translate as) "brave" not to apply to an event; it is quite another for the very idea of bravery to lose significance. When Plenty Coups said, "After this, nothing happened," I interpret him as giving voice to the breakdown of events. An event is a "now-when-X-is-happening" for some value of X. But all Crow values of X have lost intelligibility: "now-when-I-am-planting-a-coup-stick," "now-when-I-am-preparing-for-battle," and so on. So when one tries to say something like "For all X, Brave(X) or not Brave(X)," not only has the predicate "Brave( )" lost intelligibility, so have the possible values of X.

**5.** One might well wonder how common this kind of breakdown in intelligibility is. After all, if one looks from a sufficiently high altitude, the Crow are a cultural group that suffered a massive onslaught on their identity and way of life; in some sense they endured the trauma and are even now in the process of constituting themselves as a reservation and postreservation culture. Isn't this the stuff of history? To take some other examples about which we are today very aware: the capture and enslavement of Africans and their forced transportation to the United States, where they then constituted what we now think of as African American culture; Europe's two-thousand-year assault on Jews living in their midst; the subjugation and disenfranchisement of women in cultures around the world. One might well wonder: isn't the difference in what befell the Crow quantitative rather than qualitative?

Although the concerns prompting this question are of great importance, the question as it stands makes no sense. Before we can discriminate quantity from quality, we need a criterion according to which we can adjudicate the difference. The point of focusing on the Crow, from a philosophical perspective, is to bring to light a peculiar kind of ontological issue: the possibility that the intelligibility of concepts with which one has lived and understood oneself, others, and one's world might cease to be viable. These concepts no longer provide ways in which one can render oneself and others intelligible. In this essay I have tried to mark off this phenomenon from other psychological and social phenomena. The point of focusing on the Crow is not to say that they had it much worse or much easier than anyone else, but that in their case it is particularly clear that a qualitative issue—an ontological difference rather than just an ontic difference—is at stake. To put it in Heidegger's terms, it is a breakdown in the understanding of being.[12]

Now to what extent this has happened to other particular groups in other historical periods, I am not competent to judge. But I do think I have provided a criterion by which a sensitive historian might pursue these questions. If one can find what I have here called a "crisis of intelligibility," then one has evidence of a qualitative difference from a situation in which one can only find various psychological or social phenomena. And this will be so however similar or different the social situations look on the surface. I want to emphasize this: the fact that one group suffers a breakdown in intelligibility does not thereby signify that they have it worse (according to some absolute standard) than a group that does not. So, for instance, there is no reason to think that there is always more pain suffered with a breakdown in intelligibility than with other forms of assault in which intelligibility happens to remain intact. One reason I focused on the Crow was not because their experience was qualitatively different from the experience of all other groups, but because they provide an exceptionally clear case of a breakdown in intelligibility and thus of the qualitative difference between a crisis of intelligibility and other forms of psychological or social crisis.

Let me close with a concrete example that I think makes the point. Joseph Medicine Crow, the revered tribal historian now well into his nineties, gives this account of fighting in World War II:

> Naturally, I thought about the famous warriors when I went to Germany. I had a legacy to live up to. My goal was to be a good soldier, to perform honorably in combat if the occasion should occur. I did not think in terms of counting coup. Those days were gone, I believed. But when I returned from Germany and the elders asked me and the other Crow veterans to tell our war stories, lo and behold, I had completed the four requirements to become a chief.[13]

This looks like a moment of retrospective reinvention of tradition: the leaders of the tribe are trying to revitalize the activity of counting coup—which would thus provide new routes to becoming a chief. Again, from a sufficiently high altitude this looks like one more cultural adaptation to changed circumstances. But if we leave it at that, there is a danger that we collaborate in covering over the trauma the Crow had to endure. The fact is that from the time the intelligibility of counting coup broke down (with the move onto the reservation in 1884) to the self-conscious attempts to restore a meaning to the concept (with returning veterans after World War II), there was a gap of basically sixty years in which people could recount stories from their nomadic past, but no one had any idea of what could count as an act of counting coup in the present. One telling sign is that when the young Joseph Medicine Crow fought in that war, even he had no idea that anything he could do could possibly be deemed as counting coup. Indeed, even as he performed the acts that would later be looked upon as counting coup, he had no idea he was doing such. This is in dramatic contrast with the traditional past when young men knew precisely what it would be to count coup—and who certainly knew, as they acted, that they were doing something with which they could later make a claim of having counted coup. Thus, unlike the continual adaptation of a culture—and concepts within the culture—to new circumstances, in this case one needed the resurrection of a concept that had fallen into a moribund state. This is a beautiful example at the social level of *après-coup:* the retrospective decision that certain acts in the past would now be considered as counting coup.

In this regard, it is telling that the Crow hip-hop band that won the Native American Music Award is Rezawrecktion—thus condensing two or three puns into its name. The music is full of references to old warrior life but also entangled in Christian themes of hope, love, and resurrection—as well as with hip-hop concerns of contemporary street life and contemporary life on the "rez." It is explicit in their songs that Crow life needs to be understood in terms of death and rebirth. That is, it is part of contemporary Crow poetic culture that the Crow have come back from the dead. One might want to treat this as poetic license; but I think I have given the philosophical framework in terms of which one can understand Rezawrecktion, Plenty Coups, Two Leggings, and Pretty Shield as standing witness to something profoundly true.

CHAPTER FOUR

# A Lost Conception of Irony

---

**1.** On the face of it, a conception does not seem the sort of thing that is easy to lose.[1] If we think of our life with concepts in terms of our ways of going on, of categorizing and thinking about the phenomena in the world, including ourselves, it makes sense that certain concepts might lose their viability for us, and thus fall out of use. For example, we do not use the concept of *phlogiston* anymore except as a philosophical example of a concept we do not use anymore. But in this case we have not lost the concept; we just care very little about it because we no longer think it picks out anything in the universe—and that was what it was originally designed to do. We no longer have a use for the concept, but we retain a pretty good idea of how it used to function. Indeed, you can look it up in the *Oxford English Dictionary (OED)*—a reference that purports to give us the history of our use of English words, and thus the history of our use of concepts insofar as they have been thought and expressed in English.

But when I speak of a lost conception of irony, I am concerned with a use that does not show up in the list of entries under "irony" in the *OED.*

1. The expression of one's meaning by using language that normally signifies the opposite, typically for humorous or emphatic effect.
2. Dissimulation; pretence; *esp.* (and in later use only) feigned ignorance and disingenuousness of the kind employed by Socrates during philosophical discussions.
3. A state of affairs or an event that seems deliberately contrary to what was or might be expected; an outcome cruelly, humorously, or strangely at odds with assumptions or expectations.[2]

Could it be that historians of the language have simply overlooked one of our uses of the word? In which case, we could just add it to the list. But the story is not that simple. The analogy is rough, and to insist upon it would be overblown, but it is worth thinking about why Cantor's diagonal number never shows up on any list of rational numbers. The diagonal number is constructed, as it were, by "disrupting" any such list. The *OED* gives us a list of the history of our routines with words—including *irony*—but what if what we are trying to capture is a disrupter of our routines? What if the phenomenon is, intellectually speaking, tricky to capture; what if it describes a phenomenon that can be sufficiently unpleasant that we are somewhat motivated to turn away from it; and what if we are given plenty of other things to do? The second entry on the list seems to give us the "philosophical" meaning of irony—*was Socrates a deceiver or was he not?!* It would seem as though nothing is missing. There does not seem even to be room for the claim that what makes irony philosophically significant is not on the list.[3]

**2.** But consider the case of the Crow Nation, which I discussed in Chapter 3. It is now about seven generations from the cultural catastrophe that destroyed their traditional way of life. How are we to understand the suffering that endures, not just as historical memory, but as a living force in the present? We overly restrict our inquiry if we confine ourselves to looking for psychological phenomena such as trauma or sociological conditions such as levels of education or substance abuse or disproportionate levels of imprisonment relative to the population at large. All of these are important, but we are looking for something that does not show up on these lists—and is perhaps that in virtue of which these lists have the shape they do. In the course of writing my book *Radical Hope: Ethics in the Face of Cultural Devastation,* I made a number of close friends among the Crow; two tribal elders have taken me as their brother. In the course of long conversations, now extending over a decade, I realize that the Crow still face a painful practical question: what does it any longer mean to be Crow? Though members of the dominant culture have some sense of the plight of Native Americans, for the most part the culture is blind to the kind of devastation that has been inflicted upon them.

Let us consider this question:

*Among all the Crow, is there a Crow?*

I want to invite us to consider how different the question is when asked from a third-person as opposed to a first-person perspective. One reason the conception of irony I am trying to bring into focus so easily goes missing is that we tend to confuse a first-personal practical question with a third-person theoretical one. It is a fascinating fact—revealing something important about us—that, although the question has the form of a tautology, we can immediately hear that a substantive question is being asked. We hear the first occurrence of the term *Crow* as picking out the social group, the current members of the Crow Nation; and we hear the second occurrence as picking out the essence or ideal of *being a Crow,* and we hear the question as asking whether any members of the current tribe instantiate or live up to that ideal.

But from the perspective of my Crow friends, the question has a different aura. It makes them *anxious;* or rather it names a core anxiety. I mean anxiety in the literal sense of disruptive separation from the world and disorientation. It is easy *for us* to hear the question as though it were coming from the superego—a question of whether the Crow fail to live up to their ideals. But from the perspective of my Crow friends, the ideal is every bit as much in question as they are. So this is not just a question of whether they live up to the ideal; it is a question of whether there is any longer an ideal to live up to or fail to live up to. For them, it is not a theoretical question but a practical one: it centrally concerns their sense of how to live. And yet, as the ideal itself becomes problematic, they are confronted with an anxious sense that they do not know how to go on.

The question is also *uncanny* in the sense of something familiar coming back to haunt us with its unfamiliarity. My Crow friends already take themselves to be Crow. It is for each of them the most distinctive aspect of their identity; and yet, when the question arises, there is something uncanny, unfamiliar, and uncomfortable about the thought of whether they (or anyone else around them) really are Crow. The question is uncannily disruptive from the inside. And notice that the question has the structure of uncanniness: the first occurrence of the term, "Among all the Crow . . . ," has its usual familiar sense, but the second occurrence, ". . . is there a Crow?" is the return of the same, now as unfamiliar and haunting. The question is also *erotic* in the Platonic sense: my friends not only are Crow, they long to be Crow; they long to move in the direction of an ideal—if only they knew what direction that could be. They are longing *for direction*—a direction that eludes them.

**3.** My Crow friends have taught me a lot about how irony can strike us in the first-person plural. By contrast, Søren Kierkegaard, a truly ironic expositor of irony, focused on the call of irony in the first-person singular. For him, the fundamental ironic question is

> *In all of Christendom, is there a Christian?*

or

> *Among all Christians, is there a Christian?*

It is easy to hear this question in the familiar framework of a Sunday sermon. The preacher is asking his congregation whether they really live up to Christian ideals. It is also easy to hear it as humorous social critique: the clever Kierkegaard, in his detached way, is lampooning his bourgeois neighbors. This is the way irony is normally understood in contemporary culture. But the ease with which we hear the question in that way derives in part from the fact that we are looking on Kierkegaard and his times from a somewhat detached perspective. Let us try to imagine Kierkegaard asking the question in such a way that he himself is implicated. For him, it is *the* most important question of how and who to be. And, if he is enjoined to love his neighbors as himself, the question of whether any of them—who definitely live in Christendom—are indeed Christians is as pressing and demanding as it can be. And yet we need not think of this question as coming from the superego. It is not so much a question about whether we fail to live up to an ideal. Rather, when properly heard in its ironic register, it becomes an anxious question about what the ideal could possibly consist in. And it is a practical question: the proper response, from Kierkegaard's perspective, is not to undertake a census of Christendom, but rather to figure out what one's own next step will be. It is crucial to grasp what these words—"to figure out what one's own next step will be"—mean in this ironic context. What they do not mean is that I take a step back in reflection, consider the Christian ideal and my commitment to it, and in the light of that reflection consider what to do in the current circumstances. The moment of ironic experience is not a moment of stepping back to consider, but rather a moment of anxious and uncanny disruption in which the attempt to step back and consider only produces more vertigo. Because in the moment the issue is not simply how I am going to live my life in relation to an ideal; the ideal has become as enigmatic and unnerving to me as I have become to myself. And in the central case, where the question is striking me in the first person around my own sense of what is most important to me, or who I am, I am filled with a longing for direction—though I have lost a concrete sense of what that direction ought to be. I may retain a sense that, say, if I am to be a Christian, I must follow Jesus's teaching or that I must love my neighbor as myself. The problem is that the anxious uncanniness that has infected my sense of being a Christian is contagious: it infects my sense of what it would be to follow Jesus's teaching, what it would be to love, and who my neighbor is. In the experience of irony, instead of anchoring my sense of being a Christian, all of these qualifications lose their moorings. Or, rather, I lose my moorings in relation to them.

**4.** The experience of irony does not depend upon the religious nature of Kierkegaard's example. Let us take the category of *doctor.* Recently I attended a conference of medical doctors disgruntled with their profession yet trying to find ways to recommit themselves to the practice of doctoring. There is widespread discontent in the profession: doctors resent that their decisions are closely monitored (and sometimes dictated) by insurance companies and HMOs; they resent that sometimes procedures are required that they think are unnecessary, so as to avoid the possibility of a future lawsuit; and their own malpractice insurance requires them never to say they are sorry about anything, or that they wish some treatment could have gone better—for fear of creating liability. They are also demoralized by a paradigm shift in the profession. In this new paradigm, doctors are not supposed to see themselves as promoting health—that is too teleological. Rather, they are to see themselves as expert service providers. The new paradigm of the doctor-patient relation is the *contract* between the autonomous client—the person we used to call the patient—and the expert provider of a service. In a way, one can see this as society's attempt to quash any experience of irony. Ironically, it has led to its opposite: the creation of an enquiring group of doctors who spend the day asking each other the question *What does any of this have to do with medicine?*

The group had read my recent book *A Case for Irony,* and thus they explicitly asked the question, "Among all the doctors, is there a doctor?" This question is not on its own sufficient or even necessary for the experience of irony that I am trying to isolate. One can use such a question in a standard act of reflection in which one "steps back" from day-to-day practices and considers how well or how badly they fit in with one's long-term commitment to promoting health. This, one might say, is a standard superego moment. I am concerned with a different kind of moment—perhaps a moment when such standard reflection gets a bit out of hand. So imagine that you are that doctor, frustrated after a day of filling out dreadful insurance forms, ordering tests you do not believe in so you will not be sued; and you begin to wonder, *What does any of this have to do with being a doctor?* For a while, you reflect on taking up the issue with your colleagues, perhaps organizing a conference about medical values, about revisions we might make, and so on. And then a moment of anxious disruption sets in. You are struck by the idea of health—what is it?—by the very idea of one person promoting the health of another. It is a stunning idea—and here something striking happens. You are no longer stepping back to reflect on the thought that it is a stunning idea; rather, you are *stunned by the idea.* This seems to me the experience Plato was describing when he talked of us being struck by beauty.

According to Socrates in the *Phaedrus,* a person is struck by beauty here on earth and is driven out of his mind because he is reminded of the true beauty of the transcendent forms. This is the "greatest of goods," Socrates tells us: "god-sent madness [that] is a finer thing than man-made sanity."[4] Let us leave Platonic metaphysics to one side and concentrate on the experience. Plato emphasizes the importance of the disruptive, disorienting experience as that from which philosophical activity emerges.[5] Though Socrates is describing an intense moment of god-sent madness—and thus his language is dramatic—the structure of the experience fits the ironic uncanniness I have been trying to isolate. Those who are struck in this way *"do not know what has happened to them for lack of clear perception."*[6] They are troubled by "the strangeness (*atopia*) of their condition," but they also show "contempt for all the accepted standards of propriety and good taste"—that is, for the norms of the social practice.[7] Yet all along "they follow the scent from within themselves to the discovery of the nature of their own god."[8] If we demythologize this point and put it in the context of the example I have been developing, it looks like this: You have already taken on the practical identity of a doctor. You have internalized its values. This is the "scent from within": precisely by following the values of your practical identity—reflection on its norms and on how well or how badly you live up to them—you are led to a breakdown in these normal goings-on. There is something uncanny about, of all things, doctoring. It *seems* as though there is something about doctoring that transcends (and may undermine) the norms of social practice. There is something about your practical identity that breaks apart your practical identity: it seems larger than, disruptive of, itself.

In the moment you are struck by the idea of promoting health in another, you lose confidence that you know what human health really consists in. You know that in promoting health we make people better, but what would it be to make people better? Maybe a medical education should consist in training in gymnastics and physical fitness, followed by a stint of organic farming, some time as a barnyard veterinarian, several years teaching kindergarten, and several years of studying poetry and philosophy—only then may a student look at a sick human being. Maybe "making people better" will partially consist in teaching them to read those poems, or to be kind to others. In the moment of anxious disruption I am trying to describe, *all bets are off.*

Who knows, even the words of Socrates might start to seem compelling:

> And doesn't it seem shameful to you to need medical help, not for wounds or because of some seasonal illness, but because, through idleness and the life-style we've described, one is full of gas and phlegm like a stagnant swamp, so that sophisticated Asclepiad doctors are forced to come with names like "flatulence" and "catarrh" to describe one's diseases? . . . They say that the kind of modern medicine that plays nursemaid to the disease wasn't used by the Asclepiads before Herodicus.[9]

For Socrates in the *Republic,* the doctors of Athens—that is, those who put themselves forward as doctors, those who were recognized by society as doctors—were often collaborators in the corruption of souls, in the business of propping up the dissolute lives of the rich who would pay them well. To the question "Among all the doctors in Athens, is there a doctor?" Plato's answer is: there is one, Socrates, for he alone is concerned with promoting the health of those he encounters. And one of Socrates's first principles of medicine—as unusual today as it was then—is that one must treat the psyche (or soul) before one treats the body:

> [The Thracian doctor said] one should not attempt to cure the body apart from the soul [psyche]. And this is the reason, he said, why most diseases are beyond Greek doctors . . . because, he said, "the soul is the source both of bodily health and bodily disease for the whole man. . . . So it is necessary first and foremost to cure the soul if the parts of the head and of the rest of the body are to be healthy. And the soul," he said, "my dear friend, is cured by means of certain charms, and these charms consist in beautiful words. It is a result of such words that temperance arises in the soul, and when the soul acquires and possesses temperance, it is easy to provide health both for the head and for the rest of the body." So when he taught me the remedy and the charms, he also said, "Don't let anyone persuade you to treat his head with this remedy who does not first submit his soul to you for treatment with the charm. Because nowadays," he said, "this is a mistake some doctors make with their patients. They try to produce health of body apart from health of the soul." And he gave me very strict instructions that I should be deaf to the entreaties of wealth, position, and personal beauty.[10]

According to Socratic medicine, before one has surgery one ought to undergo a word-filled treatment of the psyche.

At the conference I attended, I was surprised to learn that some doctors approached the crisis they experienced in medicine by trying to incorporate their commitment to medicine within a larger context of religious devotion. This had significant consequences: giving up lucrative practices in specialized medicine in favor of primary care or general surgery, expressing regret to patients that a medical procedure did not have a better outcome (in contravention of hospital and insurance requirements), refusing to order tests or procedures when, in their opinion, the major motivation was considerations of tort rather than the health of the patient, and so on. I mention this not so much because religious commitment brings us back to Kierkegaard but because this example helps us grasp the difference between Kierkegaard's peculiar conception of irony and irony as it is commonly understood.

Imagine a medical doctor who has never felt a twinge of anxiety—who was engrossed in the contemporary social practice of medicine—observing the anxious, uncanny goings-on of these other doctors (the ones who attended the conference). How would they appear to him? It would seem that these doctors were becoming "ironically" detached from medicine in the familiar sense of irony. After all, if they care about medicine, why are they not pursuing the latest developments in cancer research or neuroscience? And if they say that the reason is that they care about being doctors, it would appear that they are being "ironic," as the culture has come to understand that term: they are being sarcastic, saying the opposite of what they mean, perhaps with the intention of being recognized as doing so by a knowing elite. The earnestness of their acts would easily be perceived as a lack of earnestness. "She isn't serious about medicine! Look, she gave up a promising career in neurosurgery; and now she's retiring into a cushy primary-care job. The next thing you know, she'll be moving to a ranch in Santa Fe! And, *can you believe it,* she says the reason she is doing this is that she wants to be a doctor! She's just being ironic."

**5.** We can now see how this experience of irony got to be called "irony." Roughly speaking, Kierkegaard became ironic about irony. At various points in the Platonic dialogues, some of Socrates's more challenging interlocutors—Alcibiades, Thrasymachus, and Callicles—accuse Socrates of deploying his typical *eirôneia.* They do so at moments when they feel caught by Socrates, taken by surprise, disrupted, frustrated, upended—even if only in the moment. That Greek term *eirôneia,* from which the English word descends, does mean putting on a mask, dissimulation. Thus there is, I think, no doubt that his interlocutors are accusing him of some kind of deception. Add to that Socrates's defense in the *Republic* of what has come to be called the "noble lie"—and it is easy to see how the debate about Socratic irony became a debate about whether or not Socrates was a deceiver. (Actually, I do not think the phrase "noble lie" is a good translation, but let us leave that to one side.[11]) The important point for now is that Kierkegaard, in his maturity, took a different tack. He had his eye on the fact that Thrasymachus, Callicles, and Alcibiades are all brilliant but also deeply flawed characters. One should expect them to be shrewd observers of the world but nevertheless to misperceive and distort the phenomena they are observing. Instead of explaining this in the flatfooted way I am now doing, Kierkegaard became ironic about *eirôneia.* Kierkegaard treats Thrasymachus, Callicles, and Alcibiades as though they were involved in a naming ceremony. He lets their use of *"eirôneia"* fix rigidly on the activity of Socrates (whatever it is) that elicits this criticism from his interlocutors. He does not expect them to understand what that activity is. And then Kierkegaard asks what Socrates was actually doing.

In his ironic treatment of irony, irony becomes a profound form of earnestness. As Johannes Climacus—one of Kierkegaard's pseudonymous authors—says, "From the fact that irony is present it does not follow that earnestness is excluded. That is something only assistant professors assume."[12] So when one of those ironic doctors says, "I've stopped seeing these patients and I certainly will not treat them, because I want to be a doctor," we can see her as saying exactly what she means, not its opposite—being ironic and earnest at the same time and in the same way. The irony is her earnestness.

**6.** Why should irony matter? To answer this question, I need to distinguish the experience of irony from a capacity for irony and to distinguish both of those from ironic existence. The experience of irony is the uncanny, disruptive, would-be directed anxiety that I have already described. In itself, it is neither good nor bad; it is a phenomenon that is, I think, intrinsic to human self-conscious life. But it is a phenomenon that can be deployed for significant uses. The capacity for irony is a capacity to occasion an experience of irony (in oneself or in another). Ironic existence is whatever it is that is involved in turning this capacity for irony into a human excellence: the capacity for deploying irony in the right way at the right time in the living of a distinctively human life. For Kierkegaard, Socrates was an exemplar of ironic existence, and Kierkegaard tried to live such a life himself. As Kierkegaard, as Johannes Climacus, says,

> Irony is an existence-determination, so nothing is more ridiculous than to suppose it to be a figure of speech, or an author's counting himself lucky when once in a while managing to express himself ironically.[13]

Irony mattered for Kierkegaard in significant part because it offered an occasion to break out of illusion. An illusion, for him, was a distorted, self-deceiving view of the world that aimed to be all-encompassing, capable of metabolizing and interpreting all experience in its terms. For Kierkegaard, Christendom—that is, the assemblage of social institutions and socially shared understandings of Christianity—was a "dreadful illusion." In other words, it provided an utterly distorted conception of what is involved in living a Christian life. Now what made the illusion *dreadful,* I think, was not simply its degree of falsity but its capacity for entangling one in a skein of self-deception from which there was virtually no way out. This is the Christian version of being at the bottom of Plato's Cave. One was born into this false world of Christianity—one had no choice over that—and before one reached the age of mature judgment, one was indoctrinated into the socially shared outlook. From the outlook of Christendom, Christendom is Christianity: the socially accepted and taught practices are put forward as what Christianity consists in. But what makes the illusion *dreadful,* from Kierkegaard's perspective, is Christendom's enormous cognitive and emotional sophistication. It is all too easy for us to caricature Christendom by thinking of hypocritical priests and the self-serving bourgeois who do not give a damn about others but do go to church on Sundays to see and be seen. To understand the importance of irony, it is crucial not to slip into this caricature. Christendom included sophisticated debates about Christian belief, self-conscious divisions of the church into different denominations, thoughtful histories of the church, and so on.

This means that one of the philosophers' favorite images of freedom only serves as a further form of entrapment. In contemporary philosophy, Christine Korsgaard, John McDowell, and Thomas Nagel have argued that our freedom importantly consists in our ability to step back and reflect—on our impulses, on the situation in which we find ourselves, or on a realm of thought that puts itself forward as true. In that reflection, they argue, we gain some distance and can then exercise our judgment. But Kierkegaard's point is that in stepping back and reflecting on Christendom, we are only making a further move within Christendom. The reflective activity of stepping back to consider will only be an illusion of stepping back. Christendom aims to be (and when it is vibrant, it for the most part is) *closed under reflection:* for its inhabitants, reflection is possible, even encouraged, but is not itself sufficient to get one outside it. The claim, then, is not that it is *absolutely* impossible to use reflection to break out of, say, Christendom, but it is unlikely. For the practices and institutions of Christendom contain and metabolize reflections upon them. So, the thought that in reflection one is thereby stepping back from the practice may itself be an illusion. In a journal entry written late in his life—December 3, 1854—Kierkegaard writes:

> To excavate in the middle of "Christendom" the types of being a Christian, which in relation to present Christians are somewhat like the bones of extinct animals to animals living now—*this is the most intense irony*—the irony of assuming Christianity exists at the same time that there are one thousand preachers robed in velvet and silk and millions of Christians who beget Christians, and so on.[14]

Imagine a serious young person trying to engage in a Christian life—but doing so by delving into Church histories and debates. This for Kierkegaard was *the* most intense irony. For precisely in the act of reflecting on Christianity this person would be entrenching himself ever deeper into the illusion of Christendom. The way out, Kierkegaard thought, was the cultivation of anxious, disruptive experiences of irony, as I have tried to describe them.

**7.** I have thus far been trying to capture the experience of irony. I would like to conclude with a preliminary account of ironic existence. Ironic existence is a form of life in which one develops a capacity for irony—that is, a capacity for occasioning an experience of irony (in oneself or another)—into a human excellence. So, one has the ability to deploy irony in the right sort of way at the right time in the living of one's life.[15] Ultimately, what this means is that one learns to embrace human finitude; and this counts as an excellence because it is a crucial form of self-knowledge.

But what is ironic existence? If ironic existence is a human excellence—a peculiar one to be sure—then there are certain lessons we can learn from Plato and Aristotle. First, we should not expect to be able to explain in any detail what the appropriate ironic thing to do is in any particular circumstances. There need be no specific behavioral manifestation that is required on any given occasion. In particular, ironic existence does not entail that a person behave in ways that are manifestly detached from established social practices. Ironic existence does not imply that one is occasioning ironic experiences all the time. Ironic existence is, rather, the ability to live well all the time with the *possibility* of ironic experience. This requires practical wisdom about when it is appropriate to deploy irony. We learn how to live with irony appropriately by learning from those who already are living an ironic existence. Our most notable exemplar is Socrates. As Kierkegaard writes in his journal, "In what did Socrates' irony really lie? In expressions and turns of speech, etc.? No, such trivialities, even his virtuosity in talking ironically, such things do not make a Socrates. No, his whole existence is and was irony."[16] Second, we can think of ironic existence as lying in a mean between excess and defect: the defect would be the familiar "ironic" wit who forever remains detached from committed life; the excess would be the perpetual disrupter of social norms, lacking good judgment about appropriateness. Ironic existence does not require alienation from established social practice. It only requires living well with the possibility of such alienation. That is compatible with passionate engagement in social life.

To grasp the peculiar ironic mean, it is helpful to return to Socrates. Socrates is often thought of as a negative figure, inflicting his method of refutation, the elenchus, on his interlocutors, reducing them to contradiction and then saying he did not know, either. Even the young Kierkegaard went along with this image, and in his *Magister's* thesis (which was translated and published as *The Concept of Irony: With Continual Reference to Socrates*), Kierkegaard says that irony is "infinite negativity."[17] Later in life, however, Kierkegaard came to reject and even ridicule this view. The mature Kierkegaard poured scorn on the young author of the phrase "infinite negativity." In a later work, *Concluding Unscientific Postscript,* the pseudonymous author Johannes Climacus criticizes "Magister Kierkegaard" for bringing out "only the one side" of irony. "As can be inferred from his dissertation," Climacus says that "Magister Kierkegaard" has "scarcely understood" Socrates's teasing manner.[18] I take the mature Kierkegaard to be making fun of himself as a young man: the *Concept of Irony* was written too much under the influence of Hegel, and thus focused one-sidedly on the negativity of irony. What we need to understand is how ironic activity can be as affirming as it is negating. In fact, what is so astonishing about Socrates's life is how effortlessly he blends positive and negative aspects of ironic existence.

So, consider Alcibiades's depiction of Socrates on the battlefield. What does Socrates do during the campaign for Potidaea? Well, for one thing, he stands still:

> One day, at dawn, he started thinking about some problem or other; he just stood outside trying to figure it out. He couldn't resolve it, but he wouldn't give up. He simply stood there, glued to the same spot. By midday, many soldiers had seen him and, quite mystified, they told everyone that Socrates had been standing there all day, thinking about something. He was still there when evening came, and after dinner some Ionians moved their bedding outside, where it was cooler and more comfortable (all this took place in the summer), but mainly in order to watch if Socrates was going to stay out there all night. And so he did; he stood on the very same spot until dawn! He only left next morning, when the sun came out, and he made his prayers to the new day.[19]

Socrates is often portrayed as absorbed in thought, as being so busy thinking a problem through that he loses track of his surroundings. Of course, in some sense that portrayal is accurate—Socrates is thinking—but if that is all there is to be said about the scene, then, philosophically speaking, it is utterly contingent that Socrates come to a halt. If all he is trying to do is think through a particularly difficult argument, then, although the portrait of him is charming, and a bit eccentric, there might have been another person just like Socrates, only one who could think and walk at the same time. The portrait becomes philosophically significant only if we add that Socrates is standing still not *simply* because he is too busy thinking, but because he *cannot walk* not knowing what his next step should be. I take this to be a moment of erotic uncanniness: *longing* to move in the right direction but not knowing what that direction is. He is uprooted only by the conventional religious demands of a new day. Yet when the actual battle comes, Socrates behaves with extraordinary bravery—*by the standard lights* of accepted social behavior. As Alcibiades says,

> During that very battle, Socrates single-handedly saved my life! He absolutely did! He just refused to leave me behind when I was wounded, and he rescued not only me but my armor as well. For my part, Socrates, I told them right then that the decoration really belonged to you.[20]

It is as though the moment of standing still invigorates him, at the right moment, to perform *extraordinary acts of conventional bravery.* And rather than them being two disparate moments in a disunified life, Alcibiades has an intimation that they form some kind of unity. In describing how Socrates bravely helped Laches in the retreat from Delium, Alcibiades says,

> In the midst of battle he was making his way *exactly as he does around town,* "with swaggering gait and roving eye." He was observing everything quite calmly, looking out for friendly troops and keeping an eye on the enemy. Even from a great distance it was obvious that this was a very brave man, who would put up a terrific fight if anyone approached him. That is what saved both of them.[21]

And yet, Alcibiades also says that Socrates's bravery cannot be compared to that of Achilles or anyone else.[22] Why not, if we are talking about battlefield bravery? The answer, I think, is that Socratic ignorance (in this case, about courage), far from being a distinct moment in Socrates's life (in the study, as it were), and far from sapping confidence in the ordinary demands of bravery, can, in certain circumstances, invigorate the enactment of the ordinary requirements. The irony must be *right there,* in the conventionally brave acts—otherwise Socrates's bravery would be comparable with Achilles's. This is what makes Socrates, in Alcibiades's words, "unique": "he is like no one else in the past and no one in the present—this is by far the most amazing thing about him." He is able to act bravely (according to the lights of social pretense), all the while holding firm to his ignorance. This is not just negativity; it is a peculiar way of *obviously* contributing to polis life. Socrates is not merely a gadfly: he is a gadfly who, on appropriate occasions, is willing to fight to the death in conventional battle.

This is similar to Socrates's classic examination of courage in the *Laches.* To be sure, by the end of the dialogue, Socrates declares the shared ignorance of all the interlocutors: "we have not discovered what courage is."[23] However, he is only able to enter the conversation because his interlocutors already trust him as a worthy interlocutor—and they trust him because he is well known for having lived courageously, according to the received norms of courage. Lysimachus says to Socrates that he keeps up his father's good reputation and that he is the best of men. And Laches elaborates, "I have seen him elsewhere keeping up not only his father's reputation but that of his country. He marched with me in the retreat from Delium and I can tell you that if the rest had been willing to behave in the same manner, our city would be safe and would not then have suffered a disaster of that kind."[24] So

Socratic ignorance is compatible with behaving with outstanding courage *as socially understood.* It is not a way of withdrawing from battle on behalf of the polis, but a way of participating in it. Even the inquiry into the nature of courage is not an abstract theoretical inquiry, but a response to an impassioned plea for help. Lysimachus and Melisius—two of the interlocutors—are the undistinguished sons of great men who are now worried about transmitting virtue to *their* sons.[25] This is a conversation born of real-life anxiety. And Socrates does not leave them empty-handed; they become convinced that they need to find a proper teacher *for themselves.*[26]

The height of his irony comes when, convicted of corrupting the youth and introducing new gods, Socrates proposes his own punishment. As conventional as he was in courageously defending the polis from external attack, he is unconventional in defending the polis from its own internal disease. It is one and the same virtue that is a manifestation of both. If the appropriate punishment is what he deserves, "Nothing is more suitable, gentlemen, than for such a man to be fed in the Prytaneum—much more suitable for him than for any one of you who has won a victory at Olympia with a pair or a team of horses. The Olympian victor makes you think yourself happy; I make you be happy."[27] The irony is utter earnestness: this *is* what he deserves. In the moment of facing death, Socrates does not deviate an iota from ironic existence.

**8.** Kierkegaard says that "no genuinely human life is possible without irony."[28] On the interpretation I have been developing, this would mean: it is constitutive of human excellence that one develop a capacity for appropriately disrupting one's understanding of what such excellence consists in. It is a human excellence to know—to practically understand—that human excellence contains a moment of ignorance internal to it. This is the self-knowledge of human finitude. Part of what it is to be, say, courageous is to recognize that one's practical understanding of courage is susceptible to ironic disruption. Part of what it is to be courageous is courageously to face the fact that living courageously will inevitably entangle one in practices and possible acts that are susceptible to the question, What does *any of that* have to do *with courage?* And yet, as we see in the example of Socrates, the recognition of the pervasive possibility for irony need not alienate or detach one from conventional acts of bravery. On the contrary, that recognition seems to have invigorated Socrates on the conventional battlefield. This is the question to which ironic existence provides an answer: how to live well with the insight into human finitude that the experience of irony bequeaths us.

CHAPTER FIVE

# Waiting for the Barbarians

**1.** Unjust societies tend to cloud the minds of those who live within them. Such societies hold themselves together not by force alone but by powerful imaginative structures that instill fear and complacency in the population. Those who, at least on the surface, profit from injustice tend to be brought up in ways that encourage insensitivity to the suffering on which their "advantaged" life depends. Unjust societies typically offer cultural vehicles that are psychologically comforting to the "beneficiaries"—narratives that say that the victims deserve the injustice they suffer. Such narratives reverse cause and effect: the misshapen state of the victims is taken to be a reason for assigning them inferior status. And those who suffer injustice can become coarse or mean-spirited through their suffering. It is as though injustice "teaches" them that injustice—in particular, selfishness—is the truth of the world: the only way to protect oneself is to look out for oneself. But the problem of injustice transcends material suffering and psychological distortion. In conditions of injustice, the possibilities of thought are themselves distorted: we lack the concepts by which we can adequately understand ourselves, and the concepts we do have distort our vision and disfigure our lives.[1]

If *we* are inhabitants of an unjust social order, it is likely that our own possibilities for thought will be tainted by the injustice we are trying to understand. Philosophical reflection on its own is limited in two ways. First, there is the danger that reflection will itself be an illusion of "stepping back" to an impartial perspective.[2] The crippled nature of our thought will be enacted in reflection, rather than addressed by it. Second, in conditions of injustice, we suffer deprivation in imagination: we fail to envisage possibilities for life and thought. Thus if we restrict ourselves to exploring the breadth, depth, and logical structure of our concepts *as we have inherited them,* we may repeat, rather than understand, unjust thought. We need to create new possibilities for thought. This would seem to require imaginative activity, even at the level of our life with concepts.

What kind of imaginative activity might that be? In this essay I will explore how an imaginative work, in this case a novel, might make an ethical difference. By *ethical difference* I mean a change in our life with others that itself expresses a transformation in the way we think and understand the world.[3] That is, I am not simply interested in novels that make a social difference as, for instance, *Uncle Tom's Cabin* galvanized the emotions of a population. I am interested in a work that can penetrate and transform the psyche of a reader. The question is how a work of literature might conceivably open new imaginative possibilities that would in turn be expressed in ethical life.

Let me clarify this question by setting aside three possible misunderstandings. First, I do not think literature needs to justify itself by appeal to anything outside itself. Great literature is of intrinsic value. Still, there is room for questions: Are there occasions when a work of fiction can influence ethical life in the community in which it arises? If so, how? Second, theoretical insight on its own is not sufficient. A work of literature might provide an insightful diagnosis of the injustice of its time. It might stand witness to truth. As such it has its own value. But I am concerned with how a work of literature might influence ethical life. If it can, we need to know the routes of efficacy. How is it that a work of literature has the efficacy it has?[4] It is not enough, for example, to claim that reading a novel can make us more sensitive. If it can, we need to know how. Finally, no novel can force a reader to read it in such a way as to make an ethical difference. A particular kind of responsiveness in the reader is also required. But then, what does this responsiveness consist in? What is it for a novel to find a reader in whom it can make an ethical difference?

In this essay I will consider a particular novel, *Waiting for the Barbarians* by John Coetzee, with these questions in mind.

**2.** As the novel opens, we readers are given direct access to the first-person consciousness of a narrator. How we have such access is unexplained. Coetzee's writing is so marvelously bleached out that it is tempting to think that he is writing a timeless parable. Kafka comes to mind. The reviewer in the *New York Times Book Review* said that the novel "tells the story of an imaginary Empire, set in an unspecified place and time."[5] But this cannot be right. From the very first sentence, we are oriented in time and space:

> I have never seen anything like it: two little discs of glass suspended in front of his eyes in loops of wire. Is he blind? I could understand it if he wanted to hide blind eyes. But he is not blind. The discs are dark, they look opaque from the outside, but he can see through them. He tells me they are a new invention. "They protect one's eyes against the glare of the sun," he says. "You would find them useful out here in the desert. They save one from squinting all the time. One has fewer headaches. Look." He touches the corners of his eyes lightly. "No wrinkles." He replaces the glasses. It is true. He has the skin of a younger man. "At home everyone wears them."[6]

Sunglasses became fashionable at the beginning of the twentieth century. So although the prose style does convey an uncanny sense of timelessness, the content locates the events of the novel approximately a century ago. We are sharing the thoughts of a narrator located at the edge of a colonial empire—with deserts and mountains on the far side—at the beginning of the twentieth century. How can we make sense of this? I would like to suggest that timelessness comes in different modes. In this case, the novel presents us with the timelessness of a dreamscape. I am not claiming that the novel is a dream, but that it is dream*like* in its presentation. It is typical of a dream that even if the dreamer has been brought up in South Africa, even if he has been powerfully affected by the events there, when he starts dreaming, all that gets left out: what remains is Empire, sunglasses, desert, nomads, and an enigmatic torturer. These are items that specify time and place, but they are uncanny in their isolation and detail. Dreams create a sense of reality for the dreamer not by depicting an entire world, but by picking out certain objects—or by staging particular scenes—and bequeathing them such intensity that the dreamer accepts the world in which they are located.

We are at the periphery of an empire at a time when it experiences itself as under duress. A torturer—Colonel Joll from the Third Bureau—has just arrived. This passage presents a fractal moment: the structure of Empire condensed into a single artifact.[7] Empires, by their nature, tend to expand out until they reach some resistance. The resistance may be other people who fight against being absorbed. Or it may be natural resistance: deserts or oceans that make it geographically difficult to go further. Or it may be some combination of the two. So, empires have a periphery. Empires also have a center. Centers are places that afford opportunities for luxury. The wealth created or stolen by Empire funnels to the center, where occasions arise for fashion, as well as for philosophy, the arts, and literature. Sunglasses begin their cultural life at the center, as a fashion for an elite who use them to protect their skin from signs of aging. "At home, everyone has them." Though they are new, they have been around long enough that the difference they can make shows on Colonel Joll's face. And yet, they are news to the narrator. Although we may not know the exact distance, *practically speaking* the periphery of the Empire is some distance from the center. Once they reach the periphery, the sunglasses acquire new uses. "You would find them useful out here in the desert." They shift from being a luxury of Empire to being a tool by which Empire sustains itself. And there is menacing irony in Joll's remark: sunglasses hide the eyes of torturers.

In writing this novel, author John Coetzee consciously deployed the craft of writing to create a dreamlike world. That does not imply that the novel offers only an *as-if* dreamscape. The novel offers readers the occasion to share the narrator's consciousness in an activity that bears a family resemblance to dreaming. A sign that the invitation is taken up is the widespread sense among readers that the novel occurs at "an unspecified place and time." As soon as one thinks about it, one can see that the space and time are specified. But that's the thing about engaging in dream*like* activity: one tends not to get around to thinking about it.[8] This would also explain why we tend to have no question of how we gain immediate access to the narrator's consciousness. The question tends not to arise. We *are just there,* in the presence of another consciousness, no questions asked. In a similar vein, *if* one were to ask about the realism of the narrator's consciousness, one would quickly have reason to doubt. It is incredible that a narrator could survive the torture he describes later in the novel with his consciousness intact. Such a consciousness would be maimed by trauma and would not be able to tell us what happened, as the steady voice of the narrator is able to do. This too is an issue that tends not to arise for the reader. Finally, the narrator is an uncanny locus of sensitivity in a world that is otherwise populated with two-dimensional sketches of human beings. How could he be *so* aware yet be the only one who is? This is the world of a dreamer's imagination.

To say that the novel is dreamlike in presentation is not to say that it is pleasant to read. It is not. The brutality of human life is reflected in the brutality of the prose that describes it. The novel confronts the reader with clinical descriptions of grotesque torture and humiliation. Readers often feel the need to put down the book. It takes fortitude just to keep on reading. Freud noticed that what we call traumatic dreams actually represent *failures* to keep on dreaming.[9] The content gets too terrible, anxiety bursts through, and we wake up in dread. This novel, then, is the opposite of a traumatic dream: it is resolute in its refusal to take out the traumatic option. The legacy of Empire needs to be dreamed *through;* it will take resolute readers to do this, and the novel is there to guide them through the appropriate imaginative activity.

Why locate the events of the novel at the beginning of the twentieth century? The novel invites readers to join the present-day consciousness of a narrator living at the time of our recent ancestors. We are in the present, but it is not our present. The mind that is alive for us is now dead and gone. And yet it is a not-too-distant past. Why this balance of immediacy and distance? Coetzee places the narrator at the temporal horizons of what can matter for us in a first-personal way. We are at the limits of a sense of entanglement. We all have ancestors going back to the Stone Age and beyond, but in an important sense they are nothing to us. Perhaps they practiced human sacrifice. So what? The fact that they did may be *interesting* to us, but the idea that we have inherited some responsibility because of our relation to them exerts no imaginative grasp. By contrast, the idea that we might somehow be caught in webs of meaning that we do not understand that stretch back to the time of our grandparents, great-grandparents, or great-great-grandparents . . . this is a thought that could come to haunt us. We are dealing with the dawn of a time that, even if it does not yet, might come to matter.

**3.** A merchant is standing at the gates of the city. A passing friend asks, "What's up?" Response: "I'm waiting for the barbarians. I want to buy their leatherwork. They're late." This familiar mode of waiting is not what this book is about. A sentry is standing at his post, and a fellow soldier comes by.

"What's up?" "I'm waiting for the barbarians. They haven't come yet, but I expect them after nightfall." This may sound more like it, but I want to argue that we miss the point if we think these are the moments the novel aims to diagnose. *Waiting for the barbarians* is not a discrete activity *in* the world; it is a structuring principle *of* the world. *Waiting for the barbarians* is the form of life of Empire. That is, all activities in conditions of Empire—whether explicit moments of waiting or not—are instances of waiting in this larger sense: they are ultimately intelligible by the contribution they make to a waiting form of life. *Everything* the citizens do is a mode and manifestation of such waiting.

I want to make the case for this claim in stages. First, consider the center of Empire in peacetime. People live in leisure; they wear sunglasses as a fashion to protect their skin. On the surface, this hardly seems like waiting. Still, as we have already seen, by its own conceptual necessity, Empire stretches out until it meets resistance. The Empire maintains itself by holding off resistance, and thus maintaining its boundary. War or *readiness* for war must be the norm. Peace at the center is dependent on the successful maintenance of conflict at the periphery. This is a conceptual matter: *periphery* is precisely the location of Empire where it is challenged; *center* is the location where, at least for a while, peace is obtained due to exertions at the periphery. So, in conditions of Empire, war is not the occasional disturbance of peace; peace is that which depends on war, or at least an ever-ready preparedness for war. Even at the center, there will be a dim recognition that "civilization needs protection"—and thus, in conditions of Empire, the leisurely achievements of culture get entangled in waiting. Even the latest fashion, sunglasses, becomes *that which is made possible and protected by waiting at the periphery.* This thought is not completely unavailable in the form of life, but it tends to be avoided; and this avoidance is itself a mode of waiting.

So, second, waiting is also manifest in efforts to avoid acknowledging it.

> We sit in the best room of the inn with a flask between us and a bowl of nuts. We do not discuss the reason for his being here. He is here under the emergency powers, that is enough. Instead, we talk about hunting.[10]

Etiquette is the unspoken regulation of what one does and does not discuss in polite society. The narrator is a country magistrate who is welcoming the newly arrived Colonel Joll. *Not* speaking about the barbarians is the shape that waiting for them takes. What does one speak about instead? Pleasantries. What do the pleasantries consist in? Horrific, gratuitous slaughter of animals on a "hunt." This is how members of the Third Bureau amuse themselves—it is how they wait—before they are actually allowed to hunt barbarians. The "genteel" activities of the social elite are themselves modes of waiting.

Third, the ever-present waiting gets expressed in fantasies, dreams, and daydreams.

> Of this unrest I myself saw nothing. In private I observed that once in every generation, without fail, there is an episode of hysteria about the barbarians. There is no woman living along the frontier who has not dreamed of a dark barbarian hand coming from under the bed to grip her ankle, no man who has not frightened himself with visions of the barbarians carousing in his home, breaking the plates, setting fire to the curtains, raping his daughters. These dreams are the consequence of too much ease. Show me a barbarian army and I will believe.[11]

As in polite discourse, ordinary life does not explicitly acknowledge *waiting*, but the waiting is going on all the same, percolating through the psyche and coming out in dreams. The narrator recognizes that dreams and daydreams can only contain the fantasy for so long. There is a cycle in which the fantasy eventually breaks out into the social world. The narrator calls this an "episode of hysteria." Once there is a social breakout, people acknowledge *then* that they are "waiting for the barbarians," but the narrator's point is that this is only a manifest endpoint of a long-term fantasy-process.

Finally, in moments of explicit crisis, the overall structure becomes clear:

> The barbarians come out at night. Before darkness falls the last goat must be brought in, the gates barred, a watch set in every lookout to call the hours. All night, it is said, the barbarians prowl about bent on murder and rapine. Children in their dreams see the shutters part and fierce barbarian faces leer through. "The barbarians are here!" the children scream, and cannot be comforted. Clothing disappears from washing-lines, food from larders, however tightly locked. The barbarians have dug a tunnel under the walls, people say; they come and go as they please, take what they like; no one is safe any longer. The farmers still till the fields, but

> they go out in bands, never singly. They work without heart: the barbarians are only waiting for the crops to be established, they say, before they flood the fields again.
>
> Why doesn't the army stop the barbarians? people complain. Life on the frontier has become too hard. They talk of returning to the Old Country, but then remember that the roads are no longer safe because of the barbarians. Tea and sugar can no longer be bought over the counter as the shopkeepers hoard their stocks. Those who eat well eat behind closed doors, fearful of awaking their neighbors' envy.[12]

In a moment of crisis, all the details of life are clearly affected. Even as simple an activity as shopping for tea falls under the penumbra. One cannot eat a meal without hiding. To be sure, this is a moment of crisis; but it is also the mode the population shifts to when it feels itself under pressure. It is an already-available possibility in a form of life structured by waiting for the barbarians. So even when in peacetime one can simply shop for tea, the possibility of hoarding—of tea disappearing from the shelves—is haunting the transaction. As a form of life, waiting structures all the possibilities of the participants. One may choose to go shopping, or one may choose not to; it may be a time of crisis, or it may not—either way, the act is informed by waiting.

**4.** Waiting is a *dreamlike* form of life. For it to thrive, this form of life must not be transparent to itself. The paranoia, the cruelty to others, the insensitive enjoyment of conditions of injustice—all of which sustain the waiting form of life—require that participants, for the most part, remain somewhat unaware of what they are doing. There are moments within the form of life when participants think of themselves as waiting for the barbarians, but they are unaware that waiting structures everything they do. That is why it is difficult to have the first-personal, present-tense thought "*We* are waiting for the barbarians" (in the relevant sense). The form of life flourishes when citizens remain in a haze about the conditions of the possibility of their own existence. The waiting form of life thus bears a family resemblance to dreaming.

In general, dream-life is a form of consciousness in which one is unaware that one is dreaming. Should the thought *"This is a dream!"* enter consciousness, it tends to wake us up. It is possible to dream that one is dreaming, but that is rare. It is a different manner of having the same thought. In the paradigm case, the recognition that one is dreaming is an awareness of one's condition that by that very awareness will change it. This is an instance of an immediate efficacy of mind that is transparent to itself. Now, the waiting form of life is dream*like* in the sense that it depends for its continued existence on not becoming fully aware of what it is.

I said earlier that the novel is dreamlike in its presentation. It now emerges that it is a dreamlike presentation of a dreamlike form of life. But it turns out to be extraordinarily difficult to have the thought "We are waiting for the barbarians" *in such a way* as to "wake us up."

**5.** In unjust times, one should not expect a hero to be a virtuous person. He has lived in an unjust environment all his life, so it is likely that he will be an amalgam of virtues and vices. This ethical ambiguity need not detract from his heroism—at least, if we think of heroism as daring indifference to consequences that moves in the direction of a noble deed—but the ambiguity will envelop his deeds in confusion. One can see the narrator struggling not just at the edge of Empire, but at the edge of Empire's use of concepts. We see this in the use of the concept *barbarian,* from which he is alienated but which he continues to use.

The Empire maintains itself via an imaginative structure. One fantasy-claim is that its geographical boundary is also the boundary of civilized intelligibility. The refusal to make sense of those who live beyond its bounds is treated as though it is *they* who do not make sense. The narrator cannot go along with this. He lives at the periphery, and that at least allows for the possibility, in quiet times, of living in an intermediate zone in which trade and other forms of interaction occur between citizens and "barbarians."[13]

> We prize barbarian leatherwork, particularly the sturdy boots they sew. . . . In the past I have encouraged commerce but forbidden payment in money. I have also tried to keep the taverns closed to them. Above all I do not want to see a parasite settlement grow up on the fringes of the town populated with beggars and vagrants enslaved to strong drink. It always pained me in the old days to see these people fall victim to the guile of shopkeepers, exchanging their goods for trinkets, lying drunk in

> the gutter, confirming thereby the settlers' litany of prejudice: the barbarians are lazy, immoral, filthy, stupid. Where civilization entailed the corruption of barbarian virtues and the creation of a dependent people, I decided I was opposed to civilization; and upon this I based the conduct of my administration. (I say this who now keeps a barbarian girl for my bed!)[14]

Others who live at the edge are able to use the concept *barbarian* unselfconsciously, but the narrator—with his temperament and sensitivity, and his long experience of life on the periphery—cannot. There is too much texture in his experience to use without qualification a concept that depends on paranoid fantasies floating free. He is aware of this.

> How can I believe that the night is full of the flitting shadows of barbarians? If there were strangers here I would feel it in my bones. The barbarians have withdrawn with their flocks into the deepest mountain valleys, waiting for the soldiers to grow tired and go away. When that happens the barbarians will come out again. They will graze their sheep and leave us alone, we will plant our fields and leave them alone, and in a few years the frontier will be restored to peace.[15]

The narrator also sees that the concept *barbarian* lends a false unity to those on the other side. As he tells Colonel Joll:

> "This so-called banditry does not amount to much. They steal a few sheep or cut out a pack-animal from a train. Sometimes we raid them in return. They are mainly destitute tribespeople with tiny flocks of their own living along the river. It becomes a way of life."[16]

The concept *barbarian* also lends a false unity to disturbing acts. If one person steals a cow, it becomes an act of the barbarians. The narrator sees that the concept *barbarian* is what makes it possible to inflict punishment on all for the act of one.

The narrator even grasps that history collaborates in keeping the citizens of Empire unaware of their waiting form of life. His insight goes deeper than the familiar thought that the victors write the history.[17] The real problem with history, the narrator realizes, lies in its temporality.

> What has made it impossible for us to live in time like fish in the water, like birds in the air, like children? It is the fault of the Empire! Empire has created the time of history. Empire has located its existence not in the smooth recurrent spinning time of the cycle of the seasons, but in the jagged time of rise and fall, of beginning and end, of catastrophe. Empire dooms itself to live in history and plot against history. One thought alone preoccupies the submerged mind of the Empire: how not to end, how not to die, how to prolong its era. By day it pursues its enemies. It is cunning and ruthless, it sends its bloodhounds everywhere. By night it feeds on images of disaster: the sack of cities, the rape of populations, pyramids of bones, acres of desolation. A mad vision, yet a virulent one.[18]

His point is not just that history facilitates unawareness by offering an ideological account of what is meaningful ("Emperor 2 came after Emperor 1") but by offering itself—*history*—as the meaningful form of temporality. By its very structure history assumes that what matters is what came after what, and what caused what to happen. But if *waiting for barbarians* is the form of life, then all the historical narratives will be subsumed under this timeless aspect of temporality. All the this-came-after-that's will be myriad instances of waiting. Waiting is the form that structures them all. The narrator grasps that if we focus on the historical narratives, the form of life will escape our notice.

For the narrator in his alienation, the linear historical narratives of Empire are part of a larger cosmic cycle of Empires rising and collapsing, and eventually being replaced by a new Empire. The proper understanding of this cycle is not to be given in a linear history—"Empire 2 came after Empire 1"—but rather as an eternal recurrence of the same. The temporality is different.

**6.** Is the narrator's alienation from the Empire's use of the concept *barbarian* an alienation from the form of life itself? Or is alienation one more mode of *waiting?* There is reason for thinking that Empire makes room for citizens who are alienated, up to a point. The narrator says,

> I did not mean to get embroiled in this. I am a country magistrate, a responsible official in the service of the Empire, serving out my days on

> this lazy frontier, waiting to retire. . . . For the rest I watch the sun rise and set, eat and sleep and am content. . . . But last year stories began to reach us from the capital of unrest among the barbarians.[19]

The narrator had sought quiet, a place to wait out his employment, and, perhaps, his life. The Empire has its cozy positions—like country magistrate—that provide a harmless place for the alienated members of a privileged class to stay at a comfortable remove from the official narratives of Empire. It is a *comfortable* alienation. The point is that certain modes of alienation feed an illusion of distance. Worldly alienation is a mode of life within Empire—one in which members of an elite deceive themselves about being detached from it. This alienation is not akin to "waking up" from a dreamlike form of life, for it still is basically a thought that waiting for barbarians is something *other people* do—namely, everyone around them. This is one way Empire contains its disaffected.

The novel charts a significant shift in the narrator's alienation: from the comfortable alienation of a country magistrate living out a sinecure to the brutally uncomfortable alienation of a tortured victim of Empire. Still, throughout his travails, the narrator's imagination is constrained. He repeatedly imagines a recurrence of the same. For him, peace is part of a cycle: after a while the soldiers go away, the nomads return, and the various groups in this intermediate zone leave each other alone. All peace can amount to for him is a recurrence of a more comfortable same. The narrator's Ozymandius moments follow a similar line. Among the dunes two miles south of town, he discovered ruins of houses, perhaps an earlier fort. It has become a hobby to excavate it, and he has found "wooden slips," some of which are legible: "in the hope of deciphering the script, I have set about collecting all the slips I can."[20] This is occasion for a melancholy "philosophic" reflection. He cannot participate in the Empire's fantasy of eternity, because he sees it as only one stage of a larger cycle. But when he looks into this ancient, enigmatic past, all he can see is the same again.

> Perhaps in bygone days criminals, slaves, soldiers trekked the twelve miles to the river and cut down poplar trees . . . built houses and forts too, for all I know, and in the course of time died, so that their masters, their prefects and magistrates and captains could climb her roofs and towers morning and evening to scan the world from horizon to horizon for signs

> of the barbarians. Perhaps in my digging I have only scratched the surface. Perhaps ten feet below the floor lie the ruins of another fort, razed by the barbarians, peopled with the bones of folk who thought they would find safety behind high walls. Perhaps when I stand on the floor of the courthouse, if that is what it is, I stand over the head of a magistrate like myself, another grey-haired servant of the Empire who fell in the arena of his authority, face to face at last with a barbarian. How will I ever know?[21]

He cannot participate in the Empire's fantasy, but in *his* fantasy, there is even an ancient precursor to himself. *He* is a repetition—at least, so he imagines. What is beyond his imagination is that perhaps the past civilization lived in a better way, some way we might learn from. His interest is basically aesthetic. He treats the wooden slips as curiosities; one might learn interesting anecdotes about how they went about doing things, but that's it. He has no sense of urgency or importance, no sense that they might have lived a very different way. Deciphering the slips is a hobby for him, a pastime. He even imagines a future repetition in which *he* becomes the discovered curiosity.

> I could lean against this ancient post with its faded carvings of dolphins and waves and be blistered by the sun and dried by the wind and eventually frozen by the frost and not be found until in some distant era of peace the children of the oasis come back to their playground and find the skeleton, uncovered by the wind, of an archaic desert dweller clad in unidentifiable rags.[22]

The narrator experiences his crippled imagination as world-weary wisdom. His alienation from Empire is a way of staying attached to it. The outlook is of an eternal recurrence of the same, which, by that very recurrence, drains any particular moment of significance. Humans strive with this or that project, but ultimately Empires come and go, and all that remains is an indecipherable fragment of a past testament to human vanity. Such a melancholic outlook is a defense with political import. It drains the will of a sense that objecting to social injustice could make a difference. No wonder such a person seeks out a comfortable position at the outskirts of Empire—a place to wait out life in an inescapably shabby world. The narrator tolerates the injustice of Empire just so long as he does not have to look at it too closely. Should he occasionally notice this or that unpleasantness, that too is part of the inevitable cycle of life. That is how it is for him—until he is disrupted from that outlook by being forced to look at it closely.

**7.** Can evil break open the structure of repetition? The novel begins with the arrival of a torturer from the Third Bureau. It can never be the First Bureau—we somehow already know that, even if we do not understand why. Nor can he come from the Torture Bureau. Empire *has* such a bureau, but it cannot be so named. It has got to be Third Bureau or Directorate of something or other. Evil is *not* banal; but it needs a banal name. Somehow—and this is the narrator's puzzle—there are some people who seem well suited to the task. Who knows what they would be doing otherwise? What we do know is: Empire gives them a uniform and something to do. But the narrator needs to know more. The torturer's evil unnerves him. There is, for him, no question of the terrible injustice of the torturer's acts—only the pressing, unignorable question of how anyone could perform them. He cannot *simply* absorb into his world-weary view that even this will happen over and over again. He needs to know why. What is it about such people that makes evil seem good to them? This question catches him and drives him. Here, for once, he cannot rest content with a melancholic *same again*—even if he cannot transcend it either. The evil is other, and he needs to know how it could be. The novel is, to a significant extent, a chronicle of his failure to satisfy this need.

The narrator's treatment of the barbarian woman deserves an essay of its own, but in terms of this inquiry, the narrator emerges as a flawed pioneer. The barbarian woman captures him, as it were, not simply because she is barbarian, but because she has been tortured. She has been maimed, scarred, virtually blinded, and forced to experience the unimaginably horrible. The narrator needs to understand what difference it has made to be marked by evil; he feels compelled to respond, but mostly he flails about with familiar ambivalent routines. He treats her poorly, as male masters have long done to female slaves; yet he tends to her scars with religious devotion. His confusion is everywhere manifest in his actions. He is all over the map in his responses, but—that's it—he basically stays on the map. To be sure, he heroically returns her to her people, at great risk and cost to himself. He gives her a moment of freedom in which she might freely return to him. But he never gives her an explanation about why such a choice would be anything other than lunacy; nor does he make an effort to get to know her or the people to whom he is returning her. And so the effort, though genuinely heroic, does not escape a familiar trope. And beyond the familiarity of the trope, there is no evidence that the narrator understands what he is doing.

The cruel irony of his situation is that the one thing he is driven to understand—evil—is not there to be understood. One can make sense of torturers up to a point. They have a different a priori. Colonel Joll explains to the narrator:

> "A certain tone enters the voice of a man who is telling the truth. Training and experience teach us to recognize that tone. . . . First I get lies you see—this is what happens—first lies, then pressure, then more lies, then more pressure, then the break, then more pressure, then the truth. That is how you get to the truth.
>
> Pain is truth, all else is subject to doubt."[23]

The torturer's method mirrors and mocks Descartes's: if overcoming all possibility of doubt is the criterion of truth, then, as the torturer sees it, inflicting pain on others is the inevitable outcome. When later in the book the narrator himself becomes one of the tortured, he says:

> No matter if I told my interrogators the truth, recounted every word I uttered on my visit to the barbarians, no matter even if they were tempted to believe me, they would press on with their grim business, for it is an article of faith with them that the last truth is told only in the last extremity.[24]

So, what from the narrator's perspective is blatant cruelty to the innocent, from the torturer's perspective is an essential moment in the search for truth. From the torturer's perspective, such pain is to be sought and hoped for. The same evidence—and let's call it what it is, *blatant* cruel injustice—counts for the torturer as justice being served. Thus there is at least a mask of intelligibility.

But how can *this* be the torturer's a priori? How can anyone live this way? This is what the narrator needs to know and cannot find out. If he were going to break out of melancholic repetition, this would be the occasion. The novel suggests that this exit route is closed.

> He deals with my soul: every day he folds the flesh aside and exposes my soul to the light; he has probably seen many souls in the course of his working life; but the care of souls seems to have left no more mark on him than the care of hearts leaves to the surgeon.
>
> "I am trying very hard to understand your feelings towards me," I say. I cannot help mumbling, my voice is unsteady, I am afraid and the sweat is dripping from me. "Much more than an opportunity to address these people, to whom I have nothing to say, would I appreciate a few words from you. So that I can come to understand why you devote yourself to this work. And can hear what you feel towards me whom you have hurt a great deal and now seem to be proposing to kill."
>
> Amazed I stare at this elaborate utterance as it winds its way out of me. Am I mad enough to intend a provocation?
>
> "Do you see this hand?" he says. He holds his hand an inch from my face. "When I was younger"—he flexes his fingers—"I used to be able to poke this finger"—he holds up the index finger—"through a pumpkin shell." He puts the tip of his finger against my forehead and presses. I take a step backwards.[25]

The problem is not so much the *psychology* of evil as it is the *nature* of evil. The narrator seeks an explanation of what is happening—he risks his life and certainly sacrifices his well-being for the sake of understanding—but explanations are themselves in the realm of the good. The response to an explanation for an evil act can only be another evil act: *that's why!* The very idea that some other kind of justification is required is mocked. The narrator is driven to understand, but the intelligible world goes dark.

The lesson is not that the true barbarians are among us, the members of the Third Bureau. There are no *true* barbarians. The concept *barbarian* is a concept designed to apply to a fantasied object. What is correct is that, from the point of view of the novel, some people perform evil acts with apparent ease, yet their acts are ultimately unintelligible. We cannot get to a satisfying explanation of why they do what they do. The concept *barbarian* is an attempt to wish this puzzle away, by placing evil on the other side of a geographical boundary. In this way, the concept *barbarian* is a defense against the difficult recognition that evil is among us but does not equally inhabit all of us. In Empire, these people are given a job to do. Insofar as Empire depends on this cruelty to maintain itself, all citizens are entangled, whether they recognize it or not. As the narrator puts it:

> I was the lie that Empire tells itself when times are easy; he the truth Empire tells when harsh winds blow. Two sides of imperial rule, no more, no less.[26]

Not understanding this is a form of not *wanting* to understand. One can see an example of this in the narrator's account of his own civility:

> But of what use is it to blame the crowd? A scapegoat is named, a festival is declared, the laws are suspended: who would not flock to see the entertainment? What is it I object to in these spectacles of abasement and suffering and death that our new regime puts on but their lack of decorum? What will my own administration be remembered for besides moving the shambles from the marketplace to the outskirts of the town twenty years ago in the interests of decency?[27]

Gentility for him consisted in placing the underbelly of Empire just out of sight. So, even if evil is ultimately unintelligible, for decorous citizens most of the time, that serves their desire not to know. As for the narrator, by the end of the novel he is in the absurd position of needing to know *and* not wanting to know *and* being shut out from any possibility of knowing. There is something about his predicament that rings true.

> If the barbarians were to burst in now, I know, I would die in my bed as stupid and ignorant as a baby. . . . To the last we will have learned nothing. In all of us, deep down, there seems to be something granite and unteachable.[28]
>
> I think: "I have lived through an eventful year, yet understand no more of it than a babe in arms. Of all the people of this town I am the one least fitted to write a memorial . . ." I think: "There has been something staring me in the face and still I do not see it."[29]

Yet there is one thing he has learned: however difficult it is to protest injustice, protesting injustice is far easier than fighting for justice.

> What, after all, do I stand for besides an archaic code of gentlemanly behavior towards captured foes, and what do I stand against except the new science of degradation that kills people on their knees, confused and disgraced in their own eyes? Would I have dared to face the crowd to demand justice for these ridiculous barbarian prisoners with their backsides in the air? *Justice:* once that word is uttered, where will it all end? Easier to shout *No!* Easier to be beaten and made a martyr. Easier to lay my head on a block than to defend the cause of justice for the barbarians: for where can that argument lead but to laying down our arms and opening the gates of the town to the people whose land we have raped?[30]

This is as far as this unjust mind can get in conditions of injustice. Even in Empire, when gratuitous cruelty stares one in the face, it is possible to recognize it. One may evade this recognition—most citizens do—but it is available. The narrator takes up this possibility and pursues it as far as he can go. Blatant cruel injustice *right before his eyes* is his bedrock. It is that against which he must protest, even as he tries to explore what it is. He thereby brings to light the possibilities of heroism in bad times and for those with a less-than-excellent character. But he can only get so far. In part, this is because of his defective character; in part, it is because of the unintelligibility of evil; but it is also because of the unavailability of adequate conceptions of goodness. In conditions of injustice, the conception of justice tends to be disfigured. Conditions of culture and of individual personality coincide in a toxic constellation. In Empire, *justice* is deployed in the service of claiming that barbarians get what they deserve, and that the advantaged members of society merit their positions. It tends to function as a signifier, with only a tinge of content. In terms of individual psychology, the person who is sufficiently alienated from the culture to see its ideological dimension is also trapped in a melancholic deprivation of imagination. He recognizes injustice and protests it, but he can only imagine the same injustice repeating itself, again and again, backward into the past and forward into the future. And really, in his melancholy, he runs out of the ability to care. The narrator has reached the limit of his desire to know, and he knows that.

**8.** I asked earlier how an encounter with a novel might make an ethical difference for a reader. The question can now be made more precise. We are concerned with a narrator's heroic, insightful but ultimately failed attempt to stand witness to his time. How might a reader's imaginative engagement with such a narrator make an ethical difference?

Freud famously suggested that mourning is melancholia's healthy twin.[31] This gives us a clue. In trying to understand the novel's possible efficacy, I have focused on two features. First, the narrator's consciousness is located at the temporal horizons of where we might, just conceivably, come to experience ourselves as implicated. Second, the novel is an occasion for imaginative activity on the part of the reader that bears a family resemblance to dreaming. If we take these two features together, what have we got? I would like to suggest: *the activity of mourning.* Or perhaps: the imaginative activity that makes mourning possible. Mourning, I will argue, is an immediate efficacy of mind. And in certain circumstances it can make an ethical difference.

Melancholia is the condition of being *stuck in repetition.* For the melancholic, everything is always already the same again—stretching back into the past, and on into the future. Mourning, by contrast, is imaginative *re-creation.* That is, it is the occasion for taking up the past way and using it as an occasion to break out of repetition and create a new future. Though it is often a painful process, it is also fertile. In mourning, the past nourishes the present and future; and the mourner ultimately says *yes* to life by saying *no* to the depressing confines of "same again forever."[32]

In the paradigm case, we mourn the death of a loved one—someone who once existed and now exists no more. The narrator, by contrast, is a fictional character. This need not make a difference to the reality of mourning. For what we need to mourn is not an individual per se but the form of life he imaginatively incarnates. We mourn, as it were *through him,* a form of life that threatens to entangle us with its ghosts. Contrary to appearances, old forms of life are not just "gone with the wind." They leave fantasy-residues that, but for the mourning, haunt the generations. Mourning, as Freud and Loewald emphasized, is a process through which we transform ghosts into ancestors.[33]

What does this mean? Freud suggests that we come to accept the loss of a person in the external world by re-creating that person imaginatively in our internal world. For the purposes of this essay, we can leave his theory of the unconscious dimensions of this activity to one side. The point is this: as readers we establish an imaginative relation with the narrator. We do not identify with him so much as sympathetically refuse to do so. That is, we refuse to take on his structure of repetition; but the manner of our refusal is an imaginative engagement with it. In relating to him in this way, the narrator becomes an integral part of our own imaginative lives. We set up an imaginative relation of sympathy and distance. Every imaginative activity is first-personal in the sense that it is one's own imaginative activity, but mourning is first-personal in the additional sense that by engaging in this imaginative activity one thereby shapes oneself. We make a loss our own. Directly, we are absorbed in thoughts of the departed other; indirectly, we change ourselves.

The ironic strategy of this novel is to mourn melancholia. That is, readers are given the occasion to mourn the narrator's melancholic attempts to make sense of life. This is a possibility the novel opens up for readers: a way to leave behind melancholic stuckness in an unjust form of life. The routes of mourning in individual readers will no doubt take idiosyncratic paths. But the paradigmatic route the novel offers is to join in the imaginative activity of making the narrator into one of our ancestors. We thereby turn his legacy into our inheritance. Such empires have existed within the horizons of a time that might come to matter to us. By crafting a novel of Empire, the author offers readers an imaginary route for creating a legacy—one of which we are conscious and for which we may take responsibility. No one needs to read the novel this way; the novel cannot force anyone to; and many will not. But the possibility is open to make such a use of the novel, and when one does, the novel can make an ethical difference.

For those who are willing to join in a mournful reading, at some point the questions arise: "Am I to live within the ambit of the narrator's imagination? Am I to be more than a future *repetition* that he has already imagined? Has he got it right that all there is are repetitions of the same again?" The answer ought to be a heartfelt but resounding *no*. The manner of the negation is important. It need not be merely a theoretical recognition that, as a matter of fact, the narrator made a mistake. Rather, we express affectionate engagement with this narrator by *committing ourselves* not to repeat his life.[34]

*Waiting for the Barbarians,* the novel, offers the reader an imaginative and efficacious way out of waiting for the barbarians: by mourning the form of life. Our imaginative engagement with the narrator may be sympathetic, but like some barely recognized ancestor whose faded photo we have seen, whose diary we have come across in a box in the attic, we relate to him by rejecting his sincere, sometimes heroic, but flawed attempt at authenticity.

This is an immediate efficacy of thought that, if one pays attention, can be self-consciously experienced.

**9.** For a novel to make an ethical difference, it depends on the right kind of responsiveness in a reader. This responsiveness is regularly resisted. When *Waiting for the Barbarians* was first published, the *New York Times Book Review* ran this headline: "A Stark Political Fable of South Africa."[35] The reviewer, Irving Howe, began:

> Imagine what it must be like to live as a serious writer in South Africa: an endless clamor of news about racial injustice, the feeling that one's life is mortgaged to a society gone rotten with hatred, an indignation that exhausts itself into depression, the fear that one's anger may overwhelm and destroy one's fiction. And except for silence or emigration, there can be no relief.

For the reviewer, it is as though the author is trying to solve his problem, not ours. And his problem is portrayed as finding "relief." No doubt authors work out various issues in writing; but it diminishes the power of a novel to place the reader in the position of judge as to how well the author is doing with his own work. Now consider the readers of the *New York Times.* Could there be anything more comfortable for such readers than to be against apartheid? It is as though the reviewer is congratulating the author on finding a literarily impressive way to adopt a position that agrees with the already-established position of readers of the *New York Times.* Readers get to pat themselves on the back for positions they already hold—and take themselves to be morally uplifted to boot.[36] In this way, the reception of a work of literature can lull an intellectual elite with a simulacrum of making an ethical difference; readers are tranquilized by an illusion of being in a moral vanguard.[37]

The problem with the *New York Times'* approach is that it distances the reader from the narrator, and that inevitably impedes the imaginative activity of establishing an imaginary relation with him. In saying that the novel is "set in an unspecified place and time," the review encourages an *empty* version of the thought

> "It could be anywhere; it could be any time; it could be us."

Even if it is sincerely thought and well meant, that does not prevent the thought from being a cliché.[38] What comes to light here is a problem of *practical conjugation:* as we get closer to the first-personal thought "We are waiting for the barbarians," the thought tends to get drained of significance. But then, how might one approach a first-personal thought without thereby emptying it of its potential to make a difference? The novel suggests that we get there obliquely, via mourning the narrator.

Consider the thought "Even *he* was waiting"—thought by a reader about the narrator. There are different ways we might have such a thought. It might be a purely theoretical recognition that our narrator, for all his alienation, suffering, and protest, did not escape the form of life. But there is also a manner of thinking this thought in which *the very thinking* is efficacious in transforming our relation to the narrator and the form of life he embodies. Thinking about the narrator's failure *in this way,* I thereby bid him a heartfelt adieu.

The narrator was able to say a heroic *no!* to injustice but was, by his own recognition, unable to say *yes!* to a justice he was not yet in a position to comprehend. Even the lineaments of the concept were too much for him. Saying *yes* to justice is another step. It is a commitment to live toward a more robust conception of justice than we may have at present. This is not at all easy to do, but a nontrivial first step is to find a significant way to mourn the refusal to do just that.

**10.** When it comes to interpretation, the *manner of thinking* makes all the difference. The *New York Times* interpretation, for all its piety that "it could be any time; it could be us," encourages us to think that *waiting for the barbarians* is something other people do. In this way, the thought short-circuits the power of the novel—consigning it to a literature of self-congratulation. But the same thought *thought differently* can be an efficacious act of mind by which one separates oneself from a waiting form of life. The novel provides the occasion for the imaginative activity by which one can make the transition from empty to efficacious thought.

If mourning is to be successful, it must bring along the imaginative, emotional, not-entirely-rational part of the soul.[39] If in the mourning process one finally resolves to say good-bye to this waiting form of life, one must be full-hearted if one is to succeed. Resoluteness of will on its own is not enough. The mourning process consists in the imaginative reworkings that allow for gathering up the soul into a unified whole.

For an interpretation to be efficacious, it must occur at the endpoint of an extended imaginative process. The interpretation functions as a concise summing-up of an imaginative process that culminates in it.[40] In the case of the novel, the *content* gives us a dreamlike presentation of the consciousness of a narrator who cannot fit into a form of life but cannot extract himself from it either. The *title* functions like an interpretation: it sums it all up, gives us a self-conscious name for it, ties us to it, and distances us from it, all at the same time. When the process is working well for a certain kind of reader, the content draws the reader into this dreamlike world and the title wakes one out of it. That is the basic structure of mourning: a dreamlike engagement—with a person, an idea, or a way of life—that needs to be bid farewell. When the activity of reading works, one gets to say full-heartedly *This is what waiting for the barbarians amounts to.* And, when it works, one thereby distances oneself from the fantasy. At this point in the imaginative process, one might think, *Waiting for the barbarians is what other people do;* but now the *manner of thinking* shifts into an efficacious distancing of oneself from the form of life one has mourned. This is one example of what it might be for a novel to make an ethical difference.

It should be clear by now that literary form is not an optional extra for an argument that could be extracted from it. It is a manner of thinking that, when successful, can make a particular ethical difference. In this case, it inaugurates mourning an unjust way of life. And in mourning we find a way of at least starting to say good-bye to an unjust form of thinking whose legacy we have inherited—and now have started to transform.[41]

CHAPTER SIX

# The Ironic Creativity of Socratic Doubt

**1.** Even after we pay due regard to his wish that the voices of the pseudonymous authors not be taken to reflect his own views, it is difficult to avoid the conclusion that the mature Kierkegaard found his early writings on irony—there is no better word for it—immature.[1] In the *Concluding Unscientific Postscript,* published in 1846, the author Johannes Climacus introduces his discussion on irony with this jibe: "What then is irony, if one wants to call Socrates an ironist, and not, like Magister Kierkegaard, consciously or unconsciously to bring out the one side only."[2] *The Concept of Irony: With Continual Reference to Socrates* is the thesis by which Kierkegaard earned his master's degree. The pain, the humor, the *irony* of looking back on oneself as a young man—the days of accepting a socially conferred title of *master!* The embarrassment gets worse when one claims to be a "master *of irony.*" Does not the claim refute itself? Would any *master* of irony be willing to let himself be called such?

Climacus complains that young Kierkegaard's account of Socratic irony is one-sided.[3] The one-sidedness consists in a portrait of relentless Socratic negativity. Here is one of many such passages:

> Socrates certainly indicated a new direction: he gave the age its direction (taking this word not so much in a philosophic as in a military sense). He went around to each one individually in order to find out if that person had a sound position; nevertheless, his activity was intended not so much to draw their attention to what was to come as to wrest from them what

> they had. This he accomplished, as long as the campaign lasted, by cutting off all communication with the besieged through his questions, which starved the garrison out of opinions, conceptions, time-honored traditions, etc., that up until now had been adequate for the person concerned. *When he had done this to the individual, the devouring flame of envy (using this word metaphysically) was momentarily slaked, the annihilating enthusiasm of negativity momentarily satisfied, and he relished the joy of irony to its fullest,* relished it doubly, because he felt himself divinely authorized, was convinced of his calling. *But naturally this was only for a moment; soon he was back to his task again.* . . . In this way he admittedly freed the single individual from every presupposition, freed him as he himself was free; but the freedom he personally enjoyed in ironic satisfaction the others could not enjoy, and it developed in them a longing and a yearning. . . . The reason Socrates could be satisfied in this ignorance was that he had no deeper speculative craving. Instead of speculatively setting this negativity to rest, he set it far more to rest in the eternal unrest in which he repeated the same process with each single individual. In all this, however, that which makes him into a personality is precisely irony.[4]

Climacus's complaint transcends issues of Kierkegaard scholarship. Working out a richer conception of irony is of enduring ethical significance. If Socratic irony is only in the service of undermining people's confidence in their ability to defend their beliefs, why think that this is in the service of a good? It is too quick to say it is a good to be robbed of falsity. Imagine Socrates's evil twin, Schmocrates: he too has that "devouring flame of envy," as Magister Kierkegaard put it, but he preys on good-hearted interlocutors who happen to be not very good at explaining their good wills. It is difficult to see how "irony" that makes a good person ashamed of his good will must be in the service of a good.

If we are to understand irony as a good, we must come to understand how the disruption it provokes can, on occasion, lead us in a good direction. This—and here I agree with Climacus—requires us to see another side to Socratic irony, one that eluded the view of the young Kierkegaard. How might irony also be positive? How might irony, even in its negativity, be put to creative and life-enhancing uses? These are the questions I want to take up in this essay.

**2.** Less than a year before his death—on December 3, 1854—Kierkegaard made this entry into his journal: "Socrates doubted that one is a human being by birth; to become human or to learn what it means to be human does not come that easily—what occupied Socrates, what he sought, was the ideality of being human."[5] This is an instance of irony as Kierkegaard understood it in his maturity. Socrates's doubt seems to be calling the obvious into question; but in the same moment we can see that is not what he is doing. We know immediately that he is not wondering whether the individual member of the species has a biologically larval moment before springing forth. Rather, the doubt is calling the category *human being* into question—and it does so in a way that is at once enigmatic, playful, and earnest.[6] Even if one does not yet understand the claim, one can see the irony is in the service of something positive: it may be that *becoming human* or *learning what it means to be human* does not come that easily—but it does come, and the intimation is that irony will help the process along. We may not yet understand Kierkegaard's journal entry, but we can already see that the mature Kierkegaard sees irony as deployable for positive outcomes—not just the emptiness and the longing of *The Concept of Irony.*

What is the irony? If Kierkegaard were simply reserving the term *human* for a person who lives up to an ideal, the claim would be straightforward but philosophically uninteresting. Why should we put up with the restriction? Obviously, someone can say of an especially humane, generous, or sympathetic person, "Now she's a *real* human being!" and we easily understand. Still, to make this kind of move the basis for a general difficulty in becoming human seems arbitrary. We ought to be able to experience the *difficulty of becoming human* not as an arbitrary imposition, but as a problem arising internally from Socratic doubt.

In explicating that doubt Kierkegaard says, "To become human or to learn what it means to be human does not come that easily."[7] Nor does understanding what this claim means. Let's start in an unlikely place, with the connective "or." This is not the "or" of either / or: we are not being invited to choose one or the other as not being that easy. Nor can "or" be functioning here as a simple truth-functional connective—for then the claim comes out as trivially true. Such a disjunction is true if at least one of the disjuncts is true. But learning what it means to be human *obviously* does not come that easily. We could then just forget the first disjunct. But what, then, happens with Socrates doubting that one is a human at birth?

An alternative interpretive possibility is to treat "or" as functioning like a conjunction. On this reading, Kierkegaard would be listing two conditions—*becoming human* and *learning what it means to be human*—and saying that each does not come that easily. On this interpretation, we have a list—where the items on the list are the associations of a genius. But if our genius is a philosophical genius, one might hope for more: that the items on the list have a deep internal relation to each other.

In this essay I would like to pursue that suggestion. I think we should read the "or" as exegetical: what follows the "or" explicates what precedes it. On such a reading, Kierkegaard is not listing two distinct conditions; he is, rather, listing one condition and explicating what that condition is. But why should *learning what it means to be human* be a mode of explicating *becoming human?*

By way of analogy, consider a craft of the type Socrates invoked—shoemaking—and let us plug the term *shoemaker* into this phrase: "Becoming a shoemaker or learning what it means to be a shoemaker does not come that easily." This makes sense *if* we take "learning what it means" in its practical guise. We are not talking about someone who has read *Everything You Ever Wanted to Know about Shoemaking (but Were Afraid to Ask)* and is now ready to ace a written exam. Practical understanding is not about a special area or subject matter—the practical; rather, it is about a special form of causality.[8] In practical thinking, the causality—in this case, making shoes—flows through the representations of that causality as they exist in the shoemaker. Becoming a shoemaker does not come that easily: one needs to apprentice oneself to a master shoemaker, learn all one needs to know about tanning leather, the shape of feet, the ultimate uses to which different types of shoes will be put, and so on. But that process of becoming is precisely what it is to learn what it means to be a shoemaker, practically understood. And so the "or" here is not linking two distinct conditions via a disjunction; it is linking two descriptions of a single condition, one of which explicates the other.

But how does one move from a craft like shoemaking to the category *human being?* One ought not simply assume that the category *human being* has the features of a craft. To be sure: *if* "learning what it means to be human" is tantamount to acquiring a practical skill, and *if* "becoming human" simply consists in acquiring that skill, then the case is made. But why think that? This is not a problem we can solve by fiat. If there is a genuine difficulty here, a difficulty in becoming human, we ought to be able to experience that difficulty, to see for ourselves how it arises within the category of the human.

**3.** Socrates *doubted* that one is a human being by birth. What is it thus to doubt? For the mature Kierkegaard, Socratic doubt must be more than the method of refutation, the elenchus; it must be more than depriving others of their previously held beliefs and opinions. That is the one-sided Socratic irony that he came to reject. But how are we to understand the multi-sided, sometimes positive, sometimes creative uses of irony to which the mature Kierkegaard points?

Climacus gives us a hint how to proceed. If Magister Kierkegaard's account of Socratic irony was one-sided, our strategy is to go back to *The Concept of Irony* and correct for its one-sidedness. To anticipate where I am going, I want to argue that Socratic doubt can be positive as well as negative because it is creative. It is creative—one might say *poetical*—in this sense: the doubting creates the doubtful. The activity of doubting Socratically that one is human at birth disturbs the concept *human* in such a way that it becomes thought-worthy that one is not human at birth. To put the point as an impossible counterfactual: the category *human being* would be an unproblematic biological category were it not for those pesky creatures who fall under the concept, who engage in Socratic doubt, and *thereby* render the category they fall under problematic. This is a movement of thought that proceeds by its own internal momentum. It is not an arbitrary imposition of a high ideal upon the category *human.*

**4.** Climacus says that the young Kierkegaard wanted consciously or unconsciously to bring out only one side of Socrates the ironist. What does this wanting amount to? In *The Concept of Irony* Kierkegaard says,

> The intention in asking questions can be twofold. That is, one can ask with the intention of receiving an answer containing the desired fullness, and hence the more one asks, the deeper and more significant the answer; or one can ask without any interest in the answer except to suck out the apparent content by means of the question and thereby to leave an emptiness behind. The first method presupposes there is a plenitude; the

> second that there is an emptiness. The first is the *speculative* method; the second the ironic. Socrates in particular practiced the latter method.[9]

In effect, this places an a priori filter over the Platonic corpus: everything that fits this image of irony emerges as "Socratic"; everything else is a Platonic addition. The method itself ensures that the "Socrates" who emerges will be one-sided.

That is not the only problem. This interpretation must fly at a high altitude—for it will not survive a consideration of textual details. Kierkegaard introduces the *Symposium* as an intermediate dialogue containing Socratic and Platonic elements: "The two kinds of presentation previously designated as the dialectical and the mythical are present in the *Symposium.* The mythical account begins when Socrates withdraws and introduces the Mantinean seeress Diotima as the one speaking."[10] But the idea of there being a moment of "Socratic withdrawal" does not fit the text. To be sure, there is a classic Socratic refutation of Agathon,[11] followed by a speech Socrates says he once heard from Diotima;[12] and this speech contains a myth.[13] This is the purported moment of withdrawal. But at the introduction of Diotima's account, Socrates says, "You see, I had told her almost the same things Agathon told me just now. . . . And she used the very same arguments against me that I used against Agathon."[14] In other words, before the purported moment of withdrawal, when Socrates is being paradigmatically Socratic, refuting Agathon, he is by his own lights repeating what Diotima did to him. It is she who teaches Socrates the "Socratic method" by subjecting him to it. And if Diotima was present before she is officially introduced, why cannot Socrates remain *after* she is?—especially since he insists that he became what he is through her teaching.

Kierkegaard sees that he has a problem: "To be sure, Socrates remarks at the close that he himself was convinced by Diotima's discourse and that he is now trying to convince others of the same."[15] But instead of allowing this insight to expose a fatal problem for his interpretation, he tries to explain it away: "In other words, he makes us doubtful as to whether this discourse, even if at second hand, is not actually his own. Nevertheless, one still cannot draw from this any further conclusion as to the historical relation of the mythical to Socrates."[16] This explanation is flawed in two ways. First, the myth that Diotima does put forward takes up only a small portion of her speech. Second, the idea that we might recover "the historical relation of the mythical to Socrates" is a misguided project. Our situation is, I think, inescapably problematic. On the one hand, we are fascinated by the idea of the actual, historical Socrates; we would like to know what he was like. On the other hand, any attempt to apply a filter to the genius of Plato is likely to give us a less interesting Socrates, not a "more real" one. The point should not be to use the Platonic texts to work one's way to "the historical Socrates," but rather to use the Platonic texts to bring forth a rich, many-sided Socrates—one who is sufficiently vibrant, persuasive, and unusual to provoke us to philosophy. All the other choices, I think, are worse ones. In particular, we should be wary of putting ourselves in a position in which we cannot be surprised or even offended by Socrates—a position in which Socrates cannot change us—because we insist that he conform to an antecedent interpretive scheme.

The elder Socrates portrays himself, as a young man, as un-Socratic and Agathon-like until he meets Diotima. That is, the text suggests that Diotima taught Socrates how to be Socrates. This is accentuated by his repeated inability to respond to Diotima's questioning:

> "So I said, 'What do you mean, Diotima?' "[17]
> "I said there was no way I could give a ready answer to that question."[18]
> " 'What do you mean?' I asked."[19]
> " 'I am beginning to see your point,' I said."[20]
> "It would take divination to figure out what you mean, I can't."[21]
> "And again I said that I didn't know."[22]
> "But that's why I came to you, Diotima, as I just said. I knew I needed a teacher."[23]

And Socrates claims Diotima as his teacher: "She is the one who taught me erotics."[24] Unusually for Socrates, he does claim knowledge: "I know nothing other than erotics."[25] But if erotics is the one thing Socrates claims to know, and if he claims Diotima as his teacher, it would seem that if we want a richer account of Socrates, Diotima's speech is an important place to look. To characterize Diotima as a contrasting figure to Socrates, representing the mythical, not only creates havoc with Socrates's claim that she is the one who taught him what he knows—as well as to his claim to have been persuaded by Diotima and now to be trying to persuade others likewise—but it also ensures that one's account of Socratic irony will remain one-sided. It is true that in the course of her speech she does introduce a myth, but the explicit myth is approximately one-tenth of her speech.[26] And if one includes Socrates's refutation of Agathon, which is a repetition of what he heard from Diotima, it is even less. Instead of dismissing it all as "the mythical non-Socratic," we should be looking at it with the question, *How might this be the teaching of a Socrates we can recognize?*

Kierkegaard does not characterize Diotima as mythical simply because she recounts a myth. It is rather because she is putting forward what he takes to be an imaginative form of thought.

> The mythical addresses itself not chiefly to cognition but rather to the imagination, requires that the individual lose himself in it, and the presentation does not become mythical until it flutters in this manner between the imagination's production and reproduction.
>
> It is assumed that the mythical presentation in the *Symposium* begins with Diotima's story. Now this is not mythical because reference is made to the myth about Eros's having been born of wealth [*Poros* (*sic.* resourcefulness)] and poverty *[Penia]* since also in earlier speeches the legends about the origin of Eros had not gone unnoticed. Here however, the characterization of Eros is negative: Eros is an intermediate being, is neither rich nor poor. At this level we have not gone beyond the Socratic development. But this negative element, which is the eternal restlessness of thinking, continually dividing and combining, this negative element that thought cannot hold on to since it is the propelling element in thought—*this negative element stops here and relaxes before the imagination, expands before intuition. Therein resides the mythical.* Anyone who has anything to do with abstract thinking will certainly have noticed how seductive it is to want to maintain something that actually is not, except when it is annulled. But this is a mythical tendency.[27]

This is a fascinating thought; but to draw a sharp division between "cognition" and "imagination" is again to set oneself up for a one-sided account of irony. And it is telling, I think, that in making his account Kierkegaard jumps over an important part of Diotima's account in order to move directly to the famous "ladder" of ascent:

> Successively the object of love is: beautiful bodies—beautiful souls—beautiful observations—beautiful knowledge—the beautiful. The beautiful

> is now defined not merely negatively as something that will appear in a far more glorious light than gold, clothes, beautiful boys and adolescents, but Diotima adds: "But what would we think if someone had the good fortune of beholding that beauty itself, sheer, pure, unalloyed, not clad in human flesh or hues or other mortal vanity, but the divine beauty itself in the unity of its essence?" The mythical clearly consists in this, that beauty in and by itself must be *beheld.* Even though the feminine interpreter has renounced all mortal taint and trappings, it is clear that these will return in the world of imagination and provide the mythical drapery. So will it always be with *das Ding an sich* if one cannot cast it away and consign it to oblivion; but instead, because one has managed to exclude it from thinking, one will now allow imagination to repair and make good the loss.[28]

Kierkegaard thus moves from the explicit myth to Diotima's "ladder" of ascent, without mentioning her intervening discussion of pregnancy. This is a significant omission.

Let us consider the broadscale trajectory of Diotima's teaching. She begins with what we would now call a Socratic refutation of the young Socrates.[29] Socrates is forced to admit that he is committed to saying that Eros is a great god, and also committed to saying he is not a god at all.[30] Perhaps we should call the elenchus a *Diotiman* refutation, for that is where Socrates says he got it. But that is only the beginning of her teaching. In effect, she explains to Socrates that there is something almost correct in his contradiction: Eros is an intermediate figure, a spirit or *daimôn,* who shuttles between gods and humans, facilitating communication between them.[31] It is only then that she introduces the myth, basically as a way of helping young Socrates (and the reader) grasp the distinction between *being a lover* and *being loved.*[32] It is then that Socrates asks a fundamental question: "If you are right, what use is Love to human beings?"[33] The rest of Diotima's teaching focuses on the place of Love in human life. She moves from the desire for beautiful things, to the desire for good things, to the desire for happiness.[34] "The main point is this," she says, "every desire for good things or for happiness is 'the supreme and treacherous love' in everyone."[35] This has the consequence that we can reflect on Love's workings *from the inside,* by reflecting on the quality of our desiring experience. Diotima then effects what I take to be an ironic reversal. It is not just that we want to possess the good but that "love is wanting to possess the good *forever.*"[36] But the only way we are going to get *that* is if *we create it ourselves.* The "real purpose of love," Diotima says, "is giving birth in beauty whether in body *or in soul.*"[37]

Socrates's response—"It would take divination to figure out what you mean, I can't"—signals that we are at a difficult but important part of her teaching. Diotima continues:

> All of us are pregnant, Socrates, both in body and in soul, and, as soon as we come to a certain age, we naturally desire to give birth. Now no one can possibly give birth in anything ugly; only in something beautiful. That's because when a man and a woman come together in order to give birth, this is a godly affair. Pregnancy, reproduction—this is an immortal thing for a mortal animal to do, and it cannot occur in anything that is out of harmony.[38]

Plato's theory of biological reproduction is false and gender-biased: he thought the embryo was contained in the male sperm—and thus it is men who first get pregnant, even biologically speaking. But we need not get hung up on this. The important points are, first, that Diotima has linked our desire for immortality with the most characteristic activity of the species; second, she effects a reversal in Socrates's initial conception of our finite dependence. What we lack and seek is not the missing good object—at least in any straightforward sense. Rather, what we lack and seek is the beautiful environment—the beautiful other—in which we can then give forth *something from deep within ourselves.* And she links this to our experience of sexual desire: "This is the source of the great excitement about beauty that comes to anyone who is pregnant and already teeming with life: beauty releases them from their great pain."[39] In effect, Diotima is offering us an interpretation: she is inviting us to understand our own experience in a certain way. She is telling us something that, in some inchoate sense, we already know.

It is in this mode that Diotima explains the distinction she has introduced between pregnancy in body and pregnancy in soul:

> Now some people are pregnant in body, and for this reason turn more to women and pursue love in that way, providing themselves through childbirth with immortality and remembrance and happiness, as they think, for all time to come; while others are pregnant in soul—because there

> surely are those who are even more pregnant in their souls than in their bodies, and these are pregnant with what is fitting for a soul to bear and bring to birth. And what is fitting? Wisdom and the rest of virtue, which all poets beget, as well as all the craftsmen who are said to be creative. But by far the greatest and most beautiful part of wisdom deals with the proper ordering of cities and households, and that is called moderation and justice.[40]

So pregnancy, according to Diotima, stretches across characteristic human activity—from biological reproduction that we share with other animals to the creative productions that mark us as distinctively human. It is remarkable that the young Kierkegaard skips over this discussion of pregnancy since it implies that we are *full*—especially those of us who experience a creative impulse. It is a familiar thought that the Platonic Socrates teaches us that because of our erotic natures we are characterized by lack. No doubt there are passages that support that thought. But here in the heart of the Platonic Socrates's discourse on eros, he says that the erotic encounter is the occasion to experience ourselves as *full.* Since Socrates says he is persuaded of Diotima's teaching, he cannot here be thinking of himself as empty—that is, as a counterexample to the teaching.[41]

This image of pregnancy has gripped the philosophical imagination for millennia. It has done so, I think, because we can recognize from our own experience that something is true about it. In speaking of "the metaphor of the mind giving birth to ideas it has conceived," Myles Burnyeat has said, "The compelling naturalness of this image is a matter of common experience and needs no argument."[42] And he continues:

> The resemblance seems so fitting, however, so familiar even, as to invite the thought that the metaphor corresponds, in some deeper sense, to psychological reality. *The response it evokes is more like recognition than ordinary appreciation,* a recognition of an aspect of one's own experience which may not be fully acknowledged. It is not only that we do often represent the originating of thoughts in terms of parturition, but that a significant emotional charge attaches to the idea that the mind is no less capable of conception and birth than the body of a woman. To take the metaphor seriously is to recognize it as embodying an important part of the meaning that the creative process can have for someone.[43]

Burnyeat is, I think, correct that Diotima is inviting Socrates (and us) to recognize something powerful and persuasive in experience. But why does Burnyeat assume that we are here dealing with a metaphor? The temptation, I suspect, arises from the thought that pregnancy is essentially tied to the body, and "pregnancy of soul" is too ethereal to be just another instance of pregnancy. But this is not Diotima's view. She insists that pregnancy of soul is stimulated by another physically beautiful person: "Since he is pregnant [in soul] then, he is much more drawn to bodies that are beautiful than to those that are ugly; and if he *also* has the luck to find a soul that is beautiful and noble and well-formed, he is even more drawn to this combination, such a person makes him instantly team with ideas and arguments about virtue."[44] It is in the presence of a beautiful other person that we give birth to our own ideas. The experience of teeming with ideas has an aura of corporeality: we experience the ideas as *inside* us, and we want *to get them out.* This is how we experience the creative process.[45] It is true that Diotima will proceed to what is now famously known as her "ladder" of ascent, a "ladder" in which one leaves beautiful bodies behind.[46] But this should not encourage us to skip over the importance of the beautiful body of the other in the stimulation of a pregnant soul. Diotima certainly does not. Before she gets to the ladder, she says,

> In my view, you see, when [the lover] makes contact with someone beautiful and keeps company with him, he conceives and gives birth to what he has been carrying inside him for ages. And *whether they are together or apart, he remembers that beauty.* And in common with him he nurtures the newborn; such people have much more to share than do the parents of human children, and have a firmer bond of friendship, because the children in whom they have a share are more beautiful and more immortal. Everyone would rather have such children than human ones, and would look up to Homer and Hesiod and the other good poets with envy and admiration for the offspring they have left behind.[47]

That is, even such immortal creations as the poems of Homer and Hesiod depended on the lovers having actually spent time in the company of the beautiful bodies of their beloveds; and all the better if the beautiful bodies are beautifully ensouled. Perhaps it is only in memory, but they are together the parents. For Diotima, pregnancy of soul is not a metaphor; it is a higher and more real form of pregnancy than the bodily pregnancy with which we are familiar.[48]

As is well known, Diotima soon introduces the so-called ladder of ascent in which a lover moves from loving a beautiful body to loving all beautiful bodies to loving beautiful souls, beautiful activities, laws, and so on.[49] And in making the transition, Diotima uses blunt language: "[The lover] must think this wild gaping after just one body is a small thing and despise it."[50] Still, it is hermeneutically unappealing to interpret her as obviously contradicting what she has just said; and there is no need to do so. Rather than being in contradiction with her previous discussion of the enduring importance of the beautiful other, it can be read as flowing from it. Let us take Diotima's example of the enduring significance of the Homeric poems. And let us assume that their creation followed her overall account—in which case, a young beautiful person *or the memory of such a person* stimulated Homer to give birth to his poems. In the creative activity, he comes to see that all this is directed at a much higher goal than he, as a young man, envisaged when he first fell for that beautiful other (his Helen? his Penelope?). What he comes to despise is not the beautiful body of the beautiful other *per se,* but the thought that the beautiful body is the aim and ultimate goal of this whole process. Diotima tells us that, through memory, the beautiful other continues to matter—even as our overall outlook develops. And it matters because it triggers something deep within us. This is not a view Diotima abandons. And it gives us a different perspective on the night Socrates spent under the same cloak with Alcibiades.[51] We have, of course, inherited the story from Alcibiades's perspective: the frustration, fury, and humiliation of being rebuffed in a sexual seduction. From this perspective, Socrates looks like a man of uncanny indifference—a purity of sorts. But from Diotima's perspective, things look different: just because Alcibiades experienced Socrates as physically unresponsive does not mean Socrates was indifferent to spending the night in close physical proximity with the beautiful Alcibiades. This could well have been a moment exciting Socrates's pregnancy, however frustrating it was for his partner.

Pregnancy of soul is not a metaphor; but it is ironic. The image itself gives birth to a richer conception of irony than young Magister Kierkegaard envisaged, but one that is in the mature Kierkegaard's journals. For if one were to ask a litmus-question testing for the presence of irony,

*Among all the pregnancies have there really been any pregnancies?*

Diotima's answer would be "Why yes; consider the pregnancies of Homer and Hesiod, of Lycurgus and Solon."[52] Diotima would be earnest and ironic at the same time.

**5.** Let us now return to the journal entry that sparked our inquiry: "Socrates doubted that one is a human being by birth . . ."[53] One should, I think, conceive of Diotima's discourse as teaching Socrates how to doubt. Doubt is not just practicing (or being stung by) elenchus—that was just the opening move in her teaching. It is her positive teaching of pregnancy that allows doubt to take hold. It allows one to see that one is not a human being by birth so much as *by birthing.* This is not simply a decision to restrict the use of the term *human* to some arbitrarily high level of accomplishment; it is an insight into the characteristic activity of human life—and it is an insight that we cannot help but have—once we have had it. To submit to Diotima's teaching, as the young Socrates did, is to allow oneself to follow a path of reflection that has its own inner momentum. We come to see—by reflecting on the quality of our experience (under Diotima's guidance)—that human life does have a characteristic activity: pregnancy and giving birth in the beautiful. That is, it is the creativity in the presence of—or in the presence of a memory of—a beautiful other person who stimulates and inspires us. Try to imagine a human being who has no pregnancy in them whatsoever, no ability to reproduce biologically nor even a spark of creative impulse. If one can imagine this at all, one is imagining someone at the far end of an autistic spectrum. This is not just another instance of a human being, but an impaired one.

Socratic doubt creates the doubtful—and it does so by ironizing the concept *human being.* We begin with what we take to be an unproblematic biological concept. It is as though we are looking on the species from the outside. Socrates and Diotima, in effect, invite us inside. We ourselves are instances of the concept *human being;* and, as such, we can become and be self-conscious that we are such. We grasp self-consciously that self-consciousness is central to our existence. Thus we come to see that if we are to grasp our characteristic activity – the characteristic activity of human beings—it is not only possible but important to consult our own experience.

Once we do that, we can no longer simply assume that "the birth of the human" occurs with the biological fetus's exit from the womb. We see from the inside that human being is characterized by creativity stimulated by our encounters with others—and that a biological instance of the kind that lacked that creativity would be a problematic instance. This is not an arbitrary high standard; it is a constitutional condition. The doubting activity itself expands the concept *human* from the inside out. That is the power of Socratic doubt.

We are now in a position to grasp the remainder of Kierkegaard's enigmatic statement: ". . . to become human or to learn what it means to be human does not come that easily—what occupied Socrates, what he sought, was the ideality of being human."[54] Since we have at least an elementary understanding of our characteristic human activity, we can plug in:

> To give birth in the beautiful or learn what it means to give birth in the beautiful does not come that easily.

If *giving birth in the beautiful* is our characteristic practical activity, then the "or" can be exegetical. Learning what it means to give birth in the beautiful is just the self-conscious understanding that we acquire in giving birth in the beautiful. It is the practical and poetical understanding that accompanies and guides the giving birth.

And "does not come that easily" hits its target—when it does—in a recognition that we are already entangled in, hooked by, irony. On the one hand, we recognize that *giving birth in the beautiful* is our characteristic human activity—an internal characteristic that pervades the human. On the other, internal to that characteristic is an aim for immortality. Diotima's argument is addressed to Socrates, Socrates repeats it to his fellow symposiasts, and, outside the fictional frame, Plato thereby gives it to us. It is an argument, I think, addressed to anyone who is pregnant in soul. The argument works by stimulating the pregnancy of the reader. We establish an erotic relation in our imagination with Socrates—that compelling figure—and as we go through the account of pregnancy of soul, we can experience our own creativity shifting into gear, just as we experience the truth of what he is saying via internal reflection on our own erotic and creative moments. And if we follow the argument, we see from the inside that in our own creative moments—our own moments of giving birth in the beautiful—there is internal to them a yearning toward immortality. Succeeding at that task does not come that easily! That is clear. What was difficult to see was that the aim was all along present in our characteristic human activity. This is the "ideality" that Socrates sought: not some impossibly high ideal imposed on us—as though Socrates were the superego for all humanity—but an ideal that is already implicit in the characteristic human activity of pregnancy and giving birth. That is, Socratic doubt poetically brings out the irony in the category *human*—a category in which we are ineluctably entangled.

I said at the beginning that I wanted to argue that "Socratic doubt" and "the difficulty of becoming human" and "the difficulty of learning what it means to be human" are three ways of describing the same reality. We have just seen the equivalence of *becoming human* and *learning what it means to be human.* But how does one link these to Socratic doubt? If we construe his doubt broadly—not confined to the elenchus but bursting out into the realm of erotics—it becomes clear that Socrates's doubt is just his way of giving birth in the beautiful. This is precisely what he does when he meets a beautiful young boy. He is *full* . . . full *of doubt!* It is an ironic fullness, to be sure—but flowing from an irony that *cannot* be one-sided. His doubting that one is a human at birth is his ironic creative activity. It is the activity of ironically opening up the concept *human*—which is at the same time his becoming human (that is, engaging in creative activity that marks us as human), as it is his learning what it means to be human—and he everywhere makes it clear that this is a difficult, if joyful, task.

**6.** The pseudonymous author Johannes Climacus relished ending his work with a revocation of everything he had just written.[55] So in tribute to him and his dear creator, I will conclude by considering a passage that might just send my interpretation up in smoke. In the *Theaetetus,* Socrates says of himself that he is an extraordinary midwife. But in common with ordinary midwives, he is "not productive of wisdom" (αγονος ειμι σοφιας—my translation) or barren of wisdom.[56] And he continues: "And the reason of it is this, that God compels me to attend the travail of others, but has forbidden me to procreate. So that I am not in any sense a wise man; I cannot claim as the child of my own soul any discovery worth the name of wisdom."[57] How are we to understand this? As a revocation of my thesis? Or should I try to take the dodge that this is a different text, that Plato changed his mind, that here it is not really Socrates speaking, and so on?

I hope by now it is no surprise that I think we should interpret this passage . . . *ironically.* That does not mean, as Climacus teaches us, that Socrates is not being utterly serious and earnest at the same time. Socrates never tells us he is barren; he tells us he is barren *of wisdom.* He cannot give birth *to any child worth the name of wisdom.* We began our inquiry with Climacus's hint that we ought to be able to find a complex, multi-sided Socratic irony, one that eluded the view of the author of *The Concept of Irony.* It would be a sad outcome if what we found was that Socrates could give birth *nonironically,* an ordinary pregnancy in soul. No, the pregnancy must itself be ironic. And if we consider Socrates's speech in the *Symposium,* we see him explicitly invoking his memory of his encounter with Diotima as he gives birth in the beautiful not to wisdom but to a conception of giving birth in the beautiful that has shaped the way the world has conceived of human creativity—again, not to wisdom but to knowledge of our ignorance; not to wisdom but to a love of wisdom. We owe it to Socrates that the very name of what we do—philosophy—has the possibility of irony built into it. And were it not for Socrates claiming that he was only a midwife, the concept of midwifery would most likely have remained in the nonironic space of biological birth. He gave the concept *midwife* its ironic immortality—and thereby changed the category *human.*

CHAPTER SEVEN

# Rosalind's Pregnancy

---

**1.** The comedy that is *As You Like It* extinguishes itself in marriage. Turning to Orlando, Rosalind says, "To you I give myself, for I am yours"—and though there is room for an epilogue, at this point the curtain can come down. What has happened to bring us to this point? We are familiar with a certain narrative of the comic: "New Comedy," Northrop Frye tells us, "normally presents an erotic intrigue between a young man and a young woman which is blocked by some kind of opposition, usually paternal, and resolved by a twist in the plot which is the comic form of Aristotle's 'discovery,' and is more manipulated than its tragic counterpart." He continues:

> At the beginning of the play the forces thwarting the hero are in control of the play's society, but after a discovery in which the hero becomes wealthy or the heroine respectable, a new society crystallizes on the stage around the hero and his bride. The action of the comedy thus moves towards the incorporation of the hero into the society that he naturally fits.[1]

This picture of comedy is illuminating in its way, and the only point I want to make is that there is nothing philosophical about it whatsoever. The problems are too well defined, and in any case they are all about overcoming obstacles *in* the world. If there is to be a way of doing philosophy *as you like it,* we must be able to experience the drama as raising a problem *with* the world. The issue would then not be about restoring the rightful political or social order, nor about overcoming the obstacles that stand in the way of love; it would be about resolving a problem that haunts the most basic concepts with which we understand ourselves and the world we inhabit.

The problem, as I see it, is Socratic in its simplicity: What is love? And, given its marks and features, is there any reason for thinking that it is a virtue, or a human excellence? Rosalind, in the guise of Ganymede, puts the point with stunning concision:

> Love is merely a madness, and I tell you, deserves as well a dark house and a whip as madmen do: and the reason why they are not so punished and cured is that the lunacy is so ordinary that the whippers are in love too.[2]

She ought to know: in these very words she assumes the role of love-crazed whipper. What value could this erotic madness possibly have? The overall structure of the comedy takes the shape of common sense: love is of value because it prepares us for marriage (and marriage is a fine state of human being.) But how could that be? Love is the name we give to a tumultuous, inconstant force that, upon the mere glimpse of another person, can drive us wild. How could that be preparation for two people to *come together,* in the stable, well-knit partnership that marriage is supposed to be? Is this a mystery that needs to be solved? Or is it an incoherence that permeates our lives with the concepts *love* and *marriage?* At stake is the possibility that we are living in a world structured by concepts that, in trying to live and understand ourselves through them, are likely to take us apart. Instead of a world in which it is at least possible to live a meaningful and fulfilling life, we would have a mere semblance of coherence that was everywhere threatened by disruptions, and emotional chaos. If we start to fathom the pain that would be common in such a world, we can at least begin to see how comedy might be the appropriate form for a resolution.

**2.** Rosalind has herself been upended by the briefest of encounters. How could it have happened, Celia asks, "on such a sudden" (1.3.22)? It happened at the wrestling match. Okay, let us grant that he is handsome, and that he does manifest bravery in his reasoned indifference to death:

> If killed, but one dead that is willing to be so . . . I shall do my friends no wrong, for I have none to lament me, the world no injury for in it I have nothing. (1.2.155–157)

Still, he has not even wrestled yet when Rosalind says, "Oh, excellent young man!" (1.2.176). And after the match she tells him, "Sir, you have wrestled well and *overthrown more than your enemies*" (1.2.216–17). She seems to have had her life turned upside down on the basis of almost nothing. When we next see her, Rosalind is close to speechless. "Cupid have mercy!" her cousin Celia says, "Not a word?" And Rosalind responds, "Not one to throw at a dog." Even if she had a word, it would not be the stuff of thoughtful speech. Celia pleads with her, "Come, lame me with reasons." And Rosalind responds, "Then there were two cousins laid up, when the one should be lamed with reasons and *the other mad without any*" (1.3.2–7).

Rosalind's thoughts turn immediately to having a child. Celia asks whether all this madness is for her father, and Rosalind responds, "No, some of it is for my child's father" (1.3.8–9). The obvious way to understand this is that in her love-struck imagination Rosalind has already leapt ahead to getting pregnant and having a baby with her lover, and she can thus now think of him as her child's father. But I would like to suggest an alternative: that Rosalind is already pregnant. She is pregnant *with the idea* of pregnancy. That idea is *already inside her,* stirring her up and driving her love-struck imaginative life. She says as much. She complains wistfully of "how full of briers is this working day world," and Celia reassures her that "they are but burs, cousin thrown upon thee in holiday foolery." Rosalind responds, "I could shake them off my coat. *These burs are in my heart*" (1.3.11–15). That is, she already has a seed inside her. It is a rough and prickly seed, a bur sticking in her heart—upsetting her calm, stirring her imagination, *driving* her to uncomfortable creativity. By her own account, Rosalind is already in the midst of a heart-filled pregnancy. It is her lovesickness, her erotic madness, that is the seed inside her—and Orlando is *this* child's father.

We began with a question: what is love such that it could possibly lead to marriage? Shakespeare's answer seems to be: love makes us pregnant, and only after we are pregnant could we possibly get married. This is a comic inversion of the love-marriage-baby routine, and I think Shakespeare is right to insist upon it.

**3.** I would like to turn for a moment from our greatest playwright to our greatest philosopher, and from one of Shakespeare's great women to Plato's greatest woman, the priestess Diotima. Socrates acknowledges Diotima as his teacher—at least, in the realm of eros. "She is the one who taught me erotics."[3] In this sense, she stands above the major figure of the dialogues. And though Socrates usually professes ignorance, this is one area where he claims knowledge: "I know nothing other than erotics."[4] Diotima taught Socrates what he knows: *eros.*[5]

According to Diotima, eros is capable of stimulating not simply pregnancy in body—as we see throughout the animal world—but pregnancy *in soul:*

> There surely are those who are even more pregnant in their souls than in their bodies, and these are pregnant *with what is fitting for a soul to bear and bring to birth.*[6]

Pregnancy in soul is usually treated as a metaphor; and since it is contrasted with pregnancy in body, it is assumed to be a somewhat ethereal "pregnancy." This reading can seem inevitable, because Diotima goes on to introduce her famous ladder of love, beginning in attraction to a beautiful body and ending in philosophical contemplation of the Platonic form of the Beautiful. Diotima may seem to be encouraging lovers "pregnant in soul" to leave behind any concern for beautiful bodies. But this is not so. One leaves behind the idea that beautiful bodies are the goal of one's pursuits. But Diotima never goes back on her claim that pregnancy in soul requires the real-life physical presence of another, beautiful human being. For Rosalind, it would be that initial meeting with Orlando. We need to give birth in the beautiful, Diotima says,[7] and the lover who is pregnant in soul "is much more drawn to *bodies that are beautiful* than those that are ugly; and if he *also* has the luck to find a soul that is beautiful and noble and well formed, he is even more drawn to this combination."[8] And when the lover "makes contact with someone beautiful and keeps company with him, he conceives and gives birth to what he has been carrying inside him for ages."[9] In Diotima's account, it is the older man's encounter with the beautiful young boy. But we do not need to stick with the age and gender stereotypes of aristocratic, homosexual ancient Athens to grasp the deeper points she is making. And in any case, Shakespeare joyously mixes up all those stereotypes. There are two important points that survive these corrections. First, Diotima insists on the importance to our own creativity of the immediate, physical presence of another beautiful human being. The physical beauty of another stimulates our creativity; and if we can, in the encounter, glimpse a beautiful soul, so much the better. Second, even though the Greek conception of pregnancy is a male-centered fantasy—the embryo is already fully present in the adult male lover—it is getting at something that is correct. When Rosalind meets Orlando, Orlando is the occasion for an explosion of creativity that is coming *from inside her.* It is not as though he has given her any ideas. He has had no education, and his poetry is terrible—and it is important that it should be dreadful. It brings into relief that he is in no way her teacher. Yet there is something beautiful about him, and she is drawn to respond—*to him.* This is the seed planted in her heart. There is something about meeting this beautiful other in the world—even in the briefest, chance encounter—that calls forth something from deep within her, that *pressures* her to create.

Diotima teaches Socrates that it is ultimately a mistake to think of love as a desire for the beautiful other. "What love wants," she tells Socrates, "is not beauty as you think it is." "What is it then?" Socrates replies. "Reproduction and birth in beauty."[10] According to Diotima—and in contrast to superficial readings of the *Symposium*—we are not lacking in the familiar sense of needing the beautiful other to complete us. That is only Aristophanes's myth. Rather, according to Diotima, we depend on the beautiful other as providing the right kind of environment for us to give birth to our own beautiful creations. It is a strange and wonderful fact about us that this beautiful environment takes the form of another, particular human being whom we find beautiful.

This image of the mind giving birth to its creations seems elemental. Certainly, it has been with us from antiquity.[11] Myles Burnyeat has suggested that "the metaphor corresponds, in some deeper sense, to psychological reality."[12] I agree with him about the psychological reality, but I want to side with Diotima and Plato that pregnancy in soul is not a metaphor. A metaphor, the *Oxford English Dictionary* tells us, is when a figure of speech is "transferred to an object or action *different from, but analogous to,* that to which it is literally applicable."[13] But for Diotima, pregnancy in soul is not a mere analogy: it is a higher and more real form of pregnancy than the bodily pregnancy with which we are familiar. It differs in certain ways from bodily pregnancy, but these are differences between species in a common genus. They need not impugn the claim that pregnancy of soul is a genuine pregnancy. And there is this reason for agreeing with Diotima: it seems nonoptional for the human imagination to conceive of its own activity not simply as getting an idea *out* but as *giving birth.* (Note how natural the use of the word "conceive" is here.) If we accept, as I think we should, that the mind's efficacy depends essentially on its own representations of its efficacy, and if the mind is more or less driven to conceive of its creativity in terms of giving birth, then there is reason for thinking that rather than a metaphor, Plato and Diotima are introducing an ironic disruption and extension of the familiar concept.[14]

**4.** Let us return to Arden. But what is Arden? It has been noted that Arden cannot be the idyllic, pastoral alternative to the foibles and corruptions of society that are so evident in the court.[15] Arden contains its own foibles and social problems that need to be worked out. C. L. Barber has suggested that Arden "is a region defined by an attitude of liberty from ordinary limitations, a festive place where the folly of romance can have its day."[16] I would like to offer a philosophical determination of what that liberty and festivity might be: Arden is a field of irony. It is a place where Orlando is free to be the beautiful beloved he is, in relation to whom Rosalind can give birth in the beautiful. And what she gives birth to is *herself*—that is, she gives birth to the ironist she becomes. Arden is the space in which she can put on the mask of being a young man, and then the further masks of being a young man playing Rosalind purportedly inducing a love-cure. And, following Socrates and Kierkegaard, I want to argue that irony is not simply a witty turn of phrase, but an important mode of human existence. Rosalind does not simply acquire a witty skill in Arden; she comes to be an ironist. In this essay, I want to discuss what this means and why it matters.

An ironist is someone who is capable of eliciting an *experience* of irony—typically in an interlocutor, sometimes in an audience, sometimes in the ironist herself. An *experience of irony* is an outburst of anxious, erotic longing that arises from the experience of a gap between what one professes oneself to be (or believe or feel) and an aspiration that is experienced simultaneously as internal to that profession and as blowing it apart.[17] With his dreadful poetry hung from trees Orlando puts himself forward as a *lover* of Rosalind. The audience can immediately detect a comic gap, but for Orlando it is going to take the entire play before he is ready to experience the irony. It is only as Rosalind comes out from her masks and declares, "To you I give myself" that he will be able to see, for the first time, that if he is to love

*Rosalind*—if he is going to receive the *she* who is right now giving *herself*—he is going to have to love the person who has just put him through all this. But the play is not about his experience of irony; it is about the birth of an ironist capable of provoking it.

We see little of Rosalind before she meets Orlando, but there is no hint of irony in what we do see. In her opening line, she tells Celia, "I show more mirth than I am mistress of," making it clear that she is attuned to the difference between appearance and reality (1.2.2–3). But the categories of appearance and reality are themselves taken for granted. Similarly, in her first moment with Orlando, when she encourages him to withdraw from the wrestling match, she says, "your reputation shall not therefore be misprized" (1.2.148–149). She wants to reassure him about the appearances; they will be maintained in stable order. It is as though she is the guardian for an unquestioned understanding of appearance and reality. This will all be upended by her as she abandons this role in the forest of Arden.

So, Rosalind becomes Ganymede, who claims that he will "cure" Orlando of his love if he "would but call me Rosalind and come every day to my cote and woo me." Orlando accepts the challenge as a test of "the faith of my love" (3.2.377–379). On a familiar reading, the audience is able to enjoy the "irony," because it can attend to the layers of appearance and reality. The audience knows that Rosalind is "there" behind her masks. It seems to me that Shakespeare makes this reading impossible, and gives us instead a Rosalind who is coming to be in her masks. Rosalind has to learn this about herself. She would have to, because there is no antecedent truth to be learned. It is precisely in coming to be such a person that she learns what she is capable of.

Before she meets Orlando in Arden, Rosalind is pleading with Celia to reveal to her the author of the poems. "Good my complexion! Dost thou think though I am caparisoned like a man I have doublet and hose in my disposition?" (3.2.176–178). It is as though the layers are clear, and the inner reality is impatience:

> One inch of delay more is a South Sea of discovery. I prithee tell me who is it quickly, and speak apace. I would thou couldst stammer that thou might *pour this concealed man out of thy mouth* as wine comes out of a narrow-mouthed bottle, either too much at once or not at all. I prithee take the cork out of thy mouth *that I may drink thy tidings.* (3.2.178–184; my emphasis)

Celia speaks beyond herself: *"So you may put a man in your belly"* (3.2.185; my emphasis). Obviously, there is the sexual innuendo, anticipating forward to some future biological pregnancy. But simply by taking in this news, Rosalind does get pregnant—at least, by her own account. Celia tries to calm her impatient interruptions: "I would sing my song without a burden. Thou bringest me out of tune." Rosalind responds,

> *Do you not know I am a woman? When I think, I must speak.* (3.2.225–226; my emphasis)

On Rosalind's theory of "woman" she would not be able to do what she is about to do—namely, keep crucial thoughts quiet. Of course, with his marvelous gender-bending and incandescent irony, Shakespeare will expose this image of "woman" as the constricting illusion that it is. And, in the figure of Rosalind, he will open up new possibilities for being a woman (and, correlatively, for being a man) that will shape the centuries. We can see this opening-up in the microcosm, in this very example. For as she works her way through Arden, Rosalind does not falsify her initial claim but transforms it. Rosalind remains someone who, when she thinks, she must speak, but her thinking has become ironized, and so has her speech.

**5.** Rosalind says that she will speak to Orlando "like a saucy lackey, and under that habit play the knave with him" (3.2.267–268). In this way, Rosalind doubles herself and in that pretense tells Orlando, "There is no true lover in the forest" (3.2.274). She is earnest in her irony. She suspects him:

> I will not cast away my physic but on those that are sick. . . . There is none of my uncle's marks upon you: he taught me how to know a man in love, in which cage of rushes I am sure you are not prisoner. . . . You are rather point-device in your accoutrements, *as loving yourself than seeming the lover of any other.* (3.2.321–343; my emphasis)

Orlando has been prevented by his brother from being "educated," in society's sense of education. This does not mean, though, that when in the first stirrings of love he tries to express himself, he does so as a "natural man"—whatever that might mean. Rather, he does so in a clumsy attempt to imitate society's expectations: poetry hung from a tree. But the problem is not going to be solved by sharpening his skills in meter and rhyme. Rosalind is right; there is as yet no true lover in the forest. Orlando needs to be educated into love, but his education will of necessity be unusual. He cannot yet love Rosalind truly, not simply because of some lack in him, but because the Rosalind he is to love is still in the process of formation. She is coming to be, in his company, in the forest of Arden.

Rosalind tells of "an old religious uncle" who "taught me to speak, who was in his youth an inland man, one that knew courtship too well, for there he fell in love.[18] I have heard him read many lectures against it." She continues:

> *And I thank God I am not a woman, to be touched with so many giddy offenses as he hath generally taxed their whole sex withal.* (3.2.308–314; my emphasis)

The irony here cannot be that she really is a woman pretending not to be one, but that in her very capacity to speak these words she shows that she could not be such a woman. Her irony is earnest: it is the form her truthfulness takes. This is crucial, for it means that in her irony she is everywhere expressing who she is.

Orlando takes up his appointed role: "Fair youth, I would I could make thee believe I love." And Rosalind responds:

> Me believe it? *You may as soon make her that you love believe it—which I warrant she is apter to do than confess she does: this is one of the points in the which women still give the lie to their consciences.* (3.2.341–348; my emphasis)

Now for Rosalind, for Celia, and for the members of the audience of the play there need be no gap between ironic performance and ironic uptake. We can all appreciate the irony in the moment. For Orlando, by contrast, as well as for the other inhabitants of Arden, Rosalind's performance is an ironic mask: they cannot yet see Rosalind in the performance. Indeed, Arden is precisely the space where Rosalind can perform her ironic self-invention, at once in Orlando's company and in relative privacy. But what Rosalind can enjoy, and we in the audience can share, is that in her irony Rosalind is telling Orlando who she is and what she is doing. For Rosalind, as well as for members of the audience, appearance and reality coincide. Rosalind is who she appears to be: someone coming into her own as someone who can express herself truthfully in her irony. That Orlando cannot see this in the moment is only a temporary impediment—though crucial for the comedy, and crucial for his education.

By the time we get to Act 4, Scene 1, Rosalind virtually breaks out into a chorus of *"And I am your Rosalind!"*:

ORLANDO: Virtue is no horn-maker, and my Rosalind is virtuous.

ROSALIND: *And I am your Rosalind.*

ORLANDO: What, of my suit?

ROSALIND: Not out of your apparel, and yet out of your suit. *Am I not your Rosalind?*

ORLANDO: . . . for I protest her frown might kill me.

ROSALIND: By *this hand* it will not kill a fly. . . .

ROSALIND: . . . but I do take thee, Orlando, for my husband. There's a girl goes before the priest, and certainly a woman's thought runs before her actions.

ORLANDO: But will my Rosalind do so?

ROSALIND: *By my life, she will do as I do.*

ORLANDO: Oh, but she is wise.

ROSALIND: *Or else she could not have the wit to do this.* (4.1.54–137; my emphasis)

She cannot stop telling Orlando that *she* is his Rosalind. On a familiar reading, the irony arises from Rosalind being there, standing behind her guise as Ganymede. But on the reading I am suggesting, the irony arises from Rosalind coming into being as the Rosalind-who-can-play-Ganymede-playing-Rosalind—for an Orlando who may or may not eventually come to appreciate all this. There is no "real" Rosalind who has, as it were, always been there behind the appearance. She is coming into being in the appearance—of someone who is capable of masking herself as a boy playing Rosalind—and *thereby* expressing exactly who she is. With irony, the reality cannot be "behind" the appearance; otherwise the irony would not show forth. Rather the "behind the appearance" must be part of the appearance. Rosalind says, *"Or else she could not have the wit to do this"*: the Rosalind who has the wit to do *this* can only be expressed by a Rosalind who is truthfully expressing herself in doing *this.* Rosalind is giving birth in the beautiful: she is giving birth to herself as an ironist.

**6.** Let us consider Rosalind's theory of sexual difference.

> ROSALIND: Now tell me how you would have her, after you have possessed her.
>
> ORLANDO: Forever and a day.
>
> ROSALIND: Say "a day" without the "ever." No, no, Orlando, men are April when they woo, December when they wed; maids are May when they are maids, but the sky changes when they are wives. I will be more jealous of thee than a Barbary cock-pigeon over his hen, more clamorous than a parrot against the rain, more newfangled than an ape, more giddy to my desires than a monkey. I will weep for nothing, like Diana in the fountain, and I will do that when you are disposed to be merry, I will laugh like a hyena, and that when thou art inclined to sleep. (4.1.124–133)

Again, I do not think we should give into the temptation to see Rosalind as "there," hiding behind her disguise as Ganymede-pretending-to-be-Rosalind, testing Orlando by inviting him to consider a prospective future—namely, life after marriage. Rosalind's language here is wondrous: Van Doren calls it "tart and vernacular," noting that there is a "rank reality in her speech, as in the speech of Shakespeare's best women always."[19] But basically, on this reading, Rosalind is repeating the cliché of "changeable woman"—one that she purportedly heard from "an old religious uncle of mine" (3.2.308–319;

361–370). But as I understand it, Rosalind is not repeating the cliché; she is ironizing it. She is not standing *behind* her disguise; she is right there *in* her disguise—ironically presenting herself as a constant young man who can pronounce with eloquence about female inconstancy. We should understand her as earnest in her irony: she *will* be "more clamorous than a parrot against the rain, more newfangled than an ape." But to understand the truth of what she is saying, one must recognize that the content of her utterance cannot be detached from its form. It is she—the constant Rosalind in the guise of her constant double—who is speaking these words, thus lending unity to the changeability she declares.

She says as much herself. Orlando protests, "Oh, but she is wise." And Rosalind responds:

> Or else she could not have the wit to do this. The wiser the waywarder. Make the doors open upon a woman's wit, and it will out at the casement; shut that, and 'twill out at the key-hole; stop that, 'twill fly with the smoke out at the chimney. (4.1.137–140)

This is only superficially about some future moment of postmarital changeableness. It is primarily about this very moment: the unity and constancy of ironic wit needed for this very performance of declaring the wit that underlies the purportedly "changeable" female nature. This *is* Rosalind, right now, being the steady ironic wit she declares herself to be.

**7.** We are now in a position to see how the end of the play can be so uncanny. "I am a magician," Rosalind tells the assembled crowd—and the denouement the next day is meant to be her magic (5.2.62–63). It would be a pretty dumb trick if it only consisted in her taking off her "doublet and hose." No, the Rosalind who emerges from her clothes is not the Rosalind who first put them on. She has in the interim transfigured herself into an ironist.

I said earlier that for Rosalind, as for members of the audience, there is no temporal distance between ironic performance and ironic uptake. She is able to enjoy herself in her ironic performance (and we in the audience can enjoy her enjoyment). But we in the audience also have to tolerate Orlando's not knowing. This too is part of our enjoyment: a tension that needs to be released. Now the moment that Rosalind emerges in her dress, *as Rosalind,* is the first possible moment of ironic uptake for Orlando, as well as for the other astonished inhabitants of Arden. Ironically, it is only at the moment of marriage that Orlando is in a position to realize that the person he is about to marry is *very* different from the person he took himself to be marrying. Orlando's erotic education essentially has two stages. Stage one is his education by Rosalind-Ganymede in the forest of Arden. This is what we in the audience see in the comic drama. Stage two is that he now needs to go back to stage one and live it all again—in memory, *nachträglich*—through the lens of the irony it always was. Whether he will do so or not is left open—outside the scope of this play. And each member of the audience is free to imagine this, as he or she pleases. But philosophy is concerned less with actuality than with possibility and necessity: less with what *is* or *will be,* more with what *might* or *must* be. In effect, the drama affects the *necessity of the possibility* that Orlando's erotic education take this form. Orlando is *confronted* with the fact that his immediate past with Rosalind is not as he had taken it to be. What he and they will do with it we will never know. But we do know that they have the possibility of a marriage that would be partially constituted by his trying to understand his engagement, all over again.

**8.** I began this essay by asking what it might be like to read *As You Like It* philosophically. I suggested that we could see it as posing a Socratic question: What is love? And how could it be of any value in human life? I further suggested that Shakespeare's answer, in broad outline, took the shape of common sense: the love affair between Rosalind and Orlando is of value because it prepares them to marry (and marriage is a form of human flourishing.) We are now in a position to see that Shakespeare ironized this answer. In conclusion, I would like to explain how this is, and why it might matter.

The philosopher Søren Kierkegaard once complained that the concept of irony had been completely misunderstood in popular culture.

> Irony is an *existence-determination,* so nothing is more ridiculous than to suppose it to be a figure of speech, or an author's counting himself lucky when once in a while managing to express himself ironically.[20]

For Kierkegaard, irony is not fundamentally about witty turns of phrase. It is, rather, a fundamental mode of human existence. Let us say that a person *exists ironically* when they have the capacity to instill an experience of irony (in themselves as well as in others) in an appropriate time and place and manner. Ironic existence is a form of living that, in the living, brings out the gap between human pretense and aspiration by inducing an anxious, erotic longing with respect to the most important concepts through which we live our lives.[21] This counts as a virtue, or a human excellence, not merely because it breaks us out of hollow, stale, or hypocritical routines, but because it can awaken us to—and enliven us as—the peculiar finite, dependent beings that we are. This means that ironic existence is an important form of self-knowledge, a manner of living up to the Delphic injunction to "know thyself." We come to understand ourselves as creatures who have a peculiar responsibility to the concepts through which we live, and in terms of which we understand ourselves and the world we inhabit.

Shakespeare is one of the world masters of ironic existence. He has the capacity to instill in us, his audience, the anxious, erotic longing that characterizes irony. In this case, he does so through this marvelous character Rosalind who we can watch fall in love, and thereby give birth to herself in irony. We all know that there are lovers and then there are lovers. How is it that our ear can immediately hear a difference between the two occasions when the same word "lovers" is repeated? We seem to be already attuned to the thought that there is something deficient in those who fall under the first occasion when the concept *lover* is invoked. More to the point, the problem does not seem to lie entirely with them. There seems to be a problem, *internal* to the concept *love,* such that by simply repeating the term, *these* lovers should suddenly show up lacking. If they do fall under the concept, how could they possibly be lacking—at least, when it comes to love? Now there is one tame way of understanding the problem that I want to mention in order to get past it. One might hear the question

> Among all our lovers, are there any lovers?

as asking whether those who fall under the socially understood category manage to live up to some high ideal of love. This is not the question Shakespeare is asking. To get closer, one needs to place ordinary usage *along with all of its purportedly "high ideals"* into the first occurrence and hear the second occurrence as anxiously asking what any of that could mean. It is, I want to claim, intrinsic to the concept *love* that there is something mysterious about it. We may use different vocabulary to try to get at it, calling it a "divine madness" or a "mystery" or "transcendent." The point right now is not to try to get the description exactly right, but to recognize that there is something internal to our life with the concept of love that *escapes the exactly right description.* It shows up, rather, as anxious erotic longing. And in the experience of irony, we get to repeat and recreate that anxious longing, from a slightly safer distance. If the question is to achieve ironic uptake, it must strike us anxiously about *our own lives as lovers.* That is, we are not here dealing with a *theoretical* question—about whether there are, after all, any real lovers in the world—but rather with an anxious practical question of how to live. It seems to be internal to our life with the concept of love that we are susceptible to anxious moments of disruption, disorientation, and longing. There are moments when we can be thrown out of our understandings of ourselves—our understandings of what matters most to us in living our lives—without there being any determinate marker or ideal in terms of which we fall short. It is as though the category of lover itself *calls us into question* by, as it were, *calling itself into question.* We experience this from the inside—that is, anxiously: a restless mystery in the concept that, because we are living the concept, shows up as a restless mystery in us.

Shakespeare can induce such moments—at least, if we as audience are receptive. So, Rosalind in the guise of Ganymede in the guise of Rosalind says to Orlando, "In her person, I say I will not have you." Orlando responds, "Then in mine own person, I die" (4.1.78–79).

> ROSALIND: No, faith, *die by attorney.* The poor world is almost six thousand years old, and in all this time there was not any man died in his own person, videlicet, in a love cause. Troilus had his brains dashed out with a Grecian club, yet he did what he could to die before, and he is one of the patterns of love. . . . *But these are all lies.* Men have died to time, and worms have eaten them, but not for love. (4.1.80–91; my emphasis)

Died for love, *eaten for love?* In a sense, yes. If we die for love, what remains of us shall be eaten; and thus, for love, we do thereby make our bodies into worms' meat. Is there a more *loveless* image than worms going at us like that? (Though it is not clear what more a worm could do to express its affection.) When this image works, it does more than shake us up about our own mortality; and it does more than shake us up about the place of love in our mortal lives; it shakes us up about the concept of love—its meaning and its value. From a *psychological* point of view, Shakespeare may help us contain this anxiety by framing it in comic form. But from a *philosophical* point of view, Shakespeare is inducing us to interrogate the meaning and value of the concept *love.* The form of interrogation is comic, anxious, erotic longing. But in that suffering there is a question: is there anything to be said for *love* beyond its being an engrossing distraction from our inevitable fate as worm food?

Shakespeare's answer, through his Rosalind, is that on occasion falling head over heels in love with another can prompt us into an ironic pregnancy. We can then work our way into an ironic existence: one in which we live *in* love and *with love* by ironically questioning its meaning and value. And this brings us to the core of our finite dependence: we are creatures who, for our very existence, depend on concepts that depend on us. We may die at the end our lives, but how can we even have lives (that end in death) if we have no meanings through which to understand ourselves, relate to others, and inhabit the world? Ironic existence is a way of embracing our lives—of celebrating our condition, of expressing our love for the peculiar kind of existence that is open to us—by *tending* to the very concepts on which we depend; in this case, expressing our love by ironically questioning the value of love. It thus makes sense to think of ironic existence as a virtue: we are creatures who flourish by actively questioning—and thus taking responsibility for—the very concepts through which we flourish.

This also gives us an ironic answer to the question of how love could prepare us for marriage. For just as we can ask about lovers, we can ask whether among all marriages anyone has ever succeeded in getting married. How, after all, could two lovers ever *come together in* marriage? Again, it tames the problem out of existence to think that the task is to divide marriages into bad marriages and good marriages, and figure out the ideals that the good marriages instantiate. Instead, put all the purported marriages, good and bad, *along with all the purported ideals,* into the first occurrence of "marriage," and hear the question asking what any of that could possibly have to do with getting married. The question begins to have ironic uptake if one can feel it anxiously raising a question about one's own possibilities for marriage. This point is not merely of psychological interest; it has philosophical import. Again, it seems internal to the concept *marriage* that there is something uncanny about it—a mystery: how could two people ever become one? And the problem shows up in vibrant form not as a theoretical question about the mystery of marriage, but practically, anxiously engaging something one experiences as uncanny in a love-relationship.

Shakespeare offers a comic resolution: two people can succeed in getting married if they can learn to celebrate together the mystery that constitutes their marriage. That celebration is irony: a shared, anxious erotic inquiry into what it could ever mean for them to be married. The play, as it were, brings us right up to the altar. The question that now confronts them is whether they can convert the experience of an ironic romance into an ironic experience of romance. That shared irony might plausibly constitute the mystery of their marriage.

**9.** Let me close with a final comment about dramatic comedy as a philosophical form. Socrates famously threw the dramatic poets out of the polis, but said that they could come back if they gave good reason why they are needed. Shakespeare gives us the material we need to construct an answer. The answer is *not* that comedy is a literary genre in which a philosophical problem can be raised. That may be true, but it is obvious; and it does not carry with it the kind of necessity we should be looking for.

Let us assume, following Aristotle and Kant, that human reason has two distinctive applications—theoretical and practical. In briefest compass, theoretical reason is knowledge of how things are; practical reason is knowledge of how things ought to be. This is not a difference in subject matter but in the form of cognition. In its practical application, reason is itself efficacious in bringing about the very thing it understands. It seems to me that Shakespeare, in *As You Like It,* opens up a subdomain of practical reason that might be called poetical. There is a difference between *theoretical* inquiry that claims that we are creatures who must tend to our concepts and a *practical* application of reason in which we actually tend to those concepts. When it comes to concepts through which we live our lives—in the case we have been considering, *love* and *marriage*—irony, I want to claim, is a poetical mode of practical reason. Reason can be efficacious in shaping these concepts via its own ironic work with them. Irony then becomes a peculiar activity of reason with its own unique "results": namely, the ironization of the very concepts it "investigates." There is no other form—say, a deductive argument or didactic essay, in which the same "result" could be achieved in a different way. Irony is *the* form in which *this* kind of activity of reason occurs. And philosophy might legitimately be conceived as a self-conscious articulation of this very activity.

So, on those occasions when a production of *As You Like It* succeeds in stirring up ironic, erotic anxiety in the audience, there really is reason for thinking that we have here an outburst of philosophy as you like it.

CHAPTER EIGHT

# Technique and Final Cause in Psychoanalysis

---

**1.** This essay is motivated by two questions that arise at opposite ends of a spectrum. At the experience-near end of a practicing psychoanalyst at work in the midst of an analytic hour, my question is: Why should I do one thing rather than another? What, if anything, grounds my choice about how to conceptualize and act in a significant moment in analysis? At the other end of the spectrum, my question is: What is psychoanalysis for? I do not have answers to either of these two questions. However, I have become convinced that these questions are interrelated—indeed, that one cannot answer one without answering the other. If one is to have a clear sense of why one is doing what one is doing in an analytic moment (as opposed to something else), one needs to have a sense of what psychoanalysis is for. Conversely, one cannot have a textured sense of what psychoanalysis is all about unless one also understands how that overall conception of its value filters down and informs the analytic moment.

I want to argue for three claims regarding which, prima facie, it might seem impossible that they could all be true together. First, if one considers a given clinical moment from different psychoanalytic perspectives, one can find genuine differences about how to approach the moment. To that end, I shall consider a single clinical moment from the perspectives of four significant psychoanalytic approaches: those of Paul Gray, Hans Loewald, the contemporary Kleinians, and Jacques Lacan. I only intend to give an account that is in the spirit of each; no doubt other formulations could be offered from each perspective. Thus, I am also not going to try to give a complete interpretation from any particular point of view, but rather to provide salient markers by which one may begin to see the same moment from different perspectives. I will argue that while there may be similarities and areas of overlap, there are also significant differences between these approaches.

Second, it is at least possible that, in trying to choose among these approaches, there might be nothing in the analysand's mind at that moment, nothing in the total transference situation, nothing in the intersubjective or interpersonal relations between analysand and analyst, nothing in the transitional space, nothing in the analysand's brain-state—in short, nothing in the present state of the analysand or the analytic situation—that could definitively settle which approach to use. It follows from this that we cannot look to the analysand's psychic history either: for if her past made a difference, it would somehow be making a difference in the present, and we have ruled that out.

Third, it is nevertheless true that there can be principled bases for making a choice among these different approaches.

But if on the one hand there are real differences among approaches, yet on the other hand no basis in the analytic present for choosing, how could there be any principled basis for choice? The answer is: we have got to go back to the future. That is, we need to consider what the analysis is aiming toward. This is what Aristotle called the final cause: that which the psychoanalytic process aims to facilitate or bring about.[1] If we grasp what psychoanalysis is for, we can then evaluate a technical approach in terms of how well or how badly it facilitates that which it is trying to bring about. I want to suggest that a wide range of analysts already agree (often implicitly rather than explicitly) that psychoanalysis seeks to promote some kind of freedom, but freedom functions as an open-ended signifier: it points us in the direction of openness but ironically is itself open-ended about what this might mean. Precisely because the concept of freedom lacks determinate, fixed boundaries, it is of special value; we are invited seriously to consider—as well as play freely with—disparate images of freedom. Toward the end of this essay, I will suggest that freedom, as it concerns psychoanalytic practice, has disparate aspects and that the different technical approaches can be evaluated in terms of which aspect(s) of freedom they facilitate. However, we are still at an early stage of thinking (working, playing) through what freedom might mean in a psychoanalytic context. One of the central aims of this essay is to invite us to think broadly and deeply about what freedom is—what its many faces are—and why it might matter. But for all the open-ended unclarity at this early stage of reflection, we are in a position to see that genuine differences among technical approaches do not imply their ultimate incompatibility. However, one can only grasp this if one takes the idea of final cause into account.

**2.** Here are four ways of looking at a clinical moment.

*From the perspective of the analysand's conscious ego defenses: Paul Gray.* One would have to go back to Freud's Dora case to find a cough that has been as commented on as that of Mr. A in analysis with Dr. Lawrence Levenson.[2] Dr. Levenson's article explains and defends the technical ideas advocated by Dr. Paul Gray.[3] I can here only give the briefest account. Mr. A had entered analysis because of anxiety, social inhibition, and a view of himself as wearing a "nice mask to hide the real, ugly, nasty, me."[4] He had difficulty with his aggressive impulses, particularly with those directed toward people in authority, and this became prominent in the transference. When toward the end of his analysis he brought up termination, he spoke in terms of "warning" Dr. Levenson or about "quitting." But he also spoke of all the gains he had made. He wanted Levenson to know how much happier, freer, and more relaxed he felt. He was pleased with the life changes he had been able to make, and he knew that these external changes were a manifestation of significant internal changes. But then there was this cough. It began with an infection, but it lingered, and it would emerge in a session when Mr. A would start talking about hostile feelings. Mr. A himself began to wonder about the meaning of his cough.

> [He] did not recognize their connection to hostile wishes until an extended fit of coughing occurred when he suddenly became intensely angry with me, saying, "Do I want to tell you to fuck off!" He then began coughing uncontrollably for several minutes, finally leaving the office for a minute to go to the bathroom for a drink of water. Returning to the couch, he asked, "Why would I want to tell you to fuck off? You haven't done anything but been here."
>
> I said, "Maybe that's why."

> "Yes, you're the doctor," he replied. "Why haven't you cured me? I've been waiting for you to fix me."
>
> This was the moment when Mr. A. experienced the full intensity of his hostility toward me in the waning months of the analysis.[5]

From this Gray-Levenson perspective, there are three important points to be made about the interpretation. First, the interpretation is meant to analyze transference of authority rather than rely upon it. Gray emphasized the importance of Freud's relatively late insight that the superego is largely a defensive structure used to inhibit and disguise aggression. What is valuable about the moment, from this Gray-inspired perspective, is that the analysis does not terminate simply with the sincere expression of gratitude. Rather, the analysand is able to see from his own vivid experience, in the here-and-now of the analytic situation, that he is also angry and disappointed. And he is at least in a position to recognize that his sincere gratitude is helping him ignore his angry feelings. Thus Mr. A can gain insight into the dynamic nature of his own feelings. Superego defenses are here analyzed rather than unwittingly relied upon. Second, the analysis is not relying upon the internalization of the analyst as a benign superego-figure. Internalization largely consists in unconscious mental processes that thus largely bypass the analysand's growing ability consciously to monitor and observe her mental activity. Gray was critical of those approaches that emphasized the replacement of the analysand's formerly punitive superego with a more benign one based on an image of the analyst. Gray argued that, while such approaches may have genuine therapeutic value, they are nevertheless based on remnants of the old hypnotic technique—which ought to be abandoned, for it ultimately compromises the possibility for the autonomy that a rigorous analysis could promote.[6] And this leads to Gray's third point: that the ultimate goal of psychoanalysis is to promote the analysand's capacity for rational autonomy. For Gray, this essentially involves the analysand's ability to observe her own mental states and processes as they are emerging in the here-and-now and assess for herself how she wants to live with them. While there has been a lively debate about how best to appropriate Gray's ideas, to what extent they are compatible or incompatible with other approaches, there is no doubt that with these points Gray made a significant contribution to our understanding of psychoanalytic technique.

*Working from the perspective of mourning: Hans Loewald.* Loewald, developing ideas from Freud, has argued that the termination phase is a process of mourning that inevitably involves internalization—for it consists in a rebuilding and reorganization of the superego-ego structure, which had been partially loosened during the analysis.[7] Obviously, there are a number of ways by which one can approach this clinical moment from a Loewaldian perspective. But when I look at this moment in the light of Loewald's work, I am struck by the phrase "Do I want to tell you to fuck off." This is a strange locution—not the way an ordinary English speaker would tell someone to fuck off, or anything else. There is room, thus, to wonder whether the purported unity of this expression is superficial. The first part of the phrase "Do I want to tell you to . . ." is the nascent stage of the explicit and conscious formulation of a wish. "Fuck off," rather than being the object of the wish, perhaps moves the speaker away from the wish, which, in the moment, was too much to speak. "Do I want to tell you . . ." is a classic expression of mourning—and its anticipation. That, for Loewald, is what the termination phase is. In imagination, as we sit by the grave of a loved one, or contemplate a love-relationship that is over, we tend to think about what we should have said to the other person, while it was still possible to do so. "I should have told her . . ." "If only we had discussed . . ." and so on. By the time we get to the "fuck off!" part of the sentence, the sentence as a whole sounds like an exclamation. But, syntactically speaking, "Do I want to tell you . . ." has the form of a question-in-the-making. So there is room to wonder whether "fuck off" not only obliterates a wish from getting expressed, but also obliterates a question from getting asked. It is not a wild stretch to wonder whether Mr. A is thinking about what he wants to say to Dr. Levenson before their relationship formally comes to an end.

It may of course be that Mr. A's wish is to tell his analyst to fuck off—in which case the asking of the question, the expression of the wish, and its gratification all come together in the same expression. But given the oddness of the overall expression, there is a question whether the last part of the locution disrupted the expression of his wish rather than expressed it. And, obviously, the 'fuck off' is gratifying some need for expression. But given the oddness of the overall expression, it seems reasonable to wonder whether the "Do I want to tell you . . ." was en route to expressing a very different wish—entangled in longing and mourning—and whether the angry outburst disrupted his emerging thoughts and feelings. In ordinary English, "fuck off" is used to repel an advance when one feels intruded upon. That is, "fuck off" is paradigmatically a negative response to someone suddenly intruding upon one with the question "Let's fuck!" But if one thinks that "Let's fuck" / "Fuck off!" are twinned as a paradigm of proposal and response, then when one suddenly hears the second part of the dyad one might well wonder, "What specific form did 'Let's fuck!' take this time?"[8] And who uttered it? In particular, does Mr. A have any experience of the analyst intruding upon him, or of somehow getting in the way of what he wants to say to him?

So, between the Loewald and Gray approaches, as I have here depicted them, there is a difference of emphasis. The Gray approach focuses on the second part of the sentence, the expression of angry and aggressive feelings, and encourages the analysand to recognize that they are his feelings. The Loewaldian approach focuses on the first part—the "Do I want to tell you . . ."—as the perhaps squelched attempt to say what needs to be said in a period of mourning. It seems to me that both approaches can agree that analytic technique ought to be directed toward, and not bypass, the analysand's own developing ego-capacity to observe and rationally assess his own mental functioning. They can agree that there is a need to stay close to the so-called surface of the analytic hour and to abjure reliance on the analyst's authority. But Sidney Phillips is right that one can accept these working guidelines of analytic technique and yet remain flexible as to what counts as "surface." Some analytic surfaces are thick or jellylike, porous or bubbling as though fed by an underwater spring. The associations of a neurotic analysand—by Freud's own theory of primary process—will be rife with possibilities. Obviously, some of these possibilities may be repressed and thus not immediately accessible to the analysand, but I agree with Phillips that one needs to be alive to possibilities that are right there—available—for one to have a viable conception of a workable surface.[9] (Gray, I believe, agreed with this point.) What is on the surface of this analytic moment is that Mr. A has conscious questions about what he wants—more specifically, about what he wants to say to Dr. Levenson. "Do I want to tell you . . ." "Why would I want to tell you . . ." From a Loewaldian perspective, I think Mr. A could be encouraged to say more about what these wants are via a line of questioning that need not be too intrusive or directive. Mr. A's curiosity centers on why he would want to tell his analyst to fuck off; my curiosity focuses on why, if that is what Mr. A wants, he used such a strange locution to express it. In response to Mr. A's question "Why would I want to tell you to fuck off?" I, in my Loewaldian persona, might say, "Do you? What you said was, 'Do I want to tell you to fuck off.' I wonder if you have a question about what you want to say to me?" Depending on what Mr. A said, this might lead to other questions about what he wants to say. Obviously, "fuck off" is the most dramatic fragment of the verbal expression—and as such Mr. A's attention is drawn to it. But perhaps Mr. A's attention is itself functioning as a resistance, leading him away from his most pressing questions. An open-ended inquiry might facilitate the resumption of a process of speaking what wants to be said. If the termination phase is essentially one of mourning, then one should expect it to be a continually disrupted and resisted process of speaking what needs to be said before the (external part of the) relation is over.

I have elsewhere argued that the therapeutic action of psychoanalysis consists in developing a capacity for irony in a special sense of that term.[10] It seems to me that both the Loewald and Gray approaches could accept this—though their emphases might differ. Irony facilitates the analysand's capacity to move freely between id-meanings, ego-meanings, and superego-meanings, embedded in a single expression. So, in this case, Mr. A's statement "You haven't done anything but been here" has the conscious, ego-meaning "You have been a steady and loyal companion on this analytic journey." In relation to the superego, it expresses the angry disappointment "You've only sat on your ass and haven't done anything to cure me." And in relation to the id, it expresses the wish and fear that Levenson make the sexual advance to which Mr. A could say "fuck off." Levenson places emphasis on Mr. A's becoming aware of aggressive feelings hidden behind sincere expressions of gratitude. A Loewaldian might emphasize psychic integration, a hallmark of the therapeutic action of psychoanalysis—but these are compatible. Dr. Levenson's comment facilitated Mr. A's building a bridge over which he could travel back and forth in thought between his ego- and superego-meanings of "You haven't done anything but been there." He is thereby able to bring together in the here-and-now his sincere feelings of gratitude with his equally sincere feelings of disappointment, anger, and even rage.

It is worth noting an important ambiguity in the claim that a certain technique or conception of therapeutic action "relies on internalization." On one reading, the claim is that a technique explicitly or implicitly encourages the internalization of the analyst as a benign, noncritical figure. These are the techniques that Gray criticized as relying upon, rather than analyzing, the transference of authority. Insofar as internalization is an unconscious process that bypasses the analysand's ego-capacity to recognize and understand what is happening, then a technique that encourages these unconscious processes will, Gray argued, inevitably shortchange the analysand's emerging capacity for analytic self-understanding. However, there is another sense in which analysis "relies on internalization": namely, that it recognizes that internalization is an inevitable part of the analytic process and thus tries to take it into account in an analytically responsible way. In this sense, analysis "relies on internalization" in the same sense that it "relies on unconscious motivation" or that it "relies on transference." That is, it is a crucial part of reality that needs to be addressed in the right sort of way. It seems to me that Loewald's conception of therapeutic action relies on internalization in this latter sense—and as such escapes Gray's criticism. Indeed, from Loewald's perspective, precisely because one takes internalization to be an inevitable aspect of the termination phase, there is all the more reason to be on the lookout for its manifestations so as to be better placed to analyze them. One may accept that internalization inevitably occurs and still be committed to analyzing it whenever manifestations of it present themselves. Thus I believe that an integration of the Gray and Loewald perspectives is possible.

*The Kleinian perspective: Working with fantasies as they manifest themselves in the here and now.* The contemporary Kleinians have concentrated on how fantasies actually work.[11] In particular, they have helped us understand how fantasies can both be "conceived" and expressed in corporeal terms. From this Kleinian perspective, Mr. A's coughing fit, his getting up from the couch, leaving the room, and going to the bathroom are clearly an enactment within the total transference situation. And the Kleinians have helped us understand that we need to grasp not only its symbolic meaning but also its actual efficacy. Projective identification and introjection have symbolic content, but they are also actual and efficacious disruptions of the mind. So from this point of view, in the coughing fit, Mr. A might be gagging on his internalization of the analyst, or he may be choking on his own expression of gratitude. It may have various symbolic meanings; but, whatever its symbolic meaning, it is also a successful attack upon and disruption of the analytic hour. It is perhaps an envious attack upon the analyst and his capacity to keep an analytic session going. Immediately before the coughing fit, Mr. A is trying to formulate an utterance whose beginning—"Do I want to tell you . . ."—looks like it will be a question about what he wants to say. There is then the expression "fuck off!" From a Kleinian perspective, we should wonder whether, rather than being a completion of that sentence, the expression was an active attack on the sentence-that-was-coming-into-being. That is, although Mr. A injected a meaningful phrase, "fuck off," he might also have burped or coughed or giggled or sneezed or felt a sudden urge to go to the bathroom. We need, thus, to distinguish two different ways in which the expression "fuck off" can be used. First, it can be used to assert an imperative: that you should fuck off. Second, it can be used to disrupt the very attempt to make an assertion. Although it is a meaningful phrase, a person can learn to use it as a form of interjection that disrupts whatever meaningful activity is in the process of unfolding. In the first case, there is the assertion of a negative thought; in the second, there is a negative disruption of the attempt to formulate a thought.

Let us suppose that "fuck off" is being used in this second way. Then Mr. A begins his locution—"Do I want to tell you . . ."—with a question that is directed to his analyst, but the explicative "fuck off" would be directed not to the analyst but to the emerging question. I wonder whether in uttering "fuck off" Mr. A is speaking to an inner voice emerging into consciousness. This could well be the voice of an internal object, perhaps an introject of the analyst. From a Kleinian point of view, one has to wonder whether voices from his inner world are starting to intrude too much into consciousness, this is causing anxiety, and Mr. A utters "fuck off!" to disrupt the whole scene. This is what Bion calls an attack on linking. On this reading, with "fuck off" Mr. A attacks his own ability to ask a question.

The coughing fit renders speech impossible. And getting up from the couch and going to the bathroom essentially closes down the analytic process. This is, I think, an example of the power of projective and introjective fantasies as contemporary Kleinians conceive them. Now when Mr. A comes back, he asks, "Why would I want to tell you to fuck off?" That is, he returns with a question about the last thing he said. There is no reference to the last thing he did, nor to the last thing that, as it were, overtook him. His question thus bypasses what, for Kleinians, would be the central manifestation of fantasy. Is his question being put to a defensive use? Mr. A is moving from thing said ("fuck off!") to a question about thing said ("Why would I want to tell you to fuck off?"), as though the issue was the aggressive content of what he had just said. This ignores the fact that between thing said and thing said there was a fantasied attack upon his capacity to say anything at all.

From this Kleinian perspective, the analyst's saying "Maybe that's why" focuses on one manifestation of aggression but, along with the analysand, ignores another. For in this moment, there is not only an expression of aggression toward the analyst, but there is an attack on his own capacity to think and to speak.

Elsewhere I have argued that we should categorize the observable mental processes that emerge in psychoanalysis as falling into two broad categories—swerve and break.[12] We see swerve in the loose associations of primary process, dream images, metaphors, and relatively free associations. We see breaks in the active disruption of swerve-like mental processes and ordinary secondary-process thinking. The aim of this distinction is not to introduce two more species of mental activity, but rather to establish genus-categories in which the already-established forms of mental activity can be located. This allows us to see a higher unity in what might otherwise look like very disparate phenomena. I take it that the minute breaks in sentence formation that Paul Gray tracks, certain (though not all) slips of the tongue and parapraxes, projective and introjective fantasies as well as projective identification that Kleinians are attuned to, and massive attacks on linking that Bion describes—all of these are instances of break.

*Jacques Lacan.* In a Lacanian spirit, I would view Mr. A's cough as an expression of an excess that stands outside (and disrupts) the chain of associations.[13] For Lacan, when the analysand is sincerely thanking the analyst for all the accomplishments of the analysis—a more genuinely happy marriage, the ability to thrive in a family, the ability to inhabit his job more wholeheartedly—this is an ego thanking its master for its alienation.[14] It would be typical of American ego-psychology, Lacan thinks, to treat this as an acceptable outcome of analysis. And, in a Lacanian mode, I would wonder whether these purported achievements express imaginary identifications, and as such block the symbolic work of the unconscious.[15] The cough is an excess that cannot be contained in this *méconnaissance.* Analytically speaking, it is an occasion for disrupting a false outcome.

The cough is an interruption in a flow of thank-you(s) and a list of identifications. It culminates in a verbal outburst, "Do I want to tell you to fuck off!" which, from a Lacanian perspective, looks like the speech of the subject breaking through. This is a highly significant transition: from cough to f-cough to fuck off![16] It is a move from disruption of a fundamental fantasy to a verbal rejection of it. The fantasy is that if Mr. A could only satisfy the Analyst's demands (through a series of imaginary identifications), He, the One who is supposed to know, would finally give him that missing thing that would overcome the lack in his being. (I use capitals for the analyst because we are not here dealing with the empirical analyst, but rather with Dr. Levenson as the embodiment of a transcendent Other whose demands and desires lie beyond the realm of mere empirical experience.) This is an analytically significant moment, for in effect the subject is telling the Analyst to get off its back. In effect, what the subject is saying is "Enough already! I'll settle for the lack of being!"

If I were a Lacanian, I would be inclined to "punctuate" the session there—that is, end the session with that verbal outburst.[17] (This is an imaginative exercise: in my analytic practice, I stick to the fifty-minute session.) The hypothesis would be that this verbal outburst was in fact a moment of unblocking of the symbolic work of the unconscious. One would leave the analysand to carry on his own unconscious symbolic activity. And one can see that to let the session continue is to allow the ego to ask its question, "Why would I want to tell you . . .?" Thus there is, from a Lacanian perspective, a danger of collaborating with the ego in covering over the subject's speech. Ironically, though, if I were (in my imagination, in my Lacanian mode) to let the session continue, I would use the very same words that Dr. Levenson used to address Mr. A's question—"Maybe that's why." But my understanding of why these words were appropriate would differ. For Gray and Levenson, the crucial issue is the continued analysis of superego defense: helping the analysand recognize how he unconsciously manages his own aggression, even in the termination phase. The aim is to expand the range of conscious ego-functioning. For a Lacanian, the virtue of this remark is that it brings the analysand back to his own words and facilitates the unblocking of an unconscious symbolic process. The aim, then, is not to facilitate autonomous ego functioning—whatever that means—but to remove obstacles from the processes of unconscious symbolization.

**3.** In my analytic work, I find myself drawn on different occasions to each of these differing approaches. Is there any principle that might justify this, or am I just moving about according to what "feels right" at a given moment? While analysts ought to be able to trust their intuitions up to a point, they also, on reflection, ought to be able to say something about it. There needs to be some basis for supporting or correcting those clinical intuitions.

The key, I think, is to recognize that, while there may be significant technical differences between these approaches, it does not thereby follow that there is a difference of technique. How, after all, do we enumerate techniques? By way of analogy, imagine someone who early in the morning goes to milk his cows; strangely, he takes some of the milk and rubs it into the cows' backs as a kind of massage; he then goes and waters the corn he is growing in his fields; he goes to his forge and makes tiny nails; he then seems to be twisting hemp; he then goes to the computer and tries to finish designing a website; then, while resting in the afternoon, he spends a long time staring at his toes. How many things is he doing? Given that this is my imagined example, I have the answer: from the point of view of technique, he is doing one thing—making shoes. He is an old-fashioned artisan. He grows a special corn to feed the cows; it produces the leather that is just right for the shoes he wants to make. The milk-massage is in order to bring out the right sort of sheen in the leather. He makes his own nails to assemble the shoes. He makes his own shoelaces. He is going to sell his shoes on the Internet. The reason we give shoes primacy here is that everything else is for the sake of making and selling them. The only reason he is growing corn is to feed the cows, and the only reason he is raising cows is to make his own leather, and the only reason he is doing that is to make and sell shoes. Were the life of an artisan to become impossible, he would give it all up.[18] Perhaps he would become a psychoanalyst.

The important point is that the only principle of unity in all these disparate activities is provided by what Aristotle called the final cause—here, shoes. It is that toward which all the activities are aiming; it is what they are for, what they are aiming to promote. If one ignores the final cause, all one can see are differences. But once one has the final cause in mind, one can see that there need be no conflict between, say, punching holes in leather and also trying to protect it. The initial appearance of conflict evaporates when one can see that toward which all these activities are aiming: a shoe made of beautiful leather with lace holes punched in just the right places. It is only by reference to the final cause that we can judge all the disparate activities to be rational or irrational. If he were just some guy who rubs milk into cows' backs, makes little nails, and stares at his toes, he would be a strange character. Without the final cause, the disparate acts are a mad hodgepodge; but in the light of the final cause, all the acts are disciplined to a unified activity of making shoes.

Moreover, once one sees that the final cause is shoes, one can see that there might in principle be different ways of reaching the same outcome. Two people might make different choices about what they do next, they might make different choices at various points along the way, but they also might ultimately agree that they have each reached the same outcome—the production of an excellent pair of shoes. In such a case, then, although there is one sense in which they are acting differently, there is another sense in which they act in exactly the same way: they are both making shoes.

Now there are two important differences between psychoanalysis and shoemaking. First, in psychoanalysis there is no finite or determinate end of the process. An act of shoemaking comes to an end in the production of a pair of shoes. By contrast, psychoanalysis lacks any such clear stopping point. Let us say that psychoanalysis aims to promote psychological health or well-being. So far, this is a formal claim, not a substantive one. "Psychological health" is thus far a signifier for that, whatever it is, which psychoanalysis legitimately aims to promote. Psychological health seems to function as an infinite end in this sense: it is not the sort of thing that once one achieves it, the process is over.[19] Rather, psychic health is manifest in the entire life of the living being while that being is living well. Second, there need be no determinate distinction between the process of achieving psychic health and psychic health itself. Thus psychoanalysis need not be conceived as a process directed toward achieving a result that is distinct from itself. On occasions, at least, psychoanalysis can itself be a manifestation of psychic health that promotes psychic health.

But these important caveats notwithstanding, psychoanalysis has a final cause—however open-ended, indeterminate, continuing, and active it may be: there is something that the psychoanalytic process aims to promote. Freedom is the final cause of psychoanalysis. Freedom is the kind of health that psychoanalysis aims to facilitate. Of course, we have not yet said that anything as determinate as freedom functions largely as an open-ended signifier. It is about this that we need to get clearer. I want to argue that the freedom that concerns psychoanalysis has myriad aspects—and that the different approaches to the analytic moment I have considered can be differentiated according to which aspects of freedom they facilitate. Thus it is a mistake to think we can evaluate these different approaches simply by looking ever more closely at the moment itself. Looking carefully at the moment in the here-and-now is important, but we also need to look more holistically at the context in which that moment is embedded. If we do, we will see that, like every successful psychoanalytic treatment, the larger context has an overall direction—from worse to better off (according to some standard of psychic well-being that still needs to be spelled out). Thus we can evaluate an approach not only in terms of how well it discloses what is already going on in the analysand's psyche, but also how well it facilitates the analysand's movement in the direction of psychic well-being. To do the former, we may look for the efficient causes of Mr. A's outburst; to do the latter, we must look to the final cause of psychoanalysis.

**4.** When we talk about psychoanalysis facilitating an emerging freedom in the analysand, we need to develop and enrich our sense of what we mean. We tend to gesture in the direction of a family of notions—freedom of mind, freedom of speech, and freedom to be and let be—all of which can be considered as aspects of freedom. (This is only a preliminary list.) If we can see the different approaches as facilitating different aspects of freedom, then we might be able to integrate them into a differentiated unity. This is a unity we could only see in the light of a final cause. This does not mean that there are no genuine disagreements among the approaches, only that there might nevertheless be ways of integrating them. Lest the reader think I am advocating eclecticism when it comes to technique, my view is this: we have no idea what eclecticism is until we have an adequate conception of unity and difference when it comes to technique. At present, this is what we lack. And we cannot address that lack adequately until we have thought more deeply about the role of final cause in psychoanalysis. If, after sustained reflection, we can see any of the approaches as involving a misconception of freedom, that would be a reason for rejecting it. The point, then, is not to advocate eclecticism but to discover whatever genuine unity and genuine differences there are in the psychoanalytic approach to human being.

*Freedom of mind.* This is itself constituted of ingredient capacities; and the approaches of Gray, Loewald, Klein, and Lacan make different kinds of contributions. Gray's technique emphasizes freedom of reflection, the ability to observe and reflect upon one's own mental states as they arise in the here and now. Loewald's emphasizes open-minded engagement with the world via the dissolution of rigid transference structures. Contemporary Kleinians focus on freedom from attack on the mind's own ability to function. Lacanians focus on the freedom of the unconscious to resume its symbolic activity. In different ways, they all make contributions to the free play of the mind. And, rather than exclusive alternatives, they seem to me to be overlapping strategies, perhaps with different foci that nevertheless contribute to an overall conception of mental freedom.

The idea that the capacity to reflect on one's mental states is a form of freedom derives from Kant. He argued that once we gain reflective awareness of a mental state, we thereby take a step back from it and gain some choice as to what to do with it. Reflective awareness thus frees us from living in the grip of our impulses. And that is why the development of this perceptual capacity is itself an expression of our increasing rational autonomy. As Gray's technique emphasizes the development of the capacity for reflective observation of one's mental states (especially defenses against split-off aggressive thoughts), the accent of Loewald's technique is on freeing the mind from the "ghosts of the unconscious," thus facilitating psychic integration and more authentic engagement with the world. Neurosis is inevitably a constriction of freedom, since a neurotic inevitably imposes on the world a distorted and confined set of meanings that he or she mistakenly takes to be reality. So, to stick with Mr. A, it seems plausible to say that, before he entered the analysis, he lived in a world in which either he had to wear "a nice mask to hide the real, ugly, nasty, me" or he would explode with fury and provoke murderous retaliation. This either/or expressed all the possibilities there were for him—and thus it expressed his world. The analysis provided Mr. A with a possibility for new possibilities. He came to understand, in an existentially vivid way, that there were possibilities for living without a mask that need not provoke retaliation, ways to express his aggression as well as his sexuality that he need not consider ugly or nasty. In short, his world opened up with new possibilities for living. This possibility for new possibilities is essentially linked to the mourning process by which old images are mourned and eventually given up. As Loewald memorably put it, in analysis:

> [the] ghosts of the unconscious, imprisoned by defenses and symptoms, are allowed to taste blood, are let loose. In the daylight of analysis the

> ghosts of the unconscious are laid and led to rest as ancestors whose power is taken over and transformed into a newer intensity of present life, of the secondary process and contemporary objects.[20]

For the contemporary Kleinians, as we have seen, the emphasis is on the mind's attack on its own ability to think. Somewhat similar to Gray, the Kleinians emphasize tracking the vicissitudes of anxiety—though they are more focused on the massive disruptions of projective and introjective fantasies. Here, the mind needs to be freed from its own attacks on its capacity to function as mind.

*Freedom of speech.* Psychoanalysis promotes the analysand's capacity to speak his mind. This is in part the capacity to say what comes into one's mind—a capacity that develops in the analytic situation as the analysand over time becomes less fearful of the analyst and of the contents of her own thoughts. But it is also, and perhaps more importantly, a capacity for taking oneself up into one's words. Thus when Mr. A first said, "You haven't done anything but been there," it was only his ego speaking. One can imagine an analytic scenario in which, after he spent some time exploring the related id- and superego-meanings, he could come back laughingly to the same phrase, infused with a vibrancy coming from all parts of his psyche. He is now able, in a profound sense, to speak his mind. Vibrancy enters his words—a living sense that he is alive in his words—that was not there before. Again, I think a capacity for irony is crucial to this capacity to speak for oneself. All the techniques we have examined facilitate freedom of speech, but with different emphases. The Gray approach facilitates an analysand's capacity to speak his aggression in emotionally vibrant ways. Loewald's approach facilitates the analysand's ability to speak of (internal and external) objects in new and living ways. The aspect of Kleinian technique I have examined seeks to restore the capacity for speech when it has been attacked, disrupted, or even shut down. For Lacan, the disruption of speech is also an occasion for the breaking-out of free speech. This is free speech by the subject, as opposed to the ego or I. Thus, as we have seen, the triumphal moment of free speech in the vignette is the "fuck off!" that blasts through what is perhaps the ego's last defensive attempt: to ask "Do I want to tell you . . .?" In the "fuck off!" it is not Mr. A speaking; it is the subject finally able to get a word in edgeways. This is a place where competing images of freedom need to be thought through more deeply than they have been thus far. Let us grant Lacan that ego-formation is in some sense a defensive structure that takes on the signifiers available in the culture at the time; let us also grant his critique that a typical use of the phrase "adaptation to reality" by at least some ego psychologists of the mid-twentieth century meant, in effect, acceptance of the bourgeois structures of American society. But Lacan is trying to make a more sweeping point: ego-formation as such is a form of imprisonment in alienating signifiers. It is instructive to compare Lacan and Loewald, for both have been influenced, and similarly influenced by Kant, Hegel, and Heidegger in the conceptualizations of subject and object-relations. For Lacan, the fact that we are "thrown" into a culture and historical epoch—and thus into a field of meanings that we did not author and in terms of which we must understand ourselves—means that we are inevitably alienated; for Loewald, it is in this thrown field that one has at least the possibility for authentic self-development and open engagement with the world. Obviously, this is a debate that needs to be pursued. But the important point for the present discussion is that the way to think this difference through is in terms of the final cause of psychoanalysis: what do we understand by freedom, and how are we to aim for it? Without this point of reference, there will only be interminable disagreement. I believe that, although there are significant differences, there are also occasions for genuine integration of Gray, Loewald, Kleinian, and Lacanian approaches. These tend to get overlooked because the question of the final cause of psychoanalysis has been ignored.

*Freedom to be and let be.* As one listens over time to analysands, one comes to hear that there are certain very basic categories in terms of which people try to make sense of their lives. That is, will they be able to make sense of themselves as someone who is capable of loving or of being loved? Will they be capable of creative engagement in the world? Can they be a friend? These categories are important psychoanalytically for two reasons. First, these are not experienced as discrete achievements or failures on the part of the analysand; rather, they are the categories in which analysands conceive of themselves as having an existence. It is in these terms that they conceive of themselves as succeeding or failing to have a life. They are subjective categories in the sense that they are the terms in which people try to shape themselves as a certain sort of subject.[21] For Mr. A, to be was to succeed at being a husband, a father, and a colleague. But, secondly, these terms need to be subjectively understood: they are not mere social roles. That is, part of what it is to constitute oneself as a lover, subjectively understood, is increasingly to determine for oneself what it is to be a lover. And that, in turn, requires that one continually be able to notice, react to, and appropriate one's own emerging impulses, thoughts, and feelings to a life so constituted. This is what it is to be able to constitute oneself as a lover.

None of the techniques we have approached specifically addresses this form of freedom, though each of them can be part of a process by which it develops. I suspect that it has been avoided because analysts want to avoid anything that smacks of the ethical for fear of imposing on their analysands an image of how to live. But freedom to be, as I understand it, is not about fitting any social role or social image; indeed, it constitutes itself as freedom precisely by its independence from any particular image. Should an analysand desire to become a person who is capable of love—a lover, for instance—the question of what that consists in will essentially be up to him.

The contemporary Kleinians have, in their discussion of envy, explicitly embraced the idea that psychoanalysis has an unavoidably ethical dimension. Envy manifests itself most notably in the attack on the creative capacities of another. In the analytic situation, there are regularly envious attacks on the analyst—from overt attacks upon the analyst's ability to minor acts of denigration like missing analytic hours, coming late. A Kleinian might well look on Mr. A's outburst as an envious attack on the analytic process itself. Now psychoanalysis cannot be neutral with respect to the question of whether it is promoting envy or helping diminish the need for envious attacks. It is not a live option for an analyst to say to herself, "This analysand seems to revel in the envious attacks upon others—especially me—so I should facilitate a process by which he can get really good at envious destruction." One of the crucial Kleinian insights is that freedom to . . . is at the same time freedom from . . .—freedom from envious attacks as well as self- and other destruction. While analysis may recognize envy, tolerate it up to a point, try to interpret it, and so on, it is constitutionally directed away from envy. It tries to understand its sources and, through analysis, diminish the felt need to deploy it. This is basically an ethical dimension to psychoanalysis. It recognizes that freedom to be inherently involves freedom to let others be. One develops one's own freedom as a subject as one can increasingly learn to recognize, tolerate, and on occasion celebrate the reality of other subjects. Psychoanalysis is inherently committed to the recognition and acceptance of the reality of other subjects—and this is an inescapably ethical commitment.

**5.** So, imagine yourself in the midst of an analytic moment with your own Mr. A: is there a right answer to which of the approaches you should choose? I think there is. Choose the approach that, given your overall understanding of Mr. A and your best grasp of what is going on in the here-and-now, best facilitates that aspect of Mr. A's freedom that you take to be most salient. On different occasions one may make different choices. The biggest mistake, it seems to me, is to think that one has to make one's decision based on what is actually in the analysand's mind in the here-and-now. Not only is it often true that, epistemically speaking, we simply do not know all that much about what is really in the analysand's mind at any given moment, but, metaphysically speaking, there may be no fully determinate answer as to what is going on. So, even if we are primarily concerned with analyzing what is going on in the here-and-now, it does not follow that the analysis of that moment ought only to make reference to materials that are themselves available in the here-and-now. To think that it does is a symptom of something that went wrong in the history of psychoanalysis: the assumption that the only scientifically respectable causes in the explanation and treatment of human beings are efficient causes. Efficient causes are those antecedent states of affairs—in this case, mental states—that are sufficient to bring about the state of affairs that needs to be explained. It is this image of scientific explanation that is responsible for so much of the controversy—as vituperative as it was fruitless—that plagued the discipline throughout the last century. The fact is that if we want to understand human action and the role of self-consciousness in human action as well as the repetitions, distortions, and disruptions of unconscious fantasy, we need a rigorous understanding of the spontaneity of the human mind as well as the role of final cause in human action.[22] Empiricism, the traditional model of scientific explanation, concerned as it is with efficient-causal explanation of a distinct object of inquiry, is incapable of providing insight into either area.[23]

Consider, for example, Freud's discussion of the condensation of ideas in primary process. Condensation is a significant psychic process: many disparate thoughts and wishes can be condensed into a single dream image. But one only discovers the condensation via an ongoing analysis, after the dream, in which the analysand continues to associate to the dream-image. The name "condensation" suggests that the meanings were already there, before the dream, and causally served to bring it about. Perhaps some did. But what really grounds our confidence that all the ideas were already there, causing the dream, as opposed to unfolding in the analytic process in response to the dream and its analysis? Of course, on occasion we will know through the analysis that a certain theme has been a long-standing concern of the analysand's. Even so, how could one know that it was actually serving a causal role in the production of the dream, as opposed to being imaginatively tied in with it later? The honest answer is that there is no satisfying way to answer this question. But this will matter only if one assumes that the only scientifically respectable form of explanation is in terms of efficient causes. By contrast, if one is also concerned with the final cause of freedom, then it will not particularly matter whether a given idea caused a dream (chicken) or the dream facilitated an association to the idea (egg). What will matter is the overall direction of the analysand's imagination: is it inhibiting or facilitating the analysand's movement toward freedom, and in what ways?

Just as Freud introduced the notion of condensation of ideas, we need to countenance the notion of condensation of strategies. Not that they all need be antecedently present in the mind as fully formed states that could be discovered as the efficient causes of what follows. Rather, they are there in the sense of being unfinished directions in which the mind might go. The aim of an analytic intervention is to facilitate a movement in the direction of (some aspect of) freedom. To do this, one needs to take the final cause into account. (To use Aristotelian language: only when we have a better understanding of the final cause of psychoanalysis [freedom] will we be able adequately to adjudicate differences about the formal cause—the technique that constitutes the form of psychoanalytic activity. For the form ought also to be [a manifestation of] freedom.)

I shall close with an unusual claim: if we want to make real advances in technique, we need to get clearer about what freedom is and why it matters to us. Thus philosophical inquiry lies at the heart of psychoanalytic technique. Even in the minutest here-and-now moment of a psychoanalytic session, how can we evaluate it properly if we have only the vaguest sense of what we are aiming for—or why we are aiming for that rather than something else? In recent decades, it has been familiar to see psychoanalysis as divided between theory and clinical practice. In fact, even to conceptualize the division in this way is a sign of the pathology of our times. It is certainly true that much writing that goes under the heading of theory is cut off from clinical experience; and it is often pursued in terms so abstract that it is hard to know what, if anything, the author is talking about. No wonder clinical practitioners feel that they do not have to pay attention, but this can encourage complacency among them. While it may be true that they do not need to attend to the latest theoretical fad, it is also true that they cannot really understand their own clinical activity if they lack understanding of what it is they are trying to bring about—or why it is worthwhile to do so. In this sense, philosophy does not lie over there, in theory; it pulses in the heartbeat of the clinical encounter.

CHAPTER NINE

# Jumping from the Couch

---

**1.** Since Freud's time, the most important development in psychoanalytic thinking has been an ever-increasing appreciation of the role of fantasy in human life. But how does fantasy work? This is a question that tends to be ignored—and there is a reason why. Consider, as a notable example, the fantasy of projective identification, first described by Melanie Klein and developed with clinical aplomb by her followers.[1] Those who accept the phenomenon of projective identification (and I count myself among them) tend to take it as a psychological primitive. Projective identification is invoked to explain certain aspects of how the unconscious mind works; there is not supposed to be a further question about how projective identification itself works. And, of course, those who do not accept it feel no pressure to explain how it works; they seek only to explain the relevant clinical phenomena in other ways.

It almost seems as though there is a question without a questioner. *Almost.* The aim of this essay is not so much to answer the question as to show what a stimulating area of inquiry this might be. Note that this project is not in the least reductive: I am not trying to explain projective identification away, nor am I interested here in whatever neurochemical mechanisms might underlie it. Rather, the questions are: In what forms of mental activity does projective identification consist? How is it efficacious—that is, how does it do what it seems to do?

There is another question that should also engage us: namely, how do these workings of the mind affect a person's overall emotional life? In other words, how does the unconscious affect the conscious? It is also a question of the relation between the microcosm and the macrocosm. Ultimately we are concerned with an analysand's ability to experience and express his/her emotional life. As we look to the trees of mental functioning, we ought to keep an eye on the forest of emotional life.

Consider this moment from Freud's treatment of the Rat Man:

> Things soon reached a point at which, in his dreams, his waking fantasies and his associations, he began heaping the grossest abuse upon me and my family, though in his deliberate action he never treated me with anything but the greatest respect. His demeanour as he repeated these insults to me was that of a man in despair. "How can a gentleman like you, sir," he used to ask, "let yourself be abused in this way by a low, good-for-nothing fellow like me? You ought to turn me out: that's all I deserve." While he talked like this, he would get up from the sofa and roam about the room, a habit which he explained at first as being due to delicacy of feeling: he could not bring himself, he said, to utter such horrible things while he was lying there so comfortably. But soon he himself found a more cogent explanation, namely, that he was avoiding my proximity for fear of my giving him a beating. If he stayed on the sofa he behaved like someone in desperate terror trying to save himself from castigation of terrific violence; *he would bury his head in his hands, cover his face with his arm, jump up and suddenly rush away, his features distorted with pain,* and so on. He recalled that his father had had a passionate temper, and sometimes in his violence he had not known where to stop.[2]

What is the Rat Man doing? In the moment, he is not sure himself. He flails about for a self-interpretation and finally hits on one that Freud says is "more cogent": the Rat Man is afraid that Freud is going to give him a beating. But why should Freud find *this* interpretation more cogent? This is a clinical moment that is as difficult as it is important to understand.

It is difficult because there are three claims that all seem to be true. First, the Rat Man is not consciously afraid of Freud; second, the Rat Man is not unconsciously afraid of Freud; and third, the Rat Man is afraid of Freud.

But how could all three claims be true? On the surface, it looks as though we are caught in a contradiction, wedded to an inconsistent triad. In fact, all three claims can be true, and in seeing how they can all be true, we shall gain insight both into how fantasy works and how it intersects with and expresses emotional life. Note that I assert that they *can* all be true and not that they *are* all true. The Rat Man is not my patient; my only access to him is through Freud's case history. The analysis, short by contemporary standards, is long since over, and there is thus no way seriously to test alternative interpretive hypotheses. But the point is not to find out what was *really* going on with the Rat Man; it is to raise a possibility about what *might* have been going on with him. If this interpretive possibility is not ruled out, then there is a chance that Freud was approaching the Rat Man at the wrong level. And, of course, the real issue is not about Freud; it is about how we approach our analysands. We need to be alive to this possibility if we are going to stay open to all the interpretive possibilities that our analysands present us with.

**2.** In the moment, the Rat Man has little conscious understanding of what he is doing. He is suffering a moment of reflexive breakdown: that is, his capacity for self-interpretation has become impaired.[3] And he later comes up with a "more cogent" explanation. He certainly does not take himself consciously to believe that the good Doctor Freud is actually about to thrash him; rather, the Rat Man has taken on the role of self-analysis and is ascribing to himself an unconscious belief.

And in so ascribing such a belief to himself, the Rat Man is implicitly following out an idea that goes back to Aristotle. Emotions are not just affective outbursts; they have complex structures. In particular, they make an implicit claim for their own appropriateness. Fear, for example, is not simply a feeling: it is constituted by a sense that one is being threatened. Fear purports to be the right response to some perceived or imagined threat.[4] It is precisely because the Rat Man does not *consciously* believe that Freud is going to beat him that, given his fearful reactions, he is tempted to ascribe some unconscious reason for his fear.

**3.** The argument in favor of the first claim might seem to provide evidence for the idea that the Rat Man is unconsciously afraid that Freud is going to beat him. For if the Rat Man is behaving fearfully yet has no conscious understanding of what he is doing, then is not that evidence that he is unconsciously afraid? Certainly, that is the line of reasoning taken by both the Rat Man and Freud.

And we do have to accept the interpretive possibility that the Rat Man is unconsciously afraid of Freud. That is, the second claim *could* be false. This would be the situation in which the Rat Man's fear of Freud was preconscious. In this case, there is an articulated fear-structure directed at Freud, though because of some inhibiting or repressing force, that fear-structure is kept from the Rat Man's conscious understanding. Perhaps this is the way it was for the Rat Man.

But if we look at the reasoning that Freud describes, another interpretive possibility suggests itself. This is that while Freud and the Rat Man take themselves to be making an empirical discovery about the Rat Man's unconscious, they are in fact following out the logic of a concept. For if one assumes that the Rat Man is afraid and there is no conscious belief that Freud is a threat, then there is *conceptual* pressure to conclude that there must be an unconscious belief.

It is in this way that the unconscious can come to be conceptualized as more rational than it is. For it is part of our concept of belief—as well as the other propositional attitudes—that one cannot have them one by one. They have to fit together in some more-or-less coherent way.[5] In this picture, irrationality can enter in only one of two ways: either unconscious beliefs and desires interact with conscious beliefs and desires in irrational ways or unconscious beliefs and desires hook onto the world in inappropriate ways.[6] It is as though the Rat Man's unconscious has beliefs that themselves hang together, but it is not very good at keeping track of time and is very shortsighted. Thus the unconscious mistakes Freud for the Rat Man's father. All this follows from the assumption that an unconscious belief is what explains the Rat Man's cringe.

In short, the Rat Man and Freud seem to think that the following interpretive inference is legitimate: from (a) the Rat Man is acting fearfully and (b) there is no conscious belief that Freud is a threat, it is valid to infer that (c) there must be an unconscious belief. But if we assume that this form of interpretive inference is valid, we will end up conceptualizing the entire unconscious along the lines of the preconscious. That is, we are in danger of attributing too much structure to the unconscious. And thus we are in danger of attributing more mental organization to our patients than they, in fact, have. Again, perhaps the Rat Man did have all this organization;

perhaps he did have an unconscious belief that Freud was about to beat him. But what if he did not?

Once one recognizes this possibility, one can see that there is a real danger that Freud is collaborating with a rationalizing defense. It may be that they are both attributing to the Rat Man more intelligibility than his acts possess. This has important consequences for technique. For if the Rat Man is acting for inappropriate reasons—and if he is able to act for those reasons because he is unconscious that those are his reasons—then the proper therapeutic technique would be to bring these reasons to light. The Rat Man would then be able to see that his hitherto unconscious reasons were bad ones. When good reasons can interact with bad, one should expect the Rat Man's fear to diminish and eventually evaporate. But if all of this is a rationalizing defense, then what at first sight looks like a therapeutic technique—"making the unconscious conscious"—on further reflection looks like the construction of a false self.

**4.** How might we otherwise conceive of what is going on with the Rat Man? And how might we otherwise think about how to help him?

To approach this clinical moment of rupture adequately, we need to go back to a moment of theoretical rupture and rethink it. By the end of the First World War, Freud came to see that there were important psychological phenomena that could not be explained in terms of the various functionings of the pleasure principle.

But he assumed without argument that what he needed to find was another principle. And perhaps he is right that there is another principle, but I do not think that we have yet figured out what it is. I have argued elsewhere in detail that Freud's argument in *Beyond the Pleasure Principle* is not sufficient to establish the death drive as a principle of mental functioning.[7] I cannot go through that argument here, but the general idea is that, given the actual empirical psychological phenomena Freud cites, the postulation of the death drive is a theoretically extravagant conclusion. The question then arises whether there might not be more austere ways to conceptualize the phenomena. Roughly speaking, I think Freud was right to think that certain phenomena—e.g., traumatic dreams, certain kinds of compulsive repetitions—are exceptions to the workings of the pleasure principle, but in trying to conceptualize them, he went off the theoretical deep end.

Let us simply abandon the assumption that if there are exceptions to the workings of the pleasure principle, then there must be a "beyond"—a hidden principle waiting to be discovered. And let us ask instead how we might characterize austerely the empirical content of Freud's important discovery. It seems to me that what Freud has shown is that, on the broadest possible scale, there are two different types of unconscious mental activity. The first is the by-now-familiar workings of the mind according to the loose associations of the pleasure principle, which Freud so brilliantly described in *Three Essays on Theory of Sexuality, The Interpretation of Dreams,* and *Studies on Hysteria.* Here we have displacement and condensation, as well as various forms of inhibition and repression, which altogether serve to diffuse our associations as well as express them in dreams, bodily expressions, and other symptomatic acts. These are, of course, all sorts of different mental activities, but they can all be summed up under one grand type: the functionings of the mind according to the pleasure principle. (From this broad perspective, the mind functioning according to the reality principle is only a variant: the search for pleasure through realistic considerations.) I call this type of mental functioning *swerve* because it exercises a kind of gravitational pull on the entire field of conscious mental functioning, bending it into idiosyncratic shapes. By way of analogy, we detect the existence of black holes by the way light swerves toward them. We detect this type of unconscious process by the ways our conscious reasoning, our bodily expressions, our acts, and our dreams swerve toward them.

Before 1920, Freud thought he could account for all the relevant pathology in terms of psychological conflicts that were themselves all instances of swerve-like mental phenomena. The kernel of Freud's discovery in *Beyond the Pleasure Principle* is that this is not so. There are significant psychological phenomena that cannot be understood in terms of any type of swerve. We need to recognize a fundamentally different type of mental activity, which is in fact the disruption of primary-process mental activity itself. I give the generic name *break* to all types of mental activity that serve to disrupt—or break apart—the ordinary functionings of the mind. So, for instance, the so-called dreams of the traumatic neuroses are instances of break because, as Freud showed, they are not really dreams. That is, they are not an ordinary manifestation of the wish-fulfilling capacity to dream but rather a disruption of that capacity. In traumatic neuroses, the ordinary swerve-like capacities of the mind are repeatedly disrupted, and the mind gets stuck in repeated disruptions.

There are three features of break that need to be emphasized. First, break is a genus concept, not a species. In conversation, colleagues have assumed that I am trying to introduce a new mental force, and then the natural response is, "Why do we need it? Don't we already have the concept of trauma?" That is like saying, "Why do we need the concept *animal* when we already have the concept *human being*?" The point of the concept *animal* is not to introduce a new species—as though we have humans, we have chimps, and now we also have animals as though it were the discovery of yet another species. Nor is it to say that now that we have the concept *animal*, we no longer need the concept *human being*. Rather, the concept *animal* allows us to see, at a higher level of generality, that there might be some salient things in common between humans and, say, anteaters. With the concept *animal*, we can see a certain unity where before we saw differences.

And so it is with the concept of break: the point is not to introduce it as something at the same level as trauma, but as additional to it; nor is the point to replace the concept of trauma with the concept of break. Rather, the point is to divide mental activity into two broad categories: those that manifest the ordinary functionings of the mind and those that disrupt them. In the broad genus of break, there are myriad species: trauma is the obvious example, but included in this category are also "attacks on linking" as well as moments to be found in projective identification, introjection, various forms of acute bodily attacks and spasms, as well as certain kinds of moments of dissociation and fugue states. In particular, it includes those that are extremely minor, nontraumatic, and difficult to detect: these are the sorts of break Gray listens for in his close-process attention.[8] One of the values of the concept *break* is that it encourages us to think about what one of Gray's minuscule breaks and a massive psychotic break might have in common.[9] I do not pretend to be able to give a complete taxonomy of all the kinds of breaks, but I think that it is a fruitful area for future research.

The second feature of break that needs to be remembered is that breaks can come from inside as well as from outside the individual mind. Another person or an event can inflict a trauma upon us that utterly disrupts mental functioning. But, on Freud's economic model, the human being is himself a repository of drives and psychic energy that can on occasion overwhelm the mind.

Third, and most importantly, a person can become active with respect to break. That is, in periods of stress and anxiety, a person can use the heightened psychic energy to disrupt his own mental functioning. In this way, break can become a primitive defense mechanism.[10] It can also be used to provoke more minor disruptions; in this way, small breaks can be incorporated into more sophisticated defenses.

Let us go back to the Rat Man. Here is what I suspect was happening.[11] As the transference with Freud is unfolding in swerve-like ways, the Rat Man's anxiety is also increasing. The anxiety becomes too much for the Rat Man to handle, and he induces a break by jumping up from the couch or cringing before Freud. It is at this abrupt and surprising moment that Freud looks to the transference to explain it. This is not strictly speaking false. But it is ironic, because a transference has been developing all along, and it is precisely when this transferential development gets disrupted that Freud looks for the appearance of transference.

If this account is correct, then simply to interpret the Rat Man's acts as fear of Freud is to go off in the wrong direction. If it makes sense to say that the Rat Man is afraid of anything, it is more likely that he is afraid of the development of his own emotional life. To put it paradoxically, he is too afraid to be afraid. Less paradoxically, the Rat Man suffers so much anxiety that he invokes break as a primitive defense, and thus he is never able to develop a mature emotional life. In particular, he is not able to get to the point where he can experience fear as a fully fledged emotion.

To say that an emotion like fear can be "fully fledged" suggests that the mature capacity to experience fear is itself the outcome of a developmental process. And like any developmental process, it can be interrupted, inhibited, or distorted in various ways. In a mature and healthy expression of fear, a person takes up the various fearful somatic responses—many of them automatic—and embeds them with good reasons. On the one hand, fear reaches down into our gut; on the other, it reaches out to the world and makes a claim that fear is the right response.

Of course, this is a complex developmental process, and thus there are many points along the way for disruption and inhibition. Now many of these truncated expressions, from a behavioral point of view, will look just like fear. And they are fearful expressions in the sense that they are the expressions of a primitive capacity that, if allowed to develop, would develop into the mature capacity to express fear. In the case of the Rat Man, the problem is that these fearful expressions are themselves being deployed to disrupt the development of the capacity to experience fear.

We are now in a position to make the case that the Rat Man *was afraid of Freud;* we need only note that in ordinary English we use emotion-words, like "fear," not only for fully fledged emotions, but also for all the truncated versions along the developmental route. When we call an infant's outburst or the Rat Man's cringe an expression of fear, we do so not simply because of the qualities of the outburst itself, but because we implicitly locate that outburst on a developmental spectrum at whose furthest end is the fully fledged expression of fear. In effect, this is to use Aristotle's distinction between fear as a *potentiality* and fear as an *actuality.*[12] Ordinary language, we note, is happy to call both cases an expression of fear. The danger that we, as analysts, must avoid is to interpret a truncated emotional outburst as, say, a fully fledged expression of fear and then feel obliged to discover all the features of the fully fledged emotion. I suspect that this is what the Rat Man and Freud do when they move from saying that the Rat Man's jump is an expression of fear to saying that there must therefore be an unconscious belief that Freud is about to beat him.

But, still, our interpretive problems are not over. For this "cringe-and-jump-from-the- couch" is not an unproblematic member of the developmental capacity to express fear. In fact, it is a disruption of that very capacity. Normally we are inclined to think that the expressions of emotional life are themselves part of a developmental process in which the emotions themselves gain in complexity and structure. But in this case, we have an affective display that, appears as fear, is deployed to disrupt and thus inhibit the development of the capacity to experience fear. In other words, in this dramatic moment, by looking at the behavioral manifestations alone, we have an emotional display about which we cannot decide whether it is an expression of the capacity to express fear or a disruption of that very capacity.

Should we call an act that disrupts the capacity to express fear itself an expression of fear? I do not think that there is a straightforward answer to this question. For psychoanalysis reveals a complexity of psychological activity that goes beyond any of our ordinary intuitions about how to employ a concept used in a natural language, such as that of fear. Nevertheless, I think that a case can be made for the Rat Man's outburst being an expression of fear. At first it seems counterintuitive that anything that disrupts the capacity to express fear should itself be considered an expression of fear. But this intuition is trumped by another: that we learn to apply the concept of fear on the basis of fairly casual observation of behavior and reports of feelings. The Rat Man's outburst is observationally identical to an outburst that would be on the developmental route to the expression of fear as a fully fledged emotion. This latter outburst would unproblematically be called an expression of fear, and the Rat Man's outburst is observationally identical to it. Thus there is reason to call the Rat Man's outburst an expression of fear. If we follow this line of reasoning, then it seems that we have to accept a surprising consequence: that emotions can be self-disrupting. The expression of fear can be used to disrupt the development of the capacity to express fear.

The danger for us analysts is that we unwittingly move from thinking that this outburst is an expression of fear to assuming that it cannot also be a disruption of the capacity to express fear. This is one reason we need specialized psychoanalytic concepts, like fantasy and projective identification: to render clearly the psychological complexity of an event that goes beyond our ordinary use of emotion-language. It seems to me that the Rat Man's outburst is a manifestation of projective identification. In the transference, the Rat Man's anxiety has been rising. There is, I suspect, an internal punishing figure—let us call it the Rat Dad—which was itself formed in fantasy by various internalizations of his father and which now performs severe superego functions. Intrapsychically, the Rat Dad is acting up, and so is the rebellious ego-figure of the Rat Child. In a burst, the Rat Man tries to relieve his anxiety by projecting a bit of himself—namely, internalized Rat Dad—out on to Freud.[13] In short, what we see in the Rat Man's jump from the couch is less a manifestation of the capacity to express fear and more a display of intrapsychic structure spread out over the analytic situation.[14] The Rat Man is cringing before his own superego.

But how does this projective identification work? Projective identification is not magic; it has real efficacy, yet it is puzzling how this efficacy is achieved. Of course, we know how to describe projective identification—in fantasy a person takes a piece of him/herself and projects it into another person—but what does this mean? How does it work? Our sense of the reality of projective identification is that a certain capacity of the person tends to go missing.[15] So, for instance, in the case of the Rat Man, his capacity to express fear has been thoroughly disrupted. This is ironic—and at first counterintuitive—because it looks as though the Rat Man is expressing fear. And yet it is part of the capacity to express fear that allows a person to be attuned to the world in the right sorts of ways—that a person can have a sense of what is salient. True fear is, of its essence, oriented to the world. It is a response to what a person takes to be genuinely worthy of fear. And if fear makes an implicit claim that it is an appropriate response, then a mature and healthy capacity to express fear ought to be sensitive to those aspects of the world that are threatening and distinguish them from those that are not.

It is just this capacity that the Rat Man so thoroughly disrupts. In the moment of the jump, he cannot tell whether he is responding to something in the world or something in himself. In projective identification, he has rendered thoroughly confusing the distinction between self and world. He has thus also disrupted his capacity for self-interpretation: in the moment, he has virtually no idea what he is doing.

It seems to me that the daunting and immediate power of projective identification comes from the fact that it is a species of break. In his jump, the Rat Man gives himself a break. That is, in response to anxiety, the Rat Man invokes break as a primitive defense and thus disrupts his emerging emotional life. He forcibly projects the Rat Dad out on to Freud; but that is just what it is for him thoroughly to disrupt his own mental functioning. For his own internal capacity for superego functioning has now gone missing. He acts as though it is now located over there, in Freud.

Then, having induced a break, he dreams and rationalizes around it in swerve-like ways. That is, he begins to imagine and to think that he must be unconsciously afraid of Freud. That is, fear of Freud is now being constructed ex post facto. It is not, then, that fear causes the Rat Man to jump from the couch; rather, it is that his jumping from the couch causes him to try to form the emotion of fear.

By way of analogy, I once had a psychotic patient who said to me, "Everything was all right until my life left me." Unlike a neurotic slip of the tongue, this patient was trying to report the outcome of a psychotic projective identification. When this person's wife left their trailer, he went into a catatonic trance and had to be taken to the hospital. In a massive psychotic break, he disrupted his own capacity for emotional life. The overwhelming power of the fantasy arises not so much because he imagines or daydreams that he has died, but because he induces a massive break. If fantasy were only a dreamlike content—or the process by which such content was formed—we would not be able to explain its remarkable power. To understand that power, we need to understand projective identification not as a swerve-like fantasy—a dream that he and his wife are one person—but rather in terms of a massive break that is induced by the loss of his wife.

The case of the Rat Man's jump and my patient's catatonic break can show us something significant about the difference between swerve and break. In particular, it is not that break is always a contentless trauma and swerve the only mental activity with content. In projective identification, a content-saturated capacity of mental functioning is forcibly disrupted. In the case of the Rat Man, his superego capacities, which are saturated with Rat Dad meanings, are forcibly disrupted; in the case of my patient, the meaning of his life—his wife—is the occasion of the disruption of his capacity to live. The difference between swerve and break, then, does not lie in the fact that in swerve there is manipulation of content and in break there is not; rather, the difference lies in the type of manipulation involved. Think of the difference between reading a journal article you strongly disagree with and saying, "That's ridiculous," on the one hand, and physically ripping up the pages of the journal, on the other. In each case, there is a manipulation of content. But in the former case, our thoughts are working through the meaning; in the latter case, we are physically destroying the vehicle of meaning, the printed word. Swerve dreams through meanings; break breaks them up.

Now, one eerie feature of projective identification that needs to be accounted for is its transmissibility. Projective identification not only has a sender, but it also has a receiver—and on occasion it can have a powerful effect on the receiver. How does this work? It is unsatisfying simply to respond, "by projective identification." We want to know how projective identification works. By way of analogy, in certain cultures, a voodoo curse can have an overwhelming impact on its target. There is no question about its efficacy. The problem lies not in the voodoo itself but in the voodoo theory of voodoo: for, in answer to the question of how it works, it can only answer, "by magic" or "by voodoo." Voodoo's efficacy is itself taken to be a primitive. As psychological theorists, we ought to be able to do better than that with projective identification. In particular, those of us who take projective identification seriously should not want it to look like magic.

In order to demystify the reception of projective identification, one can imagine my psychotic patient as himself on the receiving end of a projective identification. (I have little idea of what really happened.) Before his own break, his partner is getting herself stirred up and, in a moment of high anxiety, she projects her murderous rage into him. That is, instead of expressing her anger in a somewhat mature fashion, she actively disrupts her capacity for rage. Her own capacity for anger has gone missing, but she now experiences her partner as full of her murderous rage and she flees out the door. Perhaps she says something like "Go to hell!" and stomps out. My patient takes this message with psychotic literalness: not only is the message drained of all metaphor, but also the utterance of the words is experienced as a physical intrusion.[16] Of course, there is an important sense in which this person is right about his experience. The utterance "Go to hell!" is a physical act: The air has moved from deep inside the speaker's body; it is expelled with a collapsing chest, a moving mouth and tongue, and, perhaps, with glaring eyes. The air between them is set in motion, the sound waves penetrate my patient's ears, and a message is taken into his body. In that sense, my psychotic patient is right about what happened to him: a piece of meaning that is itself physically instantiated has been taken into him. He is mistaken about the routes of its efficacy.

What has actually happened is that my patient is psychotically attuned to his partner; in particular, he is attuned to her rising anxiety. This causes him to become more anxious himself. As she explodes in break, he follows suit. Inducing a break is his first line of defense, and, given the message, he sends himself to hell. By the time he comes for treatment, the massive break has already occurred. By contrast, the Rat Man's jump from the couch is a significant break within the analytic situation—and Freud goes looking for hidden emotions. But if the above interpretation is correct, the point of the therapy ought not to be for the Rat Man to discover the hidden contents of his emotional life, but for him to acknowledge that, in an important sense, he has not yet allowed himself to have an emotional life. For when a powerful emotion starts to develop, the Rat Man develops so much anxiety that he disrupts the whole process with a break. A *genuine* acknowledgment of this would usher in a new way for the Rat Man to relate to himself.

How might this happen? As a matter of technique, this is not an easy process to handle. After all, if this interpretation is correct, various forms of break are the Rat Man's tried-and-true defense mechanisms. They were laid down in infancy, and, precisely because they are so easily triggered, they have prevented any more sophisticated defenses from developing. It is scarcely an exaggeration to say that these primitive defenses constitute who the Rat

Man *is*. Is there, then, any hope of therapeutic action? The Rat Man induces a break when he feels anxiety, and he feels anxiety easily because he lacks more sophisticated defenses. So one initial therapeutic aim is to keep the level of anxiety low. In this way, one deprives the Rat Man of his primitive defenses, but in a benign way: one reduces the occasions for deploying them. Most likely there will be breaks no matter what one does. But the hope is that there will be more occasions in which the Rat Man learns to tolerate certain levels of anxiety—no matter how low those levels might appear from an outside perspective—without immediately resorting to a break. Thus there arise occasions in which the Rat Man can start to live with his emotional life, rather than immediately disrupt it.

A second therapeutic aim is resolutely to avoid collaborating with any rationalizing defense. Instead of joining the Rat Man in postulating an unconscious fear, one could help him see that he has just anxiously disrupted his emotional life. The fundamental attitude would no longer be one of discovery of hidden emotions; rather, it would be one of commitment to allowing emotional life to unfold.

Third, remember that some breaks can be of great therapeutic value. Precisely because break is a genus and not a species, it comes in many different flavors and intensities. Massive breaks can be destructive to the mind, but less intense breaks can be of value in breaking open rigid structures. Every core unconscious fantasy is itself an implicit metaphysical theory: it provides the person whose fantasy it is with a sense of what is and what is not possible. If a person inhabits, say, an unloving world, then everything that happens to her will be experienced as unloving. Lack of love will permeate not only everything that actually happens but it also permeates everything that *might* happen—just so long as she continues to inhabit this unloving world. For in this world, unloving possibilities are the only possibilities there are. Even when we consider a high-functioning neurotic—an "ideal" analysand—we will eventually find a core fantasies that structures this person's life and, indeed, come to structure the transference. With a high-functioning neurotic the structuring fantasy can be astonishingly protean. On the one hand, the fantasy reaches out to interpret every experience in its light—so that every experience turns out to be somehow disappointing, or somehow a lack of love—and, on the other hand, the repetition is far from automatic or rigid. The core fantasy can be quite creative in taking in new experiences and metabolizing them in terms of old structures.

So, how can we approach such a person? There are, of course, many ways. But one way is to listen for breaks. For breaks are not choosy: they will disrupt any structure, even neurotic structures. This is one reason it helps to listen with the broadscale distinction between swerve and break in mind. As we listen for swerve—in associations, dreams, and interpretations of events—we can hear the person elaborating her core fantasies. To adapt Freud, we admit swerve "into the transference as a playground in which it is allowed to expand in almost complete freedom and in which it is expected to display to us everything in the way of pathogenic instincts that is hidden in the patient's mind."[17]

One of the things we are listening for is what, for the analysand, constitutes the structure of his possibilities. It is precisely at a moment of break that this structure gets disrupted. And in what I shall call a lucky break, there opens up an opportunity for new possibilities.

So let us go back for the last time to the Rat Man's jump. The Rat Man seems to have behaved in a typical fashion: he induces a break as a primitive defense and then tries to cover it over in swerve-like ways. In the aftermath of the jump, he starts to look for hidden emotions, tries to engage Freud in finding interpretations that would rationalize his behavior, and even humors Freud by associating to his jump. Here we see swerve trying to restore ordinary mental function in the aftermath of a break.

But now let us imagine a slightly different Rat Man. Suppose Freud had already done a fair amount of analytic work with the Rat Man in such a way that the Rat Man himself had come to understand, if only inchoately, that he had a tendency to disrupt himself. Let the jump from the couch be another break, provoked by rising anxiety. But in this jump, the Rat Man can, in his very jump, recognize something ego-alien in his activity. He is going through the motions (again), but they no longer strike him as really his. Instead, he can see for himself: here I go again!

This is the same break as before, but now it is being used in a completely different way by our imagined Rat Man. In both cases, the jump is a disruption of ordinary swerve-like mental functioning, but in this latter case, the imagined Rat Man is able to experience it as such. The original Rat Man had a break too, but he immediately absorbed it into his world of possibilities. It instantly became one more example of being afraid or angry. For the actual Rat Man, *all* his possibilities were fearful or anger-filled. But the imagined Rat Man, in his jump, can see—perhaps for the first time—that not everything need be like that. This is what it is to experience a possibility for new possibilities.

What emerges—and it is no exaggeration to say so—is a new form of experience that is itself the manifestation of a new form of life. Between a Rat Man who is still searching for his hidden emotion and a Rat Man who is able to acknowledge that, up until now, he has been using his truncated emotions in the service of evading emotional life, there is not merely a difference in belief or cognitive state—it is a difference in a way of life. The two imagined Rat Men inhabit different experiential worlds. The Rat Man who continues to look for hidden beliefs is still in the business of avoiding emotional life, in the name of discovering what it is. The imagined Rat Man—who can recognize that he has been using his emotionally tempestuous life strategically to disrupt the development of a more vibrant and attuned emotional life—at last is ready to open up to life itself.

The analytic attitude is, I think, above all, a peculiar form of commitment. To spell out the complexities of this commitment is beyond the scope of this essay. But it certainly involves a commitment to allowing emotional life to unfold (under the aegis of an analytic gaze). This in turn requires that one recognize that there are ways in which one can disrupt one's own emotional life and, thereby, one's own emotional development. In short, one needs some kind of recognition, however implicit, of the phenomenon of break. One needs to learn how to avoid invoking it as a primitive defense; one also needs to learn how to use it as an occasion for opening up possibilities for new possibilities. Only in this way can a new form of experience emerge.

CHAPTER TEN

# Eros and Development

**1.** If Hans Loewald will be remembered, it will not be because of a new theory he contributed, nor because of a scientific discovery, but because of the wisdom that pervades his writing. For that reason, I do not think he will ever be fashionable; but I suspect that through the generations he will continue to attract certain readers. To appreciate Loewald requires patience and playfulness (traits that come in handy as a psychoanalyst)—a willingness to live with the unfamiliar thought of another, to allow it to take root in one's own psyche, and to return to it after some time and see how it now looks, from the changed perspective that has become one's own. Consider this passage from "Psychoanalytic Theory and the Psychoanalytic Process":

> It also needs to be said that the love of truth is no less a passion because it desires truth rather than some less elevated end. In our field the love of truth cannot be isolated from the passion for truth to ourselves and truth in human relationships. In other fields, too, the scientist is filled with love for his object precisely in his most creative and "dispassionate" moments. Scientific detachment in its genuine form, far from excluding love, is based on it. In our work it can be truly said that in our best moments of dispassionate and objective analyzing we love our object, the patient, more than at any other time and are compassionate with his whole being.[1]
>
> In our field scientific spirit and care for the object certainly are not opposites; they flow from the same source. It is impossible to love the truth of psychic reality, to be moved by this love as Freud was in his

> lifework, and not to love and care for the object whose truth we want to discover. All great scientists, I believe, are moved by this passion. Our object, being what it is, is the other in ourselves and ourself in the others. To discover truth about the patient is always discovering it with him and for him as well as for ourselves and about ourselves. And it is discovering truth between each other, as the truth of human beings is revealed in their interrelatedness. While this may sound unfamiliar and perhaps too fanciful, it is only an elaboration, in nontechnical terms, of Freud's deepest thoughts about the transference neurosis and its significance in analysis.[2]

These words were written at a historical moment when psychoanalytic writers tended to split, moving either in the direction of an image of scientific detachment or in the direction of an image of subjective engagement with the analysand. The idea that detachment and engagement could be aspects of a single form of relating was strange indeed. And within the academy, professors influenced by Freud assumed a hermeneutics of suspicion. The idea that the love of truth should be accepted without the obligatory deconstruction, and that it should be acknowledged as "no less a passion because it desires truth rather than some less elevated end"—this was not an acceptable thought within the literary humanities at the end of the twentieth century. Loewald was writing gently but firmly against the grain of an age.

As long as there is an activity worthy of the name psychoanalysis, Loewald's words will challenge any serious practitioner. Of course, the terms of the debate will change over time. There may be conflicts between conceiving the interdependence versus the dependence, the co-construction versus the antecedent reality of subjects; there may be a sense that we no longer have to think of the drives at all, since we have "moved beyond" an archaic one-person psychology, and so on. Loewald will always be there, inviting us to hold in creative tension ideas that we are powerfully motivated to see as in exclusive opposition.

One needs to pay attention here not only to what Loewald is saying, but how he is deploying his words. Within the genre of a journal article, we tend to focus on content, the claims an author is making, and his argument for those claims. We may notice in passing that the author writes well; perhaps he has a poetic flair. The background assumption of professional and academic journals is that they exist in order to provide a forum for developing the state of knowledge in a given field. But what if the aim of an article is not simply to convey new facts to the reader, but also to facilitate his psychological development? It is generally accepted that the never-ending process of developing as a psychoanalyst requires not just keeping up with the latest psychodynamic theories and debates about technique; it also requires developing one's own capacity for imaginative engagement with the analysand, one's capacity for tolerating aggression in the transference, one's capacity to analyze countertransference rather than act on it, and so on. How might psychoanalytic writing help us with that? If all psychoanalytic writing can do is tell us what to do or what to think—even if what it says is correct—it is an impoverished form of communication. For even if we know what to think and what to do, we still need to be (or become) people who are capable of thinking what we ought to think and doing what we ought to do.

However greatly psychoanalysis has contributed to our theoretical understanding of the human mind, in its essence it is a contribution to practical knowledge: it aims to intervene in human life at certain junctures in order to help people live better lives. A psychoanalyst is someone who has not only theoretical understanding, but also practical ability. This practical ability requires more than theoretical understanding; it requires personal and practical skills that are themselves manifestations of psychological development on the part of the analyst. Psychoanalytic training—including insistence on a training analysis—is designed to help us in this developmental process. But might there also be ways of writing and reading that can help us beyond just giving us the *what?* When Loewald's writing finds a reader, his words may influence the reader's beliefs, but they also spur the reader to forms of psychic activity. So, for example, when Loewald says, "In our best moments of dispassionate and objective analyzing we love our object, the patient, more than at any other time and are compassionate with his whole being," the point is not simply to describe our best moments. The air of paradox disrupts the familiar order. We can see right away that we are not simply being called to perform a difficult but well-understood task (say, a triple Salchow). Part of the difficulty involves coming to see love, objectivity, and detachment in extraordinary ways. There is no straightforward recipe for doing this. We come to understand better what the words mean as, over time, we try to instantiate them in our analytic lives. Coming to understand these concepts, then, is not just a theoretical matter; it is a life-task. Therein lies the timelessness of Loewald's writing: if the words enjoin readers at all, they will continue to engage us at different stages in our own development.

It is worth saying a word about being enjoined as a reader. If Loewald's writing is going to make a difference, a reader must, I suspect, have an inchoate sense of recognition—as though one somehow already understands the claims one does not yet understand. This enigmatic sense of recognition is, I think, a manifestation of positive transference. It can be an occasion for coming to experience from the inside the nature of the binding that it is Loewald's life-work to describe.

**2.** Loewald is a hedgehog, not a fox. Although he takes up many aspects of the psychoanalytic experience, it seems to me that he is always trying to answer a single question: what would it be to take seriously the thought that within the human realm love is a developmental force? Loewald is in the tradition that takes the human psyche itself to be a psychological achievement; and he wants to comprehend the place of love in that developmental process. In this review essay, I want to take up various aspects of Loewald's thought—of the drives, the analytic relationship, the mother–infant dyad, the transference neurosis, and, finally, the experience of time—and show how he always brings it back to the same question, the place of love as a developmental force. Loewald is in a tradition of writers that includes Tolstoy and Proust: although there are many remarkable psychological insights, when you try to count their thoughts, you never really get past number one.

Loewald's reading of Freud is an uncanny mix of loyalty and subversion. In Freud's evolving theory of the drives, the attention-getting moment was his introduction of the death-drive in *Beyond the Pleasure Principle*.[3] For Loewald, looking behind the headlines, the death drive was "nothing new."[4] It was just a reconceptualization of the old constancy principle—the tendency toward the diminution of tension—that had been part of Freud's thinking from the beginning. "What is new," Loewald tells us, "and does not seem to fit with the inertial principle is the concept of Eros, the life or love instinct."[5] Freud introduced Eros as a fitting counterpart to the metaphysically loaded death drive, but he had little to say about it. The aim of Eros, Freud tells us, "is to establish ever greater unities and to preserve them thus—in short, to bind together."[6] Freud does not tell us how Eros works and, as Loewald says, how to fit this drive into his overall theory of the drives remained for him an "insoluble problem." So, for Freud, Eros served as an algebraic marker, an *X* to be filled in by whatever it is that serves as an adequate counterpart to the death drive. This is the marker Loewald takes up—the unfinished-but-required within Freud's thought. After all, psychoanalysis cannot rest content with an account of psychopathology, no matter how acute. It must also answer the question: if one places an analysand in a room with a well-trained analyst, how is it that over time the analysand gets better? There seems to be a force field in the analytic space, a dynamic tension between analyst and analysand that can occasion a developmental process. Loewald wants to take seriously the idea of Eros or the life-drive to illuminate that process.

Part of what makes Loewald's writing arresting is that he is a self-conscious participant in the process he is trying to describe. If Eros is structuring the analytic situation, then Loewald cannot be looking on it from the outside. Loewald is, of course, a practicing analyst—a member of a number of analyst–analysand dyads; and if the therapeutic action is itself a manifestation of Eros, a movement toward differentiated unity, he is a part of that binding process. So when he says that "scientific detachment in its genuine form, far from excluding love, is based on it," he must be requiring us to rethink what we could properly mean by scientific detachment. It cannot mean what we ordinarily take it to mean: namely, observing a process from a distinct and independent perspective. The psychoanalytic process is clearly one in which two people actively interact with each other, each in the process (among other things) of trying to understand each other and themselves. Whatever Loewald means by detachment, it must be compatible with that. Detachment, for him, is a form of attachment: it is the respect one person pays another when he genuinely wants to understand him. This is of course a reciprocal, layered relationship.

At the same time, Loewald is also a psychoanalytic writer, and thus he is also inevitably entangled in a relationship with his readers. Loewald is reaching out to psychoanalytic readers, inviting us to join in the shared activity of deepening our psychoanalytic self-understanding. We are invited to learn about Eros by participating in certain kinds of erotic activity: the binding activity of forming and maintaining a community of psychoanalytic thinkers and practitioners; the binding activity of jointly developing psychoanalytic theory to new levels of complexity. We do so by immersing ourselves in psychoanalytic thinking and by doing our best to communicate with each other. This is a different style of persuasion than the familiar rhetorical form of arguing for a conclusion or presenting results. It is more like an invitation:

to consult the nature of one's own experience in the light of a certain way of seeing things. Loewald's thinking has the form of an interpretation.

**3.** In the second half of the twentieth century, a number of psychoanalytic writers—for example, Winnicott and Mahler—argued that we should comprehend infant psychological development in terms of an infant–mother dyad.[7] In Winnicott's famous phrase, "There is no such thing as a baby." Loewald is remarkable for taking this thought and weaving it into the deepest thinking in the Western tradition about the relation of subject to world.[8] Again, his tactic is to focus on an undigested morsel in Freud's thought. In general, Freud characterizes reality as hostile, impinging upon an ego besieged by internal and external demands. This is the image of ego as "frontier creature." However, there is another image that Freud briefly sketches in the first section of *Civilization and Its Discontents:* from the imagined perspective of the newborn.[9] The infant does not yet distinguish itself as ego from the world that it inhabits. There is, rather, a field of experience in which an emerging ego starts to differentiate itself from a breast that is not always available to it. It is in this way that an object gets constituted for an emerging subject. As Loewald puts it in "Ego and Reality":

> This state of affairs can be expressed either by saying that "the ego detaches itself from the external world" or, more correctly: the ego detaches from itself an outer world. Originally the ego contains everything. Our adult ego feeling, Freud says, is only a shrunken vestige of an all-embracing feeling of intimate connection, or we might say, unity with the environment.[10]

The important point, I think, is not whether Freud and Loewald are right about the details of infantile experience; perhaps infantile experience is more organized than this description suggests. The important point is structural: that ego is essentially in relation to a world it inhabits, and that the ego's level of development is understood in terms of its own ability to comprehend the complexity of that relationship.

> The psychological constitution of the ego and outer world go hand in hand. Nothing can be an object, something that stands against something

> else, as long as everything is contained in the unitary feeling of the primary, unlimited narcissism of the newborn, where mouth and mother's breast are still one and the same. On the other hand, we cannot, in the strict sense, speak of an ego, a mediator between id and an external world, where there is as yet nothing to mediate.[11]

The world of objects is thus the experiential correlate of the psychological constitution of the ego. For the ego to experience a world of objects, it must experience itself as a subject set among objects. But to experience itself as a subject is constitutive of the ego's own process of development. For Loewald, this is a paradigm of erotic activity: the development out of a tense force field of ever more complex psychological organization. To start with the infant–mother dyad:

> The less mother and child are one, the more they become separate entities, the more there will be a dynamic interplay of forces between these two "systems." As the mother becomes outside, and hand in hand with this, the child an inside, there arises a tension system between the two. Expressed in different terms, libidinal forces arise between infant and mother. As infant (mouth) and mother (breast) are not identical, or better, not one whole, any longer, a libidinal flow between infant and mother originates, in an urge towards re-establishing the original unity.[12]

This is an example of how Loewald takes a thought from Freud and uses it in his own unflashy way to turn Freud on his head. Instead of a reality that is hostile, impinging, and threatening, reality becomes a developmental task: that from which ego must differentiate itself in order to stay in touch with it:

> What the ego defends itself, or the psychic apparatus, against is not reality but the loss of reality, that is, the loss of an integration with the world such as it exists in the libidinal relation with the mother.[13]

**4.** For Loewald, the psychoanalytic relationship is a recreation at a higher level of the complexity of the infant–mother field. That is, it is a resumption of the analysand's erotic connection to the world. Loewald conceives this in terms of shifting frameworks of possibility. Here the influence of Heidegger, with whom Loewald studied as a young man, is most evident. The world, for Heidegger, is not to be understood in terms of how it actually is, nor in terms of its entire history, but rather in terms of all its possibilities.[14] To take a wildly simple example, part of what it is for an everyday object, say a particular book, to be the book that it is is for it to be impossible for it to change instantaneously into a used piece of bubblegum. The book being the book that it is is constituted not just by the actual arrangement of its pages, its binding, and so on, but by all the things it might and cannot become. Now when it comes to a human being, as opposed to a simple artifact like a book, its possibilities are constituted in part by its own sense of its possibilities. Insofar as a person's sense of his own possibilities is constrained, his life possibilities are thereby constrained. And insofar as one's possibilities are constrained, one is a more constrained person. The aim of psychoanalysis, for Loewald, is to create an environment, a force field, that facilitates a person's ability genuinely to change his sense of possibilities—and thereby change his possibilities, and thereby change himself.

This is the key to Loewald's claim that the analytic process facilitates the new discovery of objects, not the discovery of new objects:

> The essence of such a new object-relationship is the opportunity they offer for rediscovery of the early paths of the development of object-relations, leading to a new way of relating to objects as well as of being and relating to oneself. This new discovery of oneself and of objects, this reorganization of ego and object, is made possible by the encounter with a "new object" that has to possess certain qualifications in order to promote the process. Such a new object-relationship for which the analyst holds himself available to the patient and to which the patient has to hold on throughout the analysis is one meaning of the term positive transference.[15]

What is opening up here is a possibility for new possibilities. In neurotic enactments, there is, as Freud showed, a need to repeat painful emotional experiences—sometimes a need to confirm them, sometimes a wish to undo them. But there is also, Loewald argues, "a wish for re-doing the past—not exclusively a wish to do away with what happened to the patient by dint of unfeeling parents or evil fates, but also a wish to experience, to deal with whatever happened in a different way."[16] This wish is often defeated, and what then ensues is neurotic repetition. But for Loewald—and this is one significant meaning of Eros as life-drive—there is also a possibility of a restorative recreation. This is a possibility that comes to life in the analytic process.

It is an earthy, fecund, bloody birthing process. It emerges from a two-way struggle in which, on the one hand, the analysand regressively insists on treating this new possibility as an old relationship. This is transference as resistance that not only brings old ways of relating to light but also succeeds in engaging the analysand's deeper, passionate motivational currents. However obstinate this emotional connection, however difficult for analysand and analyst to endure, it is this drawing-out of the analysand's elemental life-forces that opens up the possibility for profound psychic transformation. On the other hand, by repeatedly and steadfastly interpreting transference distortions, the analyst opens up for the analysand the possibility of new forms of relating to the analyst, and thus to people in his environment.

It is here that Loewald takes an image from Freud that has never felt right to me. Referring to this second aspect of the analytic process, he speaks of "chiseling away" the transference distortions, "or, as Freud beautifully put it, using an expression of Leonardo da Vinci, *per via di levare* as in sculpturing, not *via di porre* as in painting. In sculpturing, the figure to be created comes into being by taking away from the material; in painting, by adding something to the canvas."[17] But, as I understand it, a great sculptor has a remarkable idea in mind of where he is going, of how the stone will yield to his chisel and to his mind. This image seems all wrong to me as an image of the psychoanalytic process. Loewald sees that there is a challenge here, but he thinks he can put it to good psychoanalytic use. "As in sculpture," he tells us, "we must have, if only in rudiments, an image of that which needs to be brought into its own."[18] This is an image the patient provides the analyst, through the transference distortions, "an image that the analyst has to focus in his mind, thus holding it in safe-keeping for the patient to whom it is mainly lost."[19] I find myself unpersuaded, and vaguely troubled, by this image. In my own analytic work, as I work with and interpret transference, I have a sense of possibilities opening up for the analysand as well as for the analytic relationship. It is like the curtain rising on a rich world of possibilities that had previously been shrouded; or like a horizon expanding, opening up new vistas, new ways to live. These are the metaphors that are vibrant for me. And the experience of the world opening up is something I experience with the analysand as we jointly do our analytic work. I never feel like I am chiseling away; nor do I feel that I am holding an image of the analysand's core for safekeeping. And I am suspicious of conceiving of psychoanalytic activity in these terms. How does the analyst avoid imposing on the analysand an image that he takes himself to be discovering or protecting? Loewald says, "If the analyst keeps his central focus on the emerging core he avoids moulding the patient in the analyst's own image or imposing on the patient his own concept of what the patient should become."[20] This, he thinks, requires the objectivity and love, the respect for the individual that he has all along insisted is the hallmark of psychoanalysis. My worry is that these words can be used too easily to justify bad psychoanalytic technique.

In disagreeing with Loewald in this way, I take myself to be agreeing with him in another way. I had the privilege of being in a weekly conversation with him that spanned six years. A few days before he died, he expressed the hope that there would never be Loewaldians. I do not think that he was merely expressing a personal preference. From Loewald's point of view, as I understand him, there could not be a Loewaldian, for there was no core belief or doctrine that he associated peculiarly with himself. He took himself to be explicating Freud and psychoanalysis, helping the reader grasp the vitality and depth of the thought and the scope of the activity. Thus, for him, it would be a misfire of his own life's work to be taken to be founding a new school of thought. For him, the task was to bring to light, and maintain the vibrancy, of a way of approaching human being that we have only begun to metabolize. And so, from Loewald's perspective, if a group of people started to think of themselves as Loewaldians, they would by that very act show that they were not. This does not mean it is impossible to follow in Loewald's footsteps, but that requires an unusual understanding of what it is to be a follower. It cannot be a matter of accepting this or that belief about the nature of the psychoanalytic process. It cannot be a matter of doctrine, the *what* of psychoanalysis. It must rather be the *how:* someone becomes a follower of Loewald if, inspired by reading his work, he or she takes on the responsibility of a critical, imaginative engagement with psychoanalysis. In this way, a "Loewaldian" could well be someone who strongly disagreed with Loewald on key points. This is the sense in which Loewald was a Freudian.

**5.** For Loewald, the concept of transference neurosis defines "the nature, scope and point of impact of psychoanalysis as a mental therapy."[21] On the one hand, the concept is, he thinks, an "ideal construct," and thus it "always oversimplifies." But it is nevertheless a remarkable organizing principle for what would otherwise be a chaotic constellation of events. Loewald sticks close to Freud's (1914) account in "Remembering, Repeating and Working-Through"; what is distinctive is Loewald's attempt to show how that account can be integrated into Freud's own theory of Eros. The transference neurosis is, for Loewald, "the revival of the infantile neurosis in the analytic situation"; but following Freud, it should be conceived as an "intermediate region between (old) illness and real life," "an artificial illness which is at every point accessible to our intervention."[22] The analyst, Loewald thinks, promotes neither the transference nor the defenses against it, but rather understandings of both. The so-called new transference-meaning is neither new creation nor is it discovery of hidden reality. It is recreation of old meanings taken up into new self-conscious ways of going on:

> The transference neurosis, in this sense, is the patient's love life—the source and crux of his psychic development—as relived in relation to a potentially new love object, the analyst, who renounces libidinal–aggressive involvement for the sake of understanding and achieving higher psychic organization. From the point of view of the analyst, this means neither indifference nor absence of love–hate, but persistent renunciation of involvement, a constant activity of uninvolving which tends to impel the patient to understand himself in his involvement instead of concentrating exclusively, albeit unconsciously, on the object. The resolution of the transference neurosis consists in achieving such higher psychic organization which gradually replaces the transference illness, and by virtue of which object involvement on a more mature level becomes possible.[23]

We can see the binding to higher levels of organization at several levels. Firstly, it is not that the old patterns—the repetitions—are completely undone; they are tied to new forms of understanding and new possibilities for going on. Secondly, intrapsychically, the old transferences of unconscious wishes onto familiar conscious fantasies are not completely undone; rather, they are linked to new associations, opening up new tributaries of imaginative life. Finally, in this new and emerging relation to the analyst, it is not that old (infantile) forms of relating to objects are dissolved, but they do become ever more integrated with these new possibilities for relating. That is why Loewald insists that the relation to the analyst is not the discovery of a new object but a new discovery of objects. The old is not abolished; it is erotically bound.

In discussing the indestructibility of unconscious currents in a person's psychic life, Loewald refers to Freud's allusion to Homer's *Odyssey:* they are like "ghosts which awoke to new life as soon as they tasted blood"—that is, as soon as they can make a link to some aspect of conscious life.[24] Here again there is an attempt at binding, but one that, in neurosis, gets stuck in conflicted, inhibited, repetitive patterns. But, for Loewald, this blood can be put to life-enhancing uses:

> The transference neurosis, in the technical sense of the establishment and resolution of it in the analytic process, is due to the blood of recognition, which the patient's unconscious is given to taste so that the old ghosts may reawaken to life. Those who know ghosts tell us that they long to be released from their ghost life and led to rest as ancestors. As ancestors they live forth in the present generation, while as ghosts they are compelled to haunt the present generation with their shadow life. Transference is pathological insofar as the unconscious is a crowd of ghosts, and this is the beginning of the transference neurosis in analysis: ghosts of the unconscious, imprisoned by defenses but haunting the patient in the dark of his defenses and symptoms, are allowed to taste blood, are let loose. In the daylight of analysis the ghosts of the unconscious are laid and led to rest as ancestors whose power is taken over and transformed into the newer intensity of present life, of the secondary process and contemporary objects.[25]

This is an example of Loewald's ability to take an image of haunting and turn it into a haunting image. I have found myself going back to this image countless times in my working life as an analyst. It captures the point Loewald makes throughout his work: in analysis, we do not undo our ties to the past; we redo them. There is a process by which ghosts are exhumed from the sludge of repressed memory and given a proper burial—one that ironically gives them new forms of life. Our ghosts are laid to rest as ancestors. For those of us who have worked through an analysis, it is a truth we can feel corporally, in our gut. Blood, tasting blood, the desire to taste blood: it is fitting to go back to Homer for another taste of how precious, powerful, and vulnerable the drive for life is. And it is fitting to return to Freud to see how we regularly inhibit, disrupt, and attack this drive. But if we turn our therapeutic attention onto those inhibitions and disruptions, Loewald shows us how they can be seen (and used) as developmental moments. Eros, or the life-drive, can do some of its best work when the developmental process is interrupted. From Loewald's perspective, this is the deeper meaning of Freud's famous claim that "transference, which seems ordained to be the greatest obstacle to psychoanalysis, becomes its most powerful ally."[26]

**6.** Freud famously said that the unconscious is timeless.[27] By that he referred to the enduring structures of infantile fantasy that repeatedly insist on some kind of expression, as though oblivious to the passage of historical time in the life of the person whose fantasy it is. Loewald wants to link this unconscious timelessness to a conscious experience of timelessness.[28] He is making a point about human temporality that, I have come to think, is important to the psychoanalytic experience. We are familiar with Freud's thought that in analysis the analysand's unconscious repetitions are replaced by remembering.[29] But it is easy to have a flat conception of what this means: that repetitive enactments of unconscious fantasy are replaced by historical consciousness, the ability consciously to remember certain acts as having occurred in the past. For Loewald, by contrast, remembering is an unusual blend of different forms of temporal experience. The closer a conscious experience is to the primary-process activity that feeds it, the more it is experienced as timeless. He draws a link to the *nunc stans,* the abiding now described by philosophers and theologians:

> The instant that knows no temporal articulation, where distinctions between now, earlier and later have fallen away or not arisen. All of us know, I believe, poignant moments that have this timeless quality; unique, matchless, complete in themselves and somehow containing all there is in an experience. As experience augments and grows in an individual's life course, these instants in time but not of time contain more and more meaning which is poured into the *nunc stans* in such a way that temporal and other articulating differentiations are dissolved or become condensed into oneness.[30]

Loewald alludes to religious experience, but he does not develop the thought, so I think we should concentrate on the psychoanalytic situation. His point is that, if we focus on the type of remembering that can make a therapeutic difference, we find that it contains within itself its own peculiar kernel of repeating. He begins with emotion-laden memories:

> A person gets lost, as we say, in memories of his or her past life with someone beloved who died, a parent, friend, husband, wife, a child. Often such memories are triggered by a current experience. The more we let ourselves be affected by them, the less we simply recall them in an actuarial fashion as events that took place at one time—and the more we relive them in a now that is not distinguished as present from past. . . . In poignant remembering, in a remembering that moves us, the difference between recollecting and repeating diminishes.[31]

In therapeutic moments of remembering, Loewald thinks, two very different forms of temporal experience are bound together. There is the conscious memory of the familiar sort, which purportedly supplants the need to act out in repetition. But in addition to the temporality of memory that places the event in the past, there is an experience of the timelessness of the memory—that all the while maintains a link to the ordinary temporality of historical consciousness.

One manifestation of a therapeutic process would then be that a person moves along a developmental path: from having his unconscious act as though it were timeless at one end to informing conscious acts in such a way that they are experienced as timeless at the other. This is a movement from repeating (or acting out) without remembering to remembering without the need to act out (but nevertheless containing within itself a nugget of repeating). The repetition shows up not in acting out, but in the temporal mode of experience. This, I believe, is a profound insight that needs further work. But, for Loewald, this must be yet another aspect of erotic binding, for even as one experiences a moment as timeless, one does not lose track that this moment is occurring in time. In the moment, two different forms of temporal experience are bound together.

In my analytic work, I am less concerned with memory per se and more focused on the structure and life of unconscious fantasy. But I think Loewald's point about temporality holds here as well. In regular analytic work, one can come to see the dynamics of unconscious fantasy, both as it structures a person's life and as it enters the transference. One can be analyzing the fantasy in the here and now of the analytic situation. But then there are extraordinary moments in which the fantasy seems to be right there in the speech of the analysand.[32] To take an example from a recent hour, an analysand was talking about lifelong difficulties she has had in asking people for things she wants, how she anticipates their refusal as a way of inhibiting herself from making the request in the first place. She was associating this to the difficulty she had in asking me whether I could reschedule an analytic hour. The problem was alive in the session, she was working her way toward recognizing the aggression she deployed in inhibiting herself, and then she said, "The rage I anticipate, the rage if you say no . . . no one has even said no. It feels like an eternal obstacle, a weight on my throat, keeping me from speaking." There is, of course, much to be said about this fantasy—in particular, its corporeal nature and active presence in the session. But I am concerned now with an aspect of the fantasy that is often overlooked: its timeless temporality. In that moment, the analysand was not only describing the obstacle as eternal, but she was experiencing the eternality of the obstacle. The experience of a weight on her throat keeping her from speaking may occur again and again in the historical unfolding of her life—and with analytic reflection, she may come to see the repetition. This is what it is to recognize the timelessness of the unconscious. But in this moment, she was in addition experiencing the timelessness of the obstacle.

There are moments in analysis when an analysand is not simply describing a fantasy, or associating to it, or acting it (out or in), but in which the fantasy is alive in her words. In such a moment, the fantasy is giving a verbal expression of itself. In these moments, there is a shift in the temporality of conscious experience. It is not that the analysand loses all sense of historical time; but there is a moment of timelessness that enters the analysand's historical time and takes up its own full, timeless moment. One aspect of linking unconscious fantasy to the self-conscious life of a person who can come to both understand and live with his fantasies is the binding together of different forms of temporal experience. The analysand is not simply alternating between different temporal modes of experience: he is somehow able to experience the timelessness of the moment while not losing track that he also persists through ordinary historical time. It is this astonishing integration of different forms of temporal experience that Loewald's writing does so much illuminate.

**7.** Though there is an occasional mention, there is no sustained discussion in the work of Hans Loewald of hatred, aggression, envy, or human destructiveness. One can only speculate why this might be. If Loewald were trying to give a comprehensive account of the psychoanalytic understanding of human being, this would be a grievous lapse. But, as I hope I have shown, this is not a good way to read him. Rather, we should see Loewald as struck by the beauty of an ur-observation: that when human beings are located in a field of psychological complexity, there is a tendency for them to grow in complexity themselves. The differential in complexity thus serves as the occasion for dynamism. Psychological growth is regularly blocked, inhibited, and sometimes attacked; but the tendency toward it is there. Loewald's work is an attempt to comprehend—and stand witness to—this tendency as it shows up within the psychoanalytic field.

CHAPTER ELEVEN

# Mourning and Moral Psychology

---

**1.** The ancient Greek philosophers—Socrates, Plato, and Aristotle—believed that psychology should not only explain human life but should vindicate it. For them, human excellence (*aretê*) was a real possibility, and psychology ought to be *for* it. The excellent life, they thought, was a happy life, but such a life could never be understood merely in terms of an individual's sense of satisfaction. The happy life intrinsically involved dignity and worth—and people can make mistakes about that. One aim of psychology would be to disabuse us of the misconceptions we might fall into about what happiness is, and then to promote a correct conception. Psychology would gain its worth and dignity via promoting something worthy and dignified: the happy, excellent human life. The philosophers also believed that this would help us understand, as it helped legitimate, good ways of living with others—that is, ethical life.

This outlook lends vibrancy to the somewhat tired phrase "moral psychology." Rather than being an uncritical genus-term for emotions—guilt, shame, pride, humiliation—that are used to hold us in line, *moral psychology* becomes the name of a commitment to a rigorous and truthful account of the psyche that is itself trying to promote what it finds to be good about human being. Such an inquiry would be at once objective and subjective: objective in gathering the available evidence, subjective in the sense of helping shape the psyche of the subject.[1]

The promise and danger of such an approach are, not surprisingly, related. Promise flows from the open-endedness in our understanding of what moral psychology could be. We do not know ahead of time what kind of account of the human will illuminate what makes human being valuable. The danger is that the purported vindication will be illusory. The theory may not be sufficiently robust, and a desired conclusion is reached too quickly. This is the moment when a moral psychology collapses into moralizing psychology. And it opens the possibility of a less innocent failure: a motivated illusion of excellence and happiness that serves ideological purposes.

One might think that these problems are not our problems. For this account of moral psychology is distant from what goes on in contemporary academic departments of psychology. Still, there is an ethical and cultural question: To what extent should we treat this past as *our* past? And what would it be to do so?

**2.** In outlining the conditions of an adequate moral psychology, Bernard Williams wrote:

> A non-moralized, or less moralized, psychology uses the categories of meaning, reasons and value, but leaves it open, or even problematical, in what way moral reasons and ethical values fit with other motives and desires, how far they express those other motives, and how far they are in conflict with them. Thucydides and (I believe) the tragedians, among the ancient writers had such a psychology; *and so in the modern world, did Freud.*[2]

Freud did not set out to construct a moral psychology, he had no set of ethical virtues he was trying to vindicate; thus the danger of a short circuit into moralizing is diminished. He took ordinary people as they were, and his aim was to relieve their suffering as well as reflect on what the suffering meant. He did have an overarching value that permeated his work—truthfulness, facing up to reality—but, in terms of the possibility of a moral psychology, this turned out to be an unexpected benefit. The practical manifestation of truthfulness in the minute-by-minute unfolding of the psychoanalytic situation was Freud's *"fundamental rule"*: that analysands should try as best they can to speak whatever comes into their mind without inhibition or censorship. It is astonishing what wealth of psychological insight has flowed from people trying (*and failing*) to follow such a simple rule.

It might at first seem odd to invoke Freud in the project of a moral psychology, since he is regularly brought in to debunk the Platonic-Aristotelian approach. Psychoanalysis is invoked to show that Aristotle's distinction between virtue and mere continence is illusory. There are, it is said, so many conflicting voices within a person's psyche—many of them unconscious—that the idea that they could all be "speaking with the same voice" in incredible. On this reading, we ought to abandon false images of psychic unity and think instead about how to get along without them. Moreover, on a familiar reading of Freud's *Civilization and Its Discontents,* the world is not a place that is conducive to human happiness.[3] And it is not the aim of civilization to facilitate it. Civilization may protect us against some of nature's threats, but its aim is to keep us in line. It pressures us to be "productive members of society," with no concern for the psychic costs to the individual. Civilization, on this outlook, is at the expense of our happiness.

This reception of Freud has become boilerplate; one of the joys of Loewald's writings is that he offers a different choice of inheritance. His reading of Freud opens the possibility of a fresh engagement with a broadly Aristotelian approach to moral psychology.

**3.** In "Mourning and Melancholia," Freud identified mourning as melancholia's uncanny twin. His concern was to illuminate melancholia, whose pathological workings were largely hidden from view. The strategy he hit upon was to do so by comparing it with ordinary, nonpathological mourning. "In mourning it is the world which has become poor and empty; in melancholia it is the ego itself."[4] This was Freud's route into the psychological structure of melancholia: "one part of the ego sets itself over against the other, judges it critically and, as it were, takes it as its object."[5] Freud was thus launched in his study of the superego, and of structural conflict inside the psyche.

Loewald reverses the locus of concern.[6] If melancholia is the pathological condition of psychic discord, mourning at least offers the occasion for psychic integration and development. He introduces the idea of *degrees of internalization,* "suggesting that the introjects constituting the superego are more on the periphery of the ego system but are capable of mobility within the system and may thus merge into the ego proper and lose their superego character."[7] He gives a simple example of "a son who increasingly becomes like a father after the father's death. It is as though only then can he appropriate into his ego core given elements of his father's character."[8] Before the father's actual death, the father-figure functioned at a critical distance. And there was fluidity in whether the father was located in social space—in the person of the father—or whether he became an internal figure, instigating "self-criticism," doubt, and guilt. The death of the father provided an occasion through mourning for psychic consolidation. The voice of the father is no longer set over against the ego but is integrated into the maturing character of the son. Though work needs to be done to fill out the picture, it presents the possibility of a Freudian inheritance focused on psychic integration. The fact that this possibility emerges from an unanticipated location—the details of mourning—raises the hope that we might be on the track of a robust moral psychology.

In effect, Loewald extends the concept of mourning to cover the major moments of psychological development. The human psyche, he stresses, is itself a psychological achievement, and its development consists in a series of losses and reformations: "The relinquishment of external objects and their internalization involves a process of separation, of loss and restitution in many ways similar to mourning."[9] The phrase "in many ways similar to" may suggest to a reader that Loewald is offering a useful analogy or metaphor. I do not think that is correct. In a metaphor, "a name or descriptive word or phrase is transferred to an object or action *different from, but analogous to,* that to which it is literally applicable."[10] But, as I understand him, Loewald is claiming that if we look at the psychodynamics of human development, we will see similarities to the paradigm so powerful as to justify us in thinking that we are looking at genuine cases of mourning—though ones we have hitherto not recognized as such.

Loewald is offering an interpretation. We are invited to consider our experience (which includes our experience of others) under the concept *mourning.* Since Loewald is writing for analysts, the invitation is issued in the first instance to those who have already had their own analysis and have experience analyzing others. For those who are addressed, the question then becomes: how compelling is it to see the transitional moments in human psychic development under the concept *mourning?*

So, what legitimates the thought that transition through a developmental stage should be thought of in terms of mourning? First, if we try to capture the experience of the developing subject, Loewald thinks that we must recognize that "the psychological constitution of the ego and outer world go hand in hand."[11] This means that psychological development (partially) consists in the ego giving up earlier forms of relating to objects. Care is needed in the vocabulary we choose to describe the situation. We inevitably use terms like *ego* or *self* for forms of organization that are less differentiated than the mature version. And since we are concerned with "objects" as they exist for a subject, the same holds true for objects. "It is important to recognize," Loewald says, "that when we speak of object and ego at this [early] stage of development, these terms characterize the most primitive beginnings of the later structures thus designated."[12] To take an example from early development, as the infant begins to experience the mother's breast as something distinct, something that can be absent even when need arises, the infant needs to learn to tolerate not only the disappointment, frustration, and rage that such recognition can provoke. She also needs to tolerate the *loss of this form of experiencing "objects."* There is a loss of the "primary-narcissistic breast" that had, until this developmental moment, been experienced as an appendage of the infantile ego. At every stage of development, Loewald thinks, there is a loss of objects—in the sense of the loss of a form of experiencing objects—that needs somehow to be addressed.

Second, loss of objects is compensated by an almost magical restitution. In straightforward cases of mourning the death of a loved one, there are conscious and rational modes of internalization: consolidating memories and emotions that have circulated around this person. But, following Freud, Loewald claims that there are also unconscious processes that inform these paradigm cases of mourning, and they shape psychic development. Through fantasies of introjection and identification, the "lost object" is taken into the psyche, where it takes up a new intrapsychic life. This is the irony of human development: the "acceptance of loss" in the external world is met with a corresponding recreation of the object in the internal world. This refiguration allows for more-complex relations with an emerging set of objects. Ironically, the internalization of an old form of relating to objects is the basis of a new form.

Finally, there is an internal link between developmental moments of mourning and mourning as that concept is generally understood. The former prepares us for the latter, and the latter is a repetition and recreation of the former. It is not simply that the different cases of mourning share certain marks and features. When the father actually dies, and in mourning the son becomes more like him, this is a repetition and recreation of earlier internalizations at different developmental phases. No wonder the son has been able to mourn in this way: he has already had a lot of practice. It is mourning that prepares us to mourn.

**4.** Mourning is one way we recreate our past by making it present—sometimes as memory, sometimes as psychic structure. Following Freud, Loewald gives the name *internalization* for the family of "processes of transformation by which relationships and interactions between the individual psychic apparatus and its environment are changed into inner relationships and interactions within the psychic apparatus."[13] The paradigm is the experience of eating. In eating, food is lost to us (as food) but takes up a different life inside us (perhaps as nourishment, as feelings of satiation, or as pains and bad feelings). From a psychoanalytic point of view, the infantile mind is constructed by that mind constructing an image of itself: feeding at the breast and taking in the milk that now exists inside the psyche-soma. This is an important way in which representations of inside and outside are formed; and we do not have anything like a human mind without its capacity to represent itself in terms of what is inside it and what is outside.

But psychic digestion differs from ordinary digestion. Consider Aristotle's nutritive soul: when we eat healthy food, the nutritive soul goes to work—and what we eat *becomes us*. The remainder is eliminated from us as waste. But what we eat psychically speaking becomes us *with remainder*. The introjected figure will be transformed to some extent by the digestive processes of fantasy, but the figure remains now inside us—sometimes to haunt us, sometimes to comfort us, sometimes to allow us the poetic experience of relating to an ancestor.[14] One of psychoanalysis' deepest insights is that when we take in any teaching, the teacher comes along with it. And he or she tends to remain with us, *personalizing* what we have learned. This means that our present selves are constituted not merely by memories of the past, but by *memorializations*.

**5.** Now if *mourning* is a concept that characterizes psychic development as well as the death of a loved one, one ought to expect the instances to be linked by family resemblance.[15] We cannot thus assume that a characteristic of mourning a death must be present in, say, a child's mourning in the Oedipal phase. However, the paradigm case might give us clues by which we notice intimations in other cases that might otherwise have eluded us.

Heidegger famously introduced the term *being-towards-death* to describe a manner of living: namely, how *Dasein* comports itself to the possibility of the impossibility of it having any more possibilities. I do not here want to get into Heidegger exegesis. But in terms of our concern with mourning and its place in moral psychology, a debate has arisen about the meaning of *Dasein* that deserves our attention. On the familiar interpretation, Dasein is the being for whom the question of its being is a mode of its being. "This entity which each of us is himself and which includes inquiring as one of its possibilities of its being we shall denote by the term *'Dasein.'*"[16] Usually, Dasein is understood in terms of an individual human being, possessed of the capacities for inquiry and commitment. And of course, while being-towards-death pervades human life, our self-conscious thinking about death—our own as well as our loved ones'—does tend to be pronounced at times of death and mourning. And this is one manner of being-towards-death. But there is another notion of being-towards-death that flows from an alternative understanding of Dasein. In *Dasein Disclosed,* John Haugeland argues that by *Dasein* one should understand "a living way of life" (that contains within itself an understanding of its being).[17] An individual human being is at best an *instance* or *case* of Dasein—who in authenticity may stand witness to the vibrancy or the morbidity of that way of life. The death of Dasein is then the breakdown in the intelligibility of the concepts internal to that way of life. While an investigator may theoretically grasp some aspects of that way of life, it has become unintelligible how one might realize those concepts in the living of a life. A culture breaks down via a breakdown in its own practical understanding of how to live. Authentic being-towards-death, on Haugeland's account, consists in an individual's taking responsibility for the death of a way of life. This comportment may be in place even when the form of life is vibrant. It is a responsibility one might bear, while never being called upon to exercise it.

So, now we have two distinct senses of being-towards-death, and we can see that it is precisely at the grave where these two meanings converge. One of the tasks of culture and religion is to provide—through rituals, myths, customs, and concepts—a structure of meanings that will help mourners through their grief and confusion.[18] Part of what it is to be a mourner, I suspect, is to recognize, either explicitly or implicitly, that one is at the grief-stricken limits of one's understanding. We have not just lost a loved one—we are threatened with being *at a loss:* about what to do, what to feel, what to think. We need help; and we need help with meaning. The customs and narratives of culture and religion are meant to meet that threat and provide a special kind of solace—one that provides meaning for what might otherwise be incomprehensible catastrophe.

We live in an historical period—summed up under the slogan "the death of God"—in which the possibility has become readily available for an individual to judge that a culture's structures of meanings do not work for him. I remember my father telling me, after his mother's death, that he no longer believed in God. I now think what he was getting at was not a loss of belief per se, but rather a breakdown in intelligibility. He knew how to go through the established motions of mourning, but the gestures were drained of significance for him. And yet, the fact that the rituals had gone dead did matter to him, and he felt the need to stand witness.

Here is a moment in ordinary life when the two forms of being-towards-death come together. And it is an occasion that raises an important question about the relation of mourning to separation and individuation. For, on the one hand, this would seem like a paradigmatic moment: my father, in mourning, separates himself from the culture in which he was brought up and takes his own differentiated stand. On the other hand, we cannot tell simply by looking at this vignette whether it manifested any psychic integration at all. Perhaps it did; but perhaps my father was giving voice to a painful inability to grow from this experience; perhaps he felt threatened with disintegration. So, this case of mourning seems to suggest that we are dealing with two conceptions of "individuation"—one of psychic integration and one of taking a stand with respect to social norms and customs. It would seem that mourning could be the occasion for one or the other or both or neither. But, then, what has happened to the idea that mourning is a developmental notion?

The ancient Greek project of moral psychology depended on grounding ethical life in psychological development. Our current investigation is motivated by a thought that Plato and Aristotle moved too quickly in their attempts to link the two and that psychoanalysis might give us a more robust account. Loewald linked psychological development to mourning, which he suggested binds internalization, psychic integration, separation, and individuation together. But now, in considering an ordinary case of mourning, we see that there is reason to suspect that the individuation of separation from established social roles and the individuation of psychic integration might go off on separate tracks. And thus there is reason to wonder whether something analogous might happen in psychological development. That is, there are two moments of mourning in psychological development—separation (from a previous form of relating to objects) and internalization—and there is a question why internalization, if it should happen at all, would facilitate integration rather than an internal cacophony of voices.

**6.** If integration occurs, I suspect that it is because it is promoted. If we look at the three human dramas that Loewald wants to link under the concept *mourning*—response to death, human development, and psychoanalytic treatment—we see that they are each enveloped in human caring activities that aim to shape and influence what is happening. In human development, there is parenting; with death, there is a culture's customs and rituals; in psychoanalysis, there is the caring direction of psychoanalytic technique, as embodied in the analyst and his work. All three of these activities have in common that—in different ways, and with different levels of self-conscious awareness—they grapple with the same problem: how to integrate the nonrational soul into thoughtful, self-conscious life. I want to suggest that there is a conceptual issue here: that it is internal to our understanding of mourning that it is not simply a dyadic relation between mourner and mourned, but that it also includes a mourning environment that facilitates the mourning process (more or less well). This mourning environment will typically include fellow mourners or companions, along with established customs, rituals, and activities.) It is a task of moral psychology to determine what a good mourning environment consists in.

If there is such a thing as *living well* for human beings, it must, as Plato and Aristotle saw, somehow integrate the activities of the nonrational soul. How might we do that well? At some level of understanding, this is a problem we have been grappling with since the beginning of civilization. Moral psychology is an attempt to craft an answer at a heightened level of self-conscious awareness, and so allow for justification and critique. But we should expect there to be activities that facilitate integration throughout the dramas of life.

So, the death of a loved one is expected to stir up powerful emotions and fantasies, and mourning is structured as a period of withdrawal from the ordinary demands of life. It is not unlike going to sleep in order to dream, or lying down on a couch in order to associate: the culture's customs and rituals create a space where the nonrational soul can express itself, but in a containing environment. If the death of a loved one is an occasion for unconscious fantasy, the rituals of mourning—prayers, chants, wakes—help shape fantasy in the direction of integration. All the while, the emotions, daydreams, and memories are being woven into self-conscious thought. In myriad ways, the mourning environment facilitates integration.

In the case of individual human development, Loewald speaks of the infant as born into a differentiated field of caring in which the parents reflect back to the infant his own development, at higher levels of integration. Good parenting has internal to it, however intuitive and emotion laden, a conception of what good parenting consists in. This is a constitutive element of the parents' higher level of differentiation. Parents grasp that they need to facilitate a process of growing-up, one that includes difficult periods and moments of separation and loss, but all, one hopes, ultimately in the service of human flourishing. Loewald's introduction of the concept *mourning* need not be seen merely as a theoretical contribution to our understanding of the process, but also as a practical offering for parents: a concept that might help them better understand and direct their efforts. As such, it would be a contribution to moral psychology.

Loewald is, of course, writing primarily for psychoanalysts. His introduction of mourning is meant to facilitate a movement of self-conscious awareness in the analyst of what he or she is doing. In effect, Loewald locates psychoanalysis as a middle term, linking two great moments of human life: childhood development and the adult mourning of a dead parent. Psychoanalysis becomes a repetition and recreation of the former, and an uncanny anticipation of the latter. Like classic mourning, psychoanalysis provides a space in which a person retreats from the ordinary demands of daily life. It is a space that, through its own unusual rituals, encourages the nonrational soul to express itself; and yet it is also a space that envelops those expressions in speech aimed at self-conscious awareness. At the same time, analysis is a repetition and recreation of childhood development, its losses and separations, victories and defeats.

Think of what a transformation in the analyst's self-conception the introduction of the concept *mourning* brings about. Gone is the image of the dispassionate scientist, or the detective searching the evidence for a disguised wish. The analyst becomes an unusual "companion" to the bereaved, helping the analysand face loss—reexperience it in its complexity and emotional intensity—as well as reorganize it. The analyst becomes someone who can bear the mourning of another. As in parenting, as in classic mourning, this essentially involves containing and guiding the flow of unconscious mental activity. Mourning is an occasion of psychic integration precisely because its task is to facilitate it. This is the *practical* significance of the introduction of mourning as the concept through which we understand psychoanalytic activity. From at least the time of Plato, we have understood that human happiness depends on psychic integration; but it took the painstaking work of psychoanalysis to show how such integration depends on passing successfully through mourning.

Count no man happy until he has mourned. If we think of a happy life as a complete life, and now we realize that such a life must contain significant periods of mourning within it—*not* as necessary antecedents to that life, but as essential, constituent moments of that life—we arrive at an unusual view of human happiness and its possibilities. But this is the kind of unanticipated result that a robust moral psychology ought to be able to deliver. The philosophical tradition has long been familiar with a conception of humans as finite, dependent, rational animals. Psychoanalysis reveals that this shows up psychologically as mourning. Mourning may be evaded or denied, but even as such it lies at the center of our being. Freud taught us that infantile fantasies tend toward omnipotence, and Loewald developed the thought that this occurs because the infant lacks firm boundaries between self and other, as well as between wish and reality. Over and over again, psychoanalysis finds that such fantasies are alive in adults, structuring their experience in ways they do not understand. If we are ever truly to experience ourselves as finite and dependent—that is, to grasp first-personally and self-consciously who we are—we must find appropriate ways to bid farewell to these distorting fantasies. Loewald memorably said that in analysis, "the ghosts of the unconscious are laid and led to rest as ancestors whose power is taken over and transformed into the newer intensity of present life."[19] We might add that these ghosts tend toward infinite independence: parental figures who can overwhelm us with guilt, or narcissistic figures that distort our sense of who we are and diminish the reality of others. We need to mourn them because they need to die; and we need to move on. In analysis, the analysand learns how to take responsibility for their death and burial—which is actually the death and burial of their omnipotence. And this opens the possibility for a more creative imaginative life, populated by more nuanced, and less overwhelming, ancestor figures.

It is an astonishing fact about the human mind that its capacity for imaginatively representing its own activity actually structures the mind. So, for example, to imagine a critical voice is part of what it is to have a punishing superego. As such voices fade away, *poof!* there goes the superego. In this way, mourning facilitates psychic integration. Mourning has its own efficacy, and I want to suggest that this efficacy is enhanced when the mourning becomes self-consciously grasped as such. When we understand ourselves as mourners, we become more active in taking up memories, grasping our dreams as something to be worked on, and so on. That is, self-consciously understanding ourselves as mourners can itself integrate our souls. This then becomes an important way of living up to the Socratic injunction to know oneself: it is in knowing oneself *as a mourner* that one integrates one's psyche; and we thus constitute ourselves by our own activity of self-understanding. This is a form of truthfulness—and it is difficult to see how one could come by it in any other way.

**7.** I would like to conclude with a comment about religious belief. In his essay on internalization, Loewald makes a passing remark:

> The death of a love object, or the more or less permanent separation from a love object, is the occasion for mourning and for internalization. . . . It seems significant that with the advent of Christianity, initiating the greatest intensification of internalization in Western civilization, the death of God as incarnated in Christ moves into the center of religious experience. Christ is not only the ultimate love object, which the believer loses as an external object and regains by identification with Him as an ego ideal. He is, in His passion and sacrificial death, the exemplification of complete internalization and sublimation of all earthly relationships and needs. *But to pursue these thoughts would lead us far afield into unexplored psychological country.*[20]

But if Christianity is "the greatest intensification of internalization in Western civilization," how could it be that exploring this in an essay on internalization would be taking us "far afield," and into "unexplored psychological country"? The question is whether this is far afield because it has been *made* to be far afield.

As is well known, Freud dismissed religious belief as illusion, the product of infantile wishes.[21] This had a chilling effect on the psychoanalytic profession as a whole. At the time Loewald was writing, institutes would reject applicants for training who openly professed religious conviction; and analytic thinking in this area, with a few notable exceptions, was confined to this Freudian rut. As a result, we remain impoverished when it comes to psychoanalytic insight into religious experience. And yet, when one looks back on Freud's argument with the benefit of hindsight, it is striking how brittle it is. Freud emphasizes the infantile-wishful dimension of religious experience, but then psychoanalysis teaches that there are wishful layers in all creative human endeavors. He would never use such an insight to undermine the claims of art. And when it came to art, Freud focused on humankind's greatest achievements, but when it came to religion, he focused on its most common and rundown expression. "The whole thing," he said, "is so *patently* infantile . . . that it is painful to think that *the great majority of mortals* will never be able to rise above this view of life."[22] But if what we are here dealing with is *patently* infantile, why is psychoanalysis needed to understand it? And why is Freud here dealing with the mass of humankind, as opposed to the greatest achievements of religious thought and practice? Even thoughtful defenses of religious belief were dismissed by him as "pitiful rearguard actions."[23] It seems to me that Freud was himself in the grip of a wishful Enlightenment fantasy—an illusion of the future—in which the inexorable march of reason, "our God *Logos,*" overcomes religious superstition "with the fatal inevitability of a process of growth."[24]

I have no interest in analyzing Freud, but overall this approach looks to me like a manic denial of mourning. It is beyond question that there has been a massive transformation in the form of life in Europe over the past two hundred years. I think we still lack a proper understanding of what has happened. At the time of Freud's writing, the nations of Europe took themselves to be Christian—though there were thinkers just prior to Freud, notably Nietzsche and Kierkegaard, who claimed that religious belief had degenerated into hollowed-out hypocrisy. By now, Europe is overwhelmingly atheist, agnostic, and secular (with the exception of non-Christian immigrants). It is significant, I think, that such a massive change in the form of life should be greeted with such historical triumphalism.

In this context, Loewald's comment takes on importance. It is as though he was gesturing in a direction that, until his writing, had been refused. It is also significant that Loewald did not include in his collected papers an essay he published in the *Journal of Pastoral Care* in 1953: "Psychoanalysis and Modern Views on Human Existence and Religious Experience." It is thus much less well known than his other writings. He begins by saying that analysands that have any attitude to religion at all tend to fall into two groups. One group tends to express profound disinterest in, even contempt for, religious belief, and its members tend to assume that Loewald shares their view. The other group has positive feelings, but its members tend not to want to talk about them, as they assume that Loewald does not share them, or that he would even disapprove of their view. So both sides assume that the analyst disapproves of religion. And they also share "a defensive attitude toward their childhood religion." Let us assume, for the sake of argument, that the views expressed by Loewald's analysands were typical of the time. Let us also assume that analysts of that day typically thought it appropriate to adopt Freud's attitude toward religious belief. The upshot would be that analysts unwittingly cut themselves off from a wealth of material about religious experience. Loewald seems to assume as much: "Psychoanalysis, I believe, is as yet in no position to provide anything approaching an adequate psychological understanding of such highly integrated human functions as are reached and manifested in the genuine religious experience and thought of Christianity."[25]

Loewald criticizes Freud for being "one-sided," focusing on human helplessness and the wish for an all-powerful protector, while ignoring basic experiences of trust, oneness, and belonging, also crucial to religious experience.[26] And Loewald turns an important point Freud makes against him. In *Civilization and Its Discontents,* Freud argues that modern man has become estranged from himself. Loewald suggests that Freud's critique of religious belief unnecessarily *contributes* to that estrangement.[27]

All of this suggests that if psychoanalysis is to live up to its promise of being a moral psychology—one that contributes as it comes to understand what it is to lead a full, rich, meaningful human life—it must find ways to mourn Freud's legacy and move on. Even now, we are only at the beginning of such a process.

**8.** Just before he died, Hans Loewald said to me that he hoped that there would never be any Loewaldians. I have been thinking about that remark on and off ever since; and by now I can recognize three layers of meaning. At the time, I thought that he was expressing an ironic but earnest wish that his writings not be misappropriated. Loewald devoted his life to promoting individuation, in himself and in those around him—analysands, family, friends, and colleagues. It would be a cruel fate if his legacy were a "Loewaldian school," with its own "Loewaldian" beliefs and methods. Part of what it is to be a Loewaldian is to recognize that there could never be any such thing. This is not a matter of being coy. The point is that the appropriate way to "follow Loewald" is to develop a mind of one's own.

Later, I began to wonder whether he was trying to guide my own internalizations. We both knew that he was about to die. Perhaps he was trying to help me avoid establishing an overly idealized internal figure. He did not want his memory to become a source of rigidity or slavishness in me.

But now that I have come to reflect on the religious dimension of Loewald's life, I have come to wonder whether the impossibility of becoming a Loewaldian does not also flow from intense privacy lying at the heart of Loewald's commitments. If a private and personal relation to God was at the center of Loewald's existence, then of course the only Loewaldian there could ever be is Loewald himself. Anyone else's attempt to be a Loewaldian would thus manifest a huge misunderstanding of his life. Again, it is beyond the scope of this essay to pursue these thoughts, but I hope I have said enough to make it plausible that an adequate moral psychology would be one that enabled us to do just that.

Loewald once prefaced a talk by saying that he hoped his remarks would shed a little darkness on the subject. It is worth pondering why that might be a worthy aspiration.

CHAPTER TWELVE

# Allegory and Myth in Plato's *Republic*

**1.** It is by now a terrifying commonplace—agreed to by people across the political spectrum, indeed across the divide of civilizations—that our future well-being, and that of future generations, depends on shaping the hearts and minds of the young. Why do we think this? And do we have any idea how to do it well? Plato is the first person in the Western tradition to think seriously about these questions, and it is worth going back to him—not only as a return to origins, but because there are aspects of his thought that are still not well understood.

Plato's famous account of how to educate youth comes in the immediate aftermath of a spectacular breakdown of rational argument between two adults. In *Republic I,* Socrates and Thrasymachus argue over whether it is best to be just even if one could get away with being unjust; and by the end, Thrasymachus is reduced to sarcastic silence, while Socrates "wins" what he himself recognizes as a hollow victory. It has often been suggested that Plato is here dramatizing a failure of the Socratic method, the elenchus. And no doubt Socrates does adapt his method in the remaining books of the *Republic.* But looking at the breakdown, it seems clear that what is at stake is not some *particular* form of argument—as though if we made a few adjustments it would come out all right. Rather, the problem seems to be that rational argument itself is coming too late. Thrasymachus already has an outlook on the world, and he will tend to recognize good and bad arguments in terms of that outlook. The problem, then, is not just the limitations of elenchus: there is a question of how any good argument could properly influence someone whose outlook is distorted and distorting.

So the pressing questions become: How are outlooks formed? What is it to have a good outlook? How might one go about shaping one? To address these questions, Socrates not only changes his method, but he also changes his interlocutors. Glaucon and Adeimantus are young, and they are exceptional (II.367e–368b). They are able to pose a stunning challenge to justice, and yet are not convinced by their own arguments. Socrates suggests that there is something divine about their characters that leaves them open to investigate a refutation with him. We shall investigate what this openness could be, but for the moment, it is Adeimantus who makes clear what a remarkable achievement this is. Glaucon has already challenged Socrates with an argument that what matters for happiness is only *appearing* to be just, not really being just. But it is Adeimantus who shows how this outlook is already built into normal ethical education. Fathers encourage their sons to be just because of all the societal benefits they will acquire by being known to be moral (II.363a–b). But these rewards are compatible with simply appearing to be just. And the poets suggest that the gods do not themselves behave justly. Indeed, according to the poets, rich people can buy off the gods with sacrifices (II.363e–366d). In short, the ethical outlook being instilled in contemporary Athens is unknowingly hypocritical: on the surface justice is being praised; just under the surface is the cynical message that all that really matters is appearance.

Note what a challenge this is for the idea of reflective equilibrium as a test for one's ethical beliefs. If in raising the question of how to live, we reach out to the "wisdom" of our parents—indeed to the "wisdom" of the most highly respected cultural sources—we may simply be reaching out to the accumulated prejudice of our age. And if we test this "wisdom" against our own sense of right and wrong, we may unwittingly be "testing" it against the same outlook—albeit one that was instilled in us when we were young. It will *seem* to us that we are asking and answering reflective questions, but we will simply be reinforcing the prejudices of the day.

Even philosophical debate—at least, of a familiar sort—is not going to help. So, to take a salient example, if we want to test our ethical commitments against "the skeptic," can we think of a better example than Thrasymachus? As we debate the skeptic, we *think* we are confronting a radical alternative. This encourages the illusion that we are investigating all the possibilities there are. It becomes hard to see that these positions are of a piece. Thus once an ethical outlook has been instilled, it is difficult to induce reflective discomfort. For all the debates that have occurred, Adeimantus tells us that no one has *ever* questioned justice and injustice except in terms of the reputation, prestige, and rewards they bring (II.366e).

**2.** For Plato, the human psyche is itself a psychological achievement. The infant does not have a fully formed psyche; at most, he or she has the capacity to acquire and develop psychological structures. And this formation is crucially shaped by the social environment. Cultural messages penetrate and mold the psyche in ways that are often not well understood (II.377b; III.401c–e). We need thus to understand what these meanings are and how this process works.

There is no need to dwell on Socrates's well-known critique of content: we are to eliminate tales of the gods fighting among themselves (especially intergenerational conflicts), tales that suggest that the gods are responsible for anything but the good, and tales that suggest that gods change form or deceive; we are also to eliminate tales of heroes fearing death or lamenting the loss of loved ones. Socrates says that these tales turn children into cowards as well as loosen the bonds of family and citizenship (III.387). But how? That is, what is the *process* by which these objectionable contents take hold? Socrates gives this reason for banishing these objectionable stories: "The young cannot distinguish what is an allegory (*huponoia*) from what is not, and the opinions they form at that age tend to be ineradicable and unchangeable" (II.378d–e). That is, youth lack the capacity to recognize allegory as such.

But what is this capacity that youth lack? The Greek word *hyponoia* is correctly translated as "allegory," but it also means the deeper or real meaning that lies at the bottom (of a thing). It is the deeper sense or hidden meaning: it is that which lies at the bottom of a myth or allegory.[1] *Hyponoia* is quite literally the "under-thought." Indeed, it is an under-thought in another sense: it enters the psyche beneath the radar of critical thought. (Think of the way a *hypnotist* influences another by encouraging her to suspend critical judgment.) Precisely because the child lacks the capacity to recognize allegory as such, he cannot grasp the deeper meaning of the story that is entering his soul, and thus he cannot subject it to critical scrutiny. And so it would seem that the young can take in the surface story, but they cannot recognize it *as* a surface. That is because they cannot recognize the deeper meaning, nor can they recognize that the allegory is allegorical *of* this deeper meaning. Thus they are unaware of the place of allegory in the larger structure of things. I shall therefore call this lack of capacity, which is constitutive of youth, "lack of orientation."

This lack of orientation lends extraordinary power to the stories one hears. Once one has acquired the capacity to recognize allegory as such, one can recognize a story as a surface-story and then go on to inquire into its deeper meaning. But before one acquires the capacity, it is not merely that one cannot recognize the surface-story as such, but the very idea of surface is unavailable. For one has no idea of depth with which to contrast it. It is precisely this capacity to distinguish surface from depth that one acquires as one acquires the capacity to recognize allegory as such. Thus without this capacity, the surface story takes on a weird "reality" of its own. It is too quick to say that the young treat allegories as though they were true. For we are trying to capture a state of mind in which the concept of truth itself is not yet firmly established. Part of what it is to have the concept of truth is to have acquired the capacity to discriminate reality from appearance, and in certain crucial dimensions this is what youth lack. But precisely because they lack this capacity, the experience of allegories has a kind of power that we (loosely) associate with the experience of reality.

It is difficult to capture this childhood state of mind with precision. In part, this is due to the fact that once we acquire the capacity to recognize allegory as such, it becomes difficult for us to remember the subjective quality of earlier states of mind when we lacked this capacity. Thus it is difficult for us to say retrospectively what it was like. In part, it is because the childhood state of mind itself lacks a certain definiteness. Clearly, children do have a symbolic capacity; they can distinguish symbol from thing symbolized. And they can recognize a difference between a story told and the report of a real-life event. But what difference do they recognize? Obviously, Plato was not as interested as we are in capturing the precise nature of childhood subjectivity. But he is, I think, pointing to an important characteristic of childhood experience: that even if children can *in some sense* recognize that they are being told a story, part of its thrill, part of the thrall in which it holds them, derives from the fact that they cannot quite locate the story as such.

Precisely because childhood stories float in a sea of imaginative life, they exercise a certain power—a power that we are inclined to describe as "having a reality of their own." Now if a particular story terrifies a child, parents might try to calm her by saying, "It is only a story." However, if the child lacks the capacity to recognize an allegory as such, then these words cannot be understood by the child in the way the parents mean them. The child may be calmed by her parents' words—though not because she understands the words, but because she trusts and loves her parents and accepts that they are providing some sort of explanation why she should not be scared. Indeed, the child may learn to repeat to herself, "it's only a story," and she may thereby develop a capacity to calm herself. Still, the mere repetition of the words does not *on its own* instill the capacity to recognize allegory. These words can make the right kind of difference, but only when they are embedded in the process of acquiring the capacity to recognize allegory. At that point, the words can be used to utter a judgment, and thereby locate the story as such.

And what is shocking is that even though people eventually acquire the capacity to recognize allegory, the fact that there was a youthful period in which they lacked this capacity casts a shadow over an entire life. The *Republic* begins with a fascinating conversation between Socrates and Cephalus, a wealthy merchant of ripe age who has the wisdom and moderation that would exemplify the best kind of a life, which nevertheless is organized around accumulating wealth. Socrates asks him directly what he thinks is the greatest benefit of having great wealth. Cephalus answers:

> What I have to say probably wouldn't persuade most people. But you know, Socrates, that when someone thinks his end is near, he becomes frightened and concerned about things he didn't fear before. It's *then* that the stories we're told about Hades, about how people who've been unjust here must pay the penalty there—stories he used to make fun of—twist his soul this way and that for fear they're true. And whether because of the weakness of old age or because he is now closer to what happens in Hades and has a clearer view of it, or whatever it is, he is filled with foreboding and fear, and he examines himself to see whether he has been unjust to anyone. If he finds many injustices in his life, he awakes from sleep in terror, as children do, and lives in anticipation of bad things to come. But someone who knows that he hasn't been unjust has sweet good hope as his constant companion—a nurse to his old age, as Pindar says. . . . Wealth can do a lot to save us from having to depart for that

> other place in fear because we owe a sacrifice to a god or money to a person. It has many other uses, but, benefit for benefit, I'd say that this is how it is most useful to a man of any understanding. (I.330d–331b)[2]

In other words, the stories he heard in youth were absorbed and retained by Cephalus throughout his life. They were taken in as allegories-not-recognized-as-such, and even after Cephalus acquired the capacity to recognize allegory, these stories remained for most of his life dormant within him, with little significance for him. Indeed, for much of his life, he makes fun of them. However, as he enters old age and starts to face the prospect of death, these old stories come back to haunt him with uncanny power. Here is a man who has organized his entire life around acquiring wealth, but when asked in old age what has been the value of it all, his answer is that its greatest benefit is to ward off the fears that are only now arising around stories he heard in childhood.

Cephalus is describing the structure of a traumatic cocktail.[3] The childhood stories were taken in before he had the capacity to recognize their allegorical status—and thus before he had the capacity to grasp their deeper meanings. They may provoke childhood fears, but in childhood at least, they have nothing to latch onto. However, in old age it seems that Cephalus's emerging anxiety over death needs the childhood stories to give it form and content. The elderly anxiety combines with the early childhood stories, and together they disrupt any previous self-understandings and give a new, anxious meaning to Cephalus's life. Note that Cephalus is unable to remain with Socrates and inquire into what justice really is; he has to go off to make a sacrifice (II.331d).

One would like to think that as one gets older, one matures and leaves childhood stories behind. Plato's picture, as described by Cephalus, is darker. There seem to be three developmental stages: a childhood stage when the stories are taken in but not recognized as such; young adulthood, when the stories are both recognized as such and ridiculed; old age, when the stories come to inform an otherwise amorphous anxiety over death. And so, retrospectively, we can see that childhood is a time when the seeds are planted for a terror that will explode only in old age.

Socrates is also clear that the unoriented tales we hear in youth are actually *dis*orient*ing*. The heroic tales provide paradigms for imitation, which, through the imitation, shape the psyche (III.395c–d, 401c–e; II.377b, 378b).

For they facilitate the establishment of structures of repetition: habits and dispositions whose full meaning cannot be understood at the time they are being formed. So, for instance, a little boy hears heroic tales of Achilles at a time when he lacks the capacity to recognize allegory as such. When he goes out to play his version of *hoi agathoi kai hoi kakoi* (good guys and bad guys), he assigns himself the role of Achilles. He acts out a certain image of courage before he is able to understand what courage is. This image is enacted over and over again in play, and in this way his psyche gets "Achillized." He becomes accustomed to seeing the world and acting in it from an Achillized perspective. And so, by the time he does acquire the capacity to recognize allegory as such, it is in an important sense too late. He can now recognize the Achilles tale as a story, but the tale has already done its psychic work. And by the time he tries in adulthood to think about what courage is, he is already looking out from Achilles's perspective.

**3.** It is important to recognize that lack of orientation has the same formal structure as dreaming. In dreams, we experience images without recognizing them as images and without understanding their deeper meanings. It is not quite correct to say that in dreams we think we are awake. Part of what it is to think that we are awake is to exercise the capacity to distinguish between waking and dream states, and it is this capacity that goes to sleep when we sleep. Thus dream states do have a reality and power for us, *not* because we think we are awake, but because the capacity to distinguish between waking and sleeping has temporarily shut down. So again there is disorientation: we lose the capacity to recognize our dream as a dream and thus to determine what it is about.

Socrates assigns exactly this structure to dreaming. He is talking about the lovers of sights and sounds—those who recognize many beautiful things but are ignorant of the beautiful itself. And, he asks, isn't such a person—whether asleep or awake—really living in a dream? For isn't dreaming this: "thinking that the similar thing is not similar but that it is the thing to which it is similar" (V.476c6–7; my translation)? Here the "dreamer" lacks orientation: he cannot recognize the place of the many beautiful things in the larger structure of the world. He cannot recognize a beautiful thing as an imitation of the form, nor does he know what it is an imitation of. Thus he cannot understand its deeper meaning. This condition is structurally analogous to lacking the capacity for recognizing allegory as such. In this lack of orientation, it is as though these sights and sounds are reality. This is the nature of dream experience.

It follows from these reflections that, for Socrates, entering conscious wakeful life is tantamount to entering a dream. Even if we leave aside Plato's metaphysics for the moment, his view is that it is constitutive of youth to lack the capacity to recognize allegory as such. Entering conscious life is entering into an awareness that lacks the capacity to recognize the similar thing (the allegory) as similar. But without this capacity, life has the character of a dream. And now if we do take Platonic metaphysics into account, it turns out that as young men and women acquire the capacity to recognize allegory, they "wake up" from one dreamlike state only to enter another. Ironically, the newly acquired sense of reality—"that was only a story!"—is precisely that which disorients us all over again. For we now plunge into the adult world of cultural artifacts, social practices, and physical objects—and we take it to be the real thing. As we acquire one version of the capacity to recognize the similar as similar, we enter a new level of experience where there is another version of this capacity that we lack.

**4.** It is time to take another look at the Noble Falsehood. Socrates thinks that the inability to recognize allegory as such is constitutive of childhood. Thus for him the task cannot be to avoid all allegories—that is impossible—but to find the right kind of allegory not to be recognized as such.[4] That is, in choosing which stories to tell children, we ought to make use of our knowledge that, in the first instance, they will not be able to recognize the allegory as such. Obviously, there may be various grounds for criticizing Socrates's candidate, but by now it should be clear that, given the overall outlook, there is one position that is not available: simply speak the truth to our children. This is not due to a lack of fortitude on our part, nor to dishonesty. It is *constitutive of the adult-child* situation: children cannot possibly understand our words as we mean them. Either we remain unaware of this ourselves, or we try to take it somehow into account. Our children lack orientation, so can we tell them things that will not positively disorient them? Even better, can we hope to orient them in the right sort of way?

Socrates distinguishes a verbal falsehood (*to en tois logois pseudos*) from "true falsehood" (*alēthos pseudōs*), and it is clear that a verbal falsehood has essentially the same structure as an allegory-not-recognized-as-such. For a verbal falsehood is basically a form of words that comes to rest in the soul *without* being connected to its "deeper meaning." Plato calls it an imitation, or an image of a "true falsehood." Now a true falsehood is like that "deeper meaning"—it is actually a condition of a person's soul when she is living in falsity. And it is a condition everyone wants to avoid. A verbal falsehood, like an allegory-not-recognized-as-such points to—or imitates—this deeper meaning *without* actually being connected to it. That *lack* of connection is what keeps the falsehood in its verbal form. And in this sense, Socrates thinks it can be used as a medicine (*pharmakon*). Clearly, this is a potentially dangerous drug. How can we use it for medicinal purposes? To answer this question, perhaps it is useful to ask What is the "disease" from which children need to be "cured"?

The aim is to implant an allegory not recognized as such that will help children with the fact that they live in a condition of not being able to recognize allegories as such.

> I have to try to persuade first the rulers themselves and the soldiers, and then the rest of the city, that the entire upbringing and education we gave them was after all merely a dream. (III.414d)

In other words, we are to implant an allegory not recognized as such that in effect "says" that the entire content of our experience up until now has been in a condition in which we cannot recognize allegories as such. It is a dream about dreaming and waking up. And unlike standard myths about the gods or ancient heroes, this myth is explicitly about the people to whom it is being told. In this sense, it serves as a dreamlike wake-up call *for them.*

It is important to recognize that this Noble Falsehood is protophilosophical in two ways. First, it attempts to give an account of the totality of our experience (up until now). It claims that *all* experience (up until now) can be understood under the concept *dream.* Insofar as philosophy attempts to comprehend the whole, this myth is an imitation of that aspiration. Compare that to the familiar Homeric myths, from which this aspiration is absent. There is thus reason to think that it would have a very different effect on the young psyche than the standard fare of the day. Second, the myth inherently sows the seeds of discontent. It opens us to the idea that all our experience until now is somehow inadequate. And though we do not yet know precisely what this allegory means, we do know that it is classifying all our experience (until now) as somehow second rate as far as being well oriented to reality. Thus it is a myth that introduces the philosophical distinction between appearance and reality—and it tells us firmly that up until now we have been living in appearance. In this way, the myth prepares us for philosophy.

It has often been remarked that the Noble Falsehood is a politically conservative myth: it claims in essence that people are born with innate and distinctive natures suited for different social and political roles.[5] It also reinforces the idea that citizens are indebted to the existing political order, the *kallipolis*. However, what is less understood is that while the Noble Falsehood may be *politically* conservative, it is *epistemically* revolutionary. It is meant to instill discontent with one's entire current epistemic condition. Moreover, the allegory is authored by someone who explicitly understands that children lack the capacity to recognize allegory as such. Thus one should expect the myth to be tailored to play to this lack of capacity. At the end of the Noble Falsehood, Socrates asks Glaucon, "Is there any way of persuading them of this myth?" And Glaucon responds, "No way with those people you tell it to; but with their sons and with future generations" (III.415c–d; my translation). Glaucon recognizes that the proper way to "believe" a myth is to hear it before one acquires the capacity to recognize allegory as such. For once one acquires that ability, allegories lose their "quasi-realistic" power. Thus there is no way you can get an adult to "believe" your myth.

At first one might think that, from the perspective of living within the truth, the original adults who hear this myth are the best placed. For they can immediately recognize the allegory as an allegory—and, after all, that is what it is. The succeeding generations will all in some sense be misled, for they will all take in the allegory before they can recognize it as such. And the power that the myth will have for them will depend essentially on having heard it before they were in a position to understand its true nature.

But for Socrates the situation is the reverse of what it seems. For while the original adult generation will immediately be able to recognize the allegory as such, that recognition will occur in a life that is fundamentally disoriented. For this is a generation that assumes that the physical objects and artifacts in its midst are the real thing. They lack the capacity to recognize the familiar couch on which they lie as an imitation of the form (X.596–598). Thus they are in a position structurally analogous to that of the child who cannot recognize allegory as such. They cannot recognize the "deeper meaning" of the familiar couch; they cannot even recognize that it has a deeper meaning. Thus the physical couch will inevitably seem more real to them than it in fact is. As we have seen, Socrates says that such people are in effect dreaming. And the Noble Falsehood cannot, for them, function as a wake-up call precisely because they immediately recognize it as an allegory. Ironically, the allegory gets located as such, but in a sea of disorientation.

But for the children, grandchildren, and subsequent generations, we should expect the myth to have the kind of two-stage effect we saw in the case of Cephalus. In childhood, the myth is laid down as an allegory-not-recognized-as-such. But even as a surface story, the myth begins to teach the child to be hermeneutically suspicious of the other myths he has heard in childhood. After all, is has all been just a dream up until now. Thus one can think of the Noble Falsehood (told in childhood) as itself beginning to inculcate the capacity to recognize allegory as such. For it is an allegory told to us when we cannot recognize allegory as such, but one that *right on its surface* tells us that the other allegories we have already heard (and by hypothesis have not yet recognized as such) are really only dreams. In that way, the Noble Falsehood embeds an antifundamentalist message about all other myths: none of them should be taken literally.

Now we have reason to think that the Noble Falsehood will be told to *all* the children in the polis, for it is told to the rulers, the soldiers, and *the rest of the city.* But we can imagine it having a special belated effect on the future rulers of the city. The Noble Falsehood sets them up for a later aha!-experience. Just as the stories Cephalus heard in childhood set him up for a later explosion of terrible fears about death in old age, so the Noble Falsehood one hears in childhood sets one up in adulthood to be open to the reality of the forms. Think of young men and women who have the same outstanding character as Glaucon and Adeimantus but who have been brought up since childhood in the right sort of way. In particular, they were exposed in childhood to the Noble Falsehood. As they grow up, the finest young men and women among them will be exposed in their education to the reality of the forms. Because earlier, in childhood, they were told the Noble Falsehood, they are now also in a position to feel, "Aha! So *that's* what the myth was really about." In their education, they are being exposed to the true nature of reality for the first time, but their souls have already been set up to embrace it with gusto. It's like getting a joke many years after you hve heard the punch line. Only in this case the joke is the idea that ordinary physical objects constitute reality. From a certain Platonic perspective, that is very funny. And if you have heard the Noble Falsehood in childhood, you're in a position to let out a real belly laugh as an adult. (If that seems implausible to you, you can reflect on the fact that you did not hear the Noble Falsehood as a child.)

Thus it is superficial to think of the Noble Falsehood *simply* as a myth that is designed to make children loyal to the established political order in the kallipolis. It may in fact do this, but it is also concerned with orienting children toward the truth. Socrates is trying to take explicit account of the fact that we are born into a culture and that by the time we can reflect on it, that culture has already shaped our souls. In particular, it has shaped our souls in ways that will influence our reflection. What is striking about the Noble Falsehood, in contrast with other myths and ideologies that are meant to legitimate the status quo, is that this allegory does its work by generating dissatisfaction. It teaches us to be dissatisfied with all the myths we have heard, at least insofar as we have taken them to have more than dreamlike status. Indeed, it teaches us to be dissatisfied with all of our experience up until now insofar as we have taken it to be experience of reality. This is not how legitimating myths normally work.

**5.** It is now possible to see that Socrates's account of the Cave is a repetition and recreation of the Noble Falsehood. As is well known, this image is meant to characterize us in terms of "the effect of education—or lack of it—on our nature" (VII.514a). Again, it is essentially about those to whom it is being told: it is designed to describe their fundamental condition. And it is protophilosophical in the same ways that the Noble Falsehood is. First, it is trying to capture the totality of our experience up until now, the moment this story is introduced. It claims that all of our experience until now can be understood under the concepts *seeing shadows* or *hearing echoes* (and mistaking them for reality). Second, the account is designed to instill dissatisfaction with the current level of experience. It introduces in imagistic terms the philosophical distinction between appearance and reality, and it gives us "grounds" for "thinking" both that we are living in appearance and that we should be unhappy about that. The dissatisfaction is thus not about this or that belief—this is not a process of rejecting false beliefs—but rather dissatisfaction with the sum total of experience (up till now).

Both the Noble Falsehood and the Cave thus intentionally create reflective disequilibrium—they build an inherent discontent with the current level of experience. Unlike existing myths—say Homer's presentation of Achilles, which, in Plato's view, gives a fixed, false, and thus imprisoning image of courage—the Socratic allegories encourage the idea that the current state of experience ("knowledge," etc.) is unsatisfactory. Life up until now, unbeknownst to us, has been a dream. Life up until now, unbeknownst to us, has been a prison in which we are mistaking shadows for the real thing. The Socratic allegories, unlike the Homeric myths, inherently encourage dissatisfaction with the existing state of affairs. They thus motivate us to try to go on in some different way. If Socrates is right that we have been living in a dream, then these allegories serve as a wake-up call. If he is right that, unbeknownst to us, we have been living in prison, then in becoming aware of that we begin to chafe at the chains.

Note that the problem we began with was the idea that our best attempts at achieving reflective equilibrium might be a sham. This was in effect Adeimantus's challenge: as we try to test our ethical beliefs, we end up reaching out to the (disguised) prejudices of the day. Here finally are allegories that are not intended to legitimize the values of the day, but rather to instill suspicion with respect to them. They do this not by criticizing this value or that, nor by taking on the role of "moral skeptic," but by making us uncomfortable with our entire mode of acquiring beliefs and values. Whatever else might be said about these myths, they are clearly not meant to keep us locked into current images of goodness, beauty, courage. Rather, they create an inchoate sense of discomfort with those images.

After Socrates describes the Cave, Glaucon says, "A strange picture. And strange prisoners." Socrates responds, "No more strange than us" (VII.515a). The Greek word for "strange" is *atopos,* which means more literally "out of place"; most literally it means "without a place, unlocated." But "unlocated" is precisely the "position" of an allegory-not-recognized-as-such: we do not yet know its place in the scheme of things. Insofar as we, as children, lack the capacity to recognize allegory as such, *we* shall be unlocated, for we cannot orient ourselves with respect to these allegories. Now the story of the Cave is ostensibly being told to Glaucon, who does have the capacity to recognize allegory as such. But he stands in relation to ordinary experience—to physical objects, artifacts, contemporary beliefs about the good life—as children stand to allegories: he cannot yet locate them as imitating the forms. As a young adult, he lacks the capacity to recognize the allegorical nature of ordinary experience. He cannot locate his experience in relation to reality—to the forms—and thus he remains unlocated, *atopos.* The Cave is an allegorical attempt to get him to recognize that.

As such, the Cave seeks to instill a new form of Socratic ignorance. As is well known, in the *Apology,* Socrates says that he discovered that he was the wisest among humans because he knew that he did not know. But the Cave is a story that is designed to put Glaucon, and anyone else ready to hear it, into a position in which they can begin to recognize that they do not know. Socrates says that education is not a matter of putting knowledge into souls, but of turning the whole soul away from the darkness and toward the light (VII.518c). Certainly, what we are turning away from are images, shadows, echoes, allegories *not recognized as such.* Thus we are turning away from a dreamlike state. And what we are turning toward is a recognition that if we are to understand these images, we must grasp that they are images, and we must struggle to understand what these images are images of. Indeed, the process of turning away is constituted by coming to recognize the "allegorical" nature of ordinary experience. We may not yet be able to say what the deeper meanings are—thus we remain ignorant—but we are able to glimpse that the images are pointing toward deeper meanings; and thus we at least know that we are ignorant. So the allegory of the Cave facilitates a Socratic movement from being ignorant, yet ignorant of one's ignorance, to being ignorant but aware that one is ignorant. And insofar as ordinary life is like a dream, then as we move toward Socratic ignorance, we begin to wake up.[6]

It is important to keep in mind to whom the Cave is addressed. Ostensibly it is addressed to Glaucon and Adeimantus—and it is addressed *directly* to them. That is, the Noble Falsehood is told to Glaucon and Adeimantus, but in the context of an inquiry into what stories we should tell the members of the kallipolis. The Cave, by contrast, is told directly to Glaucon and Adeimantus and is explicitly for them. I suspect that in this way the Cave is addressed to the ideal reader of the *Republic.* For, as we have seen, Glaucon and Adeimantus are exceptionally fine people who have had the historical bad luck of having been born into a bad society. The *Republic* is a book for such people. There are two features of such readers that command our attention. First, they have already been exposed in childhood to the misleading myths and stories of their culture—though given their fine natures, they have not been as misshapen by them as other members of society. In particular, they are capable of going through a process of questioning their myths, much as Glaucon and Adeimantus do in Books II and III. Second, by the time they are told about the Cave, it is too late for them to experience the allegory in the way a child does; they already have the capacity to recognize allegory as such. So there is reason to think that the allegory is meant in the telling to be essentially denatured: it is not meant to have on the intended recipients the kind of power it would have had if it had been told in youth. But, then, what kind of effect is it supposed to have?

Earlier in the day—or earlier in the reading of the book—Glaucon, Adeimantus, and the ideal reader have been exposed to the Noble Falsehood. They are in a position to recognize that it could not possibly affect them as it is meant to affect the young members of the kallipolis. At best, they are left to imagine what effect it might have on a young soul in a good society. But now, when they hear the Cave, they are hearing basically the same story for the second time—only now they are hearing an age-appropriate version. I am going to indulge the fantasy that *we* are ideal readers of the *Republic.* Obviously, it is too late for the Cave—or any other story—to have the same effect on us as it would have had if told to us in youth.

Nevertheless, the fact that we are first told the Noble Falsehood then the Cave means that we are put in a position in which we can reenact in adult life a process by which a child acquires the capacity to recognize allegory as such. Ostensibly the Noble Falsehood is *for them;* the Cave is *for us.* But what is really for us is *the movement* by which we go from hearing the Noble Falsehood (which is for them) to the Cave (which is for us). For the fact that we have just heard the Noble Falsehood sets us up for an aha!-experience when we hear the Cave. Retrospectively we can say with emotion and conviction, "So *that's* what the Noble Falsehood is about!" We are now able to locate the Noble Falsehood in a way we could not earlier—and this is an adult surrogate to the childhood process by which we first learned to recognize allegory as such.

Prospectively, the Cave gives us an inkling of something we recognize that we can at best only glimpse. In effect, the story tells us that as we leave childhood behind and enter adulthood, we are, in effect, entering a second childhood. For the Cave invites us to picture our situation as one of seeing images and shadows and mistaking them for reality. It is an imagistic story in which we are told that we lack the capacity to recognize *reality* as such. Just as the children in the kallipolis will be told the Noble Falsehood *before* they have acquired the capacity to recognize allegory as such—and thus are left with an uncanny sense that they will soon be experiencing things in nondreamlike ways (whatever that means)—so we will be told the Cave before we have acquired the capacity to recognize reality as such. And thus we are left with an uncanny sense that *we* may soon be experiencing reality in nondreamlike ways (whatever that means). The Cave intimates to us our own future selves. At least, it intimates our own best possible future selves.

Note also that someone in Glaucon's position who had been exposed to the allegory of the Cave would be in a better position to tell the Noble Falsehood to children. If the kallipolis is ever going to be established, it will have to be by someone like Glaucon, though someone who is better placed in terms of power and historical opportunity. So it is someone like Glaucon who is the projected inaugural teller of the Noble Falsehood. Now the founder of the kallipolis will be the first-generation teller of the Noble Falsehood, so he is not in a position in which he can believe it, nor was he ever in a position in which he did "believe" it. By contrast, the children who hear the Noble Falsehood will be able to transmit it to their children with added verve.[7] Thus this original transmission will be the weakest in terms of producing the intended effect. However, if we arm the founder of the kallipolis with the picture of the Cave, we have, as it were, given him an age-appropriate allegory—and one that has the same basic structure as the Noble Falsehood he now has to tell. This puts the original teller of the Noble Falsehood in a position in which he himself has accepted an allegory that has the same basic structure as the one he is about to tell. And thus he can speak with a conviction that might otherwise be lacking. Although this is the first transmission of the Noble Falsehood to children, the earlier transmission of the allegory of the Cave to adults secures as much efficacy as is possible within the context of this original telling.

**6.** The *Republic* is a work of astonishing depth, so there are obviously a number of ways to read it. But it certainly can be read as an occasion to work through the power of allegories and myth. At the very beginning, we the readers are exposed, through Cephalus, to the uncanny power that childhood myth can have in adult life. Insofar as Cephalus's situation is not unusual, *we* have reason to feel vulnerable. What myths that *we* have heard in childhood are ticking away, deep inside our souls, ready to explode our happiness at some future date? The myths Cephalus heard disturbed him, and the fact that he was disturbed should disturb us.

It is in such a disturbed state that we come to the Noble Falsehood—which we recognize as a cure that could not possibly help us. The Noble Falsehood itself provides a prophylactic *for children* against all the other misleading myths they might have heard. For it claims that *all* their experience up until now has been a dream. But the myth is useless when told to adults. Many students who come to the *Republic* for the first time express pleasure that they have not been subjected to such "lies," and that response is understandable. But when we come to understand the deeper motivation of the Noble Falsehood, there is also room for a certain wistfulness that such lies could no longer do us any good.

But then there is the Cave, an allegory specifically designed for a young adult reader or interlocutor. At last we have an allegory that is *for us,* yet it is also a recreation of the Noble Falsehood to which we have already been exposed. As we have seen, even in our original encounter with the Cave, we are coming to it for the second time. There is thus reason to think that the *Republic* is not merely an account *of* the proper mythic education of youth—an education we could never experience—but it is also a form of mythic therapy for us. For we are told a story (the *Republic*) of being told a myth in childhood (the Noble Falsehood), followed by being told an allegory (the Cave) of the same basic structure but appropriate for us as adults.

It is this whole movement that *for us* does the therapeutic work. Although it is impossible for us to create a myth that would have the effect on us that it would have had if we had heard it in youth, there is reason to think that the allegories we do create—in particular, the Noble Falsehood and the Cave—will be prophylactic against the untoward effects of the myths we have heard in youth. The allegories we are now hearing are essentially *reactive.* They are not myths about the creation of the universe, nor are they about the gods or heroic ancestors who founded civilization as we know it. Rather, they are about our epistemic condition; and they say that all previous myths we have heard are really only a dream, a shadow, an echo. Insofar as we take the earlier myths to have more reality than that, we are deluded. The Noble Falsehood and the Cave are allegories to correct for all previous myths. We first see this corrective in a version that, we imagine, we would have heard if only we had been children at the founding of the kallipolis. Later we encounter a version that is more appropriate to our age and actual historical circumstance. In short, we move from the ideal to the real, from a fantasy of what a great childhood would be like to a more realistic appraisal of what our actual condition is. But all this is accomplished within the movement of allegory. I suspect that Plato thought it would work like an antidote: the outcome of this movement is to put ourselves in the best possible position we could be in—given the realities of our early life in a flawed culture—to counteract the later effects in adult life of early childhood myths. This cannot all be accomplished at the level of reasoned arguments: we need to use imagination to counter the belated ill effects of earlier imaginative products. But with the prophylactic tales of the Noble Falsehood and the Cave, we have done the best we can to avoid the kind of horror that, in late age, struck Cephalus.

Having accomplished this, we are in a position to revisit a healthy version of the type of myth that came to torment Cephalus. This, in effect, is the myth of Er. Thus the *Republic* ends as it began, with a myth of justice and retribution in the afterlife. Er was supposedly a hero from a foreign land, killed in battle, who twelve days later came back to life and thus was able to report on life after death. There are two important emendations that Er makes to the myths that torment Cephalus. First, the myth confirms Cephalus's fear that he would be punished for his injustices, but it is worse than he feared (X.615a–b). For not only is a person punished ten times—indeed, punished ten lifetimes—for each offense, but there is also no hope of buying off one's injustices with money. The idea that Cephalus in this life could buy his way out of punishment in the next is exposed as a merchant's fantasy. Second, the myth reveals that Cephalus's version is only partial. Cephalus cannot get beyond the punishments he might suffer in the next world. But Er declares that after an extended period of punishment, there is then a chance to reenter life—only one must choose lots for what kind of a life one will lead. This is the most dangerous and fraught part of the cycle: even the shape of one's soul is at stake, for the soul is affected by the kind of life it chooses to live (X.618b).

Now what role does this myth play in the closing moments of the *Republic?* It seems to me that the myth is both therapeutic and argumentative at the same time. Therapeutically speaking, we know from the case of Cephalus that we ourselves have been implanted with childhood stories of retribution that are set to "go off" in old age. We need to do something now that will prevent these stories from later having a deleterious effect upon us.

This is just what the myth of Er is designed to do. For it takes up the stories that come to haunt Cephalus, but it points us in a different direction.

> It looks, my dear Glaucon, as if that is where the whole danger lies for a man. It is why the greatest care must be directed towards having each and every one of us disregard all other branches of study, and be a follower and student of this branch of ours, in the hope that he can learn and discover who it is who will give him the ability and knowledge to distinguish the good life from the bad, and choose always and everywhere out of all those possible, the life which is better. *He must take into consideration all the things we have talked about here today.* (618b–c)[8]

The day began with everyone hearing of Cephalus's fears, but by the end of the day we can see that these fears led him off in the wrong direction. The late-blooming effect of childhood myth on Cephalus was to make him anxiously try to pay off debts and make (no doubt expensive) sacrifices to the gods. And this prevents him from doing the one thing he should be doing if he wants to make a genuine contribution to his future happiness: spending the day with Socrates to inquire what a good life might really consist in. Cephalus cannot stick around for the discussion because "it's time I was doing something about the sacrifices" (I.331d).

By the time we hear basically the same kind of myth at the end of the day we are ready to move in a very different direction. The therapeutic action of the myth of Er runs along two dimensions—conscious and unconscious. Consciously, the myth sheds light on all the previous myths and allegories we have heard in this remarkable day. Not only does it illuminate what is going wrong in Cephalus's reception of his myth, but it also sends *us* back to the Noble Falsehood and the Cave. For if the all-important task is to be able to determine what is (and what is not) a good life, these earlier myths help free us from the illusion that we already know the answer. And the myth of Er is there to show us how important that is.

But it is reasonable to assume that the myth will also have unconscious effects on us. Yet, if the effects are unconscious, how are we to investigate them? Obviously, the route needs to be indirect and can be no more than hypothetical. My hypothesis begins with a conscious phenomenon and treats it as a symptom. I have often heard readers express disappointment that the *Republic* ends with a myth; my suggestion is that the experience of disappointment is in some sense correct, but that it has fastened onto the wrong object. For if we are ideal readers of the *Republic,* then part of the process of coming to grips with the text must be the realization that *we* are in various ways flawed. After all, if we have grown up in less-than-ideal historical and social circumstances, there is now reason to think that this has taken a toll on our souls. To give one salient example: it is likely that in childhood we too were subject to terrifying stories of hell, just as Cephalus was. Certainly, Plato would have thought that this was the childhood legacy of his ideal reader. Thus the reader would have to be living with unconscious "time bombs" that are likely to "go off" in old age. The myth of Er takes up these childhood stories and diverts them down a different stream. We now have implanted within us a story that takes up previous punishment stories and emends them—locating them in a larger story of coming back to life, of personal responsibility, and of the importance of choosing well.

Thus there does seem to be some basis for the experience of disappointment; but we have not thought through our own relation to the book if we experience it as disappointment with the book rather than with ourselves. What *is* disappointing—though to dwell on it would be self-indulgent—is that by the end of this marvelous book, we, even as ideal readers, still need a myth.

I have heard readers complain that, by ending the book with a myth, Plato is admitting a kind of argumentative defeat. After all, was not the challenge to Socrates to argue that the just life is the best one? And if his argument has succeeded, why does he need a myth to prop it up? This complaint does not take sufficient account of the role a myth might play inside an argument. It seems to me that Plato could have reasoned like this: When it comes to justice, the universe of possibilities breaks up into three broad classes. Either we live in this life and when we die, that is the end of it; or, after we die, we go into some kind of afterlife; or, after we die, we go into some kind of afterlife and somehow return to this life. Those are all the possibilities there are. The main argument of the *Republic* covers the first possibility, and the main argument plus the myths cover the other two.

And one should not be surprised that an argument that includes possibilities of life after death would make recourse to myths—for the actual conditions of life after death are not things we can know anything about. From an argumentative point of view, the recourse to myth itself is not problematic just so long as it covers all the possibilities there are. This, I suggest, is precisely what the myths of the *Republic* set out to do. *If* there is life after death, the unjust will be punished; *if* there is life after that, the just will be better off. Thus Plato's recourse to myth at the end of the *Republic* in no way gives up argumentative rigor—and disappointment with the book on that basis is thus misplaced.

Plato has used myth not to argue for an actuality, but rather to cover the universe of possibilities. One way or another, these are the ways things have to be; unless, that is, there is a fourth possibility—namely, that the world is essentially a bad place, an occasion for despair. In this world there would be an afterlife in which the just would be mocked and tortured by malevolent gods. Virtually all of the rhetorical power of the *Republic*—the allegories and myths, the arguments and images—is designed to cure the reader of the temptation to think that this is a real possibility. Reality and intelligibility itself are structured by the Good. Thus, while there may be grounds for *pessimism,* there can never be grounds for *despair.* How successful Plato was in eliminating this temptation is a task for each reader to decide—less as an academic exercise than as an approach to the question of how to live.

CHAPTER THIRTEEN

# The Psychic Efficacy of Plato's Cave

**1.** In the interpretation of the *Republic,* there are two outstanding questions that, I want to suggest, have the same answer. First, is there a distinctively philosophical significance to Plato's use of myth and allegory? In recent years, there have been enlightening investigations of Plato's use of dialogue form, his use of myth, and his literary style.[1] And we have been encouraged to recognize that there is much more to do in relation to these texts than try to extract the so-called arguments of the philosophers. Still, the question remains: aside from literary value, is there any distinctively philosophical contribution that myth and allegory make? I do not think it sufficient to say that there is no firm distinction between literary value and philosophical contribution. If, on the one hand, we think of philosophy as constituted by rational argument, it is hard to see what place myth and allegory could have. If, on the other, philosophy somehow outstrips rational argument, we need to know what this means. In a word: how could recounting myths and allegories be philosophy?

The second question is: what does psychic harmony consist in? In the *Republic,* we learn that justice, whether in city or soul, consists in each of the parts doing its own thing. But this is not just parallel play. In the case of the city, justice is also characterized as a "power" (*dunamis*) to bring this condition about and to sustain it (IV.433b–c, d; cp. 434c). So if we follow Socrates's suggestion that we ought to be able to find the same condition in the soul that we find in the city (435b–c; II.368e–369a), then justice ought to be not merely a state in which each part sings the right note, but a power of the soul to sustain that harmony. What is this power? And what would its exercise be? Socrates does give us some clues. So, for instance, he says that it is appropriate for reason (*to logistikon*) to rule "because it is wise and exercises foresight on behalf of the whole soul" and thus that it is appropriate for spirit "to obey and be its ally" (IV.441e).[2] He says that it is a mixture of musical and physical training that makes these parts concordant (*sumphôna*). But what does this mean? What does this concordance consist in; how does it work? Similarly, he says that with the temperate person, not only do the parts have "friendly and concordant relations," but the ruler and its two subjects "share the same belief" (*homodoxôsi*) that *to logistikon* should rule (442c–d). Again, we need to know the nature of this cognitive agreement. Consider the difference between a telephone poll that reveals that all the respondents believe that *P* and a baseball game in which all the fans in the stadium believe *that the White Sox should win.* In the former case, I want to say, there are as many beliefs as there are respondents, though each of the beliefs has the same content; in the stadium, there is only one belief, which all of the fans share. It is this sharing that helps bind them as a group. I believe that Socrates wants to capture a psychic condition that more resembles this latter example than the former. Spirit and appetite do not simply each believe that reason should rule—they all share the belief; this is part of what the unity of the psyche consists in. The challenge is to gain a less metaphorical insight into what this might mean. Socrates is clear that justice requires an enormous amount of psychic activity on behalf of the just person—activity in which harmony and unity is instilled and maintained:

> [The just person] does not allow the elements in him each to do the job of some other, or the three sorts of elements in his soul to meddle with one another. Instead he regulates well what is really his own, rules himself, puts himself in order, becomes his own friend and harmonizes the three elements together, just as if they were literally the three defining notes of an octave—lowest, highest and middle—as well as any others that may be in between. He binds together all of these and, from having been many, becomes entirely one, temperate and harmonious. (441d–e)

What does all of this activity consist in? If we cannot answer this question, we cannot really say what justice is. Socrates, as is well known, contrasts the just person with someone who merely appears to be just. The oligarchical personality, for example, is someone who "has a good reputation and is thought to be just." He has the power to hold the various parts of his soul together in such a way that he can pass himself off as just. But this is mere appearance precisely because harmony is lacking: "Something good of his is forcibly holding in check the other bad appetites within; not persuading them that they had better not, nor taming them with arguments (*logôi*), but using compulsion and fear, because he is terrified of losing his other possessions" (VIII.554c–d).

But this last quotation ought to give an attentive reader pause. How could bad appetites possibly be tamed by argument? Though appetite does have certain sophisticated cognitive abilities, it is notoriously a nonrational part of the soul, so it is not clear why or how it should be susceptible to rational argument at all.[3] There are two ways to make the point I want to make. One way is to say that appetite is not tamed by argument but by *logos*—and that the form logos takes is allegory and myth. The way I prefer is to say that appetite can indeed be tamed by argument, but that we must extend our conception of argument to include certain forms of allegory and myth. The hypothesis I want to put forward and investigate in this essay is that philosophy, as it is manifested and discussed in the *Republic,* is concerned not simply with the rational investigation of the good life, but with using that rational inquiry to facilitate the ability of readers and interlocutors actually to live a good life. Precisely because the soul is shown to have three parts, rational investigation and facilitation cannot be identical. For two parts of the soul—spirit and appetite—are not immediately susceptible to rational persuasion; and if we wish to facilitate the good life, they somehow need to be brought along. The point of myth and allegory is to find a way for reason *mediately* to persuade the nonrational parts of the soul. Allegory and myth is the way reason uses logos to talk to spirit and appetite. It is one of the ways in which reason unifies the soul.

**2.** The hypothesis I want to explore is that the *Republic* is not simply a book that discovers *that* spirit and appetite are distinct parts of the soul, but that it facilitates the process by which they come into line with reason—at least, for a special reader. That is, the *Republic* is, and is meant to be, a therapeutic activity for the right kind of reader. We shall need to learn more about who the right kind of reader is. For the moment, let us say that he or she is someone like Glaucon—who I take to be an ideal interlocutor in the conversation. And let us consider the allegory of the Cave, which is widely considered to be the most powerful image in all of philosophy. I want to claim that, for the right kind of reader, the Cave is not merely a powerful image or a captivating literary device; it is an imaginative activity that justifies the soul. By "justify" I do not here mean, "provide a rational defense of," but rather *bring the soul into the condition of justice,* harmonize the parts. If I may bring the two meanings together: the justification (rational defense) of myth in a philosophical work like the *Republic* is that it serves to justify the soul—that is, bring spirit and appetite into line with reason. It is thus part of the activity—should we be ideal readers—by which we constitute ourselves as integrated persons.

By and large, the scholarly investigation of the Cave has focused on what it means. For example: What are the shadows? Who are the puppeteers, and what are the artifacts they are carrying? What makes us prisoners, and how does our education contribute to our imprisonment? Where on the divided line are the shadows of the Cave located? What is the fire, and how does it relate to the analogy of the sun? How are we to interpret the claim that, in Kallipolis, the philosophers who have ascended out of the Cave will be compelled to go back down?[4] And so on. This is a fruitful line of inquiry; but taken as a genre, it can encourage the impression that this is the universe in which all scholarly inquiry occurs. In this way, a different form of inquiry gets overlooked. Because, in addition to the question of what the Cave means, there is also a question of *how* it means. That is, how does it grab our souls and change us?

Once one becomes attuned to the question of psychic efficacy, it becomes strange that it has been overlooked. For if the overall message of the *Republic* is the overwhelming importance of psychic unity, wouldn't it be a demerit in the book if it spoke to reason alone? It is conceivable that the book should be addressed to reason and give reason instruction on how to proceed with spirit and appetite. And Socrates certainly does give explicit instructions about the cultural, musical, and gymnastic education the future guardians should receive. By way of analogy, we do not expect a cookbook actually to fill our stomachs, but rather to give us instructions on how to feed appetite. I take it that the *Republic* is often read in this spirit. It is as though the only real question is one of content: what is this book really saying? It is of course well known that Plato was concerned with rhetoric, the forms of legitimate persuasion. But this seems to me to have an implication: I would expect that a brilliant author like Plato, concerned with rhetoric, as he works out the theory of the tripartite soul, would wonder whether there were forms of literary persuasion that might serve to bring appetite and *thumos* into harmony with reason's outlook.[5] If so, it could not be rational argument, since the challenge is to persuade the nonrational part of the soul. It would have to be reason's production of images and appearances, which are known to sway spirit and appetite.

Plato was well aware of the limitations of writing as a stimulus to philosophical activity.[6] And in the *Republic,* Socrates describes personality-deformations—notably in the lover of sights and sounds and the democratic personality—that are perfectly capable of "taking up philosophy" in order to gratify certain appetites and thumoeidic ambitions. And though he was not acquainted with the contemporary social form, the academic conference, he would surely not be surprised by the spectacle of lovers of sights and sounds getting together to present papers to each other, perhaps on the meaning of the Cave. Plato was not a magician—and there is no form of writing that can defeat the possibility of such a spectacle. But there is reason to believe that Plato wanted his writing not merely to describe health, but to promote it. And he recognized that this would require imaginative activity on the part of the (right kind of) reader.

**3.** As is well known, in *Republic* X, Socrates returns to the topic of mimetic poetry. And he justifies this return by saying that the damage it does is even more evident now that we have a conception of the parts of the soul (595a–b). There are various ways in which it has a bad effect on the nonrational part of the soul and serves to instill a bad constitution in the soul—for example, encouraging lamentation and pity (604d–605c). But for our investigation, the crucial point is that poetry produces images that are at odds with reason's understanding of what is good and is true (605c). The nonrational part of the soul—spirit and appetite—is swayed by images and appearances; but as nonrational, it is not directly susceptible to reason's rational grasp of what is true and good. But, then, might there not be an indirect way of reason reaching the nonrational part of the soul? If myth and allegory were fashioned so as to promote reason's understanding of the good and the true, then if the nonrational part of the soul were swayed by these images, it would thereby facilitate psychic harmony—that is, actually bring it about. Myth and allegory would be serving as vehicles through which reason could speak to the nonrational parts of the soul in a way that was psychically efficacious. This would provide a vindication of one type of poetic activity (607c). And it would also escape Socrates's criticism of the mimetic poet that he fixes his eye on appearances and thus creates the metaphysically inferior product of an appearance of an appearance (600e–601c, 602c–603). The philosophical "poet" would have his eye fixed on the good and would create appearances with the aim of orienting the nonrational part of the soul in the right direction.

It is clear that Plato thought that the poetry of his day had a disintegrating effect on the human soul. But it is also clear that in Book III—before he introduces the tripartite theory of the soul—Socrates leaves room for a good type of poetic *mimêsis* that would promote the healthy and virtuous development of the human soul (394e–398a). In terms of the Book III discussion, the real danger of bad *mimêsis* is that it encourages multifariousness in people, a kind of psychic dispersion.[7] Good *mimêsis* by contrast would promote the unity of a good person (395b–d; 397d). But once Socrates has developed the tripartite theory of the soul, it becomes possible for him to develop a more nuanced account of what that unity consists in. Psychic unity now requires psychic harmony between disparate parts, two of which are not directly susceptible to rational argument. The question is whether he used that insight to craft an integrating alternative. In the remainder of this essay, I shall look at the allegory of the Cave with this hypothesis in mind. But already we can see certain advantages to the hypothesis.

- The *Republic* would be a better book by its own lights if, in addition to rational argument, it could provide appropriate poetic creations to bring along the nonrational parts of the soul.
- It would give a persuasive reason for why there are myths and allegories in the *Republic.*
- There would be a newfound harmony between what Plato says about poetry and what he does with myth and allegory.
- There would be a new-found harmony between what Plato says about the human soul and what he does with myth and allegory.
- Finally, we would gain insight into Plato's conception of the nonrational

parts of the soul. For if the allegory of the Cave is meant to be an "image" that appeals to appetite and *thumos,* we can gain insight into the types of nonrational persuasion Plato thought possible.

**4.** *Republic* VII famously opens with the allegory of the Cave. Socrates is speaking to Glaucon, and, according to the Reeve translation, he says,

> Next, then compare (*apeikason*) the effect of education (*paideia*) and that of the lack of it on our nature to an experience like this. Imagine (*ide*) human beings living in an underground, cavelike dwelling. (514a1–3)

The verbs are both second-person aorist imperative active: in other words, Socrates is not here simply having a conversation with Glaucon; he is addressing him directly and enjoining him to engage in a certain kind of imaginative activity. The verb *apeikazô,* which is translated as "compare," also means (and was used by Plato to mean) to form from a model, represent, or copy. The injunction to imagine is the aorist imperative of *oîda*—and thus it can be understood as an injunction to see with the mind's eye. The use of the aorist suggests a discrete mental activity. The imperative injunction to imagine is repeated in the same introductory paragraph:

> Imagine (*ide*) that along this road a low wall has been built. (514b5)

And Glaucon's first response is one of compliance and imaginative success:

> I am imagining it (*horô*). (513b8)

The verb is *horaô,* and thus we can understand Glaucon as saying, "I see it, I have it before my mind's eye." Socrates responds,

> Also imagine, then (*hora toinun*), that there are people alongside the wall. (514b9)

Again, the verb is second-person aorist imperative, and it seems reasonable to interpret the *toinun* as a response to Glaucon's immediately preceding declaration of imaginative uptake. Thus, in effect what Socrates is saying is, "Since you have succeeded so far in imagining the Cave (or bringing it before your mind's eye), therefore (*toinun*) continue on by seeing the prisoners' situation in this way."

The important point here is that the significance of the Cave is not exhausted by its content or by figuring out what its content means. Socrates is the tour director of an imaginative trip: he is telling Glaucon what to do with his soul. Glaucon reports that he is successfully following orders; he is active with his soul in just the way Socrates tells him to be, he is creating the images Socrates tells him to create. In effect, Socrates has found a way to speak to the nonrational parts of Glaucon's soul. By enjoining Glaucon to create mental images, he is getting Glaucon to engage in imaginative activity that will be appealing to spirit and appetite. I hypothesize that, for Plato, the ideal reader of the *Republic* would be someone like Glaucon (what this means needs to be investigated) and that the proper way to read this passage would be to submit oneself to the imaginative activity that Glaucon is himself enjoined to carry out. Thus as ideal readers we would not simply be reading *about* a Cave; we would be engaging in our own Cave-ish psychic exercise. And so, while the Cave does provide a comparison with our education (and lack of it), it does so in a way that is particularly comprehensible to spirit and appetite. The Cave is basically reason's report to spirit and appetite on how *paideia* (education, culture) has misshaped them. But to call it a "report" is still a bit misleading, for that suggests a passive accounting in an imagistic language that spirit and appetite can understand. Socrates's use of the second-person aorist imperative address, however, means that if we were to follow his orders, we would engage in active imagining—and this imagining would itself be an act of bringing spirit and appetite into line. The Cave, imaginatively enacted by the right sort of reader, ought to be an act of psychic integration.

Glaucon says,

> It is strange image (*atopon eikona*) you are describing (*legeis*) and strange prisoners. (515a4)

Socrates is not so much describing as he is *speaking* an image—an image that is now before Glaucon's mind's eye and on which Glaucon is commenting. This is an imaginative trip. Socrates responds, "They are like us (*homoious hêmin*)" (515a5). This exchange shares the same formal features as an oracle.

In its paradigmatic form, an oracle (a) is addressed to a recipient, (b) purports to tell the recipient some important feature about his life, and (c) is enigmatic. It is these three features that give oracles their psychic power: There is something about being directly addressed with enigmatic content purporting to tell us who we are that *grabs* us. We are intrigued and curious and imaginatively alive. We want to know how the oracle hooks up to life as we understand it. So when Socrates says, "They are like us," I take him not merely to be describing the fact of a certain similarity between us and the prisoners, but to be indexically *targeting* us as the recipient of this enigmatic image.

Now if the image is directed primarily to the recipient's appetite and *thumos,* it ought to be captivating; it ought also to paint an unappetizing and ridiculous portrait of the prisoners. That it is captivating is beyond question: it has entranced readers for millennia.[8] I have argued elsewhere that the allegory of the Cave is protophilosophical in that it purports to give us—in imagistic form—an account of the totality of our experience (with respect to education and cultural *paideia*) and characterizes that totality as some sort of illusion (imprisoned without realizing it, living amid shadows not recognized as such).[9] But it is also an appetitive and thumoeidic turnoff.

**5.** In terms of spirit, as soon as Socrates has described the prisoners, he asks what it would be like for them to be released from their bonds and "cured of their foolishness" (*aphrosunê*) (515c4–5). He asks Glaucon what he thinks a newly released prisoner would think when we told him that his previous experience of shadows was "silly nonsense" (*phluaria*). Glaucon indicates that initially at least he would be puzzled and not yet able to recognize the truly ridiculous for what it was (515c–d). But after he makes the painful ascent and looks back at "what passed for wisdom there," he will "feel pity" for the others.

> And if there had been honors, praises, or prizes among them for the one who was sharpest at identifying the shadows as they passed by; and was best able to remember which usually came earlier, which later, and which simultaneously; and who was thus best able to prophesize the future, do you think that our man would desire these rewards or envy those among the prisoners who were honored and held power? Or do you think he

> would feel with Homer that he would much prefer to "work the earth as a serf for another man, a man without possessions of his own," and go through any sufferings, rather than share their beliefs as they do? (516c–d)

The image here is of a transformation of the ridiculous. But in the right sort of reader, the image ought actually to transform his sense of the ridiculous. For it is by consulting this image that he can now *see* what is truly ridiculous. The image is an occasion for the transformation of *thumos.* It serves to alienate *thumos* from its earlier attachments and direct it onto new sorts of activity.[10]

There is also an attempt to inoculate *thumos* against the ridicule of others. If a person returned from his ascent into the cave and had "to compete" (*diamillâsthai*) in recognizing shadows, Socrates asks, "wouldn't he provoke ridicule (*gelôs*)?" (517a2). Socrates shows how the prisoners' ordinary sense of the ridiculous serves to keep them in their bonds. And he suggests that this organization of *thumos* has a menacing side: "And as for anyone who tried to free the prisoners and lead them upward, if they could somehow get their hands on him, wouldn't they kill him?" Glaucon responds, "They certainly would" (517a). In terms of the interpretation I am trying to work out, the most striking fact about this exchange is that, in Glaucon's soul, surprise at the murderous outcome has been drained away. After all, the prisoners are "like us" in terms of education and cultural upbringing (*paideia*)—and yet it is no longer surprising that people "like us" would put such a fine person to death. This suggests that both Glaucon and we (the intended readers) are no longer "like us"—in the sense that we can see this as a shameful injustice committed by people who do not understand what they are doing.

The lack of surprise is used as a hallmark of psychic transformation. Socrates invites Glaucon to join him in a further thought: "you should not be surprised" (*thaumazô*) that those who ascend from the Cave want to stay there and do not want to occupy themselves with human affairs (517c). Nor is it surprising if someone who comes from looking at the divine "appears completely ridiculous" (*phainetai sphodra geloîos*) when he is compelled to compete (*agônizesthai*) among the shadows or shadows of justice (517d). Glaucon responds, "It is not surprising at all" (*Oud' homôstioûn thaumaston*) (517e2). Thus not only is Glaucon (and the intended reader) no longer "like us" in terms of *paideia,* but the truly absurd behavior of those who still are "like us"—the prisoners—is, for him, only to be expected.

Socrates continues that "anyone with any sense" (*ei noun ge echoi tis*) would not "laugh absurdly" (*alogistôs gelôi*) when he saw someone coming from the light to the dark (518a).[11] Instead, he would ask whether the person's eyesight was confused because he was coming from light to dark or from dark to light. The first soul he would consider happy; the second soul he would pity (*tên de elêseien*). And then Socrates adds,

> But even if he wanted to ridicule [this second soul], at least his ridiculing it would make him less ridiculous than ridiculing a soul that had come from the light above. (518b)

So by now there is a complete revolution in the sense of the ridiculous from that which those who are "like us" in terms of *paideia* have inherited. And Glaucon responds, "That's an entirely reasonable (*metriôs*) claim" (518b6). In other words, Glaucon has been able to make a journey by which his current sense of the ridiculous now stands at 180 degrees from the sense of the ridiculous of those who are "like us" in terms of education and cultural inheritance. No doubt his soul was in various ways ready to make this journey, but he needed an image to bring *thumos* along. If we think of a Socrates-figure entangled in the courts of law, he will, from the perspective of ordinary cultural influence, cut a ridiculous figure. From that perspective, he seems oafish—unable to give "clever" arguments, unrepentant and arrogant, lacking in tears and lamentation.[12] Now a rational understanding of this situation will correct for this misleading appearance. Reason will comprehend that the Socrates figure is oriented toward the good: he cannot give a "clever" argument in the sense that a good person cannot commit a bad act. But how can reason convince *thumos* of this? By creating an image that frames this Socratic behavior in a different context. The image of the Cave allows *thumos* to see what reason understands. In this way, the Cave can serve as a "spiritual exercise" in the literal sense that it can help modify what spirit—*thumos*—values and desires.

**6.** That the Cave is also structured so as to facilitate a revolution in appetite can be seen from the following. Appetitive desire can desire almost anything. Indeed, it *pushes* for variety. Left unchecked, appetite will lead us politically to the fevered city where there are not only the couches, relishes, and chickpea desserts of the healthy city, but also pastry cooks, whores, and fashionmongers who tempt us with wigs, makeup, and stiletto shoes (II.372e–373c). It will lead to the democratic city, where one can shop for different constitutions as though one were at a market, where license to pursue the appetite of the moment is called "freedom." One can even choose philosophical theories according to taste. The democratic constitution itself encourages "multifarious people" who live according to unchecked appetite (VIII.557c, 561c–e). Socrates tells us that appetite is so voraciously multiform that even the name *appetite* does not really capture its nature. It is called "appetite" because certain intense instances—hunger, thirst, sexual desire—serve as paradigms (IX.580d–581a). Part of appetite's multiplicity stems from its ability to transfer desire onto new objects. So, appetite begins desiring money because money can buy the food, drink, and sex that appetite desires; but appetite comes simply *to desire money.* Thus appetite comes to be known as the money-loving or profit-loving part of the soul (581a).[13]

If we consider simply the hurly-burly world in which we tend to live, appetite can lust after almost anything. What doesn't it want? Shadows it can recognize as such. We want *the burger,* not the shadow of it cast by the overhead light.[14] When we go to order a sandwich at Subway, it would be astonishing for someone to say, "On second thought, I'll just take the plastic model of the sandwich on display." Even if looking at the plastic sandwich causes us to salivate—that is certainly possible—our appetite clearly reaches beyond the model and out to the sandwich that the model represents. We do not find ourselves salivating *for* the plastic. This seems obvious, but there is an important interpretive point here that tends to get overlooked. First, let us remind ourselves of the obvious. If we are speaking nonallegorically and simply try to describe appearances, there is of course such a thing as the *appearance of a shadow*—that is, a shadow visually recognized as such. We see one every time we see shadow and see that it's a shadow—that is, almost all the time. Second, and only slightly less obvious, this distinction between reality and shadow is readily available to the appetitive part of our soul—and, thus, readily available to us if we happen to be appetitive personalities. As is clear from the above burger example, appetite easily and regularly makes the distinction between burger (which it wants) and shadow of burger (which it does not care about). And that means that there is a distinction within the realm of appearances between "real thing" and "shadow" that appetite can recognize. But now we get to the third and more interesting point: this obvious visual distinction within the realm of appearance can be used for an appetitive counterpart of the philosophical distinction between reality and mere appearance. It is precisely because, literally speaking, appetite can recognize shadows as such that an allegory about prisoners who cannot recognize shadows as such *can be recognized by appetite* as a negative image of the prisoners. This, I think, is what the allegory is for. It is an imaginative meal that Socrates feeds to Glaucon's appetite that will help bring it into line with what Glaucon's reason is discovering in the course of their rational inquiry. If appetite had no traction on the reality/shadow distinction, the allegory would not be able to appeal to it in the way that it does.

Obviously, within the allegory, the prisoners cannot recognize the shadows they see as such. But what this means is that the prisoners take the world of appearances—that is, the world in which appetite functions, and which includes Big Macs as well as shadows of Big Macs recognized as such—to be reality. What the prisoners cannot recognize is the metaphysically derivative status of the world of appearances. And thus they cannot recognize that the entire physical world (comprised of things and their shadows) is, philosophically speaking, shadow. Appetite is incapable of grasping this distinction, which transcends the realm of appearances in which it operates. So insofar as a person is dominated by the appetitive part of his soul, he will remain a prisoner. However, if a person is leaving his prisoner status, he needs an image that will bring appetite along. One way to do this is to provide the image of a distinction that appetite can grasp, in order to bring it into line with a distinction whose true meaning is forever beyond its grasp.

Therefore, for the allegory of the Cave to be psychically efficacious, it is important that even at the level of appetite, appetite go after what it takes to be real and can distinguish its own version of reality versus shadow. From a higher perspective, we may see that it is lusting after mere appearances, shadows—but that is not how it seems from the point of view of appetite. So if one could get appetite to see shadow where before it only saw food, drink, sex, and glamour, that would be part of the process by which appetite is turned around. The Cave transforms the entire realm of ordinary appetitive desires into an image of lusting after shadows (that are now, in the telling of the allegory, recognized as such). In this way, it defeats appetite's desire for variety. Instead of the heady brew of moving from pastries to sex to glitzy clothes and fashionable speeches, that entire mix is painted with a gray uniformity. It is all more of the same—shadow after shadow. This is an appetite suppressant.[15]

And insofar as appetite is tempted by the new, by getting that glittering object that it can see over there but cannot yet reach, then the Cave-image gives appetite a new primordial desire: getting to the sun, which is out there, just beyond the horizon, lighting it up. In *Republic* VI, shortly before he introduces the allegory of the Cave, Socrates claims that every soul pursues the good, "and for its sake does everything." He continues: "The soul has a hunch that the good is something, but is puzzled and cannot adequately grasp just what it is" (505e). The image of the sun is perfect for orienting appetite in the right direction.

**7.** In the midst of the allegory of the Cave, Socrates argues for the need for conversion. I think this gives us instruction on how to read the allegory. "Education," Socrates tells us, "is not what some people boastfully claim it to be":[16] they think knowledge is something you could put into souls, as though one could put sight into blind eyes. But what the "present account" (*ho de ge nun logos*) shows about the power to learn, which is present in everyone, is that "it must be turned around (*periakteon*) from what comes to be *together with the whole soul* (*sun holêi têi psychêi*), until it is able to bear to look at what is and at the brightest thing there is" (VII, 518c4–9; my emphasis). But in the light of Socrates's theory of the tripartite soul, the only way one could turn the *whole* soul would be to turn appetite and *thumos* in the same direction as reason. It is, I think, inconceivable that Plato could be concerned with turning the whole soul, recognize that the whole soul is importantly constituted by appetite and spirit, and not have on his mind the question of how to turn appetite and *thumos*. Socrates speaks of a *technê*—a craft—of soul-turning (*tês periagôgês*) (518d3–4); but if there were going to be a craft that turned appetite and *thumos,* it would have to be a craft that, at least in significant part, appealed to them through images and appearances. As I have already hypothesized with respect to Glaucon, the allegory of the Cave is an instance of that craft—an occasion for the very soul-turning he is talking about. In this instance, turning the whole soul around and bringing about psychic harmony are one and the same activity. By means of the allegory, appetite is alienated from its ordinary world via an unappetizing image of shadows and lured in the direction of reality (the forms) via a glittering picture. The allegory is an instance of reason speaking to appetite; and on the occasions when appetite is responsive, appetite is thereby "listening" to what reason has to say. In this way, appetite is turned around and—another way of describing the same activity—reason and appetite are brought into harmony. In the *Phaedrus,* Socrates famously claims that rhetoric should be a *technê* that functions as a certain kind of leading of the soul by means of *logoi* (*psuchagôgia tis dia logôn*).[17] If one wants to take seriously the idea of such a *technê* in the light of the tripartite theory of the soul worked out in the *Republic,* it would seem that the soul-leading *logoi* of rhetoric must be broadened to include certain instances of *muthos* and *muthologia:* the myths and allegories that will lead the nonrational parts of the soul in the right direction.

**8.** This interpretation also helps us understand the much-discussed claim that the philosophers in Kallipolis will be "compelled" (*prosanankazô*) to return to the Cave and take care of others (VII.520).[18] How are we to understand this "compulsion"? Socrates makes three claims in this passage: (a) that the young philosophers have incurred a political obligation to the polis, due to their upbringing; (b) that the polis overall will be better run by people like them who have seen the truth about the fine and grasp the significance of everyday political life in terms of that truth; and (c) that the requirement is just and thus the philosophers will carry it out willingly because they are just. Indeed, Glaucon explicitly says that the reason the young philosophers will adhere to the requirement is that "we'll be giving just orders to just people" (VII.520d). But if the obligation is just, if it falls on just people who are able to appreciate its justice, and that is the basis of their action, why talk of compulsion? This would seem to be a paradigm of free and willing action in relation to political obligation. Sure, Socrates wants to make the point that if it were not for this obligation, the philosophers would much prefer to hang out with the Form of the Good rather than exercise political rule. But if that is all that is meant, why didn't he just say so?

An idea that makes sense of this somewhat excessive language is that Socrates is here addressing the appetitive side of Glaucon's soul. (And correlatively Plato is addressing the appetitive side of the ideal reader's soul.) After all, we have here an image of the philosopher being "compelled" to return to the Cave, to the world of shadows. But, before one is released from those bonds, that world is appetitive heaven: it is the world of wine, sex, song, and fast chariots. Why not treat the return as appetitive vacation?! The image of compulsion blocks that option. It is an image of being forced to go where you really do not want to go, in contrast to the glittering prizes that lie outside the Cave. Understanding that the "compulsion" here is the compulsion of rational freedom—the "compulsion" of the just man happily carrying out a just act—is something that reason can grasp. But how do you get the point across to the nonrational parts of the soul? By painting an unappetizing picture about a "compelled" return to the land of shadows.

**9.** It is an unsettling thought to wonder whether the *Republic* has ever helped anyone become a better person or live a better life. I want to think that the answer must be yes; but what is my evidence? And just as Socrates directly challenges Homer, as though he were a conversation-partner—"My dear Homer!"—isn't it incumbent upon us, who spend a significant portion of our lives reading and teaching the *Republic,* to say, "My dear Plato! Tell me, has reading the *Republic* ever influenced human practices, whether public or private, for the better?" (cp. X.599c–600a). Socrates tells us that a philosopher-king, able to bring about the changes required for happy political life, though a real possibility, is extraordinarily rare (V.471c–e; VI.499c–d, 502a–d). And when I think of the forced march of city-dwellers into the Cambodian countryside, where approximately two million died from starvation and other forms of hardship, I wonder with nausea whether the Khmer Rouge leaders, while studying in Paris, were influenced by *Republic* VII, 540e–541a. There is, of course, nothing in the written word that can defeat a tyrant's desire to put a book to tyrannical use, nor even stop a lover of sights and sounds turning the *Republic* into the latest academic fashion. Plato was aware of this. But then what *good* could it do anyone who did not live at such a propitious time, who had no chance of being or being near a philosopher-king—what good could it do such a person simply to read the *Republic?* By the theory of the *Republic* itself, it could do the reader no good unless the reading somehow facilitated integration in his soul. If the *Republic* only reached the reader's reason, it is hard to see how he could be improved by reading it. Perhaps those extraordinarily rare people who are both *already* just and have not been corrupted by society, who have perhaps constituted themselves according to a divine model, could use the *Republic* to understand their situation better; or perhaps they could use it cookbook-style for how to give instructions to appetite and *thumos* that are already basically in line (VI.496b–d; IX.592b). But if that is the only good it does, it would seem to be pretty much superfluous, for these are people who are able to constitute themselves as just in the face of massive cultural influence to the contrary; it does not seem like they need the *Republic.*

The hypothesis I have been exploring is the idea that for some readers—rare, but less rare than the philosopher-king or the miraculously just person—an imaginatively engaged reading of the text can promote psychic harmony. I have hypothesized that Glaucon provides a model of the right sort of reader; and I want to conclude with a brief speculation about what makes him so. Socrates tells us that Glaucon's personality is dominated by spirit: he is like the timocratic man, at least in terms of love of victory (VIII.548d). And Socrates famously says that something godlike (*theion*) must have affected him, and his brother Adeimantus, if they are not persuaded by their own arguments that injustice is better than justice (if you can get away with it) (II.368a). How are we to understand this ability not to be persuaded? In terms of the tripartite theory of the soul, it would seem that Glaucon's reason is not persuaded by his own argument (even though he cannot yet see what is wrong with it), nor do his appetites seem to be inflamed by the claim that it would be better to get more (if you could get away with it). This seems to confirm Socrates's diagnosis that Glaucon is a man dominated by spirit and—this is what is godlike—for whatever reason, his spirit seems to be somehow oriented toward what is truly honorable. He is a proud person who wants the right sort of victory. For such a person, the arguments of the *Republic* can at least begin to orient reason in the right direction; and the images provided by myth and allegory can direct and solidify the orientation of appetite and *thumos.* In this way, the *logoi* of the *Republic* not only talk about the good life, but they facilitate it.

CHAPTER FOURTEEN

# The Ethical Thought of J. M. Coetzee

**1.** What is ethical thought? For starters, let us say that thought is ethical when it facilitates or promotes the living of an ethical life. It would seem, then, that ethical thought cannot be captured by its subject matter. It is easy enough, for example, to imagine a rundown social practice that consists in discussing ethical topics in empty ways. Imagine someone who devotes his professional life to writing articles about, say, the difference between just and unjust wars but whose soul is made coarser in the process. There might be a journal—let us fictionally call it *Ethics and Politics*—in which professors from different universities vie to place their articles, none of which make any difference in how countries go to war. It is, of course, possible that the reflection that went into those articles helps authors, readers, and students become more ethically sensitive, and this possibility should not be diminished. However, it is easy to imagine a different scenario: one in which the journal functions mainly as a credentialing agency for university jobs. People who publish there would write "outside letters" for other people who publish there so that deans who care nothing about the field (other than that their university should be "ranked high") will approve appointments and promotions.

To make the problem more vivid, imagine a moral or political issue that matters to you—racism, gerrymandering, campaign finance, gay rights, religious liberty, the Middle East, Islamic extremism, mistreatment of animals, the destruction of indigenous cultures. Then imagine that the social circumstances surrounding you shift in such a way that this issue becomes fashionable: clever articles about it appear in the best op-ed pages and book reviews, it is discussed over dinner and at cocktail parties, certain individuals attain celebrity for advocating the cause—and yet the whole social whirl is somehow cut off from making a difference. In such circumstances, we have the *appearance* of ethical thought, and it is this very appearance that can mislead participants. In such a situation, we would most likely take ourselves to be thinking about ethical issues. After all, we have just read, discussed, or even contributed the latest article on *X.* Ersatz ethical thought would give us the sense that the space for ethical thought was already filled.

The situation is even worse with novelists. No one is better positioned to profit—in the mundane, literal sense of earning large sums of money, or by winning distinguished literary prizes—from a "sensitive" portrayal of an ethically charged topic, like torture or war. Let us leave to one side the cynical author who uses an ethically charged topic like torture to seek fame and fortune. The problem is more pressing if we imagine a sincere, morally engaged author who would like his writing to correct an injustice. How might that work? Can we not imagine that, precisely as a result of the author's success as a writer, he will be taken up as a celebrity, and that being "against torture" might become a fashion item among the intelligentsia? It is not impossible that something good should come of this. But it is easy enough for the whole public event to serve as a fashionable substitute for ethical thought, rather than as an instance of it. (Imagine the publication party for a book against global warming that ends early so the guests can catch a plane.)

J. M. Coetzee's literary style is, I think, an attempt to defeat this possibility. And I think we can understand the complexity of his literary form if we see him as trying to communicate ethical thought. That is, he is trying to stimulate genuinely ethical thought in other people. In this essay, I want to give at least a preliminary indication of how this might work. In the first instance, I will give a broad overview of how Coetzee's literary form fits into a philosophical tradition concerned with the contribution of form to ethical thought. Then I will examine one of the central arguments of *Diary of a Bad Year* concerning the shame of torture, and I will try to show how the form of the book facilitates a reader's relation to that shame.

**2.** There has been speculation in reviews about the relation between JC, the protagonist of *Diary of a Bad Year,* and J. M. Coetzee, its author. JC is, after all, a South African novelist who has recently immigrated to Australia, and hanging on the wall of his bedroom (as seen by his Filipina secretary, Anya) is "a framed scroll in some foreign language (Latin?) with his name in fancy lettering with lots of curlicues and a big red wax seal in the corner."[1] We know he is JC because that is how he signs two letters—one imploring Anya to come back to his employ after they have had a blowup, the other inviting her and her lover, Alan, to dinner to celebrate the completion of the book he has been writing. In private discussion between Anya and Alan, Anya refers to JC as "Señor C" and "El Señor," and Alan refers to him as "Mr. C." At the dinner party, when Alan gets drunk, he calls him "Juan" to his face. As anyone who has read Coetzee's novel (or even just reviews of it) knows, almost every page is divided into two or three sections, each section written in (and representing) a different voice. The top section is the official voice of the author, JC, the exposition of moral opinions that will eventually find their way into his book. Many of them sound as though they could be taken for the voice of Coetzee.

But there is this crucial difference between JC and J. M. Coetzee: JC is willing to publish his *Strong Opinions* as a freestanding book; Coetzee is not. Coetzee is only willing to publish the opinions as authored by JC in the context of a novel in which those very opinions—as well as the act of writing them down and publishing them—are questioned by JC himself as well as by Anya and are mocked by Alan. Not only that, but JC and his book are embedded among other sections of Coetzee's book that include JC's personal musings (from a diary?) about his attraction to Anya and his growing sense of infirmity. What is the meaning of this difference? It is a mistake to treat the different voices represented in these sections simply as a display of literary virtuosity. The reviewer in the *New York Times Book Review* said that we readers "are manipulated by a form that is coy as well as playful."[2] This claim is, I think, mistaken. The aim of the style is not for Coetzee to show off—to demonstrate that he, unlike the melancholy, infirm, single-voiced JC, can do postmodern hip. Rather, it is an attempt to defeat the reader's desire to defer to the "moral authority," the "novelist" J. M. Coetzee. In an article in the *New York Times,* Rachel Donadio writes, "In a country [South Africa] where every inch of physical and moral ground is contested, Coetzee has been criticized for refusing to play the role of writer-as-statesman, one more easily played by his fellow Nobel laureate, Nadine Gordimer."[3] The wording is marvelous: for Coetzee has never been explicitly accused of failing to play a role. He has been accused of racism, of letting South Africa down, of not being a moral exemplar. But when I read the criticism, it seems to me that Donadio got it right: what irks people about Coetzee is his refusal to conform to their image of how he should behave as a "South African writer," "Nobel Prize winner," "moral conscience." We need to see this same refusal in his literary style.

JC writes, "Authority must be earned; on the novelist author lies the onus to build up, out of nothing, such authority" (149). But Coetzee's authority lies in his ability to divest himself of authority: this is not manipulation, it is certainly not coy, and if "playful" is meant to be the opposite of moral seriousness, it is not playful either. The questions are why he does it and how he does it. Why he does it is, I think, straightforward: he wants to defeat ersatz ethical posturing and promote genuine ethical thought in his reader. How he does this is tricky, and requires some attention.

**3.** Within the Western philosophical tradition, there have been a number of attempts to use literary characters—most notably, at the beginning, in Plato's dialogues. At the center is the figure of Socrates, who claims to know only that he does not know. Not only does Plato, as authority figure, disappear behind his characters, but the central figure distinguishes himself by eschewing authority when it comes to ethical knowledge. There are of course many other characters, some with worked-out ethical views, but the dialogues are set up so that there is always some question about how those views should be received. This is not simply a literary device to sustain the reader's interest; it is an ethical strategy, an attempt to provoke thought in the reader by defeating any easy desire to defer to the author or to any surrogate for the author in the text. Even the figures within the text need to be handled with dialectical delicacy. If a respected character were to say, "When it comes to ethics, you really need to think for yourself," one can imagine the response "Anything you say, boss: I really must think for myself!"

Plato was also suspicious of writing as a medium for philosophical activity. In a famous passage at the end of *Phaedrus,* Socrates recounts an Egyptian tale of an ancient time in which King Thamus warns Theuth, the inventor of writing, that students "will imagine they come to know much while for the most part they know nothing."[4] Socrates's worry seems to be that writing, by its very nature, tends to defeat ethical thought. People can read the words, think they know what is at stake, pass the words along to others who think they are being taught—all without friction. There is a mimicking of ethical thought: the reading, reproduction, and transmission of "ethical arguments" that make no difference to how anyone lives. It stands to reason that a philosopher so aware of the dangers of writing would try to find a literary form that would defeat the transmission of ersatz thought.

Entranced as I am with Plato, I think I see a problem with the dialogue form. It can encourage in the reader a sense that he is in the audience, watching the characters debate as though they were up on stage. Rather than being thrown into philosophy's midst, challenged to examine one's beliefs, one can feel like an arbiter, able to choose one's position from among the many presented according to taste. One does not have to read the dialogues this way, but (and perhaps this is a reflection of the times and culture we live in) I have seen generations of students incline toward it.

It has crossed my mind to wonder whether this problem motivated Kierkegaard, a devoted student of Plato, to create pseudonymous authors. Although Kierkegaard wrote many works under his own name, the most famous ones—*Fear and Trembling, Either/Or, Repetition, Sickness Unto Death, Philosophical Fragments, Concluding Unscientific Postscript*—were all published under pseudonyms. But, in the *Postscript*, Kierkegaard makes it explicit in a document signed under his own name that the pseudonyms are not pseudonyms for him. Rather, he, Kierkegaard, has created pseudonymous authors who have themselves gone on to write their books. If it could work, the pseudonymous authorship would be an ingenious improvement on the dialogue form, precisely because it breaks down the division between stage and audience. Instead of me watching as two characters debate with each other "on stage" and adjudicating points to one or the other of them, it is as though one of the characters has come down from the stage—in fact, there is no longer a stage, no longer a character—and he is confronting *me*. "My pseudonymity," Kierkegaard tells us in "A First and Last Explanation," "has not had an *accidental* basis in my person . . . but an *essential* basis in the *production* itself."[5]

But why did Kierkegaard write "A First and Last Explanation"? That Kierkegaard felt the need to explain his authorship is, I think, an indication that he thought it had failed. Perhaps the demands made on the reader are too strenuous. Perhaps it is too easy to assume that the pseudonym is just a pen name and too difficult to sustain the recognition that one is being addressed by a literary character.

Might there not be a more forgiving (and thus more successful) way to use this literary form—one that would not require the selfdefeating gesture of a first and last explanation? Perhaps one might put the pseudonymous author along with his book inside a novel in which author and book are both commented upon by various voices. If this is a literary style aimed at provoking ethical thought in the reader, standing, as I think it does, in a tradition that goes back to Plato's dialogues and continues through Kierkegaard's pseudonymous authorship, then it is a misunderstanding of the form to think that it is a clever or irritating literary feat—one in which, if Coetzee were less clever, or less irritating, he would come out from behind his mask and tell us what he meant. But what if his concern were that our concern with what he meant would distract us from our concern with how we should be? If *Diary of a Bad Year* is ethical thinking in action, if it is directed toward stimulating ethical thought in the reader, then it would be a misstep for Coetzee to "step out from behind his mask" and tell us what he meant—not in the sense that he would be exercising bad political or literary judgment, but because there ought to be no mask out from which to step. There would be no content withheld, nothing more to say, and thus an attempt to say what that content was would be to attack the production itself. This is what it would mean to say that the pseudonymous author JC does not have an accidental basis in Coetzee's person—that is, he is not showing off—but an essential basis in the production itself.

**4.** One reason to divide a page is that it gives Coetzee a way to address different parts of our soul at more or less the same time. In *Phaedrus,* Socrates claims that rhetoric is a peculiar craft of leading the soul through the power of logos—that is, through speech and argument.[6] And in the *Republic,* he says that education should not be thought of in terms of putting something into another person, but rather as turning the whole soul around.[7] I think we need to see the split page of *Diary of a Bad Year* as a rhetorical move in this Platonic sense. This is Coetzee's attempt to lead the whole soul.

For the sake of simplicity (and brevity), I am going to focus on two broad movements. If one reads across the top section, one is ostensibly reading *Strong Opinions,* the book that JC will publish in German translation. (One will later read what Anya calls his "Soft Opinions" and JC calls his "Second Diary," which JC does not publish but does share with Anya.) Reading across like this, one is confronted by what I shall call the *dialectic of responsibility.* I am tempted to say that this is the level of rationality, but that is not quite right. As we shall see, not all of JC's arguments are rational. But this is the level at which we are presented with (and entangled in) argument. The movement works through logos. However, when we read downward, we encounter a *spectacle of embedding.* That is, we see how the moral stances that are officially to be presented in book form are embedded in the fantasies, happenings, musings, and struggles of the author's day-to-day life. It is that from which a normal book of moral essays would be cut off. I suggest that this imaginary embedding is meant to draw along parts of the reader's soul that would not be led by argument alone. "That from which" is a phrase Aristotle used to pick out the matter of a living organism.[8] A living human being, for example, is a form-and-matter unity in which the stuff of human life—blood, guts, flesh, and bones—realizes itself in self-maintaining form, in human being. The stuff of life is that from which its form emerges and that in which life maintains itself. I want to suggest that *Strong Opinions* has the *form* of argument, but that form is an aspect of a living form-and-matter unity that consists of JC's arguments embedded in the stuff of his life. JC gives us the form; Coetzee gives us the form-and-matter unity. Now why an apprehension of moral arguments as embedded in the life of a fictional character should defeat ersatz ethical thought, and perhaps even promote ethical thought in some, is a puzzle. But to solve that puzzle is to grasp the rhetorical strategy of the book.

**5.** *Diary of a Bad Year* opens at the very same place as the purported book *Strong Opinions,* whose author we will later learn is JC. It is an excursus on the origins of the state.

> Every account of the origins of the state starts from the premise that "we"—not we readers but some generic we so wide as to exclude no one—participate in its coming into being. But the fact is that the only "we" we know—ourselves and the people close to us—are born into the state; and our forebears too were born into the state as far back as we can trace. The state is always there before we are. (3)

JC's official voice is one of reminder and recognition. He invites us to share his skepticism about how certain forms of philosophical argument implicate us in the formation of the state. In the polis version of chicken and egg, we are told that we came first and, out of our needs, created a state. JC reminds us that there is no "we" that we can recognize as ever wanting or needing to do that. It does not follow that JC's voice is therefore antiphilosophical. Philosophy is regularly constituted by questioning the uses to which philosophy can be put. Nor is JC scorning all uses to which a state-of-nature argument might be put. Rather, he is questioning a particular use, one that locates our responsibility in the wrong place. If we bear responsibility, it is not because of some original sin, a mythical act of mythical ancestors who lived outside the state but nevertheless count as "us." I suspect that the intended reader (that is, the reader Coetzee has in mind, whom I will simply call the reader) is one who will enjoy this opening criticism—who will enjoy the recognition that I or we are not part of a nonexistent "we" who purportedly carried out this bogus act. That is, we begin with a satisfying recognition that we are not who this vindicating story of the state says we are. We are not people who owe allegiance to the state's actions because "we" formed it—and we are not going to accept an argument that tries to implicate us on such shabby grounds.

As we move toward the lower part of the page, we also move to the lower part of the body—and, not incidentally, the "lower" part of the soul.

> My first glimpse of her was in the laundry room. It was mid-morning on a quiet spring day and I was sitting, watching the washing go around, when this quite startling young woman walked in. Startling because the last thing I was expecting was such an apparition; also because the tomato-red shift she wore was so startling in its brevity. (3)

What could be more ordinary, homogeneous, self-contained than sitting in one's laundry room (as, no doubt, he had often done) watching the washing go around? But this is a world that can be disturbed by a glimpse. There is no doubt that the glimpse is erotic. A week later he happens to see her again "only fleetingly as she passed through the front door in a flash of white slacks that showed off a derriere so near to perfect as to be angelic. God, grant me one wish before I die, I whispered; but then was overtaken with shame at the specificity of the wish, and withdrew it" (8). If this were only a report of JC's sexual fantasies, he would stand in an odd relation to his own imagination. What, after all, is it to have a wish and then "withdraw" it? For JC's act to make sense, we must take his whispering to be not merely the expression of a wish, but a plea to God. Wishes are not the sort of thing one can withdraw; requests are. But now that the divine has been invoked, we are not just within the realm of sex (are we ever?), but approaching something significant, difficult to name or understand, that, at least in the moment, makes it feel instinctively appropriate to call on God for remedy. JC calls it a "metaphysical ache":

> As I watched her an ache, a metaphysical ache, crept over me that I did nothing to stem. And in an intuitive way she knew about it, knew that in the old man in the plastic chair in the corner there was something personal going on, something to do with age and regret and the tears of things. (7)

If you have never felt a metaphysical ache yourself, or if you are unable to use this occasion to feel such an ache vicariously, or if you are unable to use this occasion imaginatively to anticipate the future onset of such an ache, then this book is not for you. But then why are you wasting your time reading a novel? We need to take seriously the idea that the ache is metaphysical. Though it is a psychological occurrence, it is not merely that. It is, rather, an ache that can lead us to a richer grasp of what kind of being we are.

In the *Symposium,* Socrates tells of a conversation he had with the priestess Diotima, who taught him the art of love. "All of us are pregnant, Socrates, both in body and soul, and, as soon as we come to a certain age we naturally desire to give birth."[9] But pregnancy and reproduction are the ways in which mortal beings participate in immortality. This is a godly affair, and it must occur in beauty, which is in harmony with the divine. Now when someone is pregnant in soul, "he too will certainly go about seeking the beauty in which he would beget." "In my view, you see, when he makes contact with someone beautiful and keeps company with him, he conceives and gives birth to what he has been carrying inside him for ages."[10] Now, for the beautiful young boy of ancient Greek aristocratic society, substitute the Filipina woman in her startlingly brief tomato-red shift and "thongs of the kind that go on the feet" (6). Much later in the book, toward the end of the *Strong Opinions* section, JC writes in the middle section of the page:

> Was Anya from 2514 in any but the most farfetched sense the natural mother of the miscellany of opinions I was putting down on paper on commission . . . ? No. The passions and prejudices out of which my opinions grew were laid down long before I first set eyes on Anya, and were by now so strong—that is to say, so settled, so rigid—that aside from the odd word here and there there was no chance that refraction through her gaze could alter their angle. (124–125)

In one way, this fits the Socratic conception well. For the beautiful other is not a contributor to the pregnancy but the occasion for a long-standing pregnancy to come to term. On this picture, what we would see on the upper part of the page is that to which JC gave birth in the presence of the beautiful Anya. In the lower two sections, we would be witness to the birthing process. The book *Strong Opinions* is then a kind of husk: the externalization into the world of what used to lie inside JC's pregnant soul. Perhaps one reason that published "moral opinions" can fall flat in terms of ethical thought is that they are cut off from the birthing process.

But in another way JC provides a significant variation on the Socratic theme. For JC is not just erotically bowled over by Anya's beauty; he is preoccupied with his own aging, physical decay, and death. To be sure, there are intimations of this in Plato: it is because we are mortal creatures that we stretch ourselves to become immortal. It is because we humans know in some sense that we are mortal—we live in the light of that mortality—that our births-in-beauty can be symbolic. Yet JC's birthing is more mired in anticipations of physical decay and death than anything Plato imagined. Let's face it: JC is looking for a way to die. JC's metaphysical ache is the living recognition that in his erotic longing, in all its wild inappropriateness, he is a creature who will soon not be. From the middle section: "Last night I had a bad dream, which I afterwards wrote down, about dying and being guided to the gateway to oblivion by a young woman. What I did not record is the question that occurred to me in the act of writing: Is she the one?" (59).

Diotima talks of giving birth in beauty; JC is giving birth in beauty in the valley of the shadow of death. He has a fantasy of dying in a whorehouse and being dumped unceremoniously in an alley; after reporting this, he continues, "But no, if the new dream is to be trusted it will not be like that. I will expire in my own bed and be discovered by my typist, who will close my eyes and pick up the telephone to make her report" (65). It is clear that Anya picks up on the importance of this fantasy. Later, in the lower section, she reports: "He told me one of his dreams, I said to Alan. It was really sad, about dying and his ghost lingering behind, not wanting to leave. I told him he should write it down before he forgets, and work it into his book" (77). Is Anya here giving advice to JC or to Coetzee? Coetzee writes about it in *Diary of a Bad Year,* but JC leaves it out of *Strong Opinions.*

One might say that she is giving advice to them both, or that Coetzee is the one able to take up her advice; but I do not think either option is correct. Anya is Coetzee's creation—who knows in whose presence he gave birth to that beauty. What we have in the fictional world is Anya giving advice to JC, and I think it is helpful to think of JC as following it after his own fashion. JC's *Strong Opinions* is written in the light of his own decay and death, in the presence of the beautiful Anya. *Strong Opinions* is JC's own being-toward-death: it is what he elects to put forward into the public world in the light of his own imminent demise. His own decay is not what he wants to talk about—that is Coetzee's preoccupation. JC wants to utter the ethical word in the public domain. That is how he wants to spend his last days on earth: in the public domain, writing *Strong Opinions;* in private, entangled with Anya as quasi-Platonic lover. What all this means is far from clear. But the fact that Coetzee lets us see how JC's ethical words are embedded in his living-toward-death allows us at least to explore, in gut-open ways, why taking such a stance might matter.

It is clear from the moment they meet that JC and Anya are in close intuitive contact. As we have already seen, the moment he feels the metaphysical ache, "in an intuitive way she knew all about it." It was something "which she did not particularly like, did not want to evoke," but she could recognize it, feel it. And JC recognizes that she feels it, and is even able to grasp the meaning it has for her: "Had it come from someone different, had it a simpler and blunter meaning, she might have been readier to give it welcome; but from an old man its meaning was too diffuse and melancholy for a nice day when you are in a hurry to get the chores done" (7).

In short, this metaphysical ache is not the private property of JC's imagination: it reaches out to Anya, is instantly recognized by her and responded to in her own imaginative act that is itself immediately recognized by JC. The question is whether this ache is able to reach out, off the page, and entangle the reader. My own sense is that it does; and it helps us import an ethical ache into the *Strong Opinions.*

Even at this early stage, one can see in the form of communication a strategy designed to defeat ersatz ethical thought. In particular, any tendency in the reader to transfer authority to the author is undermined twice over. Not only is the author of *Strong Opinions* not Coetzee—and thus whatever admiration one has for him cannot directly transfer into admiration for the opinions expressed—but even the purported author, JC, is shown to be entangling himself in a somewhat melancholy, perhaps pathetic, erotic outreach to a woman he happened to glimpse in the laundry. Who knows what place his moral musings have in relation to this human drama? We know immediately that these "strong opinions" are being embedded in a larger context, but we have no idea what the significance of this embedding is. The "strong opinions" do seem to be what JC wants to put in the public domain during a period when he is contemplating his own decay and demise. This we can see not from *Strong Opinions* but from *Diary of a Bad Year.* But is this a final word that he needs to speak, or is it simply an empty motion he is going through as he pursues what really matters to him—a relationship with Anya? There is no answer to this question in the text. Thus there is no easy way for a reader to take on the strong opinions simply by taking Coetzee's or JC's word for it. If we think of ethical thought as something that cannot be accepted on authority, then this is a literary form that defeats a typical way in which ethical thought is itself defeated.

For a similar reason, the form also works against ethical thought becoming routine. With transference of authority, the problem is not only that we are taking a so-called expert's word for it; the word we take tends to lose vitality. So, to take an example that we shall presently consider in more detail, if we were to take JC's word for it that "torture is a national dishonor," how would that stand with our own sense of dishonor? This is the irony of "strong opinions": opinions cannot be strong simply in virtue of their content. It is possible to "accept" the opinion, yet the strength of the opinion is drained off in the transmission. Certainly, there are many warnings in *Diary of a Bad Year* that the "strong opinions" may just be ersatz ethical thought. JC himself calls the invitation to write *Strong Opinions* "an opportunity to grumble in public, an opportunity to take magic revenge on the world for declining to conform to my fantasies: how could I refuse?" (23). Anya warns him that he has "a tone that really turns people off. A know-it-all tone. Everything is cut and dried: *I am the one with all the answers, here is how it is, don't argue, it won't get you anywhere.* I know that isn't how you are in real life, but that is how you come across, and it is not what you want" (70). And of course Alan, in his obnoxious tirade, says that *Strong Opinions* is being published in Germany because that country is the last on earth that has any interest in the shriveled musings of a white-bearded guru. Each of the charges has some plausibility. Thus if JC's voice—that is, the voice of *Strong Opinions*—is going to gain authority with the reader, it can only come after the reader has grappled with all the warnings against assigning it any authority at all. Ironically, *Diary of a Bad Year* inoculates *Strong Opinions* against being ersatz ethical thought by warning the reader that it might be just that.

**6.** Let us return to the dialectic of responsibility, which I have associated with reading horizontally across the pages of *Strong Opinions.* In an entry on Machiavelli, JC writes:

> Necessity, *necessità,* is Machiavelli's guiding principle. The old, pre-Machiavellian position was that the law was supreme. If it so happened that the moral law was sometimes broken, that was unfortunate, but rulers were merely human, after all. The new, Machiavellian position is that infringing the moral law is justified when it is necessary.
>
> Thus is inaugurated the dualism of modern political culture, which simultaneously upholds absolute and relative standards of value. The modern state appeals to morality, to religion and to natural law as the ideological foundation of its existence. At the same time it is prepared to infringe any or all of these in the interest of self-preservation. (17)

JC sees that Machiavelli has trickled down into "ordinary life." The only people who somehow don't get it are people he calls "liberal intellectuals":

> The kind of person who calls talkback radio and justifies the use of torture in the interrogation of prisoners holds the double standard in his mind in exactly the same way: without in the least denying the absolute claims of the Christian ethic (love thy neighbor as thyself), such a person approves freeing the hands of the authorities—the army, the secret police—to do whatever may be necessary to protect the public from enemies of the state.

> The typical reaction of liberal intellectuals is to seize on the contradiction here: how can something be both wrong and right, or at least both wrong and OK at the same time? What liberal intellectuals fail to see is that this so-called contradiction expresses the quintessence of the Machiavellian and therefore the modern, a quintessence that has been thoroughly absorbed by the man in the street. (18)

But who are the "liberal intellectuals" JC describes? And to whom is he speaking? Since he talks about them in the third person, it would at least initially seem that JC, in his writing, does not take himself to be addressing them. Rather, he seems to take himself to be addressing a different group—we the intended readers (whoever we turn out to be)—and he is talking about "liberal intellectuals" with us. The sense that we readers are not "liberal intellectuals" is enhanced by JC's claim "What liberal intellectuals fail to see . . ." JC implies that we (his readers) can see, merely by his pointing it out, what liberal intellectuals fail to see. And if it were that easy for "liberal intellectuals" to see what they purportedly fail to see, why could not JC call them "you"? Why could he not then address them directly, as he does us (his readers)? He could then say, "What some of you fail to see is . . ." I suspect that JC cannot address "liberal intellectuals" directly—cannot simply point out to them what they have hitherto failed to see—because what they fail to see, they cannot see. That is, they suffer from a kind of blindness. And so if one were somehow to bring this failure to see to the attention of those who are failing to see (that is, to the attention of liberal intellectuals themselves), one would have to use a less direct method than simply pointing to something one already knows they cannot see.

In contemporary political discourse, when someone talks of "liberal intellectuals," he or she is a conservative commentator, and the point of mentioning them is to pour abuse upon them for the satisfaction of other like-minded conservatives. But this cannot be what JC is doing. His outrage at Guantanamo, to take just one example, means that he does not fit the standard mold of a conservative commentator who takes Guantanamo to be a necessity of war. And the fact that he assumes that his readers will be sympathetic with his views means that this cannot be the standard derogatory usage of "liberal intellectual."

Precisely because JC's use of "liberal intellectuals" does not fit this mold, it ought to raise some curiosity in the reader as to whom he is talking about.

And why is he talking about them to us? I would like to suggest that we construe "liberal intellectuals" broadly to include a group that meets three criteria: they are relatively well educated by contemporary standards (that is what makes them "intellectuals"); they place special concern on the dignity and rights of the individual (this is the core value of liberalism); they have some confidence in reason's ability to understand the world and to give humans the basis for making good decisions (we have seen that they object to the contradictions that "ordinary people" accept as a matter of course).

Note that on this characterization, "liberal intellectuals" would cut across the standard left-right divide. For example, the late Robert Bartley, the legendary editorial-page editor of the *Wall Street Journal,* called himself a "liberal" in the traditional sense of the term right up to the end of his distinguished conservative career. In the conservative version of liberalism, it is the right of the individual to make up his mind in the marketplace; the left-wing version valorizes the dignity of the individual that argues in favor of universal health care. In each case, what is at stake is some vision of the rights and dignity of the individual. The opposition JC is establishing, then, is not between left and right, but between "liberal intellectuals" and "ordinary people." What I think JC wants to investigate is the role of the intellect—at least, as it is given social expression in terms of privileged education—among those who take themselves to value the the individual.

Although JC sets up an opposition between "liberal intellectuals" and "ordinary people," it is noteworthy that against neither group will a moral appeal against torture succeed. "If you wish to counter the man in the street, it cannot be by appeal to moral principles. . . . Ordinary life is full of contradictions; ordinary people are used to accommodating them" (18). In effect, the "ordinary" response to torture is: "yes, torture is a moral outrage; but sometimes it is necessary." For "liberal intellectuals," moral appeal fails for a different reason: it is experienced by them as superfluous because they are already against torture and do not need to be told that it is an outrage. JC tells us how we might nevertheless reach "ordinary people." Instead of making a moral appeal, "you must attack the metaphysical, supra-empirical status of *necessità* and show that to be fraudulent" (18). If one can show that torture is not really necessary for the state's survival, if you can show that the claim is a fraud, then ordinary people will not need a further moral argument to be against it. But this kind of rhetorical move will not work against "liberal intellectuals," precisely because they do not think they need convincing. If there were going to be a rhetorical strategy that worked with them, it would have to be one that elicited from them recognition that, after all, they do need convincing—that being absolutely against torture does not preclude the possibility that they are somehow for it. This would be especially difficult for them to see if, as intellectuals, believers in logic, they assumed that their opposition to torture thereby ruled out the possibility that they are somehow also in favor of it.[11]

**7.** JC thinks that Americans are entangled in a national curse—a modern, secular version of bloodguilt. Actually, JC is more concerned with shame—the transmission of dishonor—than with guilt. In this modern version, shame is transmitted not through blood, but through citizenship. We are shamed, JC thinks, by the fact that we are citizens of a nation that engages in torture. Of the Bush administration, JC writes:

> Their shamelessness is quite extraordinary. Their denials are less than halfhearted. The distinction their hired lawyers draw between torture and coercion is patently insincere, pro forma. In the new dispensation we have created, they implicitly say, the old powers of shame have been abolished. Whatever abhorrence you may feel counts for nothing. (39)

It is here, in JC's opinion, that each individual American faces the challenge of ethical thought: "how, in the face of this shame to which I am subjected, do I behave? How do I save my honor?" (39). But how does the shamelessness of the Bush administration trickle down and shame me? There are a number of peculiarities in the dynamics of shame. To begin with, shamelessness is shameful. But if the administration is, as JC alleges, shameless, then they will never feel the shame that, JC alleges, attaches to them. That is, there is objective shame that attaches to the administration because of their shameless behavior; but there is also a subjective shame—the experience of being ashamed—that they will never feel (because they are shameless). When it comes to shamelessness, objective and subjective shame come apart. But now there is a further problem with JC's claim that the shame has somehow become my shame, something in relation to which I must figure out how to live. Again, there is a split between JC's claim of objective shame, which attaches to me, and subjective shame, which I cannot yet figure out why I ought to feel it. Is this puzzlement my very own form of shamelessness, manifesting itself in a belief that I do not deserve to feel shame? JC is, I think, trying to block the assumption that because I oppose George Bush, loathe the administration's tactics of skirting the law, and abhor torture, I am therefore not responsible for what the government does. On this picture, my ethical thinking has already been done, and though I may be disturbed by my government's actions, I am comfortable with my judgment of myself. For JC, this tactic will not work, and he tries to instill in the reader a sense that it is not working.

> Dishonor is no respecter of fine distinctions. Dishonor descends upon one's shoulders and once it has descended no amount of clever pleading will dispel it. In the present climate of whippedup fear, and in the absence of any groundswell of popular revulsion against torture, political actions by individual citizens seem unlikely to have any practical effect. Yet perhaps, pursued doggedly and in a spirit of outrage, such actions will at least allow people to hold their heads up. Mere symbolic actions, on the other hand—burning the flag, pronouncing the words aloud "I abhor the leaders of my country and dissociate myself from them"—will certainly not be enough. (40)

JC is attacking the liberal idea that the individual can be judged on his own terms, in isolation from the nation into which he happens to be born. His point is not that the nation or the culture will have influenced him or shaped his outlook and thus his complicity. Rather, his claim is that even if the nation has had no influence on him at all, the shame is still his. It attaches to him simply by virtue of his being a citizen. There are thus, for JC, severe limits to an individual's ability to ward off shame by saying, "It is not mine." Worse, at least from the point of view of the liberal imagination, these limits may not be rationally justifiable. This is what "liberal intellectuals" cannot see: the fact that I can reason my way out of the shame—after all, I did nothing to deserve it—does not mean that it is not mine. It is there, like a curse or an oracle. It attaches to me simply by virtue of my nationality. JC cites the "deep theme" of Faulkner: "The theft of the land from the Indians or the rape of slave women comes back in unforeseen form, generations later, to haunt the oppressor" (48). And he quotes the classicist J.-P. Vernant on the way the structure of tragic guilt arises from a clash between an ancient religious conception in which an impious act can defile an entire race and a newer legal conception in which the guilty one is the individual who breaks the law (49). On JC's nationalist conception, shame transmits not just across generations, but it also trickles down within a single generation from the political class that sanctions the taboo act to the citizens who may have had little or no say in how the political class operates. How is it fair, one wants to ask, that I should bear the guilt for acts I abhor, committed by leaders I voted against and over whose behavior I have no control? JC's answer: whether you understand it or not, the shame is yours.

In short, JC plays jujitsu with the liberal imagination. The liberal sensibility wants to start out with the individual—his rights, dignity, and responsibilities—and then ask, "How am I responsible?" JC begins with an accusation of shared shame: "You are dishonored, simply by being part of this tainted 'we.' Now figure out how to behave as an individual: for it is given to you to figure out how to deal with the shame you have inherited for acts you did not perform, for acts you abhor."

**8.** In reading JC's strong opinion, many reactions are possible. One might, for example, dismiss JC as a nutcase given to oracular pronouncements we could well live without. Or one might "agree" with JC in the service of bolstering a complacent sense of self-righteousness. Really, only one avenue of reaction is blocked: the one that tries to object to JC's accusation by saying, "The shame could not be mine, because I did nothing to deserve it." This is essentially the reaction of the "liberal intellectual." And it cannot be an objection, because JC begins with the premise that this is a shame that attaches to you whether or not you did something to deserve it. One wants to say that it does not make sense that there should be such a thing as shame that genuinely attaches to me even though I have done nothing to deserve it. But JC already agrees that this shame does not make sense: he does not think it open to rational assessment in this way. Rather, he thinks one must recognize it as there; it attaches to me by virtue of my nationality, independently of my deeds. JC's accusation may be one I refuse to accept, but I cannot refuse it on *standard* rational grounds. For the accusation does not claim to be rational—in other words, to make sense according to contemporary standards of responsibility. It claims to be true.

What if this accusation were somehow to resonate with me? Would that not only show that I was susceptible to irrational appeals? Perhaps. But it might also serve to bypass a defensive use to which reason can be put. Rationalization is a process that purports to determine on the basis of reasons alone whether or not, say, I ought to feel shame, but it is actually structured so as to arrive at the conclusion I want. To take a salient example, torture is forbidden by U.S. law. And there is widespread agreement that it would be shameful for this country to engage in torture. So, to the question "Should we feel shame because our government engages in torture?" the official answer is "Absolutely not; our government clearly forbids the use of torture." However, in ruling out torture, the law also leaves it unclear what interrogation techniques count as torture. At the time of writing this essay, the interrogation technique known as waterboarding has neither been conclusively ruled in nor conclusively ruled out. Or, as we shall see, in a peculiar way it has been both ruled out and ruled in. One might think, if torture is so horrible, if engaging in it would be a national disgrace, is it not a matter of urgency for us to make up our minds about waterboarding? After all, if waterboarding is not torture, it is certainly an effective interrogation technique, and we could perhaps engage in it more often. If it is torture, we ought to make that determination as soon as possible, so as to ensure that it is never used again. Instead, the situation is such as to leave us in a murky limbo. Again, on the one hand, waterboarding is absolutely forbidden to the U.S. military. The Detainee Treatment Act forbids "cruel, inhuman, or degrading treatment or punishment" of detainees, and requires that interrogation techniques be restricted to those authorized in the Army Field Manual. The Army Field Manual explicitly prohibits waterboarding. On the other hand, waterboarding has been used by the CIA. It was approved by a presidential finding in 2002 and then prohibited in 2006 by a directive of the CIA director, Michael Hayden. Even so, at the time of this writing, it has not yet been ruled to be torture. It could presumably be restored as a CIA interrogation technique, should a new director issue a countermanding directive.

This is a complex structure of prohibitions and permissions. It almost looks like the solution to a complex algebraic equation: solve for a situation in which (a) torture is forbidden, (b) waterboarding is forbidden, (c) waterboarding was permitted and could be permitted again, and (d) there is no contradiction. What is this complexity for? It seems to me that it is the last condition, (d), that gives the game away. The law goes to great lengths to avoid the explicit Machiavellian contradiction that JC says "ordinary people" are used to accommodating, namely:

> Torture is absolutely forbidden.
> Torture is permitted when necessary.

It is as though this complex system were written for those who cannot tolerate this contradiction: that is, for the people JC calls "liberal intellectuals." It is an attempt to capture all that is needed in the Machiavellian moment without admitting to it. Why not just admit to it? The only answer I can think of is that admitting to it brings with it a sense of shame. The liberal intellectual, as we have seen, is committed to the rights and dignity of the individual; he is also committed to the use of reason. There is thus no way he can both forbid torture and then take it back without disgracing himself (in his own eyes). But then reason is working not merely to determine whether or not a situation is shameful, but also to ward off shame by whatever means possible. It is as though reason has been given a task: torture is forbidden; now use all your resources to show that all of our behavior (including waterboarding) has been consistent with the prohibition.[12]

Note that this strategy is very different from a more straightforward one that argues that waterboarding is not torture, and thus ought to be permitted. Then one would allow the military to engage in it as well. It is also different from a strategy that argues that in certain cases torture is necessary. By contrast, the strategy in use is one that forbids torture, but then goes to great lengths to obscure whether waterboarding is or is not torture and gives mixed messages about whether it is or is not permitted. The contradiction is avoided, just so long as we do not look too closely into what is going on or what we are doing.

The national debate has not been explicitly about shame, but about consistency with the law. Three events that have occurred while this essay was being written speak to this point. First, Michael Mukasey was confirmed by the U.S. Senate as attorney general of the United States despite the fact that he refused to say whether or not he considered waterboarding to be torture. He did say that personally he found it repugnant, but he left open the question of whether or not it counts as torture.[13] One would think that if waterboarding might be torture, we should get clear about whether it is or it is not; and should then determine whether a nominee was on the right side of such an important issue before confirming him as attorney general. But in this instance, being on the "right side" of the issue means being on neither side. Second, according to an AP report of January 2008, the Director of National Intelligence has made the remarkable claim that waterboarding would be torture if used against him, but he "declined for *legal reasons* to say whether the technique categorically should be considered torture."[14] This is what today counts as judiciousness. Again, one might ask, if Mr. McConnell is so sure that waterboarding would be torture if used against him, how could he, as a matter of legality, remain unclear about whether it is torture for others? And if, as a matter of legality, it is not clear, why does that legality not apply in his case? As anyone who has worked his way through these contortions can see, the issue is not that the law is unclear and thus they cannot decide; the law has been written and interpreted so that they can say that they cannot say. JC's point is that consistency with the law has become a fetish whereby "liberal intellectuals" can ward off a sense of shame. Evidence in favor of JC's claim is provided by the third recent event, the report of the CIA's destruction of videotapes of interrogations using waterboarding.[15] Officially, the destruction occurred in order to protect CIA interrogators from retaliation; and there has been some speculation in the press about whether it might also have been done to protect them (or the CIA) against legal redress. But another explanation suggests itself: the CIA (or those who ordered the destruction) correctly understood that its activities should not be seen. The gaze is that under which one experiences shame. And the CIA is part of a complex structure that avoids shame not by avoiding the shameful act but by making it impossible for the public to gaze upon it. If the public were to see the act, they would no longer be able to allow their public leaders to remain vague about whether it was or was not torture. But if public leaders must remain vague, then these images must not be seen. This entire complex edifice—the dance around whether waterboarding is or is not torture—would collapse if the practice became visible to the public.

JC's accusation of national shame blows this kind of casuistry out of the water. In effect, his accusation says, "It does not matter what kind of reasons you can find, the shame is yours all the same. It does not matter what the legal technicalities are, the shame is yours all the same. It does not matter whether the videos have been destroyed, because they have been destroyed for your sake, to protect you from feeling the shame that is yours all the same. Shame on you for using your reason to try to find consistency in your acts. Consistency will not protect you against the shame that is yours all the same."

And to the individual who says, "I do not see why I should bear the shame; I abhor torture," we can now see that this is a repetition of what the law says about itself. The law abhors torture and yet has somehow tolerated it. We abhor torture, but what have we tolerated? Can anyone be confident enough to believe that his own "opposition" does not have the same defensive structure as the law? Thus, although JC is officially talking to us (his readers) about "liberal intellectuals," the thought begins to dawn: Might he be talking to us, about us? Might we not have a complicity we do not yet recognize?[16]

**9.** Having worked through one instance of the dialectic of responsibility, let me briefly recap its moments.

First, the task is to help us see that we are entangled in motivated structures of not-seeing. This cannot be done simply by pointing it out. We think we can see the situation as it is; we think we are already against torture.

Second, we are told of a group, the "liberal intellectuals," who fail to see the Machiavellian world in which they are entangled precisely because they refuse to accept its contradiction.

Third, we come to see that the law and its complex structure of enforcement and nonenforcement seem to be in place in order to placate the so-called liberal intellectuals' need for consistency. If the law simply reflected ordinary people's understanding, it would be much simpler: torture is forbidden, except when it is necessary. But, then, who are these "liberal intellectuals" whom the law is going to such efforts to pacify? And why should they be the people who feel that they have no responsibility for the law?

Fourth, JC makes the accusation that we are entangled in this national shame, irrespective of our reasons, solely by virtue of citizenship. I take this to be an intentionally scandalous claim. In effect, it says, "Your use of reason does not matter at all; it will not get you off the hook." In a funny way, this provides a certain kind of relief. If our reasons do not matter, then we can at least momentarily take a break from using them to try to justify our innocence. We can at least begin to inquire into how reason has been used to tolerate and sustain this shameful situation.

Finally, this question begins to dawn: have I used reason to tolerate this shameful situation by giving myself reasons to think that I am not implicated in this national shame? It is at this moment that I begin to wonder whether I am an instance of the "liberal intellectual" I have been reading about. But it is also at this moment that I cease to be a "liberal intellectual," precisely because I can now see what the "liberal intellectual" fails to see.

Note that this dialectic requires neither that JC be right that we share shame solely by virtue of our citizenship nor that we agree with him. JC and his accusation serve merely as a catalyst for a process by which we slowly come to see that our own reason has been implicated in a motivated structure of not-seeing. What matters is that the accusation—perhaps by its scandalous nature—stimulates us to make this movement. In general, JC seems to think that human injustice requires motivated structures of not-seeing. So, to take another example dear to his heart, the fact that meat ends up on our dinner table requires that we remain satisfied with at best a vague understanding of how it got there. His strategy helps us see that we are motivated not to see.

**10.** Now what does the spectacle of embedding have to do with all of this? That is, what is Coetzee's strategy here, as opposed to JC's? It seems to me that the structure of the answer is obvious: there is something about seeing JC's opinions embedded in the travails of his life that makes those very opinions come to matter to us in ways they might not otherwise. The difficulty is in figuring out how this might be so. Here a comparison with Kafka might be illuminating. Kafka is more concerned with guilt; JC is more concerned with shame. Guilt is more associated with the voice, and Kafka is at his most powerful when he isolates the voice of judgment—"You are guilty!"—from any embedding. Shame, by contrast, requires a gaze. JC's writing provides us with many images to gaze upon. As he himself says, Guantanamo Bay "is more a spectacle than a prisoner-of-war camp: an awful display" (21). But if we are not merely to look upon shameful situations, but ourselves participate in that sense of shame, we need some imaginative sense of being gazed upon. Arguably, this cannot be provided by a bare gaze (what is that?), as the voice of guilt can be provided by a bare voice. We need to have a sense of who is gazing upon us if we are to think that under his gaze we ought to feel shame. As Bernard Williams pointed out in *Shame and Necessity,* shame must be experienced under the gaze of someone we could imaginatively respect.[17]

And JC earns our respect not simply because of the content of his strong opinions, but because of the honesty with which he faces up to his stumbling efforts to live through what he recognizes to be the end of his life. As readers, we are familiar with the novelistic technique of embedding a moral argument in a larger human drama. For instance, there is the hypocritical preacher whose sermons are at odds with how he lives his life. Or, to take an example closer to home, it is easy to imagine a David Lodge novel in which a philosophy professor travels all over giving lectures on how ethics is just a projection of our own values onto the world—and has an affair in each town in which he gives the lecture. We might, then, wonder about his psychology: how much does the content of his lecture flow from his desire for extramarital affairs? By contrast, JC's drama deals with more than his personal psychology. He is facing up to his own death. He is trying to understand—and live out—the place of love and creativity as one moves toward death. These are issues that confront us all insofar as we are human. And it is as such that we are moved by him. We are struck not so much by his personal idiosyncrasies as by the demands of being human.

This leads to the final point: the demands of being human require that we respond to metaphysical ache. This is not JC's peculiarity; we are creatures susceptible to metaphysical ache. And, I want to suggest, there is something about the realistic portrayal of metaphysical ache in another that can serve to stimulate it in ourselves. Though Anya may have been the occasion of JC's metaphysical ache, she cannot on her own have been its balm. Nothing on its own could have done that. To grasp JC's metaphysical ache, we need to look at the entire movement of *Diary of a Bad Year.* This includes not only the moral cries of *Strong Opinions,* but also the worry that they are ersatz. It includes also the semi-Platonic love affair that develops between JC and Anya. What changes? JC says that the opinions he publishes have not changed, but his opinion of his opinions has. And he goes on to write a second diary, not for publication but to share with Anya—a diary that is more personal and passionate than anything in *Strong Opinions.*

There is much in the second diary that is very moving, and we are led to believe that it is his acquaintance with Anya that transformed these thoughts and feelings into written words: "The best proof we have that life is good, and therefore that there may perhaps be a God after all, who has our welfare at heart, is that each of us, on the day we are born, comes to the music of Johann Sebastian Bach. It comes as a gift, unearned, unmerited, for free" (221). There is also awe, reverence for Tolstoy and Dostoyevsky in an homage as passionate as any I have read. Anya, for her part, is able to dump the crude Alan, but she is also able to develop into a person who wants to provide the aging author with the company he seeks for his death. The moment of love is the moment of death, around which both lives become organized.

Whatever the residues of JC's political incorrectness, I am struck by this "soft opinion":

> Why is it that we—men and women both, but men most of all—are prepared to accept the checks and rebuffs of the real, more and more rebuffs as time goes by, more humiliating each time, yet keep coming back? The answer: because we cannot do without the real thing, the real real thing: because without the real we die as if of thirst. (179)

It is here, I think, that JC names the metaphysical ache, by saying what it is ultimately for: reality. JC is a prime example of how it gets more humiliating: this time around he is caught up in the desire to grasp the reality of his own decay. The ache *for* reality is, in his case, also the ache that is the reality of his demise. But as he falls apart, he also wants to stand witness to the reality of others: in particular, those nameless others who have been and perhaps still are being tortured, just beyond the horizon of collective awareness. How humiliating is it for us this time, to come back to this reality? Here, I think, we can move from JC to J. M. Coetzee. The entire rhetorical strategy of *Diary of a Bad Year* is devoted to turning this into a genuine ethical question—one to which we will not be comfortable giving an ersatz ethical answer.[18]

CHAPTER FIFTEEN

# Not at Home in Gilead

**1.** What is it like for life to seep out of a way of life? We are familiar with abrupt moments of cultural trauma, but there are times when a form of life is hollowed out from the inside, with people barely noticing. We see this in Marilynne Robinson's epic tale of the passing of the Protestant Reformation in the American Midwest. One sign of the courage in her writing is that we would most likely not see that this was her theme if we read only one of her companion novels, *Gilead* or *Home,* on its own. Taken together, the two books establish an uncomfortable intermediate space in which the theme broadens out from what we believe it to be in either novel. Robinson does not talk about the decline of Protestant reform (a topic whose discussion could so easily be a manifestation of that very decline), but rather instills a dawning sense of loss.

I have come to think of the character Jack Boughton—who in *Gilead* is seen through the eyes of the narrator, Reverend Ames, as a sinister, perhaps even diabolical figure who commits petty crimes for "the sheer meanness of it" and who, in *Home,* is seen as the prodigal son who could not return home—as a Christian martyr.[1] He is not a saint, but in a somewhat perverse way he stands witness to Christian values. It is a sign of the rundown nature of the so-called Christian world of Gilead that neither his father nor his godfather (the Reverend Ames) nor his neighbors can see this in him; nor can he clearly see this about himself. But for all his confusion, he is also resolute. His significance is not to be found in his psychology, but in the peculiar stand he takes.

It is tempting to think of Jack as a "pale criminal." Consider, for example, his sister Glory's impression of him when he returns to Gilead:

> She saw that wary look of his, caution with no certainty of the nature of the threat, and with no notion at all of a possible refuge. He realized he did not please his father, did not know how to please his father. He would probably have liked to believe he had done something wrong so that he could at least orient himself a little, but she had told him a terrible thing, that he had done nothing to offend, that his father [Robert] had found fault with him anyway, only because he was old and sad now, not the father he thought he had come home to.[2]

What if Glory was wrong to attribute Robert Boughton's attitude to his old age? What if she put her finger on something ancient, a sense of fault reverberating through the generations, organizing the family in ways it did not quite understand? Dostoyevsky, Nietzsche, and Freud tell us that the structure of crime and punishment can be the reverse of what common sense dictates: there are some who do not feel guilty because they have committed a crime, but rather commit a crime because they feel guilty. The crime provides temporary relief from an inchoate sense of guilt, because it offers a rationalization. And, of course, if Jack can, through his acts, justify his father's faultfinding, then he protects the ultimate goodness of his father, the world, perhaps even God. To what extent is Jack martyring himself with his misbehavior?

But Jack is no pale criminal. According to Freud, the pale criminal suffers from a punishing superego that makes him suffer guilt in ways he does not understand. But the superego is an internal representative of the normative order. For Freud, the pale criminal has too much civilization inside of him, albeit intensified by aggressive fantasies. Thus the guilt searching for a crime. But Jack's problem is different. He has not internalized the established normative order as superego. In that sense, civilization has failed to get its hooks into him. On the contrary, he is a walking legitimacy crisis for the civilization that surrounds him.

As he becomes closer to his sister Glory, he confesses:

> If I had to do it all over again, I mean adolescent criminality, I'd try to restrict myself to doing things that were explicable. Or at least appeared to be explicable. I'm serious. It's the things people cannot account for that upset them. The old gent used to ask me, "Why did you do that, Jack?" And I couldn't even tell him I did it because I felt like it. Even that

> wouldn't have been true. What did I want with an old baseball mitt? Nothing. But there wasn't really much to steal in this town. It would have been hard to find anything to want, anything that might make it seem as though I had a motive. So all my offenses were laid to a defect of character.[3]

What would it be like to view Jack as a Christian critic of the normative order? There is an honesty that shines through his petty criminality. It was not enough for him to do things that were explicable—that would have been digestible by all around him (whatever pain it also caused). Nor was it enough to confine himself to acts that had the *appearance* of explicability. That too would have been digestible by family and neighbors, for they would have taken the appearance to be real. Though he may not fully understand why, Jack needs to put the inexplicability of his acts on display.

Jack stole the Greek New Testament off the Reverend Ames's desk. "If ever there was a thing on earth so little worth the trouble of stealing I don't know what it would be."[4] He stole Ames's reading glasses, a photograph of his first wife, a baseball glove—though all would eventually find their way back to their owner. "He's just mean," Ames would conclude.[5] When Jack tries to engage him in a conversation about predestination, Ames feels he is "deviling" him.[6] And even as Ames is being dishonest with Jack, he attempts to excuse himself by saying that he has a right not to be "deviled." Jack even blew up Reverend Ames's mailbox. But what if Jack dimly grasped that he had a message that would blow up Gilead's normative order? Ames's mailbox—is there any artifact more redolent of the established order?—could not contain it; indeed, blowing up the mailbox was Jack's message.

Gilead is a town that over two generations has lost its formal and its final cause, its essence and guiding goal. Gilead was founded by a westward migration of the Protestant Reformation, by settlers who were determined to serve God by abolishing slavery. The town served as a staging post for emigration into Kansas as well as for raids upon Kansas slaveholders, so that Kansas, which was then just a territory, should enter the union as a free state. It was also an important station on the Underground Railroad, a network of safe houses and white abolitionist conductors who would help runaway slaves escape to freedom. Ames writes to his son, "There have been heroes here, and saints and martyrs, and I want you to know that. Because that is the truth, even if no one remembers it."[7] Ames here misunderstands the situation he is in. It is not simply that people do not remember past heroes; they have lost a sense of the meaning of Gilead. This is not just about their past, but about their present: no one any longer has a clear sense of what, if anything, holds them together. So when Ames continues,

> To look at the place, it's just a cluster of houses strung along a few roads, and a little row of brick buildings with stores in them, and a grain elevator and a water tower with Gilead written on its side, and the post office and the schools and the playing fields and the old train station, which has pretty much gone to weeds now.[8]

he *thinks* he is describing a false appearance. He assumes an underlying unity that escapes this appearance, and about that he is mistaken. There has been a failure of transmission through the generations, and the principle of unity that held Gilead together has lost its animating force. With the principle desiccated, Gilead is nothing more than its appearance: a mere "cluster of houses strung along a few roads." Gilead no longer exists; all that remains is an illusion of unity that goes by the same name.

Ames comes to recognize this for himself toward the end of his meditation. I suspect that it is this recognition that turns his meditation into a repentance and opens him up for a genuine blessing of Jack.

> I woke up this morning thinking this town might be standing on the absolute floor of hell for all the truth there is in it, and the fault is mine as much as anyone's. . . . It seems to me now we never looked up from the trouble we had just getting by to put the obvious question, that is, to ask what it was the Lord was trying to make us understand. . . . Well, we didn't ask the question, so the question was just taken away from us. We became like people without the Law, people who didn't know their right hand from their left. Just stranded here. A stranger might ask why is there a town here at all. Our own children might ask. And who could answer them? It was just a little outpost in the sand hills, within striking distance of Kansas. That's really all it was meant to be.[9]

But I want to go back to the prerecognition period, to examine the structure of illusion.

Freud and Kierkegaard describe illusion in different ways, and it is important to see how they are related. For Freud, an illusion is a psychological state of an individual: he defines it as a belief caused by a wish. For Kierkegaard, by contrast, an illusion is a whole structure of social institutions, cultural rituals, ways of going on that serves to keep participants deluded about the true nature of their situation. He used the term *Christendom* to refer to the large-scale structures that embedded and expressed a social understanding of Christianity; and he argued that it was a "dreadful illusion."[10] By this he meant that the culturally available routes for expressing one's Christian faith were actually serving to tranquilize any sense of what a Christian life required. Gilead is the midwestern incarnation of Christendom. This is why Ames's grandfather abandoned the town in disgust. It also helps explain why Ames's older brother, Edward, left, why Ames's father eventually followed him, and why the few "colored" families who were still there in Ames's time also left. "It wasn't a big fire," Ames wrote about the fire someone set behind "the Negro church":[11] "a little nuisance fire";[12] "it was only a small fire. There was very little damage."[13] The illusion of Christendom also explains why Della, Jack's longtime lover, who is black, could never think of settling in Gilead—as well as why she and Lila, the Reverend Ames's young wife, would take with them what might otherwise have been the town's next generation. We do not know why the Boughton children all decamped, but there was certainly no sense of liveliness keeping them there. As Robert Boughton says of his children, "All of them call it home, but they never stay."[14] Christendom is the illusion that has killed off Gilead; people do not quite realize it, and yet in some inchoate ways they do.

Against this backdrop, Jack does not look as much of an outsider as he and everyone around him take him to be. And his criminality can be seen as a protest against a normative order that is corrupt but does not recognize itself as such. In a way, his life is given over to standing witness to this corruption. He does not quite know this, yet he sort of does. For the moment, let us put to one side his alleged great crime—impregnating and abandoning a young girl—and consider his other crimes. Arguably, these acts would not show up as crimes in a Christian world. There is no evidence he ever stole anything he wanted. Unlike Reverend Ames, Jack did not covet. Glory thought his "thievishness might involve some subtle derangement of mine and thine."[15] Does not Christianity demand precisely that: a derangement of mine and thine?

Ames writes that his grandfather "rarely stole except from his own family," and something similar can be said of Jack: he tended to keep his "thievishness" focused pretty close to home.[16] The men share a similar unworldliness when it comes to material goods. Jack has the suit on his back, and that is about it. He does not want to have more than forty dollars, for money might get him into trouble. Ames's grandfather had the explicit belief that God would provide; and though Jack has doubts about God's existence, he lives in a similar way. They differ, of course, in that the grandfather was always giving the stolen goods away to those who needed them; he was always acting in the name of a good cause. Jack is deprived of that final cause, and he is confused about what he is doing. But if he cannot give a reason for what he is doing, his acts bear uncomfortable witness to the fact that neither can anyone else. No Christian can ultimately justify this arrangement of mine and thine. And yet Christendom is only working as an illusion if this lack of justification remains just over the horizon of conscious awareness. Jack is forever disturbing the illusory order—and in a vague way, he and everyone else grasps this.

Jack is the only person in Gilead who evidently feels compassion for the plight of black people in 1950s America. In this sense too he is closer in spirit to Ames's grandfather—and thus to the raison d'être of Gilead—than any of the other characters. Racism is a fault line running through the constitution of the United States, and in this issue one can see most clearly the power of illusion. On two occasions when Jack is watching the television news reporting the racial struggle in the South, he says, "Jesus Christ!" In the first, police are using riot sticks, fire hoses, and dogs to beat back black protesters;[17] in the other, a young woman is being prevented from entering the University of Alabama.[18] "That kind of language has never been acceptable in this house," says his father.[19] He thereby changes the subject from massive and evident social injustice to family propriety, through the ostensibly serious issue of taking the name of God in vain. I am not an expert on this, but it is difficult to think of an occasion in which the invocation of Jesus's name would be more appropriate. What is more, I have the sense that Jack is fully present in his words. We do not know the last time such a heartfelt cry to Jesus occurred in Gilead, but in the topsy-turvy world of illusion, his father experiences it as the casual blasphemy of a reprobate.

At one point Jack circulates to Ames and his father an article on religion in America from a 1948 copy of the *Ladies' Home Journal.* Jack represents the article as calling into question the seriousness of American Christianity given the appalling racism in the country. But his father and Ames both invoke Christian categories to dismiss it. The old men agree that the author is too quick to judge others, as though the real issue is the sin of pride of the author rather than the disgraceful condition he describes. Or the author displays religious self-righteousness in the very act of condemning it. The two old men enjoy discussing how poorly argued it is.

I was able to find a copy of the article in the University of Chicago library. It is a rich article, more complex and argumentative than anything we would find today in the equivalent popular journalism. The *Ladies' Home Journal* went to the expense of commissioning a Gallup poll on religious attitudes in America. They gave the results of that survey to three nationally prominent religious leaders—a Protestant, a Catholic, and a Jew—and invited them to respond. Finally, the journalist, Lincoln Barnett, was invited to present the material as he saw fit.

The statistics are striking: 95 percent of the American people said that they believed in God; 71 percent thought that God observed our actions and rewarded or punished us for them; and 73 percent believed in some kind of afterlife. Still, only 5 percent said they ever prayed for forgiveness, "suggesting," as the author puts it, "perhaps that they have no sins to forgive."[20] The respondents were also asked if they thought they could fulfill the command to love one's neighbor as oneself if one's neighbor happened to be, say, of a different race. A full 80 percent said they could, with only 12 percent thinking they could not and 8 percent having no opinion. This in spite of the fact that there were virtually no integrated churches throughout the United States. It seems that it is not so difficult to love your black neighbors so long as you make sure you do not have any.

This article sheds light on what Kierkegaard meant by calling Christendom a *dreadful* illusion. His point is not merely about the degree of its falsity, but about its ability to metabolize challenges to it. The problem with Gilead is not merely that its inhabitants share a false outlook of what their Christianity requires. It is that even when the falsity of their outlook is plainly pointed out to them, it seems to make no difference. The challenge to Christendom is itself dismissed as unchristian.

That is why Jack's challenge matters. It pierces the armor of the illusion. The elders might try to dismiss it as delinquency, sheer meanness, or devilment, but they cannot thereby contain it. There is a remainder that troubles them, makes them ill at ease with their illusory lives.

Ames writes to his son:

> This is an important thing, which I have told many people and which my father told me and his father told him. When you encounter another person, when you have dealings with anyone at all, it is as if a question is being put to you. So you must think, What is the Lord asking of me in this moment, in this situation? If you confront insult or antagonism, your first impulse will be to respond in kind. But if you think, as it were, this is an emissary sent from the Lord, and some benefit is intended for me, first of all the occasion to demonstrate my faithfulness, the chance to show that I do in some small degree participate in the grace that saved me, you are free to act otherwise than as circumstances would seem to dictate. You are free to act by your own lights. You are freed at the same time of the impulse to hate or resent that person. He would probably laugh at the thought that the Lord sent him to you for your benefit (and his), but that is the perfection of the disguise, his own ignorance of it.[21]

If the Lord did send Jack in his ignorance to break through the veil of Ames's illusion, then at least by the time he leaves town for good, he has started to succeed. But the period of Jack's life in Gilead is pervaded by unfreedom. The letter's words have been passed down from grandfather, to father, to son; and now there is an attempt to pass them on yet again, to the son's son. But at each stage of transmission, the words seem to be evacuated of meaning. It is as if these words of freedom—their repetition—are taking the place of the freedom that the words enjoin. The words ring so true when they are spoken, yet it becomes easy not to notice that they are not being lived. Much of Ames's letter is given over to showing us, whatever he says, that he cannot treat Jack as an emissary of the Lord. Or perhaps that he *will* not. And yet he cannot rest content with his dismissal of Jack either. This restless unease is the solvent of illusion.

This conception of freedom has an external as well as an internal aspect. Ames eloquently describes the internal aspect: in treating our neighbor as the Lord's emissary, we are freed from the natural impulse to retaliate or feel resentment. But we thereby also create an external space—a space of neighborliness—in which we are both freed up to act toward each other in new and kindly ways. Jack is largely deprived of this external space of freedom—notably by his father, Boughton, and his godfather, Reverend Ames. I do not mean to diminish their own suffering or their attempts at sincerity, but for all the talk of forgiveness and all the rituals of prayer, there is no evidence that Boughton ever forgave his son for anything. And for Ames to conclude—or at least attempt to conclude—that Jack is "just mean" is an attempt to close down the very process of opening up that he verbally commends. Unbeknownst to themselves, the two older men are doing everything in their power to keep Jack confined to a realm of unfreedom. It is the opposite of the Christian love that they both teach. What makes this so poignant is that they are not cynical or blatantly hypocritical; in some sense, they both mean well. Ames is a man who is capable of compassion and genuine soul-searching. And he is not a pedestrian conformist: in the case of his marriage, he is able to transgress social convention and marry a woman much younger than himself, of uncertain social class and unknown past. And while Boughton's love for his son is troubled and conflicted, his attachment to Jack clearly runs deep.

**2.** What if Jack had been born into the space of freedom described by Ames? What if, at the moment he had what he described as a conversion experience and wanted to go to the Congregationalist Church, he had been genuinely welcomed rather than subjected to an envy-filled sermon about fathers who abandon their children? There are a thousand such what-ifs that we will never be able to answer. Nor will we ever know the depths of Jack's motivation. But it does help to consider what Jack says he wants—to settle in Gilead with his African American partner and their child—for it helps us see what happens to desire in a realm of unfreedom. "What about this town?" Jack asks Ames. "If we came here and got married, could we live here? Would people leave us alone?"[22] In a hopeful moment, he says to Glory, "I believe I could see myself here. Jack Boughton, honest working man. Little wife at home, little child—frolicking with his dog, I suppose. Not unthinkable."[23] But this desire cannot stand up against real-life experience. A little while later, he tells her, "A diligent and humiliating search for employment has persuaded me that I must look beyond Gilead. I'll need a car if I am ever to become a respectable man."[24] His point, of course, is not that one needs a car for respectability, but he needs a car to get away from a space that will never grant him respectability. At one point Jack describes himself as "deranged by hope": "I guess I thought [Ames] might look down upon me from his study window and say to himself, 'He's a cad and a bounder, but I appreciate his attention to my son.' . . . That won't happen.

No need to worry about that. What a stupid idea."[25] He says to Glory, "I came back thinking we might be able to make a life here, she and I. Why did I think that? . . . I was clutching at a straw, coming to Gilead. No doubt about that. I've had some experience with them. Straws."[26]

But what is it that makes the straw straw? It is worth dwelling on this for a moment, for it helps us understand how Freud's conception of illusion fits together with Kierkegaard's. Jack wants to settle down with his longtime lover and partner, the mother of his child; he would like to get a job in town, and virtually any job will do; and he would like to raise his child in Gilead. What is so unrealistic about that? In ordinary circumstances, this would be a modest and easily fulfillable set of desires. But in the Gilead of Jack's tenure, living such a life is out of the question: there is no way a black woman would be allowed to settle into the town, at least in the same class as the other residents; no way that an interracial couple would be accepted; no way that the town would forgive Jack and welcome him back into their community as a responsible citizen. One thinks of Jack's aspiration as illusion in the Freudian sense only because the town of Gilead is living in illusion in the Kierkegaardian sense. This suggests that a certain externalism is necessary to grasp Jack's psychological state. Remember, Freud thought of illusion as an outlook that is caused by a wish rather than reasonably formed beliefs about how the world is. But the way to determine whether Jack is suffering from an illusion is not to look deeper into his mind to see whether his beliefs are caused by a wish, but rather to look out into the social world to see how rigidly distorted it is by illusion, in Kierkegaard's sense. It is because the social world refuses to accommodate Jack that his desires end up getting labeled wishful, and his overall project an illusion. And the social world refuses Jack because it is enmeshed in an illusion of Christian life—for example, an outlook that requires "Negroes" to worship at their own church. Here is the heart of the illusion: the day-to-day acceptance of the thought that "separate but Christian" is a viable expression of Christian worship. If that is how things *ought* to be, a division based on race not creed, then it is not surprising that other consequences flow from it. For example, that Reverend Ames never meets the "Negro pastor" until he is about to leave town—in spite of the fact that Gilead is the tiniest of midwestern towns. It is not simply that an interracial couple could not possibly settle down and be accepted in this town; it is that this impossibility is an expression of what the town takes to be its core Christian values. In this case at least, the Freudian illusion is tied inextricably to Kierkegaardian illusion.

Indeed, the two are in agonistic tension with each other. It is not difficult to imagine that Jack, with all his illusory hopes, is doing God's work, unsettling this illusory world of Christian life. We have already seen that introducing into the town a magazine article that describes its own hypocrisy is not the least bit disruptive. It is at most an occasion for conversation and dismissal, thus reinforcing the illusion. But what would be unnerving would be Jack trying to live out his hopes. If Jack were to decide ahead of time that his desires were merely illusion, that they had no hope of success, he would thereby be depriving the town of Gilead of its possibility for freedom—at least, according to the norms of freedom that Reverend Ames has been preaching. Jack is Gilead's possibility for doing things differently than the town's inclination would dictate, and doing so because the town residents come to see Jack as posing a question sent by God. Jack does get rebuffed—by his father, by Ames, by the townspeople who refuse him employment, by his lover, Della, and by Della's father—and in these rejections he comes to see his hopes as illusory. That is the cost of testing out the shared illusions of the social world. This is a remarkable example of how large-scale structures in the social world can affect the intimate details of private life—and, possibly, vice versa.

I recently traveled to Tabor, Iowa, the town on which the fictional town of Gilead is loosely based, and I visited the home of Reverend John Todd, the abolitionist preacher who serves as a model for the figure of Ames's grandfather. Todd's home was a station along the Underground Railroad; he protected John Brown, fought to abolish slavery his whole life, and founded Tabor College, which from its inception in the mid-nineteenth century was meant to be racially integrated and coeducational. One can still visit the crannies where he hid slaves, as well as walk through the cornfields where slaves hid when slave masters came looking for them. Then I drove back to the airport in Omaha, Nebraska, an hour away, and while I was waiting for my flight, I saw a black woman shining shoes. I decided to get my shoes shined, and we started talking. She asked me what I was doing there, and I told her that I had made a trip to Tabor. She said, "Oh, I would never go over to Iowa. It's too dangerous for people like me." I told her that Tabor had been a center for the abolitionist movement before the Civil War, that its preachers had been leaders of the antislavery movement. She was surprised. "I'm going to read about Tabor," she said, "but I'll never go there." I was reminded of Della thinking that she had to get out of Gilead before dark.

**3.** Jack is, I think, a Christian hero in that, by his very way of being, he pounds on the illusion of Christendom. He will break it apart or be broken by it. Theoretically speaking, we cannot be sure that there would be any successful way to live with Jack. But, in my limited understanding of Christian requirements, the point is not to make a theoretical assessment, but a practical commitment. *Practically* speaking, the only way to live with Jack successfully would be genuinely to extend Christian love to him. Nothing less is going to work. This, of course, does not make Jack a virtuous man. He is not, and that is not the kind of heroism I am talking about. He is rather a challenge, an occasion for others either to display or fail to display their Christian charity; with Jack there is no middle ground.

Jack's two love affairs expose the illusion of Christian life in Gilead. The first, with a white girl from an impoverished rural background, transcends the bounds of class; the second transcends the bounds of race. Neither distinction would matter in a Christian world. Indeed, neither distinction would even show up. These distinctions do not seem to matter to Jack; they certainly do not serve as barriers. To be sure, he behaved disgracefully by impregnating his first lover and then simply abandoning her to go off to college. But there is at least the possibility that, in his confusion and immaturity, he thought that the way to love his father was to go into self-imposed exile. In this way, he would not merely save his father embarrassment, but he would avoid breaking apart his father's class-structured world. Ames says of his and Boughton's trip to see the father of the young girl, "Her father clearly assumed that we were going to so much bother and expense in order to keep Jack out of trouble. And while no one ever said such a thing or even hinted at such an idea, I can't say he was altogether wrong."[27] But who was really being kept out of trouble here? They were paying to spare Boughton the trouble of having to welcome his granddaughter and the mother of his granddaughter into his family. What Boughton actually said was, "I am Robert Boughton. I understand that my family has some responsibility to your daughter and her child. I have come to let you know that we are aware of our obligation and ready to assume it."[28] He then handed over an envelope of money. This is a man who experiences himself as speaking across a chasm of class division. The only thing that could possibly cross that divide is money—certainly not love and welcome. This is what young Glory cannot understand: why is this child not an occasion for joy? But what Jack understands, however dimly, is that he must leave if he is not going to blow his father's world apart. It is not, I think, an exaggeration to say that he was sent away, exiled, though it was also important for the person who expelled him to remain almost in the dark about what he was doing: "Years later [Glory] had heard her father say in the depths of his grief, 'Some things are indefensible.' And it was as if he thought a great gulf had opened, Jack on the far side of it, beyond rescue or comfort. . . . He had come to the last inch of his power to forgive, and there was Jack, still far beyond his reach."[29]

With Della, it seems that there is great affection between them, a sympathetic connection, and, if you do not insist that love require maturity, then you could call it love. It is not true, I think, to say that Jack's love is color blind: the fact that Della is black does matter to him. What remains systematically unclear is whether his own sense of being an outsider gives him a remarkable capacity for sympathy with other excluded people or whether his remarkable capacity for sympathy with excluded people makes him into an outsider. Either way, the established normative order is not his friend. And when the blowup comes once again, the normative order stays in place, at least for a little while longer; and Jack goes into his second exile.

His exile sheds some light on his capacity for love, and the relationship of his love to his truthfulness. I have wondered whether one of Jack's faults lies in his inability to love the world as he finds it—to accept it, with all its hypocrisy, callousness, and corruption as nevertheless God's creation. Why could he not focus on the beauty that was also there, the love his family did extend to him? I do not know the answer. But his acts are consistent with this possibility: that he feared his father could not take his truthfulness and that he fled out of a misguided conception of love for him. Around every major issue in his life, Jack tells the truth. He is open with Ames, even as Ames does not speak the truth to him. He describes his confrontation with Della's father this way: "I wished very much at the time I could have been, you know, a hypocrite. But I just didn't have it in me. My one scruple."[30] And of the project of deceiving his dying father into thinking he had found faith, he says, "I didn't try though. Did you notice that? To lie to him. I lost my nerve."[31] Nor is there any prevarication about his paternity of his first child—with his father, at least. If the issue has been hushed up in the family, it is by the father. And as he contemplates his second exile, Jack confesses to Glory that he is concerned about his father: "I'm not exactly a pillar of strength. And if I went wrong, it would be better if I did it somewhere else. Better for Papa."[32] On this reading, it is not that Jack suffered for lack of love, but for a misguided sense of love's requirements. He feared that his father could not withstand his truthfulness: Jack could not remain in his father's hypocritical world without trying to bring it down, and he cared for his father too much to do that. Thus he left.

If we can give any traction to this thought, it sheds new light on Jack's juvenile criminality. One might see him as searching for a compromise: is there a way that he might stand witness to a different normative order while not utterly alienating himself from the community? Perhaps petty crime might do the trick. "I used to stir up a little trouble to make sure the old fellow was still keeping an eye on me."[33] This is a kind of inverse love affair—performing little bad deeds to keep winning his father's disapproval. Perhaps that is as close to winning approval as Jack could get, for to perform the deeds that would actually win his father's approval would have required him to enter a normative order that was alien to him. Petty criminality was an unstable compromise formation, an attempt to live in some relation to the established normative order without either going along with it or abandoning home altogether. When that compromise formation broke down, he had to leave.

**4.** It is time to confront the hopelessness Jack expresses at the end of his conversation with Glory. "I think hope is the worst thing in the world. I really do. It makes a fool of you while it lasts. And then when it is gone, it's like there is nothing left of you at all. Except what you can't get rid of."[34] Glory goes back to an ancient memory: "It was the loneliness that none of them could ever forget, that wry distance, as if there were injury for him in the fact that all of them were native to their life as he could never be."[35] And she describes his appearance in his current hopelessness this way: "He looked like destitution. He looked like the saddest fantasy she had ever had of the worst that might have become of him, except that he was breathing."[36] Jack says, "Now you know me." And he continues a little while later: "Reverend Miles, Della's father and my biographer, told me I was nothing but trouble.

I felt the truth of that. I really am nothing. . . . Nothing with a body. I create a kind of displacement around myself as I pass through the world which can fairly be called trouble."[37]

This is a self-portrait of despair. And the question is whether Jack is right about himself. He is hopeless in this moment, but is he correct that this hopelessness expresses who he really is? Is he really *nothing*, nothing with a body? There are basically two ways to go: accept Jack's self-interpretation or reject it. If one were to accept it, one would have to accept that at his core is emptiness, an inchoate nausea at being itself. The expressions of hopefulness that one does see in Jack throughout his conversation with Glory—his attempt to return to Gilead, work in the garden, restore the car, look for a job, have a conversation with Glory—one would have to interpret as a brittle defense, a fragile and ultimately futile attempt to keep despair at bay. On this reading, the hopeful Jack is the false Jack, a mask over nothing except perhaps envy at other people's attempts to find beauty in life. If this is Jack, the world in all of its goodness makes him sick.

The other way to go is to accept Jack's hopelessness but deny his self-interpretation. In the moment, Jack's capacity for hope has broken down, an experience that makes him feel as though he has no capacity. But this experience need not be true. A temporary breakdown in one's ability to feel in touch with one's hopefulness may simply *feel* like a permanent condition.

There is reason to support this second interpretation, though it is not based on any claim to have a deeper insight into Jack's soul. This reason can be expressed both in secular and in religious terms. Secularly speaking, the point is about the legitimate limits of psychological interpretation. However much we have come to know a person, we are never in a position legitimately to claim that at his core there is nothing, just despair and envy. This is beyond the bounds of human knowing. As an imaginative exercise, it helps to think of Reverend Ames's second wife, Lila, as a person very much like Jack, having spent decades wandering the earth in her selfimposed exile. When she finally wanders into the church in Gilead, meets Reverend Ames, and is baptized by him, she is, for whatever reason, able to accept the balm Gilead has to offer. Perhaps that explains the ease with which she understands and sympathetically accepts Jack: she is a veteran of the battles he is still fighting. In the heat of his inquisition about predestination, Jack asks his father and Ames, "I don't mean to be disrespectful. My question is, are there people who are simply born evil, live evil lives and then go to hell?"[38] And he sums up what he hears them saying as, "People don't change, then."[39] It is Lila who breaks in and says, "A person can change. Everything can change."[40] One needs to imagine her speaking from the depths of her own experience. Who knows what Lila's past was, but no one is in a position legitimately to rule out this imagined past as impossible for her. And imagining this even as a possibility makes Ames's refusal of Jack's myriad attempts to connect with him all the more heartrending.

Since Marilynne Robinson is a Christian writer, let me try to put the religious formulation of the reason that supports our second interpretation in Christian terms. These are the terms in which Ames would have understood his own obligation. In the *Institutes of the Christian Religion,* Calvin writes a section, "Love of neighbor is not dependent upon manner of men but looks to God," that includes this passage:

> Say, "He is contemptible and worthless"; but the Lord shows him to be one to whom he has deigned to give the beauty of his image. . . . Now if he has not only deserved no good at your hand, but has also provoked you by unjust acts and curses, not even this is just reason why you should cease to embrace him in love and to perform the duties of love on his behalf [Matthew 6.14, 18.35; Luke 17.3]. You will say, "He has deserved something far different from me." Yet what has the Lord deserved? While he bids you forgive this man for all sins he has committed against you, he would truly have them charged against himself.[41]

In this formulation, to see Jack as *really nothing, nothing with a body,* is to fail to see the way in which Jack is created in God's image. In attributing nothingness to Jack's core, one is unwittingly and indirectly pointing out the finite limits of one's own ability to see. On this religious interpretation, this is Jack's own condition; not that he has finally been able to see and declare who he really is—he absolutely lacks authority for that—but that in the moment he has lost the ability to be in touch with something good in his soul. This is the form Jack's suffering takes.

Marilynne Robinson's novels are a slow burn. She writes as though she knows it is going to take time to wake up her readers and get them to see what they—we—have barely noticed about our own hollowed-out forms of life. I am not myself a Christian, and I do not try to live by Calvin's injunction. Rather, I think that life is short, my own resources limited, and there are better ways to live, even when helping others, than engaging with very difficult people. It is a different way of embracing human finiteness than the one Calvin recommends. Yet what Marilynne Robinson has taught me through her novels, among so much else, is that there are serious costs attached to living as I do.

# Notes

## INTRODUCTION

1. Plato, *Republic* IV.441e. For English translations using "to rule," see, e.g., Plato, *Republic,* trans. C. D. C. Reeve (Indianapolis: Hackett, 2004); *Republic,* trans. G. M. A. Grube, rev. C. D. C. Reeve, in *Plato: Complete Works,* ed. John M. Cooper (Indianapolis: Hackett, 1997); *Republic,* trans. Christopher Rowe (New York: Penguin, 2012); *Republic,* trans. Robin Waterfield (Oxford: Oxford University Press, 1993); *The Republic,* trans. Tom Griffith, ed. G. R. F. Ferrari (Cambridge: Cambridge University Press, 2000).

2. Throughout this book I use the words "psyche" and "soul" interchangeably. "Soul" is an adequate translation for the Greek term "*psyche*"; as is the English word "psyche". I follow Aristotle in thinking that psyche is the principle of life in a living organism.

3. Freud, *Introductory Lectures on Psycho-analysis, Standard Edition of the Complete Psychological Works of Sigmund Freud* (London: Hogarth Press, 1956–1974) (hereafter *SE*) 16, 284–285. See also, "A Difficulty on the Path of Psycho-analysis," *SE* 17, 141.

4. Plato even had a conception of unconscious desire: he thought that dreams express unruly desires of which we are unaware in waking life. In *Republic* IX, Socrates says of such desires: "These are the ones that wake up when we are asleep, whenever the rest of the soul—the rational, gentle and ruling element—slumbers. Then the bestial and savage part, full of food and drink comes alive, casts off sleep, and seeks to go and gratify its own characteristic instincts. You know it will dare to do anything in such a state, released and freed from all shame and wisdom. In fantasy, it does not shrink from trying to have sex with a mother or with anyone else—man, god or beast. It will commit any foul murder, and there is no food it refuses to eat. In a word, it does not refrain from anything, no matter how foolish or shameful" (Plato, *Republic* IX.571c–d, trans. C. D. C. Reeve).

5. As is well known, in some forms of psychosis people speak their minds without inhibition. But that is not the same thing as trying to follow a rule. In a different way, they cannot follow the rule either.

6. Freud, "On Beginning the Treatment," *SE* 12, 134–135n.

7. And so, the development of freely unfolding self-consciousness in a person typically (though not necessarily) requires the help of another—in an unusual, asymmetrical I-thou relation we have come to know as the psychoanalytic situation.

8. See, for example, Freud, *Fragment of an Analysis of a Case of Hysteria, SE* 7, 112–122.

9. *Oxford English Dictionary Online*, 2016.

10. Aristotle, *Nicomachean Ethics* (hereafter *NE*), trans. C. D. C. Reeve (Indianapolis: Hackett, 2014), II.6, 1107a11–16.

11. See Søren Kierkegaard, *Fear and Trembling: A Dialectical Lyric by Johannes de Silentio,* ed. C. S. Evans and S. Walsh (Cambridge: Cambridge University Press, 2006).

12. See Plato, *Republic* VIII; and Cora Diamond, "Losing Your Concepts," *Ethics* 98, no. 2 (1988): 255–277.

## 1. WISDOM WON FROM ILLNESS

1. Aristotle, *Nicomachean Ethics* (hereafter *NE*) VI.7, 1141b1–4;. For the Greek text: *Aristotelis: Ethica Nicomachea* (Oxford: Clarendon Press, 1975). For translations of all Aristotle's works into English: *The Complete Works of Aristotle: The Revised Oxford Translation*, ed. Jonathan Barnes (Princeton: Princeton University Press, 1984). See also *Metaphysics* I.1, 981b28.

2. *NE* VII.3, 1147a23–b5.

3. *NE* VI.7, 1041a20–b23.

4. On the earlier view see Freud, *The Interpretation of Dreams, SE* 4, 100–101; "Freud's Psychoanalytic Procedure," *SE* 7, 251–252; and *Five Lectures on Psychoanalysis, SE* 11, 31–32. On the later view, see "The Dynamics of Transference," *SE* 12, 107; *Five Lectures,* 33; "Recommendations to Physicians Practicing Psychoanalysis," *SE* 12, 115; and "On Beginning the Treatment," *SE* 12, 134–135.

5. Freud, "Remembering, Repeating, and Working-Through," *SE* 12, 147.

6. Freud, *The Interpretation of Dreams,* 98n (added in 1914).

7. For a brief sample: W. R. Bion, "Attacks on Linking," *International Journal of Psychoanalysis* 40 (1959): 308–315; Bion, *Attention and Interpretation* (London: Tavistock, 1970); C. Botella and S. Botella, *The Work of Psychic Figurability: Mental States without Representation* (London: Routledge, 2005); A. Green, *The Fabric of Affect in Psychoanalytic Discourse* (London: Routledge, 1999); Green, *The Work of the Negative* (London: Free Association Books, 1999); Green, *Key Ideas for a Contemporary Psychoanalysis: Misrecognition and Recognition of the Unconscious* (London: Routledge, 2005); Green, *Psychoanalysis: A Paradigm for Clinical Thinking* (London: Free Association Books, 2005); H. B. Levine, G. S. Reed, and D. Scarfone, eds., *Unrepresented States and*

*the Construction of Meaning: Clinical and Theoretical Contributions* (London: Karnac Books, 2013); B. Joseph, "Transference: The Total Situation," and "Projective Identification: Some Clinical Aspects," in *Psychic Equilibrium and Psychic Change* (London: Routledge, 1989), 156–180; Edna O'Shaughnessy, "W. R. Bion's Theory of Thinking and New Techniques in Child Analysis," and "The Invisible Oedipus Complex," in *Melanie Klein Today: Volume 2: Mainly Practice,* ed. E. B. Spillius (London: Routledge, 1988), 177–205; H. Rosenfeld, *Psychotic States: A Psychoanalytic Approach* (London: Hogarth, 1965); Rosenfeld, *Impasse and Interpretation* (London: Tavistock, 1987); D. W. Winnicott, "Ego-Distortion in Terms of True and False Self," in *The Maturational Process and the Facilitating Environment* (London: Hogarth Press, 1960), 140–152.

8. Freud, *New Introductory Lectures on Psychoanalysis, SE* 22, 80.

9. Freud, *The Ego and the Id, SE* 19, 17–18.

10. See David Finkelstein, *Expression and the Inner* (Cambridge, MA: Harvard University Press, 2008); and Sebastian Rödl, *Self-Consciousness* (Cambridge, MA: Harvard University Press, 2007).

11. See Jean Laplanche, *Essays on Otherness* (London: Routledge, 1999); and Jonathan Lear, *Happiness, Death, and the Remainder of Life* (Cambridge, MA: Harvard University Press, 1999).

12. Freud, "On Beginning the Treatment," 135n.

13. Freud, *The Ego and the Id,* 17–18. "We must admit," Freud says, "that the characteristic of being unconscious begins to lose significance for us. It becomes a quality which can have many meanings . . ." Ibid.

14. Freud, "On Beginning the Treatment," 135.

15. Ibid.

16. Matthew Boyle, "Essentially Rational Animals," in *Rethinking Epistemology,* ed. G. Abel and J. Conant (Berlin: Walter De Gruyter, 2012); and "Additive Theories of Rationality: A Critique," *European Journal of Philosophy,* http://nrs.harvard.edu/urn-3:HUL.InstRepos:8641180. Accessed March 28, 2014.

17. *NE* I.13, 1102b13–14.

18. *NE* I.13, 1102b25–28. See Chapter 2, "Integrating the Nonrational Soul."

19. *Republic* IX, 571c–d, my emphasis.

20. Freud, "The Unconscious," *SE* 14, 187.

21. Thomas Mann, "Freud and the Future," in *Essays of Three Decades* (London: Secker and Warburg, 1938), 411–428.

22. Donald Davidson, "Paradoxes of Irrationality," *Philosophical Essays on Freud,* ed. R. Wollheim and J. Hopkins (Cambridge: Cambridge University Press, 1982), 289–305; J. Lear, "Jumping from the Couch," *International Journal of Psychoanalysis* 83 (2002): 583–595; and Lear, *Freud* (London: Routledge, 2015), pp. 29-60..

23. The German is *Widerspruchlosigkeit.* Freud, "Das Unbewußte," in *Gesammelte Werke* 10, ed. M. Bonaparte, A. Freud, E. Bibring, W. Hoffer, E. Kris, and O. Isakower (Frankfurt: Fischer, 1969), 286.

24. See, e.g., Christine Korsgaard, *The Sources of Normativity* (Cambridge: Cambridge University Press, 2006); and *Self-Constitution: Agency, Identity, and Integrity* (Oxford: Oxford University Press, 2009).

25. Freud, "The Dynamics of Transference," 108.

26. Ibid., my emphasis. See also Freud, *Fragment of an Analysis of a Case of Hysteria, SE* 7, 117. "Transference, which seems ordained to be the greatest obstacle to psychoanalysis, becomes its most powerful ally, if its presence can be detected each time and explained to the patient."

27. Freud, *The Ego and the Id,* 26; and Freud, *Negation, SE* 19, 237.

28. G. E. M. Anscombe, *Intention* (Cambridge, MA: Harvard University Press, 2000).

29. Stephen Engstrom, *The Form of Practical Knowledge: A Study of the Categorical Imperative* (Cambridge, MA: Harvard University Press, 2009); Rödl, *Self-Consciousness;* Michael Thompson, *Life and Action: Elementary Structures of Practice and Practical Thought* (Cambridge, MA: Harvard University Press, 2008).

30. Rödl, *Self-Consciousness,* 47–49.

31. *NE* I.13, 1102b27–28; VI.1, 5.

32. *Metaphysics* IX.6, 1048b18–35.

33. *De Anima* II.1, 412a20–21.

34. *NE* I.7, 1098a3–20.

35. *NE* I.7, 1097b22–33. The Greek word *ergon* that I here translate as "characteristic activity" or "characteristic work" is often translated as "function."

36. *NE* I.7, 1098a3–7; I.13, 1102a27–1103a10.

37. Jonathan Lear, *A Case for Irony* (Cambridge, MA: Harvard University Press, 2011).

## 2. INTEGRATING THE NONRATIONAL SOUL

1. Aristotle, *Nicomachean Ethics* I.13, 1102b13–14. *Aristotelis, Ethica Nicomachea,* ed. I. Bywater (Oxford: Oxford University Press, 1912).

2. *Nicomachean Ethics,* trans. W. D. Ross and J. O. Urmson, in *The Complete Works of Aristotle: The Revised Oxford Translation,* ed. Jonathan Barnes (Princeton: Princeton University Press, 1984), 1741; *The Nicomachean Ethics,* trans. H. Rackham, Loeb Classical Library (Cambridge: Harvard University Press, 1990), 65; and *Nicomachean Ethics,* trans. Christopher Rowe (Oxford: Oxford University Press, 2002), 110. The same problem arises with the Ostwald translation (Upper Saddle River: Prentice Hall, 1999), 30–31. The Irwin translation gets it right that a nature is involved (Indianapolis: Hackett, 1985), 31. I follow standard practice in translating *psychê* as either "soul" or "psyche," and I follow Aristotle in considering soul to be the principle of life in a living organism.

3. *NE* I.13, 1102b27–28. Liddell-Scott-Jones also gives "speak the same language" for *homophôneô,* which is fine for my interpretation as well, though, as I shall argue, there

are reasons for thinking that Aristotle is here drawing upon the literal idea of speaking with the same voice. H. G. Liddell, R. Scott, and H. S. Jones, *A Greek-English Lexicon* (Oxford: Clarendon Press, 1968), 1228. LSJ cites this particular line and gives "chimes in with," which, again I shall argue, is not a good translation. And, like Wittgenstein's account of buying a second copy of the newspaper, the fact that it is so cited here lends no more authority to this translation than the original decision of the translator.

4. *NE* I.13, 1103a3–10; cp. VI.2, 1138b35–1139a6.

5. So, for example, in *History of Animals,* Aristotle uses the term to compare the grunts of wild boars during periods of copulation, birth, and taking care of their young. *History of Animals,* trans. d'A. W. Thompson, in *The Complete Works of Aristotle: The Revised Oxford Translation,* ed. Jonathan Barnes (Princeton: Princeton University Press, 1984), 578a32. Aristotle also describes in this passage how wild boars castrate themselves, but that topic is beyond the scope of this essay. He also uses it to describe the voice of birds (593a3–4). And he distinguishes the voice (*phônê*) of animals from other types of sounds that animals make (535b13–32). So, for example, certain fish make noises that *appear* to be voice but are not; and the scallop, when it moves along the ground, makes a whizzing sound; and the wings of flying birds make sounds—but none of this voice.

6. *NE* I.13, 1102b13–14; 1103a1–3.

7. Ibid., 1103a3–10.

8. Aristotle follows Plato in thinking that we are psychologically complex creatures, and in this essay, I want simply to assume this tradition and work within it, though I recognize that there are other psychological approaches. As is well known, Plato in the *Republic* valorizes psychic harmony, and he uses the Greek terms *harmonia* and *euharmostia*—but he also uses the term *symphônia,* regularly translated as "concord" or "harmony," which at least carries a connotation of agreement in voice. See, e.g., *Plato's Republic,* trans. G. M. A. Grube (Indianapolis: Hackett, 1974); and *Republic,* trans. C. D. C. Reeve (Indianapolis: Hackett, 2004). It is not unreasonable to think that Plato had this meaning in mind, because he used this term not just to describe intrapsychic concord, but also as a quality of the stories we tell each other. So, for example, poets will not be allowed to say that the gods are the cause of bad things, because we already know that they are only the cause of good; and such stories are not only impious and disadvantageous, "neither do they speak with the same voice / nor are they in agreement with each other" (. . . *oute symphôna auta hautoîs*). *Platonis: Republicam* II, ed. S. R. Slings (Oxford: Clarendon Press, 2003), 380c3–4. The stories are not in concord with each other because they are *saying* different things. And when Socrates famously concludes that it is appropriate for reason to rule because of its wisdom and foresight for the whole soul, he goes on to say that this will be possible in virtue of a musical and physical education that makes the elements of the soul "speak with the same voice" (. . . *symphôna auta poiêsei*) (*Rep.* IV, 441e7–8). Socrates is here calling for concord in the soul. But it would be a lesser achievement if that consisted merely in reason singing, "Do X!" and the nonrational parts harmoniously singing, "Let's do X!" If we are to

make robust the idea of reason *ruling*, it would be preferable for reason to be in some form of successful communication with the nonrational parts of the soul. The concord would then be a manifestation of intrapsychic communication.

9. Bernard Williams, "Naturalism and Morality," in *World, Mind, and Ethics: Essays on the Ethical Philosophy of Bernard Williams,* ed. J. E. J. Altham and R. Harrison (Cambridge: Cambridge University Press, 1995), 202–205.

10. *NE* I.13, 1102b31–33.

11. *NE* I.13, 1102b31–32, 1103a3.

12. Williams, "Naturalism and Morality," 202, my emphasis. See also, *Ethics and the Limits of Philosophy* (Cambridge, MA: Harvard University Press, 1985), 30–53; and *Shame and Necessity* (Berkeley: University of California Press, 2008).

13. Freud, "The Unconscious," *SE* 14, 187.

14. David Finkelstein, *Expression and the Inner* (Cambridge: Harvard University Press, 2003), 115.

15. Ibid., 119, my emphasis.

16. Richard Moran, *Authority and Estrangement* (Princeton: Princeton University Press, 2001), 85. My emphasis.

17. *NE* I.4, 1095a30–b4.

18. Aristotle, *Posterior Analytics* (in *Complete Works*), 71b19–72a5.

19. See Chapter 1, "Wisdom Won from Illness," for relevant quotations from Freud.

20. Freud, "Recommendations to Physicians Practising Psycho-analysis," *SE* 12, 115. "On Beginning the Treatment," *SE* 12, 134–135; *Five Lectures on Psychoanalysis, SE* 11, 31–32; "An Autobiographical Study," *SE* 20, 40–41.

21. John Wisdom, a former president of the Aristotelian Society, wrote: "No doubt the unconscious is irritatingly like ectoplasm—gone whenever the light is strong enough to see it. But still, provided a psychologist's prescription for settling his claim is clear, we must continue to be patient, however complicated it is." *Philosophy and Psychoanalysis* (Berkeley: University of California Press, 1969), 192. By tying psychoanalysis to its method, as opposed to any particular dogmatic claim, I think we approach the kind of clarity Wisdom was looking for.

22. Analysands have reported to me that, if they pay attention, they can *feel* thoughts escaping their consciousness; with effort they can draw them back. They can see for themselves that the thought they were about to lose was not an indifferent one, but an unwanted thought—one that was about to lead in uncomfortable directions. That is, when the analyst is working with the analysand at the level of the analysand's own conscious experience, the analysand will on occasion experience repression as a conscious experience.

23. Freud, "On Beginning the Treatment," *SE* 12, 135n.

24. Freud, *The Ego and the Id, SE* 19, 17.

25. Ibid., 18.

26. This also helps us understand the one legitimate sense of psychic determinism of the unconscious. Psychoanalytic practice does not put us in a position to say with

confidence that event A in childhood caused state of mind B, which then later in life led inexorably to C. This is the chain of *efficient* causes; and we open ourselves to legitimate criticism when we try to make any such claims. However, what we do see all the time in psychoanalysis is the psychic determinism of *formal* cause: that no matter what life's unfolding events, a person will have a tendency to experience them, say, as a "green light" around which he feels wary or a "red light" about which he feels envy that other people can go through it and get away with it. The unconscious is gifted at drawing unfolding events into its formal structures.

27. Plato saw in *Republic* that even simple acts of inhibiting oneself (say, from getting a drink when one is thirsty) can express express a world-view (439b-d). For the inhibition expresses an overall sense of appropriateness.

28. See Stephen Engstrom, *The Form of Practical Knowledge: A Study of the Categorical Imperative* (Cambridge: Harvard University Press, 2009). I discuss this also in Chapter 1, "Wisdom Won from Illness."

29. *NE* I.13, 1103a3–10.

30. *NE* VI.12, 1144a24–36.

31. *NE* VI.13, 1144b1–25.

32. *NE* VI.13, 1144b26–28.

33. *NE* VI.13, 1144b28–30.

34. *NE* I.9, 1099b32–1100a2; X.8, 1178b24. *EE* I.1117a21–29.

35. Christine Korsgaard, *The Sources of Normativity* (Cambridge: Cambridge University Press, 1996), 92–102. John McDowell, "Two Sorts of Naturalism," in *Mind, Value and Reality* (Cambridge: Harvard University Press, 1998), 170–171.

36. Korsgaard, *Self-Constitution: Agency, Integrity and Identity* (Oxford: Oxford University Press, 2009).

37. See Korsgaard, "Self-Constitution and Irony," and my response in Jonathan Lear, *A Case for Irony* (Cambridge: Harvard University Press, 2011), 75–83, 84–102.

38. See Matthew Boyle, "Essentially Rational Animals," in *Rethinking Epistemology*, ed. G. Abel and J. Conant (Berlin: Walter De Gruyter, 2012). See also Michael Thompson, "Apprehending Human Form," *Royal Institute of Philosophy Supplement* 54 (2004): 47–74.

39. See the discussion of adultery in the Introduction; and *NE* II.6, 1107a14–17.

40. Jacques Lacan, *The Ethics of Psychoanalysis, 1959–1960* (London: Routledge, 1992).

41. See Freud, *Civilization and Its Discontents, SE* 21, 64–145.

42. See Freud, *Beyond the Pleasure Principle, SE* 28, 7–64.

43. *NE* I.2, 1094a18–b11; I.3 1095a1–12; I.13, 1102a7–25. *Politics* I.1, 1252a1–7; I.2.1252b29–30; III.6, 1278b17–24; III.9, 1280b39; VII.2, 1325a7–10.

## 3. WHAT IS A CRISIS OF INTELLIGIBILITY?

1. Elizabeth Anscombe, *Intention* (Cambridge, MA: Harvard University Press, 2000), 57–58.

2. I have written at length about these statements in *Radical Hope: Ethics in the Face of Cultural Devastation* (Cambridge, MA: Harvard University Press, 2006). This essay is a continuation of a meditation on those themes. For an outstanding history of this period, see Frederick Hoxie, *Parading through History: The Making of the Crow Nation in America, 1805–1935* (Cambridge: Cambridge University Press, 1997).

3. Frank B. Linderman, *Plenty Coups, Chief of the Crows* (Lincoln: University of Nebraska Press, 1962), 311; my emphasis.

4. Peter Nabokov, *Two Leggings: The Making of a Crow Warrior* (Lincoln: University of Nebraska Press, 1967), 197.

5. Alma Hogan Snell, *Grandmother's Grandchild: My Crow Indian Life* (Lincoln: University of Nebraska Press, 2000), 42.

6. It is heartrending to visit the massive collection of Crow coup-sticks and shields in the basement of the Field Museum of Natural History in Chicago. They were sold to the curator and anthropologist Charles Simms, who made a trip to the northwest plains at the turn of the twentieth century, because the Crow no longer had any use for them.

7. See Fred W. Voget, *The Shoshoni-Crow Sun Dance* (Norman: University of Oklahoma Press, 1984); Michael O. Fitzgerald, *Yellowtail: Crow Medicine Man and Sun Dance Chief* (Norman: University of Oklahoma Press, 1991).

8. Snell, *Grandmother's Grandchild*, 42.

9. See Anscombe, *Intention;* and Sebastian Rödl, *Self-Consciousness* (Cambridge, MA: Harvard University Press, 2007).

10. Michael Dummett, "Bringing about the Past" and "The Reality of the Past," in *Truth and Other Enigmas* (Cambridge, MA: Harvard University Press, 1978), 333–350, 358–374. See also his *Elements of Intuitionism* (Oxford: Clarendon Press, 1977) and *The Logical Basis of Metaphysics* (Cambridge, MA: Harvard University Press, 1991).

11. The Crow word for "brave" is *alaxch-iaa:* See Ishtaléescgua Báchiaa Héeleetaalawe, *A Dictionary of Everyday Crow* (Crow Agency, Montana: Bilingual Materials Development Center, 1987).

12. As another illustration, consider three different ways in which marriage might become "unintelligible."

(1) Standing in front of the mirror shaving, I realize I no longer love my wife. Indeed, it no longer makes any sense to me how we ever got married. It is as though I am detached, looking down from a great distance, with utter bewilderment at this stranger: whatever have we been doing all these years? We have each been living in the same house, but have we been living together? We have each been sleeping in the same bed, but have we been sleeping together? I no longer have any idea.

(2) Standing in front of the mirror shaving, the very idea of marriage becomes unintelligible to me. I can see clearly that there are all these people living in pairs in houses and apartments, calling themselves "married" and so on, but whatever are they talking about? What *are* they doing? I no longer have any idea.

(1) and (2) describe odd and unusual states of affairs, but they are basically psychological phenomena. By contrast:

(3) This historical institution of marriage goes out of existence. The associated rituals are suppressed, the act is successfully forbidden, there is genetic intervention in population to suppress the desire to remain with any one partner, the memory of the institution becomes one of something that now seems quaint, on the level of driving chariots and wearing togas. And so on. In such a situation, there is no longer any legitimate way to represent myself (to myself or to another) as married. This has nothing to do with my psychology: it has everything to do with the viability of a form of life that I have hitherto inhabited. And in such a situation my earlier married state might well remain intelligible in theoretical terms. It is this third mode of unintelligibility that is the focus of this essay.

13. Joseph Medicine Crow, *Counting Coup: Becoming a Chief on the Reservation and Beyond* (Washington, D.C.: National Geographic, 2006), 107; my emphasis.

## 4. A LOST CONCEPTION OF IRONY

1. But see Cora Diamond, "Losing Your Concepts," *Ethics* 98, no. 2 (1988), 255–277.

2. *Oxford English Dictionary Online,* 2016.

3. And in a social world in which philosophy has become a profession—one in which getting a job, getting promoted, getting tenure depends on procuring a list of publications that few may read but that deans feel they need—there is plenty to keep us busy in trying to decide whether Socrates said what he meant. In participating in this professional form of life, we ourselves fall into a routine.

4. Plato, *Phaedrus,* (*Complete Works*) 244a–d, 245b–c, 249d–e.

5. See, for example, Socrates's account of how the prisoners in the Cave break their bonds (*Republic* VII, 515c–d). The prisoner is *suddenly* (εξαιφνης) compelled to stand up (515c6) and is pained and puzzled (απορειν; 515d6) to turn around. And see Alcibiades's description of Socrates's disruptive effect upon him in *Symposium,* (*Complete Works*), 215d–216d.

6. Plato, *Phaedrus* 250a–b.

7. Ibid., 251e.

8. Ibid., 252e–253a.

9. Plato, *Republic* III, 405c–406a.

10. Plato, *Charmides,* (*Complete Works*),156e–157c.

11. The Greek is "*gennaios pseudos*"—and "*pseudos*" can simply mean falsehood. Thus any fiction no matter how well meaning, high-minded or instructive is strictly 'false' in the sense of its being a fiction. In Socrates's so-called "noble lie" there is no evidence of any intention on Socrates's part to deceive. Or, at the very least, it is not difficult to read him as lacking any such intention. Thus to characterize his fiction as a lie is to tilt

the text pretty heavily in one direction. Thus I prefer "fine fiction" or "noble fiction". I think Socrates takes himself to be offering a truthful myth that has political value.

12. Johannes Climacus [Søren Kierkegaard], *Concluding Unscientific Postscript to Philosophical Fragments,* trans. H. V. Hong and E. H. Hong (Princeton: Princeton University Press, 1992), 277n.

13. Climacus, *Concluding Unscientific Postscript,* trans. Alastair Hannay (Cambridge: Cambridge University Press, 2009), 422.

14. *Søren Kierkegaard's Journals and Papers,* ed. H. V. Hong and E. H. Hong, vol. 2, *F-K* (Bloomington: Indiana University Press, 1970), 277; my emphasis.

15. It would take an essay of its own to follow out this possibility, but the case of the Crow Nation that I discussed earlier raises the possibility of ironic excellence in the first-person plural. In a sense, the Crow had irony forced upon them. On the one hand, they survived as a social unit: they still exist as "The Crow Nation" or the "Absalokee" (Children of the Large Beaked Bird). On the other hand, the question "What can it any longer mean to be Crow?" has been forced upon them as a result of cultural devastation. This is not simply a question of how they can any longer live up to Crow ideals; it is a question of what Crow ideals can any longer be. And to understand the question *as forced* on them, one must try to imagine it not as a theoretical question, but as an urgent, anxious practical question, filled with longing yet lacking clear determination or orientation. We come closer to understanding one way in which cultural devastation endures as we grasp the continued suffering embodied in this question. But the possibility of ironic excellence *for the group*—perhaps fostered by poetic and creative individuals in that group—might be a way of providing an answer to the ironic question of Crow existence.

16. *Kierkegaard's Journals,* 278.

17. Søren Kierkegaard, *The Concept of Irony with Continual Reference to Socrates,* trans. H. V. Hong and E. H. Hong (Princeton: Princeton University Press, 1989), 279.

18. Climacus, *Concluding Unscientific Postscript* (trans. Hong and Hong), 503, 90n.

19. Plato, *Symposium* 220c–d.

20. Ibid., 220d–e.

21. Ibid., 221b; my emphasis.

22. Ibid., 221c–d.

23. Plato, *Laches,* (*Complete Works*), 199e.

24. Ibid., 181a–b.

25. Ibid., 178c–d.

26. Ibid., 201a–c.

27. Plato, *Apology,* (*Complete Works*), 36d–e.

28. Kierkegaard, *The Concept of Irony,* 326. See also Thesis XV, p. 6: "Just as philosophy begins with doubt, so also a life that may be called human begins with irony."

## 5. WAITING FOR THE BARBARIANS

1. I am indebted to the work of Cora Diamond and Alasdair MacIntyre. See Diamond, "Losing Your Concepts," *Ethics* 98, no. 2 (1988): 255–277, and "The Difficulty of Reality and the Difficulty of Philosophy," in *Partial Answers: Journal of Literature and the History of Ideas* 1, no. 2 (2003): 1–26; and MacIntyre, *After Virtue: A Study in Moral Theory* (South Bend, IN: University of Notre Dame Press, 1981).

2. I discuss this problem in *A Case for Irony* (Cambridge: Harvard University Press, 2011) and in the Introduction to the second edition of *Freud* (London: Routledge: 2015).

3. In practical thought, as Aristotle and Kant understood it, self-conscious thinking is itself efficacious in bringing about that which it is thinking. See Stephen Engstrom, "The Will and Practical Judgment," in *The Form of Practical Knowledge: A Study in the Categorical Imperative* (Cambridge: Harvard University Press, 2009), 25–65.

4. Bernard Williams warned us of the danger of moral psychology collapsing into a *moralizing* psychology—one that tacitly assumes the categories it is trying to vindicate. See Bernard Williams, "Naturalism and Morality," in *World, Mind, and Ethics: Essays on the Ethical Philosophy of Bernard Williams,* ed. J. E. J. Altham and R. Harrison (Cambridge: Cambridge University Press, 1995), 202–205.

5. Irving Howe, "A Stark Political Fable of South Africa," *New York Times Book Review,* April 18, 1982.

6. John Coetzee, *Waiting for the Barbarians* (New York: Penguin, 2010), 1.

7. For Freud, condensation is one of the hallmarks of dream-activity. *Interpretation of Dreams, SE* 4, 279–304. A single item—in this case, sunglasses—can stand for the intelligible structure of a world.

8. See D. W. Winnicott, "Transitional Objects and Transitional Phenomena," and "The Location of Cultural Experience," both to be found in *Playing and Reality* (London: Routledge, 2005).

9. Freud, *Beyond the Pleasure Principle, SE* 18, 7–64. I discuss this in the second chapter of *Happiness, Death, and the Remainder of Life* (Cambridge, MA: Harvard University Press, 1999), 61–105, and in *Freud* (New York and London: Routledge, 2005), 154–161.

10. Coetzee, *Waiting for the Barbarians,* 1.

11. Ibid., 9.

12. Ibid., 120.

13. See Richard White, *The Middle Ground: Indians, Empires, and Republics in the Great Lakes Region, 1650–1815* (Cambridge: Cambridge University Press, 2010).

14. Coetzee, *Waiting for the Barbarians,* 43.

15. Ibid., 152.

16. Ibid., 4. Or, as he reminisces to himself: "The people we call barbarians are nomads, they migrate between the lowlands and the uplands every year, that is their way of life" (56). And: "The barbarians who are pastoralists, nomads, tent-dwellers . . ." (16).

17. Even torturers understand *that.* As Col. Joll tells the narrator, "You want to go down in history as a martyr, I suspect. But who is going to put you in the history books? These border troubles are of no significance. In a while they will pass and the frontier will go to sleep for another twenty years. People are not interested in the history of the back of beyond." Ibid., 131.

18. Ibid., 153–154.

19. Ibid., 8–9.

20. Ibid., 16.

21. Ibid., 17.

22. Ibid., 116.

23. Ibid., 5–6.

24. Ibid., 111.

25. Ibid., 135–136. See also, e.g., pp. 145–146:

> "Wait! Listen to me a moment longer. I am sincere, it has cost me a great deal to come out with this, since I am terrified of you, I need not tell you that, I am sure you are aware of it. Do you find it easy to take food afterwards? I have imagined that one would want to wash one's hands. But no ordinary washing would be enough, one would require some priestly intervention, a ceremonial of cleansing, don't you think. Some kind of purging of one's soul too—that is how I have imagined it. Otherwise how would it be possible to return to everyday life—or sit down at table, for instance, and break bread with one's family or one's comrades?"
>
> He turns away, with a slow claw-like hand I manage to catch his arm. "No, listen!" I say. "Do not misunderstand me, I am not blaming you or accusing you, I am long past that. Remember, I too have devoted a life to the law, I know its processes, I know that the workings of justice are often obscure. I am only trying to understand. I am trying to understand the zone in which you live. I am trying to imagine how you breathe and eat and live from day to day. But I cannot! That is what troubles me! If I were he, I say to myself, my hands would feel so dirty that it would choke me—"
>
> He wrenches himself free and hits me so hard in the chest that I gasp and stumble backwards. "You bastard!" He shouts. "You fucking old lunatic! Get out. Go and die somewhere!"

26. Ibid., 156.

27. Ibid., 137.

28. Ibid., 164–165.

29. Ibid., 178–179.

30. Ibid., 124–125.

31. Freud, "Mourning and Melancholia," *SE* 14, 243–258. Freud was more concerned with the intrapsychic structure that underlies melancholia, the object relations and internalizations that lead up to it. We can leave all this to the side. In particular, we are not attempting the absurd task of trying to psychoanalyze a fictional character. Rather,

we are looking at structures of living that are all on the surface, available to anyone who wishes to observe them.

32. See Hans Loewald, "Internalization, Separation, Mourning, and the Superego", in *Papers on Psychoanalysis* (New Haven: Yale, 1980), 257. And see my "Mourning and Moral Psychology," *Psychoanalytic Psychology* (2014).

33. Hans Loewald, "On the Therapeutic Action of Psychoanalysis," in *The Essential Loewald* (Hagerstown, MD: 2000), 249. Freud, *Interpretation of Dreams, SE* 4–5, 553n.

34. It is possible for this commitment to be practical knowledge. That is, it can be an efficacious resolution to defeat in oneself such an outlook on life. Such knowledge is practical in that it is an understanding that is itself efficacious in bringing about that which it understands. And it counts as knowledge insofar as what it understands is genuinely a good way to be. For just as theoretical knowledge aims at the true, practical knowledge aims at the good. See Engstrom, *The Form of Practical Knowledge,* op. cit.

35. *New York Times Book Review,* April 18, 1982.

36. It is difficult to imagine a more ironically cruel fate for an author who seeks to make an ethical difference than to be recognized as a "great writer" in this way. John Coetzee is "known" for avoiding social events, being reticent, even "reclusive." It is worth pondering to what extent this is a quirk of personality and to what extent it manifests a commitment to a certain kind of authorship. Cp. Søren Kierkegaard, *The Point of View of My Work as an Author: A Report to History* (Princeton: Princeton University Press, 1998); and Kierkegaard [Johannes Climacus, pseud.], "A First and Last Declaration," in *Concluding Unscientific Postscript to the Philosophical Crumbs* (Cambridge: Cambridge University Press, 2009).

37. See, e.g., Marcuse's conception of repressive tolerance in *One Dimensional Man: Studies in the Ideology of Advanced Industrial Society* (Boston: Beacon Press, 1991).

38. It is a secular counterpart to "We are all sinners." One hears it in a sermon, and as one walks out of church starts to think about what's for lunch. It is not impossible for one to have a shocking moment of reversal and recognition in which one is taken aback by the thought *we are waiting!*—but such a moment would be highly unusual. Aristotle says that in a paradigmatic tragedy there is reversal *(peripateia)* and recognition *(anagnorisis). Poetics,* 1450a2. This cannot consist simply in his coming to believe, "After all, I am the one who killed my father, Laius, and thus married my mother, Jocasta." He has to come to believe this in a manner appropriate to the tragedy. So, Oedipus does not need a *further* thought to put out his eyes; putting out his eyes is the manner in which he expresses his thought that he is his father's murderer and mother's lover. I am suggesting that the novel offers the reader a gentler, more forgiving, route to recognition.

39. Aristotle famously said that there is a part of the soul that is nonrational but *in a way* listens to reason. He was thinking of our emotional and imaginative capacities. *Nicomachean Ethics* I. 13, 1102b13–14, 1103a1. He further claimed that ethical virtue is an excellence of this part of the soul. Ibid., 1103a3–10.

40. By way of analogy, in psychoanalysis an enormous amount of shared imaginative work, with analysand and analyst working together, must occur before one or the

other can sum up in concise explicit words what they have been working on together. We call this last statement the "interpretation," but the interpretation would have no efficacy were it not the fruition of this imaginative process.

41. I would like to thank James Conant, Gabriel Lear, Sarah Nooter, Mark Payne, Robert Pippin, and David Wellbery for valuable comments on a previous draft.

## 6. THE IRONIC CREATIVITY OF SOCRATIC DOUBT

1. Søren Kierkegaard [Johannes Climacus, pseud.], *Concluding Unscientific Postscript to Philosophical Fragments,* trans. Alastair Hannay (Cambridge: Cambridge University Press, 2009), 527–529.

2. Ibid., 422; and *Concluding Unscientific Postscript to Philosophical Fragments,* trans. H. V. Hong and E. H. Hong (Princeton: Princeton University Press, 1992), 503.

3. Climacus also complains that "Magister Kierkegaard . . . to judge from his dissertation, has scarcely understood" Socrates's approach to prayer. *Concluding,* trans. Hannay, 76n. He misses Socrates's "teasing manner." *Concluding,* trans. Hong and Hong, 90n.

4. Kierkegaard, *The Concept of Irony with Continual Reference to Socrates,* trans. H. V. Hong and E. H. Hong (Princeton: Princeton University Press, 1989), 175–176; my emphasis.

5. Kierkegaard, *Søren Kierkegaard's Journals and Papers,* ed. H. V. Hong and E. H. Hong, vol. 2, *F-K* (Bloomington: Indiana University Press, 1970), 278.

6. As is by now well known, Climacus tells us that earnestness can, on occasion, best be expressed in irony: see, e.g., "From the fact that irony is present it does not follow that earnestness is excluded. That is something only assistant professors assume." *Concluding,* trans. Hong and Hong, 277n; for a slightly different translation, see *Concluding,* trans. Hannay, 232n.

7. *Kierkegaard's Journals,* 278.

8. See Elizabeth Anscombe, *Intention* (Cambridge, MA: Harvard University Press, 2000); Stephen Engstrom, *The Form of Practical Knowledge: A Study in the Categorical Imperative* (Cambridge, MA: Harvard University Press, 2009); and Sebastian Rödl, *Self-Consciousness* (Cambridge, MA: Harvard University Press, 2007).

9. Kierkegaard, *Concept of Irony,* 36.

10. Ibid.

11. Plato, *Symposium,* trans. Alexander Nehamas and Paul Woodruff (Indianapolis: Hackett, 1989), 199c–201c. All quotes are taken from this translation, unless otherwise noted.

12. Ibid., 201d.

13. Ibid., 203b–204b.

14. Ibid., 201e.

15. Kierkegaard, *Concept of Irony,* 36. The reference is to *Symposium,* 212b.

16. Ibid. Similarly, Kierkegaard says, "Although the relation between the dialectical and the mythical is not as markedly conspicuous in the *Symposium* as it is, for example, in the *Phaedo* and *although for that reason it is less useful for my purpose,* it nevertheless does have the advantage that it so definitely accentuates what Socrates himself says and what he has heard from Diotima." Ibid., 42; my emphasis. But he does not use this insight to impugn his method. In a similar vein, see his discussions at 105–108.

17. *Symp.,* 201e.

18. Ibid., 204d–e.

19. Ibid., 205b.

20. Ibid., 205d.

21. Ibid., 206b–c.

22. Ibid., 207c.

23. Ibid., 207c

24. Ibid., 201d5; my translation.

25. Ibid., 177d7–8; my translation. The term I am translating as "erotics"—*ta erôtica*—is often translated into English as "the art of love" or "the rites of love." But, first, there are good reasons for thinking that Plato and Socrates did not think of erotics as an art or a craft (a *technê*). To be taught a *technê* is to possess first-personal practical knowledge; take, for instance, the shoemaker's practical knowledge of how to turn leather into a shoe. But when it comes to *eros,* we are often more like the leather than we are like the shoemaker. Imagine one intelligent piece of leather who had understanding of what was about to happen communicating with another intelligent piece of leather (who lacked that understanding) what was to happen to them both, as they saw the shoemaker arriving. For the shoemaker, who has the practical knowledge, his activity will be the art of shoemaking, but for the leather it is "the stuff that has to do with shoes coming to be." To be sure, erotics is an intermediate case: there are things we can understand and things we can do as a result of our understanding. But that is an understanding and an acting that emerges from suffering, undergoing passion. It does not truly qualify as a *technê.* Second, "rites" suggests ritual; and Diotima and Socrates are not here particularly concerned with ritual. It is rather the undergoing and the activity that typically express an erotic situation. Literally, *ta erotica* are the things having to do with eros. As "physics" is the standard translation for *ta physica*—the things having to do with nature—so "erotics" is a cognate translation.

26. Ibid., 203b–204a.

27. Kierkegaard, *Concept of Irony,* 105–106; my emphasis.

28. Ibid., 107.

29. *Symp.,* 201e–202e; cp. 199c–201c.

30. Ibid., 202b–c.

31. Ibid., 202e–203b.

32. Ibid., 204c.

33. Ibid., 204c–d.

34. Ibid., 204d–205a.
35. Ibid., 205d.
36. Ibid., 206a; my emphasis.
37. Ibid., 206b; my emphasis.
38. Ibid., 206c.
39. Ibid., 206d–e.
40. Ibid., 208e–209a.
41. Ibid., 212b.
42. M. F. Burnyeat, "Socratic Midwifery, Platonic Inspiration," *BICS* 24 (1977): 8.
43. Ibid.; my emphasis.
44. *Symp.*, 209b–c.
45. See Richard Wollheim, "The Bodily Ego," in *The Mind and Its Depths* (Cambridge: Harvard University Press, 1993), 64–78; and "The Mind and the Mind's Image of Itself," *On Art and the Mind* (Cambridge: Harvard University Press, 1974), 31–53.
46. *Symp.*, 210b–c. It is, I think, ultimately unsatisfying to try to separate Socrates from Plato; and yet it is difficult to resist weighing in. My sense is that at Diotima's introduction of the so-called ladder, the author gives a heavy clue: " 'Even you Socrates could probably come to be initiated into these rites of love. But as for the purpose of these rites when they are done correctly—that is the final and highest mystery, *and I don't know if you are capable of it.* I myself will tell you,' she said, 'and I won't stint any effort. And you must try to follow if you can.' " Ibid., 209e–210a; my emphasis.
47. Ibid., 209b–c; my emphasis.
48. On Diotima's account, Kierkegaard and Regine Olsen would be the joint parents of many of Kierkegaard's works.
49. Ibid., 210a–212a.
50. Ibid., 210b.
51. Ibid., 219b–d
52. Cf. ibid., 209d–e.
53. *Kierkegaard's Journals*, 278.
54. Ibid.
55. See *Concluding*, trans. Hannay, 520–526.
56. Plato, *The Theaetetus*, trans. M. J. Levett, revised by Myles Burnyeat (Indianapolis: Hackett, 1990), 150c.
57. Ibid., 150c–d.

## 7. ROSALIND'S PREGNANCY

1. Northrup Frye, *Anatomy of Criticism* (Princeton: Princeton University Press, 1957), 44.
2. William Shakespeare, *As You Like It*, ed. David Bevington (Toronto: Broadview Press, 2012), 3.2.355–358. All references in this chapter are to act, scene, and line of this edition and are cited in the text.

3. *Symposium,* 201d5: I prefer "erotics" for *ta erôtika* over the familiar translation "the art of love." See Chapter 6, note 25 for an explanation.

4. *Symp.*, 177d7–8.

5. Indeed, when she questions the young Socrates, his answers sound remarkably like Orlando's responses to Rosalind: "What do you mean, Diotima?" (201e); "How could you say this!" (202c); "I am beginning to see your point" (205d); "Diotima: 'What is the real purpose of love, can you say?'—Socrates: 'If I could I wouldn't be your student!' " (206b).

6. *Symp.*, 209a.

7. *Symp.*, 206d.

8. *Symp.*, 209b–c; my emphasis.

9. *Symp.*, 209c.

10. *Symp.*, 206e.

11. See David D. Leitao, *The Pregnant Male as Myth and Metaphor in Classical Greek Literature* (Cambridge: Cambridge University Press, 2012).

12. M. F. Burnyeat, "Socratic Midwifery, Platonic Inspiration," *Bulletin of the Institute of Classical Studies* 24, no.1 (1977): 8.

13. *Oxford English Dictionary Online,* s.v. "metaphor," last modified June 2015; my emphasis.

14. If one were to ask the ironic question, "Among all the pregnancies and giving birth, has there ever been a real pregnancy, a real giving birth?" Diotima clearly answers in the affirmative, citing the pregnancies of the poets Homer and Hesiod, and the lawgivers Lycurgus and Solon as the clearest and most exemplary instances of giving birth (*Symp.*, 209d–e).

15. Mark Van Doren, *Shakespeare* (New York: New York Review of Books, 1939), 127–135.

16. C. L. Barber, *Shakespeare's Festive Comedy: A Study of Dramatic Form and Its Relation to Social Custom* (Princeton: Princeton University Press, 2012), 253.

17. I discuss this in *A Case for Irony* (Cambridge MA: Harvard University Press, 2009).

18. I cannot argue for this, but I read this as Shakespearean irony: Rosalind's uncle is Shakespeare, and she is here referring beyond the play to her author.

19. Van Doren, *Shakespeare,* 132–133.

20. Kierkegaard, *Concluding Unscientific Postscript* (A. Hannay, trans.), 422. Although Johannes Climacus is the pseudonymous author, this is a case in which I am confident that this statement expresses the mature Kierkegaard's view.

21. See *A Case for Irony.*

## 8. TECHNIQUE AND FINAL CAUSE IN PSYCHOANALYSIS

1. Aristotle, *Physica* (Oxford: Clarendon Press, 1950), 192–200; *Physics, The Complete Works of Aristotle* (Princeton: Princeton University Press, 1984), 329–342; and Jonathan

Lear, *Aristotle: The Desire to Understand* (Cambridge: Cambridge University Press, 1988), 15–54.

2. Lawrence Levenson, "Superego Defense Analysis in the Termination Phase," *Journal of the American Psychoanalytic Association* 46 (1998): 847–866; S. H. Phillips, "Paul Gray's Narrowing Scope: A 'Developmental Lag' in his Theory and Technique," *Journal of the American Psychoanalytic Association* 54 (2006): 137–170.

3. Paul Gray, "Developmental Lag in the Evolution of Technique for Psychoanalysis of Neurotic Conflict," *Journal of the American Psychoanalytic Association* 30 (1982): 621–655; reprinted in Gray, *The Ego and Analysis of Defense,* 2nd edition (Lanham: Aronson, 2005), 27–61.

4. Levenson, "Superego Defense Analysis," 855.

5. Ibid., 857–858.

6. Gray, "Developmental Lag," 52; James Strachey, "The Nature of the Therapeutic Action of Psychoanalysis," *International Journal of Psychoanalysis* 50 (1934): 275–292.

7. Hans Loewald, "On the Therapeutic Action of Psychoanalysis," *International Journal of Psychoanalysis* 41 (1960), reprinted in Loewald, *The Essential Loewald: Collected Papers and Monographs* (Hagerstown, MD: University Publishing Group, 2000), 221–256; Loewald, "Internationalization, Separation, Mourning and the Superego," *Psychoanalytic Quarterly* 31 (1962), reprinted in *The Essential Loewald,* 267–276; Jonathan Lear, *Therapeutic Action: An Earnest Plea for Irony* (New York: Other Press, 2003), 89–133; compare Phillips, "Paul Gray's Narrowing Scope."

8. Phillips gives as an example of the idea that there is sexual content in this moment: the word "fuck" occurs twice in two sentences, each of which also has the phrase "I want" and an explicit reference to "you," the analyst. And he notes Loewald's claim that, in the termination phase, male analysands regularly sexualized internalization fantasies—such as fellatio of or impregnation by the analyst. Phillips, "Paul Gray's Narrowing Scope", 157; Loewald, "Comments on Some Instinctual Manifestations of Superego Formation", *Essential Loewald,* 327.

9. Ibid., 158.

10. Lear, *Therapeutic Action;* and "Socratic Method and Psychoanalysis," in *The Blackwell Companion to Socrates,* ed. R. Kamtekar and S. Rappe (Oxford: Blackwell, 2006), 442–462.

11. For example, W. R. Bion, "Attacks on Linking," *International Journal of Psychoanalysis* 40 (1959): 308–315; *Learning from Experience* (London: Maresfield, 1962); R. D. Hinshelwood, *Clinical Klein* (London: Free Association Books, 1994); Betty Joseph, "*Psychic Equilibrium and Psychic Change* (London: Routledge, 1989); Donald Meltzer, *The Psychoanalytic Process* (London: Karnac, 1978); Edna O'Shaughnessy, "W. R. Bion's Theory of Thinking and New Techniques in Child Analysis," in *Melanie Klein Today: Developments in Theory and Practice,* ed. E. B. Spillius, vol. 2: *Mainly Practice* (London: Routledge, 1988), 177–190; Herbert Rosenfeld, *Impasse and Interpretation: Therapeutic and Anti-therapeutic Factors in the Psychoanalytic Treatment of Psychotic,*

*Borderline and Neurotic Patients* (London: Tavistock, 1987); Hanna Segal, *Introduction to the Work of Melanie Klein* (London: Hogarth, 1982); and *Dream, Phantasy and Art* (London: Tavistock, 1991); E. B. Spillius, ed., *Melanie Klein Today: Developments in Theory and Practice,* 2 vols. (London: Routledge, 1988–1989); Spillius, *Encounters with Melanie Klein* (London: Routledge, 2007); R. Wollheim, *The Thread of Life* (Cambridge, MA: Harvard University Press, 1984); *The Mind and Its Depths* (Cambridge, MA: Harvard University Press, 1993); and *On the Emotions* (New Haven: Yale University Press, 1999).

12. Lear, *Happiness, Death, and the Remainder of Life* (Cambridge, MA: Harvard University Press, 2000), 114–135; and *Freud* (London: Routledge, 2005), 154–163.

13. Jacques Lacan, *The Four Fundamental Concepts of Psychoanalysis* (New York: Norton, 1978); *Le séminaire, livre 7, L'éthique de la psychanalyse* (Paris: Seuil, 1986); *Le séminaire, livre 8, Le transfert* (Paris: Seuil, 1991).

14. Lacan, *The Seminar of Jacques Lacan,* Book 1, *Freud's Papers on Technique, 1953–1954,* ed. J.-A. Miller, trans. J. Forrester (Cambridge: Cambridge University Press, 1988); *The Seminar of Jacques Lacan,* Book 2, *The Ego in Freud's Theory and in the Technique of Psychoanalysis, 1954–1955,* ed. J.-A. Miller, trans. S. Tomaselli (Cambridge: Cambridge University Press, 1988); and *Ecrits: A Selection,* trans. Bruce Fink (New York: Norton, 2006).

15. Bruce Fink, *A Clinical Introduction to Lacanian Psychoanalysis: Theory and Technique* (Cambridge, MA: Harvard University Press, 1997); and *Fundamentals of Psychoanalytic Technique: A Lacanian Approach for Practitioners* (New York: Norton, 2007).

16. This marvelous formulation is due to Dr. Nancy Olson (in a comment that is no longer available online).

17. Lacan, *Ecrits: The First Complete Edition in English,* trans. Bruce Fink (New York: Norton, 2006), 313; Fink, chaps. 3–4, *Fundamentals.*

18. Elizabeth Anscombe, *Intention* (Cambridge, MA: Harvard University Press, 1963); Michael Thompson, *Life and Action: Elementary Structures of Practice and Practical Thought* (Cambridge, MA: Harvard University Press, 2008); Candace Vogler, *Reasonably Vicious* (Cambridge, MA: Harvard University Press, 2002).

19. Sebastian Rödl, *Self-Consciousness* (Cambridge, MA: Harvard University Press, 2007).

20. Loewald, "Therapeutic Action," in *The Essential Loewald,* 249.

21. Lear, *Therapeutic Action,* 31–88.

22. Rödl, *Self-Consciousness;* Thompson, *Life and Action.*

23. Rödl, *Self-Consciousness.*

## 9. JUMPING FROM THE COUCH

1. Melanie Klein, "Notes on Some Schizoid Mechanisms," in *The Writings of Melanie Klein,* vol. 3: *Envy and Gratitude and Other Works* (London: Hogarth Press, 1975), 1–24;

Hanna Segal, "Notes on Symbol Formation," *International Journal of Psychoanalysis* 38 (1957): 391–397; *Introduction to the Work of Melanie Klein* (London: Hogarth Press, 1964); Donald Meltzer, "The Relation of Anal Masturbation to Projective Identification," *International Journal of Psychoanalysis* 47 (1966): 335–342; Herbert Rosenfeld, "Contribution to the Psychopathology of Psychotic States: the Importance of Projective Identification in the Ego Structure and the Object Relations of the Psychotic Patient," in *Problems of Psychosis,* ed. P. Doucet and C. Laurin (The Hague: Excerpta Medica, 1971), 115–128; Betty Joseph, "Projective Identification: Some Clinical Aspects," in *Projective Identification,* ed. J. Sandler (Madison, CT: International Universities Press, 1987), 65–76; Joseph, *Psychic Equilibrium and Psychic Change* (London: Routledge, 1989); R. D. Hinshelwood, *Dictionary of Kleinian Thought* (London: Free Association Books, 1989); Hinshelwood, *Clinical Klein* (London: Free Association Books, 1994).

2. Sigmund Freud, "Notes Upon a Case of Obsessional Neurosis," *SE* 10, 209; my italics.

3. Sebastian Gardner, *Irrationality and the Philosophy of Psychoanalysis* (Cambridge: Cambridge University Press, 1993); Jonathan Lear, "Restlessness, Phantasy, and the Concept of the Mind," in *Open-Minded: Working Out the Logic of the Soul* (Cambridge, MA: Harvard University Press, 1998).

4. Aristotle, *Rhetoric,* in *The Complete Works of Aristotle: The Revised Oxford Translation,* ed. J. Barnes (Princeton: Princeton University Press, 1984), II.5, 1382a22–23; Lear, *Love and Its Place in Nature: A Philosophical Interpretation of Freudian Psychoanalysis,* (New Haven: Yale University Press, 1998).

5. Donald Davidson, *Essays on Actions and Events* (Oxford: Clarendon Press, 1980); *Inquiries into Truth and Interpretation* (Oxford: Clarendon Press, 1984).

6. Davidson, "Paradoxes of Irrationality," in *Philosophical Essays on Freud,* ed. R. Wollheim and J. Hopkins (Cambridge: Cambridge University Press, 1982); Lear, "Restlessness, Phantasy."

7. Lear, "Death," in *Happiness, Death, and the Remainder of Life* (Cambridge, MA: Harvard University Press, 2000).

8. Paul Gray, *The Ego and Analysis of Defense* (Northvale, NJ: Aronson, 1994); Marianne Goldberger, *Danger and Defense: The Technique of Close Process Attention, A Festschrift in Honor of Paul Gray* (Northvale, NJ: Aronson, 1996).

9. There is a tendency to assume that the primitive mental phenomena Melanie Klein describes must be utterly different from the minuscule disruptions Paul Gray describes in his close process monitoring of high-functioning neurotics. The generic concept of break enables us to see something in common.

10. What Bion calls an attack on linking is one type of such a defense mechanism. See W. R. Bion, "Attacks on Linking," in *Melanie Klein Today,* vol. 1: *Mainly Theory* (ed. Bott Spillius, London: Routledge, 1988).

11. Though, as I said, my argumentative aim is only to establish an interpretive possibility.

12. Lear, "Restlessness, Phantasy," 93– 98. I make the case that Aristotle's distinction between matter and form is also of great help in understanding this clinical moment.

13. This mental act is strategic, but it is not intentional. See Mark Johnston, "Self-deception and the Nature of Mind," in *Philosophy of Psychology: Debates on Psychological Explanation,* ed. C. Macdonald and G. Macdonald (Oxford: Blackwell, 1995); and Lear, "Restlessness, Phantasy."

14. Brian Bird, "Notes on Transference: Universal Phenomenon and the Hardest Part of Analysis," *Journal of the American Psychoanalytic Association* 20 (1972): 267–301; Hans Loewald, "The Transference Neurosis: Comments on the Concept and the Phenomenon," in *The Essential Loewald: Collected Papers and Monographs* (Hagerstown, MD: University Publishing Group, 2000); Lear, "Restlessness, Phantasy."

15. Hinshelwood, *Clinical Klein.*

16. Segal, "Symbol Formation."

17. Freud, "Remembering, Repeating, and Working-Through," *SE* 12, 154.

## 10. EROS AND DEVELOPMENT

1. Hans Loewald, "Psychoanalytic Theory and Psychoanalytic Process," in *The Essential Loewald: Collected Papers and Monographs,* ed. Norman Quist (Hagerstown, MD: University Publishing Group, 1970), 297.

2. Ibid., 297–298.

3. Sigmund Freud, "Beyond the Pleasure Principle," *SE* 18, 3–64.

4. Loewald, "Review: Max Schur, the Id and the Regulatory Principles of Mental Functioning," in *The Essential Loewald,* 62.

5. Ibid.

6. Freud, "An Outline of Psychoanalysis," *SE* 23, 148.

7. D. W. Winnicott, *The Child, the Family, and the Outside World* (London: Tavistock, 1964); Winnicott, *Through Pediatrics to Psychoanalysis* (London: Hogarth, 1982); Winnicott, *The Maturational Processes and the Facilitating Environment* (London: Hogarth, 1982); Margaret Mahler, "Thoughts about Development and Individuation," *Psychoanalytic Study of the Child* 18 (1963): 307–324; Mahler, "On Human Symbiosis and the Vicissitudes of Individuation," *Journal of the American Psychoanalytic Association* 15 (1967): 740–763; *The Psychological Birth of the Infant* (New York: Basic Books, 1975).

8. See, e.g., Immanuel Kant, *Critique of Pure Reason,* trans. and ed. Paul Guyer and Allen Wood (Cambridge: Cambridge University Press, 1998), 219–266; G. W. F. Hegel, *Phenomenology of Spirit,* trans. A. V. Miller (Oxford: Clarendon Press, 1977), 104–138.

9. Freud, *Civilization and Its Discontents, SE* 21, 64–73.

10. Loewald, "Ego and Reality," in *The Essential Loewald,* 5.

11. Ibid. See also Loewald, "On Motivation and Instinct Theory," in *The Essential Loewald,* 102–137.

12. Loewald, "Ego and Reality,", 6.

13. Ibid., 12; see also Loewald, "The Problem of Defense and the Neurotic Interpretation of Reality," in *The Essential Loewald,* 21–42.

14. Martin Heidegger, *Sein und zeit* (Tübingen: Niemeyer, 2001).

15. Loewald, "On the Therapeutic Action of Psychoanalysis," in *The Essential Loewald,* 225.

16. Loewald, "Review," 67.

17. Loewald, "Therapeutic Action," 225–226.

18. Ibid., 226.

19. Ibid., 226.

20. Ibid., 229.

21. Loewald, "The Transference Neurosis: Comments on the Concept and the Phenomenon," in *The Essential Loewald,* 312.

22. Loewald, "Therapeutic Action," 245; "Transference Neurosis," 310. Freud, "Remembering, Repeating, and Working-Through," *SE* 12, 154.

23. Loewald, "Transference Neurosis," 311.

24. Freud, *The Interpretation of Dreams, SE* 4, 553n. Loewald, "Therapeutic Action," 248.

25. Loewald, "Therapeutic Action," 248–249.

26. Freud, "A Fragment of an Analysis of a Case of Hysteria," *SE* 7, 117.

27. Freud, "The Unconscious," *SE* 14, 187.

28. Loewald, "The Experience of Time," in *The Essential Loewald,* 138–142; Loewald, "Perspectives on Memory," in *The Essential Loewald,* 143–173; and Loewald, "Comments on Religious Experience," in *Psychoanalysis and the History of the Individual* (New Haven: Yale University Press, 1978), 55–77.

29. Freud, "Remembering, Repeating, and Working-Through."

30. Loewald, "Religious Experience," 65; see also "Experience of Time," 141.

31. Loewald, "Religious Experience," 66; see also "Primary Process, Secondary Process, and Language," in *The Essential Loewald,* 199–204; "Superego and Time," in *The Essential Loewald,* 45; "Internalization, Mourning and the Superego," in *The Essential Loewald,* 259.

32. Jonathan Lear, *A Case for Irony* (Cambridge, MA: Harvard University Press, 2011). See esp. chap. 2.

## 11. MOURNING AND MORAL PSYCHOLOGY

1. This sense of *subjective* is Kierkegaard's use, and it stands at some distance from contemporary use of the term. See Søren Kierkegaard (Johannes Climacus, pseud.), *Concluding Unscientific Postscript to the Philosophical Crumbs,* trans. Alastair Hannay (Cambridge: Cambridge University Press, 2009); and Jonathan Lear, *Therapeutic Action: An Earnest Plea for Irony* (New York: Other Press, 2003).

2. Bernard Williams, "Naturalism and Morality," in *World, Mind, and Ethics,* ed.

J. E. J. Altham and Ross Harrison (Cambridge: Cambridge University Press, 1995), 202; my emphasis.

3. See, e.g., Jacques Lacan, *The Ethics of Psychoanalysis* (London: Routledge, 1992).

4. Sigmund Freud, "Mourning and Melancholia," *SE* 14, 246.

5. Ibid., 247.

6. Hans Loewald, *Papers on Psychoanalysis* (New Haven: Yale University Press, 1989).

7. Ibid., 257.

8. Ibid., 271–272.

9. Ibid., 258.

10. *Oxford English Dictionary Online*, 2015; my emphasis.

11. Loewald, *Papers*, 5.

12. Ibid.

13. Ibid., 262.

14. Ibid., 248–249.

15. Ludwig Wittgenstein, *Philosophical Investigations*, 4th ed., trans. G. E. M. Anscombe, P. M. S. Hacker, and Joachim Schulte (Hoboken: Wiley-Blackwell, 2009).

16. Martin Heidegger, *Being and Time*, trans. John Macquarrie and Edward Robinson (New York: Harper and Row, 1962), 27.

17. John Haugeland, *Dasein Disclosed: John Haugeland's Heidegger* (Cambridge, MA: Harvard University Press, 2013).

18. I am using the term *myth* nonpejoratively to describe a fundamental and organizing narrative. By using the term I take no stand on whether the narrative is true or false.

19. Loewald, *Papers*, 249.

20. Ibid., 260; my emphasis.

21. Freud, *The Future of an Illusion*, *SE* 21, 5–56.

22. Freud, *Civilization and Its Discontents*, *SE* 21, 74; my emphasis.

23. Ibid.

24. See *Future of an Illusion*, 54 and 43. I discuss these issues in "The Illusion of a Future: The Rhetoric of Freud's Critique of Religious Belief," in *On Freud's "The Future of an Illusion,"* ed. S. Akhtar and M. K. O'Neil (London: Karnac, 2009), 83–97.

25. Loewald, "Psychoanalysis and Modern Views on Human Existence and Religious Experience," *Journal of Pastoral Care* 7, no. 1 (1953): 8.

26. Ibid., 9.

27. Ibid., 13.

## 12. ALLEGORY AND MYTH IN PLATO'S *REPUBLIC*

1. See the entry in *A Greek-English Lexicon*, ed. H. G. Liddell and R. Scott (Oxford: Clarendon Press, 1977), 1890.

2. Translation is from Plato, *Republic,* trans. G. M. A. Grube and C. D. C. Reeve (Indianapolis: Hackett, 1999).

3. This is basically the structure that Freud assigns to trauma. See, e.g., Freud, "Project for a Scientific Psychology," *SE* 1, 347–359. See also Jacques Lacan, e.g., *The Seminar of Jacques Lacan: Book I: Freud's Papers on Technique, 1953–1954* (Cambridge: Cambridge University Press, 1988), 34–35, 189–197, 232, 283.

4. This is what Jean Laplanche would call a seduction. See "The Unfinished Copernican Revolution," in *Essays on Otherness* (London: Routledge, 1999); and my *Happiness, Death, and the Remainder of Life* (Cambridge, MA: Harvard University Press, 2000).

5. I take it that Plato thought that these claims were true. Thus the Noble Falsehood is at worst a verbal falsehood, not a true one. If one is capable of grasping the true allegorical meanings of the Noble Falsehood, one can grasp its truth: that people are "rooted" in the polis—in the sense of political obligation—that they do have different innate natures, and that their experience until now has been "dreamlike" in the sense elaborated in this essay. However, the Noble Falsehood is to be told to children who do not yet have the capacity to grasp the allegorical meaning; and insofar as it is grasped literally, the claims are false. (Obviously, this interpretation requires its own argument, which is beyond the scope of this essay.)

6. One can now see in a new light why Socrates, at the end of the *Republic,* wants to expel imitative poets from the kallipolis. For the poets have the effect of recreating this childhood condition in adults. The imitative poet does not act as though he is narrating a story about Achilles; he speaks as though it is Achilles himself who is speaking. Thus the literary form induces a dreamlike state: instead of our thinking that A (Homer) is similar to B (Achilles), it is as though A is B. In this way the imitative form collapses spatial, temporal, and narrative distances. Every time someone reenacts Homer's poem, he will not only be saying the same words as Homer, but it will again be as though Achilles is speaking. Thus the imitative form again pulls us in the direction of taking in an allegory not recognized as such. That is, it is a regressive force, pulling us back to the incapacities of childhood.

7. Think about the difference between adults who never believed in the Santa Claus myth versus those who in childhood were in the myth's thrall each telling their children about it a generation later.

8. Translation is from the *Republic,* trans. Tom Griffith (Cambridge: Cambridge University Press, 2000); my emphasis.

## 13. THE PSYCHIC EFFICACY OF PLATO'S CAVE

1. See, for example, Ruby Blondell, *The Play of Character in Plato's Dialogues* (Cambridge: Cambridge University Press, 2002); Andrea Nightingale, *Genres in Dialogue: Plato and the Construct of Philosophy* (Cambridge: Cambridge University Press, 2000).

2. Unless otherwise noted, translations are from C. D. C. Reeve, *Plato: Republic* (Indianapolis: Hackett, 2004). For the Greek text, I rely on S. R. Slings, *Platonis: Rempublicam* (Clarendon Press: Oxford, 2003).

3. For an account of appetite's cognitive sophistication, see Hendrik Lorenz, *The Beast Within: Appetitive Desire in Plato and Aristotle* (Oxford: Clarendon Press, 2006). (In another context, consider the difficulties involved with the charioteer using rational argument on the black horse in the myth in *Phaedrus,* 253c–254e.)

4. Since almost the entire literature on the Cave focuses on what it means, references are too numerous to include in a footnote; but for an introduction, see, e.g., James Wilberding, "Prisoners and Puppeteers in the Cave," *Oxford Studies in Ancient Philosophy* 24 (2004): 117–140; Malcolm Schofield, "Metaspeleology," in *Maieusis: Essays in Honour of Myles Burnyeat,* ed. Dominic Scott (Oxford: Oxford University Press, 2007); John Malcolm, "The Line and the Cave," *Phronesis* 7 (1962): 38–45; Malcom, "The Cave Revisited," *Classical Quarterly* 31 (1981): 60–68; R. C. Cross and A. D. Woozley, *Plato's Republic: A Philosophical Commentary* (London: Macmillan, 1964), chap. 9; Alan Bloom, *The Republic of Plato* (Chicago: University of Chicago Press, 1968), 405–408; Julia Annas, *An Introduction to Plato's Republic* (Clarendon Press: Oxford, 1981), 253–271; J. R. S. Wilson, "The Contents of the Cave," *Canadian Journal of Philosophy,* sup. vol. 2: *New Essays on Plato and the Presocratics* (1976): 111–124; J. Raven, "Sun, Line and Cave," in *Plato's Thought in the Making* (Cambridge: Cambridge University Press, 1965) chap. 10; C. D. C. Reeve, *Philosopher-Kings: The Argument of Plato's Republic* (Princeton: Princeton University Press, 1988), 50–58; V. Karamanis, "Plato's *Republic:* The Line and the Cave," *Apeiron* 21 (1988): 141–171; R. Robinson, *Plato's Earlier Dialectic* (Oxford: Clarendon Press, 1962), 183–201; H. W. B. Joseph, *Knowledge and the Good in Plato's* Republic (London: Oxford University Press, 1948), 31–41.

5. Certainly, at the beginning of Book II, Glaucon and Adeimantus make it clear that they have not been persuaded by the arguments thus far, and though they want to be persuaded rationally, they want to be *persuaded;* and this is going somehow to require defusing the persuasive power of the poets (357a–367e). For example, Adeimantus tells Socrates that the poets "persuade not only private individuals, but whole cities that there are in fact absolutions and purifications for unjust deeds" (364e5–6). But if, by the end of the *Republic,* all parties recognize that poetic persuasion depends on certain appeals to the nonrational part of the soul, how could Plato think that the text was a sufficient response to Glaucon's and Adeimantus's request for genuine persuasion unless there was some alternative, legitimate appeal to the nonrational part of the soul?

6. *Phaedrus,* 274d–279.

7. See Gabriel Lear, "Plato on the Ethics and Aesthetics of Doing One Thing" (forthcoming).

8. There is, I think, some recent evidence to suggest that this captivation is a manifestation of the appetitive part of the soul. If one thinks of freshman-level surveys of Western

philosophy, the curriculum will typically spend one or two weeks on the *Republic.* The syllabi seem to me basically appetitive in nature: aimed to give a prospective lover of sights and sounds, or a democratic person, a *taste* of Plato—before they go into a career in government or business. One moves through the syllabus too quickly for anything else to occur. I am reminded of the *Saturday Night Live* character Father Guido Sarducci (Don Novello) who wanted to establish the "Five-Minute University," which would teach you everything you would learn in college—and remember five years later. Tuition would be $20. When I survey alumni of distinguished universities and ask them what they remember of Plato's *Republic,* I routinely get the answer, "Something about a cave." This is evidence, I think, that it is appetite that has been captivated. (To see Father Sarducci speak for himself, see: http://www.youtube.com/watch?v=kO8x8eoU3L4. See also the Wikipedia entry at: http://en.wikipedia.org/wiki/Father_Guido_Sarducci.)

9. See Chapter 12, "Allegory and Myth in Plato's *Republic.*"

10. This, I think, provides the basis for an answer to the puzzle David O'Connor raises in his fascinating essay "Rewriting the Poets in Plato's Characters" in *The Cambridge Companion to Plato's Republic,* ed. G. R. F. Ferrari (Cambridge: Cambridge University Press, 2007), 55–89. Speaking of the above-quoted passage, O'Conner notes: "This is Socrates' second recitation of the lament of Achilles' soul, and it presents us with a puzzle. For now Socrates uses Homer's words exactly to undermine the attachment of one particular man to political leadership and to the affairs of any city. These very words had been censored [see *Rep.* III, 386a–387b] for their tendency to produce precisely the effect Socrates wants to produce here: they tend to undermine one's wholehearted attachment to politics and the city. The guidance Socrates gives Glaucon now flatly contradicts the pedagogy he and Adeimantus had agreed to earlier," p. 58. O'Connor is right that there is a real puzzle here; but he goes too far when he says there is a flat contradiction. For in Book III, the issue is about providing principles for educating youth in Kallipolis; but in Book VII, Socrates is directly addressing Glaucon and Adeimantus. The latter have already been exposed to the bad literature that the youth in Kallipolis would never hear. Thus there is reason to think that Socrates needs to do something to counteract Glaucon's prior exposure to harmful stories. O'Connor is right that there is a very different pedagogy here, but one needn't think of it as flatly contradictory. And I think we can see the different pedagogies in an illuminating way if we consider them in terms of the tripartite theory of the soul. For in the first case, the poet (Homer) does not have his eye on the good, but on appearances. Rather than his reason grasping the good and preparing an appropriate image of it for *thumos,* Homer's *thumos* is creating a thumoeidic appearance for *thumos.* That is, through poetry, *thumos* is basically reinforcing its own misapprehension that death is a terrible misfortune. And Homer makes cowards of us all. But when Socrates uses the same quote in the allegory of the Cave, he has his eye on the good—that is, reason grasps the good and fashions an image designed to bring *thumos* into line. O'Connor has deftly shown how Plato appropriates poetry for his own use. But I think we can here see the intrapsychic difference that appropriation makes.

11. Or: laugh thoughtlessly.

12. Cp. *Apology,* 34b–35c, 37a; *Gorgias,* 486.

13. My teaching assistant Charles Comey suggested to me that it is a hallmark of appetite being nonrational that it cannot keep track of the means-end distinction. Thus appetite begins by desiring money as a means, but it is incapable of keeping its instrumental role clear, and so comes simply to love money.

14. Vegetarians: for *burger* please read "lentil pie." And please forgive me for trying to speak to those whose appetites have not already undergone the training into vegetarianism.

15. I'm surprised Weight Watchers has not yet incorporated the allegory of the Cave into its program.

16. VII.5185b8. *Tines epangellomenoi phasin.* See the note in Adam's commentary on *epaggellómenoi:* it is used to note a sophistic profession. James Adam, *The Republic of Plato* (Cambridge: Cambridge University Press, 1929), vol. 2, 97–98, n. 14. It is reasonable to wonder whether the use of this verb is in the service of revising *thumos.*

17. *Phaedrus,* 261a7–8; see also 271d10–c2.

18. This passage has provoked interpretations that, I think, are importantly mistaken in that they lead to a misreading of the book as a whole. One paradigm is the idea that young philosophers-to-be need to be seriously deceived so that when they grow up they will be indoctrinated to follow orders and act against their own desires and best interests. For an example of a fine argument for what I take to be a mistaken position, see Malcolm Schofield, *Plato: Political Philosophy* (Oxford: Oxford University Press, 2006), 284–309; and his "The Noble Lie," in *The Cambridge Companion to Plato's Republic,* ed. G. R. F. Ferrar (Cambridge: Cambridge University Press, 2007), 138–164. Obviously, I cannot make the case for this claim here (though I hope to do so on a future occasion), but I do think I've provided an alternative way in which the discussion of "compulsion" can be understood.

## 14. THE ETHICAL THOUGHT OF J. M. COETZEE

1. J. M. Coetzee, *Diary of a Bad Year* (London: Harvill Secker, 2007), 47. All references in this chapter are to this edition and are cited in the text.

2. Kathryn Harrison, *New York Times Book Review,* December 31, 2007.

3. Rachel Donadio, "Out of Africa," *New York Times,* December 31, 2007.

4. Plato, *Phaedrus,* 275a–b. Translation (modified) from *Phaedrus,* trans. Alexander Nehamas and Paul Woodruff, in *Plato: The Complete Works* (Indianapolis: Hackett, 1997), 506–556.

5. S. Kierkegaard [Johannes Climacus, pseud.], "A First and Last Explanation," in *Concluding Unscientific Postscript to the Philosophical Fragments,* ed. H. V. Hong and E. H. Hong (Princeton: Princeton University Press, 1992), 625–630.

6. *Phaedrus,* 261a7–8; *"psuchagôgia tis dia logôn"*; see also 271d10–c2.

7. *Republic* VII, 518c409; *"periakteon* . . . sun *holêi têi psychêi."*

8. *"To ex hou."* Aristotle obviously also used the term *hulê.*

9. Plato, *Symposium,* 205d, 206c. Quotes are from *Symposium,* trans. Alexander Nehamas and Paul Woodruff, *Complete Works,* 457–505.

10. *Symp.*, 209b–c.

11. While reading *Diary of a Bad Year,* a memory came back to me of my first assignment as a student journalist, trying out for the *Yale Daily News.* The article was about alleged branding (that is, like cattle) of students as a rite of initiation into a fraternity. George W. Bush, 1968, the past president of DKE, called the branding "insignificant." Stating that there is little pain, Bush said, "There's no scarring mark, physically or mentally" (Jonathan Lear, "No Intervention for Fraternities," *Yale Daily News,* November 7, 1967).

12. From the *Yale Daily News* story: The head of the Inter-Fraternity Council "said it was more like a cigarette burn and goes away after two or three weeks. Labeling the branding as minor, he stated that it has never caused any medical complications. 'It's not as bad as it sounds,' he said. He asserted that the definition of a physically and mentally degrading act was 'a matter of interpretation.'"

13. See, e.g., "Mukasey Sworn in as Attorney General," *New York Times,* November 9, 2007.

14. My emphasis. The story is by Pamela Hess of the Associated Press and thus ran in many newspapers on January 13, 2008.

15. See, e.g., "Justice Dept. Sets Criminal Inquiry on C.I.A. Tapes," *New York Times,* January 3, 2008.

16. Looking back at that *Yale Daily News* story now, my attention is drawn to a completely different place than it has been before. "Fraternities will be allowed to 'put their house in order' without interference from the Yale administration, said Richard C. Carroll, Dean of Undergraduate Affairs, yesterday. Dean Carroll expects to let the Inter-Fraternity Council have complete jurisdiction 'solving its own problems,' according to Carroll. . . . 'I suspect the hazing has been sensationalized just a little more than the facts warrant: it may not be as horrendous as it seems. I think there may be an exaggeration of the total picture,' said Carroll." This seems to me a perfect specimen of a certain type of academic dean: in the name of giving students responsibility for how they conduct themselves, he absolves himself of responsibility for directing them in any particular way. What if, in response to that incident, Dean Carroll had gone on a loud and public crusade? What if, in his remarks to me, he had said instead, "What these young men have done may look innocent, but it is in fact very dangerous. It is a step along the way to coarsening their souls. Here are people who may be future leaders, and they should not be taught to be indifferent to the pain they are inflicting on others. I hope Mr. Bush will come to see this for himself and apologize to those on whom he inflicted pain, even if it was meant to be 'in fun.' This cannot be fun; it is morally very serious. His ability to make moral discriminations is at stake." Such a scenario would have seemed strange at the time, but I cannot help wondering what good it might have done.

17. B. Williams, *Shame and Necessity* (Berkeley: University of California Press, 1994), 81–85.

18. I am grateful to John Coetzee, James Conant, and Gabriel Lear for extended conversations on the philosophical topics discussed in this chapter. Obviously, only I can be held responsible for the views expressed here. But I should like to state explicitly that I have never had a conversation with Coetzee about his literary style.

## 15. NOT AT HOME IN GILEAD

1. Marilynne Robinson, *Gilead* (New York: Farrar, Straus and Giroux, 2004), 183.
2. Robinson, *Home* (New York: Farrar, Straus and Giroux, 2008), 76.
3. Ibid., 202.
4. *Gilead,* 183.
5. Ibid., 184.
6. Ibid., 150.
7. Ibid., 173.
8. Ibid., 173.
9. Ibid., 233–234.
10. Søren Kierkegaard, *The Point of View on My Work as an Author,* ed. H. V. Hong and E. H. Hong (Princeton: Princeton University Press, 1998), 41–44.
11. *Gilead,* 36.
12. Ibid., 231.
13. Ibid., 171.
14. *Home,* 296.
15. Ibid., 311.
16. *Gilead,* 174.
17. *Home,* 97.
18. Ibid., 155.
19. Ibid., 97.
20. Lincoln Barnett, "God and the American People," *Ladies' Home Journal* (November 1948), 232.
21. *Gilead,* 124.
22. Ibid., 231.
23. *Home,* 88.
24. Ibid., 106.
25. Ibid., 199.
26. Ibid., 208.
27. *Gilead,* 163.
28. *Home,* 56.
29. Ibid., 55–56.
30. Ibid., 144.

31. Ibid., 297.
32. Ibid., 166.
33. Ibid., 276.
34. Ibid., 275.
35. Ibid., 249.
36. Ibid., 249.
37. Ibid., 288–289.
38. Ibid., 225.
39. Ibid., 226.
40. Ibid., 227.
41. John Calvin, *Institutes of the Christian Religion,* ed. J. T. McNeill, trans. F. L. Battles (Louisville: Westminster John Knox Press, 1960), III.7.6, 606–697.

# Acknowledgments

The essays in this book are the fruit of longstanding conversations: with my wife, Gabriel Lear, with Matthew Boyle, John Coetzee, John Haugeland (now deceased), Sean Kelsey, Irad Kimhi, Hans Loewald (now deceased), Alasdair MacIntyre, Anselm Mueller, Edna O'Shaughnessy, Sebastian Rödl, Candace Vogler, Bernard Williams (now deceased), and Katherine Withy. I am deeply grateful to them all. I could not have put this book together without the editorial help of two remarkable research assistants, Isabela Ferreira and Skomantas Pocius. I would like specially to thank the Andrew W. Mellon Foundation for its Distinguished Achievement Award. This award allowed me the time to explore the avenues of thought expressed in this book, and I doubt I could have written it without this support. I am also grateful to my colleagues—faculty, students, and co-workers—at the Committee on Social Thought, the Department of Philosophy, and the Neubauer Collegium for Culture and Society at the University of Chicago. This list is indefinitely long, but let me specially mention James Conant, David Finkelstein, Sarah Nooter, Thomas Pavel, Mark Payne, Robert Pippin, Eric Santner, Josef Stern, Mark Strand (now deceased), Rosanna Warren, David Wellbery, and Adam Zagajewski. For a certain sort of person, the University of Chicago is heaven on earth. Over the past two decades, I have discovered that I am such a person.

I thank the publishers and journals that have granted me the permission to republish some of the essays contained in this book.

Chapter 1: "Wisdom Won from Illness: The Psychoanalytic Grasp of Human Being," *International Journal of Psychoanalysis* 95, no. 4 (August 2014): 677–693.

Chapter 2: This chapter is a significant revision of a paper by the same name: "Integrating the Non-Rational Soul," *Proceedings of the Aristotelian Society* 114, no. 1, pt. 1 (April 2014): 75–101, copyright © 2014 The Aristotelian Society. I added a different clinical example, to avoid overlap with Chapter 1 and to give added clinical nuance.

Chapter 3: "What Is a Crisis of Intelligibility?" in *Appropriating the Past: Philosophical Perspectives on the Practice of Archaeology,* ed. Geoffrey Scarre and Robin Coningham (Cambridge: Cambridge University Press, 2013), 141–155.

Chapter 4: "A Lost Conception of Irony" was originally published in the online journal *Berfrois* (January 4, 2012), http://www.berfrois.com/2012/01/jonathan-lear-lost-conception-irony/. It was previously delivered as a lecture given at Stanford University (November 30, 2011) and the University of Kansas (November 14, 2011).

Chapter 5: First published as "Waiting with Coetzee," in *Raritan* 34, no. 4 (Spring 2015): 1-26.

Chapter 6: "The Ironic Creativity of Socratic Doubt," *MLN* 128, no. 5 (December 2013): 1001–1018. An earlier version of the paper was presented at Aarhus University, Denmark, in a conference to celebrate the two hundredth birthday of Søren Kierkegaard.

Chapter 7: "Rosalind's Pregnancy," *Raritan* 34, no. 3 (Winter 2015): 66–85. An earlier version was presented at the Bridge Foundation for Psychotherapy and the Arts, The Tobacco Factory, Bristol, UK, March 15, 2014.

Chapter 8: "Technique and Final Cause in Psychoanalysis," *International Journal of Psychoanalysis* 90, no. 6 (December 2009): 1299–1317. Earlier drafts were presented as lectures to the Western New England Psychoanalytic Institute; at a conference organized by the Psychoanalytic Unit at University College London; as the Robert Stoller Lecture at the New Center for Psychoanalysis, Los Angeles; as a keynote lecture to the European Federation of Psychoanalysis; and as the Paul Gray Lecture at the Baltimore–Washington Psychoanalytic Institute.

Chapter 9: "Jumping from the Couch: An Essay on Phantasy and Emotional Structure," *International Journal of Psychoanalysis* 83, no. 3 (June 2002): 583–595. Copyright © 2002 Institute of Psychoanalysis.

Chapter 10: "The Thought of Hans Loewald," *International Journal of Psychoanalysis* 93, no. 1 (February 2012): 167–179. Copyright © 2011 Institute of Psychoanalysis.

Chapter 11: "Mourning and Moral Psychology," *Psychoanalytic Psychology* 31, no. 4 (October 2014): 470–481.

Chapter 12: "Allegory and Myth in Plato's *Republic,*" in *The Blackwell Guide to Plato's Republic,* ed. Gerasimos Santas (Malden, MA: Blackwell Publishing, 2006), 25–43. It is a revised version of "The Efficacy of Myth in Plato's *Republic,*" *Proceedings of the Boston Area Colloquium of Ancient Philosophy* 19, no. 1 (2004): 35–56. The ideas presented in this paper have been in gestation for several years, and an earlier version appeared in the Boston Area Colloquium in Ancient Philosophy.

Chapter 13, "The Psychic Efficacy of Plato's Cave," is published for the first time in this volume.

Chapter 14: "The Ethical Thought of J. M. Coetzee," *Raritan* 28, no. 1 (Summer 2008): 68–97. A version was also published as "Ethical Thought and the Problem of Communication: A Strategy for Reading *Diary of a Bad Year,*" in *J. M. Coetzee and Ethics: Philosophical Perspectives on Literature,* ed. Anton Leist and Peter Singer (New York: Columbia University Press, 2010), 65–88.

Chapter 15: "Not at Home in Gilead," *Raritan* 32, no. 1 (Summer 2012): 34–52.

# Index

Achilles, 77, 212, 218
Adeimantus, 207–208, 218–220, 243
Alienation, 75, 78–79, 90–99; Lacan on, 147, 154
Allegory: definition of, 208; in childhood, 208–214, 218, 220; recognizing, 208–216, 219–221, 239; philosophical significance of, 214–217, 219, 227, 229, 235, 243; as therapy, 222–224; and psychic transformation, 230–243. *See also* Myth of Er; Noble Falsehood; Plato's Cave
Anscombe, Elizabeth, 51
Anxiety: and irony, 65–69, 133–136; disruption of psychic functioning, 84, 146, 153, 165–166, 168–173. *See also* Fear
Appearance, 231–232, 238–239
Appearance and reality, relationship between, 126, 129–30, 209, 215, 217, 238–239
Appetite, 228–235, 237–243
Argument: and literary form, 102; myth as a form of, 223, 225–226, 229–232, 241, 243; nonrational soul and, 229, 231–233, 243, 250
Aristotelian ethics, 47–49
Aristotle, 3; on intrapsychic communication, 2–3, 17–18, 24–25, 30–33, 43–45; on happiness, 5–6, 12, 43–46; on virtue, 8, 30–33, 43–44; on practical and theoretical wisdom, 11–12, 23, 43; on characteristic activity of humans, 16–17, 27–28
Autonomy, 141, 152

Barbarian, concept of, 88–89, 95
Being-towards-death, 197–198.
Birthing, 112–119, 123–125, 130, 252–253
Blindness, 4, 257, 266, 284
Break, 147, 164–166, 169–174
Burnyeat, Myles, 113–114, 124

Calvin, Jean, 284–285
*Case for Irony, A* (Lear), 68
Cephalus, 210–211, 216, 221–224
Christendom, 66, 73–74, 273–275, 278–280

Climacus, Johannes (pseud.), 72, 75, 103–104, 107, 118–119
Coetzee, J. M., 246–247; literary form of, 81, 83–84, 245–247, 249–250, 254–256, 266–268; *Waiting for the Barbarians*, 81–97, 99; *Diary of a Bad Year*, 245–247, 249–261, 263–268
Comedy, 120–121, 135–136,
Concepts: basic/core, 9–10, 15, 50–51, 120–121, 135–137, 154, 177; distortion of, 9–10, 80–81. *See also* Injustice
Crow, 51–53, 60–62, 64–66; way of life of, 52–55, 57–59, 61–62; planting/ counting coup, 53, 59, 61–62

Death drive, 47, 163, 178–179
Defense mechanism, 92, 95, 140–141, 146–147, 153–154, 166, 171–173; rationalization as, 163, 172–173, 262, 270
Desires, unruly 2–3, 17, 20, 44. *See also* Appetite; Unconscious
Devastation, cultural, 9, 51, 55–56, 62, 64
*Diary of a Bad Year* (Coetzee), 245–247, 249–261, 263–268; JC, 245–247, 249–261, 263–268; Anya, 246, 253–256, 267–268; dialectic of responsibility in, 250, 256, 265; "liberal intellectuals," 256–261, 263–266; "ordinary people," 258, 263, 265; shame in, 259–261, 263–266
Diotima, 108–116, 122–125, 252–253. *See also* Birthing; Pregnancy
Disorientation, 56, 65, 134, 209, 212–213, 215–216
Disruption: of mental functioning, 7, 38, 142, 145–147, 164–174; of concepts, 64–65, 78, 134; and philosophy, 68–69
Doctoring, 67–71; Socrates and, 69–70
Dreaming, 82–84, 87–88, 212–214
Dreams, 17, 163–164

Education: in love, 127–129, 132; of youth, 206–207, 216; not putting in but turning around, 219, 240, 249
Efficacy: psychoanalytic, 22–23, 25–26, 28, 42–43, 46; of mind, 23–26, 28, 42–43, 46, 81, 98–102, 125, 202; literary, 81, 98, 230, 232; of practical reason, 136–137; of projective identification, 145, 159, 168, 170–171
Efficient cause, 20, 156–157
Ego, 16, 38–39, 140–142; not master in its own house, 5–6; development of, 180–181, 194–195
Emotional life, 34, 159–161; development of, 166–168, 172, 174; mature and primitive, 166–169, 171; disruption of, 168–169, 171–172, 174
Empire, 82–85, 88, 90–93, 95–97; form of life of, 84–87, 89–91
Empirical stance and psychoanalysis, 3–4, 36–38, 175–176, 179, 200–201
*Energeia*, 26–27, 46–47
Envy, 155–156
Eros. *See* Love
Erotic longing, 65–66, 76, 113, 117, 133–134,
Ethical: life, 5–6, 81, 244; difference, 81, 97–102; thought, 244–250, 253–256, 259–260, 268

Ethics: Ancient Greek, 5–6, 8, 32, 74, 191; and psychoanalysis, 8–9, 47–49, 155–156, 193
*Eudaimonia. See* Happiness
Evil, 93–97

Fantasy, 86, 91–92, 145–148, 159–161, 168–169, 189; basic/core, 18–22, 25, 40–42, 172–173, 187; of omnipotence, 21, 201–202
Fear, 160–162; primitive, 166–167; mature, 166–169
Final cause, 149–151; in psychoanalysis, 139, 150–151, 154, 156–157. *See also* Freedom
Finkelstein, David, 35
First-person authority, 35, 38, 52, 57
Formal cause, 20, 257
Form of life, 50–51, 53–55, 60, 197, 269; waiting, 84–87, 89–91; extrication from, 98–102, 173–174
Freedom, 18, 47, 139, 150–151, 242, 276–277; as stepping back in reflection, 44–45, 73; of mind, 151–153; of speech, 153–154; to let be, 154–156
Freud, Sigmund, 3–5, 10; "Remembering, Repeating and Working-Through," 12, 185; development of, 12–14, 16, 36–39, 163–164, 178–179; legacy of, 14–15; as supplementing Aristotle, 34, 39, 43–44, 47–49, 192–193; on mourning, 98, 193; "Notes Upon a Case of Obsessional Neurosis," 160–163; on illusion, 203, 272–273, 278–279; on religion, 203–204; on the pale criminal, 270
Frye, Northrop, 120
Fundamental rule. *See* Psychoanalysis

*Gilead* (Robinson), 269, 271–274, 276–277, 280
Glaucon, 207, 215, 218–221, 229, 233–237, 241, 243
Gray, Paul, 140–141, 143–145, 148, 151–153, 165

Happening, 52, 54, 60
Happiness, 5–6, 12, 43–48, 111, 191, 193, 201
Haugeland, John, 197
Health: ancient conception of, 5–6, 11–12; psychological, 12, 27, 150–151; idea of, 68–70; promoting through literature, 231–232
Heidegger, Martin, 50, 54, 61, 181–182; Dasein, 197
*Home* (Robinson), 269–271, 273, 277–278, 280–284
Homer, 114–116, 186, 218
Human: flourishing, 2, 9, 12, 27, 47–48, 135; condition, 3–4, 6–7, 10–12, 15, 17–18, 50, 135, 267; finitude, 4, 74, 78–79, 201, 284–285; category of, 15, 26, 105–107, 116–119, 165; vulnerability, 20–21; characteristic activity of, 27–28, 112–113, 116–118; becoming, 28–29, 105–107, 116–118

Illness, 11–12, 27, 283
Illusion: breaking through, 72, 74, 275–76, 279–280; and irony, 72–74; Kierkegaard's conception of, 72–74,

Illusion *(continued)* 272–273, 275, 278–279; and reflection, 73–74, 80, 207–208; Freud's conception of, 203, 272–273, 278–279
Imagination, deprivation of, 80–81, 91–92, 97
Imaginative activity, 81, 98–102, 230–231, 233–234
Injustice, 9–10, 80–81, 96–97, 101, 245, 266
Intelligibility: loss of, 50–62, 197–198; lack of, 53–57, 59, 94–96; difference from possibility, 54–56
Intentional action, 23–24
Internalization, 141–142, 144–145, 196; and mourning, 193–196, 198–199; and Christianity, 202
Interpretation, 112, 179–180, 194; "deep," 12–13, 36–37, efficacy of, 102
Intrapsychic communication, 2–3, 30–34, 43, 46, 48–49; as speaking with the same voice, 17, 23–25, 30–33, 38–39, 43–49, 193
Ironist, 125; Socrates as, 103, 107–108; in *As You Like It*, 125–127, 130–131
Irony: richer conception of, 9, 63–64, 104–105, 115–116; and philosophy, 63–64, 68, 119–120, 137; common conception of, 63–64, 71, 126, 129–130, 132–133; and the Crow, 64–66; in relation to superego, 65–66, 68; experience of, 66–69, 71–72, 74, 125, 133–134; and earnestness, 71–72, 78, 127–131; as an excellence, 72, 74, 78, 133, 135; capacity for, 72, 74, 78, 144, 153; and ironic existence, 72–75, 78–79, 133–135; as poetical mode of practical reason, 136–137. *See also under* Kierkegaard, Søren; Socrates

Justice, 207–208, 225–230. *See also* Injustice; Myth of Er

Kant, Immanuel, 43, 136, 152
Kierkegaard, Søren: on irony, 66–67, 70–74, 78, 103–105, 115–116, 132–133; on Christianity, 66–67, 73–74, 273, 275; on Socrates, 71–72, 75, 103–105, 107–108; Johannes Climacus (pseud.), 72, 75, 103–104, 107, 118–119; on illusion, 72–74, 272–273, 275, 278–279; on the mythical (Diotima), 108–111; and pseudonymity, 248–249. *See also* Human: becoming
Kinesis, 26, 46
Klein and Kleinians, 145–147, 152–153, 155–156, 159. *See also* Projective identification

Lacan, Jacques, 147–148, 152–154
Law of excluded middle, existential version, 58–60
Levenson, Lawrence, 140–141, 144, 148
Literary form, 102, 245–249. *See also under* Coetzee, J. M.; Kierkegaard, Søren; Loewald, Hans; Plato
Loewald, Hans, 175, 178, 190: on mourning, 98, 142, 193–196, 198–202; psychoanalytic approach of, 142–145, 152–154, 181–189; on

internalization, 145, 193–196, 198–199, 202; writing style of, 175–180, 194, 200; main ideas of, 175–190; and relationship to Freud, 176, 178–179, 204; on erotic activity, 178–179, 181, 183–187; and followers, 184, 204–205; and religious belief, 202–204
Logos, 1–2, 229, 249–250. *See also* Reason
Love, 110–112, 114–115, 121–124, 132–135, 179; Christian, 67, 276–277, 280–282, 284; of truth, 175–176; as developmental process, 178–187. *See also* Erotic longing

Marriage, 120–122, 132, 135–136
Melancholia, 98–99, 193
Metaphysical ache, 252–254, 267–268. See also *Diary of a Bad Year* (Coetzee)
Mind: capacity of, 1–4, 9, 42–43, 152–153, 196; efficacy of, 23–26, 28, 42–43, 46, 81, 98–102, 125, 202. *See also* Psyche; Soul
Modernity, 47–48
Moral psychology, 25, 33, 191–192, 199–201; psychoanalysis as, 18, 34, 43–44, 192–194, 198, 200–201, 204; moralizing, 33, 48–49, 192
Moran, Richard, 35–36
Mourning, 98–99, 101–102, 142–144, 152–153, 193, 197–198; and psychological development, 193–196, 198–202
Mr. A, 140–148, 152–156
Mr. B, 39–42, 44–45
Ms. A, 18–23, 25
Myth. *See* Allegory; Argument: myth as a form of; Myth of Er
Myth of Er, 223–225

Nietzsche, 12, 270
Noble Falsehood, 71, 213–224
Noble lie. *See* Noble Falsehood
"Notes Upon a Case of Obsessional Neurosis" (Freud), 160–163

Oracle, 234–235

*Phaedrus* (Plato), 68, 241, 247, 249
Philosophy, 132, 214–215, 227, 229, 235, 251; challenge to, 3, 18, 20; contemporary, 35, 44, 73; and irony, 63–64, 68, 119–120, 137; at the heart of psychoanalysis, 157–158
Plato, 1, 12, 108–109, 201; *Republic*, 1, 12, 69, 206–208, 210–243, 249; and conception of eros, 65, 113; *Phaedrus*, 68, 241, 247, 249; *Symposium*, 108–116, 122–125, 252; on the formation of outlooks, 206–226; and therapeutic writing, 229–237, 239–243; and dialogue form, 247–249. *See also* Allegory; Argument; Diotima; Socrates
Plato's Cave, 73, 217–224, 230, 233–237, 239–242
Pleasure principle, 163–164
Plenty Coups, 51–52, 54, 56–57, 60
Poetical, 9, 28, 46–48, 107, 117, 136
Poetry, 9–10, 231–232

Possibilities: creation of new, 10, 28, 81, 127, 152, 173–174, 182–183; for thought, 80–81
Practical question, 64–66, 134, 136
Practical reason, 11, 25, 43, 51, 55, 106, 136–137
Practical understanding. *See* Practical reason
Pretty Shield, 52, 56–57
Preconscious, 162
Pregnancy, 112–119, 122–124, 135, 252–253
Process. *See* Kinesis
Projective identification, 145–147, 159, 165, 168–170
Psyche, 1–2, 27, 196, 202; as an achievement, 178, 194, 208. *See also* Mind: capacity of; Soul
Psychic change, 4, 25–26
Psychic conflict, 16–17, 38, 193–194
Psychic harmony. *See* Psychic unity
Psychic unity, 6, 9, 17, 27, 32–33, 193, 227–228, 232; and integration, 8, 24–5, 43, 144; as jazz, 28, 49; and mourning, 193–194, 198–202; and literature, 228–232, 240–243
Psychoanalysis, 10–12, 27–29, 46; analyst-analysand interaction in, 3, 36–38, 179, 200–201; misconceptions of, 4, 6, 35–38, 156; as Copernican revolution, 5–6; fundamental rule of, 6–8, 12–17, 25, 37, 40, 192; therapeutic process of, 7, 13, 175–177, 181–188; as cure, 7–8, 22–23, 173–174; and ethics, 8–9, 47–49, 155–156, 193; technique of, 12–15, 36–37, 140–149, 151–157, 163, 171–173, 183–184; aim of, 13–14, 20, 25–26, 138–139, 141, 150–158, 182; working-through in, 23, 42; approaches of, 138–151; and writing, 175–180, 194, 200. *See also* Freud, Sigmund; Moral psychology
Psychological development, 177–183, 185–187, 190, 193–196, 198–202
Psychology, 1, 56; ancient, 5–6, 18, 191, 198. *See also* Moral psychology

*Radical Hope: Ethics in the Face of Cultural Devastation* (Lear), 53, 55–56, 64
Rationality, 2, 17–18, 44–45, 47. *See also* Reason
Rat Man, 160–163, 166–174. *See also* Superego
Reality, 220–221, 226, 268; and dreams, 82, 212–213; in psychoanalysis, 152, 180–181, 201. *See also* Allegory; Appearance and reality, relationship between
Reason, 1–3, 46; as ideological tool, 1, 47–48; and ruling, 1–2, 4, 48, 228; false image of, 1–2, 4–5, 48; participating in, 3, 17, 30–33; capacity for, 4, 32, 39, 44; theoretical, 55, 59, 136; relation to appetite and *thumos*, 223, 228–232, 234–243; as defense, 258, 262–266. *See also* Practical reason; Rationality
Reflective stance, 44–45, 66–68, 73–74, 80–81, 152, 207. *See also* Illusion
"Remembering, Repeating and Working-Through" (Freud), 12, 185
Repression, 16–17, 36, 38–39, 162, 186

*Republic* (Plato), 1, 12, 69, 206–208, 210–243, 249; as therapy, 229–237, 239–243
Resistance, psychological, 13, 16, 36–37, 100–101, 144, 183
Robinson, Marilynne, 269, 284–285; *Gilead*, 269, 271–274, 276–277, 280; Gilead (the city), 269, 271–280; *Home*, 269–271, 273, 277–278, 280–284; Jack Boughton, 269–271, 273–284; Reverend Ames, 271–280, 283–284
Rodl, Sebastian, 24

Scientific detachment. *See* Empirical stance and psychoanalysis
Self-consciousness, 1–2, 4, 7, 14–15, 24, 46; and psychoanalytic therapy, 7, 13–16, 22–23, 25–28, 37–38, 42, 46–47, 199–200; opposition to and disruption of, 7, 16–18, 20, 38–39, 45, 50; efficacy of, 23–26, 28, 42–43, 46
Self-knowledge, 74, 78, 133, 179–180, 202
Shakespeare, William, 122, 127, 132–136; *As You Like It*, 120–132, 134, 136; Rosalind, 120–135; Arden, 125, 128
Shame, 259–267
Shoemaking, 106, 149–150
Sickness. *See* Illness
Socrates: on reason ruling, 1–2, 4, 227–229; and poetry, 9, 136, 231–232; method (elenchus) of, 47, 75, 108, 111, 206; and doubt, 47, 105, 107, 116–118; ignorance of, 63, 77–78, 123, 219; irony of, 63–64, 71–72, 75–79, 103–105, 107–108, 118–119; as doctor, 69–70, 214; and Diotima, 108–113, 115–116, 122–124, 252; in the *Republic*, 206–208, 210–220, 224, 227–242. *See also* Allegory; Kierkegaard, Søren: on Socrates; Plato
Soul, nonrational, 9, 18, 25, 30–34, 41, 44, 200, 229–243. *See also* Intrapsychic communication; Psyche; Psychic unity; Unconscious
Spirit. See *Thumos*
Superego, 140–142, 144, 148, 193–194, 202, 270; and ethical life, 5–6; Rat Man's, 168–170
Swerve, 147, 164, 169–170, 173
*Symposium* (Plato), 108–116, 122–125, 252

Taking responsibility for ourselves, 26–29, 46–47, 99, 133–135, 197, 201–202
Temporality, 19, 89–91, 187–189. *See also* Timelessness
*Thumos*, 228–231, 234–237, 240, 243
Timelessness, 19, 34, 41, 81–2, 90, 187–189. *See also* Temporality; Unconscious
Torture: making sense of, 83–84, 94–95; opposition to and implication in, 245, 256, 258–262
Transference, 22, 25, 41–42, 166, 181–187
Trauma, 9, 56, 165, 269
Traumatic dreams and neuroses, 84, 163–164, 211

Truthfulness, 23, 202, 281–282; as fundamental value of psychoanalysis, 8–9, 47, 192; in irony, 128–130

Uncanny, 65, 67–69, 76, 136
Unconscious, 4, 16–17, 39, 162; form of activity of, 4, 7, 18, 22–23, 34, 41, 45, 148, 164; exemption from contradiction of, 18–20, 34; timelessness of, 18–21, 34, 41, 187, 189; belief, 160–163
Unintelligibility. *See* Intelligibility

Virtue, 8, 121, 191–193; irony as, 72, 74, 78, 133, 135

*Waiting for the Barbarians* (Coetzee), 81–97, 99
Western humanistic tradition, 15, 23, 26,
Williams, Bernard, 33–34, 43, 192, 266–267
Winnicott, Donald, 180
Wisdom: theoretical, 11, 28; practical, 11–12, 18, 23–24, 28, 43, 75
Wonder, 4